# KIERKEGAARD'S INFLUENCE ON
# SOCIAL-POLITICAL THOUGHT

*Kierkegaard Research: Sources, Reception and Resources*
*Volume 14*

*Kierkegaard Research: Sources, Reception and Resources*
is a publication of the Søren Kierkegaard Research Centre

# Kierkegaard's Influence on Social-Political Thought

*Edited by*
JON STEWART

Routledge
Taylor & Francis Group

LONDON AND NEW YORK

First published 2011 by Ashgate Publishing

2 Park Square, Milton Park, Abingdon, Oxon OX14 4RN
711 Third Avenue, New York, NY 10017, USA

*Routledge is an imprint of the Taylor & Francis Group, an informa business*

First issued in paperback 2016

**British Library Cataloguing in Publication Data**
Kierkegaard's influence on social-political thought.
  Volume 14. – (Kierkegaard research)
  1. Kierkegaard, Søren, 1813–1855 – Influence.
  2. Kierkegaard, Søren, 1813–1855 – Political and social views.
  I. Series II. Stewart, Jon (Jon Bartley)
  198.9–dc22

**Library of Congress Cataloging-in-Publication Data**
Kierkegaard's influence on social-political thought / [edited by] Jon Stewart.
    p. cm. — (Kierkegaard research ; v. 14)
  Includes indexes.
  ISBN 978-1-4094-3491-7 (hardcover : alk. paper) 1. Political science—Philosophy—History—20th century. 2. Political scientists—History—20th century. 3. Kierkegaard, Søren, 1813–1855—Influence. 4. Kierkegaard, Søren, 1813–1855—Political and social views. I. Stewart, Jon (Jon Bartley)
  JA83.K48 2011
  320.092—dc23

                                                                              2011026578
ISBN 978-1-4094-3491-7 (hbk)
ISBN 978-1-138-26161-7 (pbk)

Cover design by Katalin Nun

Transferred to Digital Printing in 2014

# Contents

# List of Contributors

**Leif Bork Hansen**, Kirkestræde 10 A, DK-2800 Kgs. Lyngby, Denmark.

**Michael O' Neill Burns**, Department of Philosophy, School of Humanities, University of Dundee, Dundee DD1 4HN, United Kingdom.

**Marcio Gimenes de Paula**, University of Brasilia, Department of Philosophy, University of Brasilia, ICC Ala Norte, Campus Darcy Ribeiro, P.O. Box: 04661, Brasilia – DF, Brazil, CEP: 70910-900.

**Nigel Hatton**, School of Social Sciences, Humanities & Arts, University of California, Merced, Merced, CA 95343, USA.

**Peter Brickey LeQuire**, Committee on Social Thought, The University of Chicago, 1130 East 59th Street, Chicago, IL 60637, USA.

**András Nagy**, University of Pannonia, Faculty of Modern Philology and Social Sciences, Department of Theatre Studies, Egyetem u. 10, H-8200 Veszprém, Hungary.

**Robert Puchniak**, Delbarton School, 230 Mendham Road, Morristown, NJ 07960, USA.

**Marcia C. Robinson**, Department of Religion, 501 Hall of Languages, Syracuse University, Syracuse, NY 13210, USA.

**Bartholomew Ryan**, European College of Liberal Arts, Platanenstraße 24, 13156 Berlin, Germany.

**J. Michael Tilley**, Department of Philosophy, Georgetown College, 400 E. College Street, Georgetown, KY 40324, USA.

**Gerhard Thonhauser**, Department of Philosophy, University of Vienna, Universitätsstraße 7, 1010 Vienna, Austria.

**Jennifer Elisa Veninga**, St. Edward's University, 3001 South Congress Avenue, Austin, Texas 78704, USA.

# Preface

Søren Kierkegaard has long been known as a multifaceted writer and thinker. His works possess the rare virtue of appealing to various kinds of people specialized in different fields of study. While scholars have traditionally recognized his important contributions to fields such as ethics, aesthetics, philosophy of religion, philosophical psychology, and hermeneutics, it was long thought that he had nothing meaningful to say about society or politics. This has rendered the importance of his work for social-political thinking somewhat problematic.

There are indeed many reasons for the neglect of this aspect of his work. Kierkegaard has been traditionally characterized as a religious writer who focused more or less exclusively on the faith of the individual. According to this view, what is of supreme importance is the inward religious life of each individual believer, and this cannot be meaningfully shared with others in a religious community. Thus, first, Kierkegaard appeared to be interested only in religion, or specifically Christianity, and not politics or the social order, and, second, his view of Christian faith was thought to be radically individual and to exclude any meaningful theory of the group, be that religious, social, or political. Indeed, one does not have to look too hard to find passages in his authorship which seem to support some version of this view. For example, in one of his NB journals he discusses as follows the relation of religion to the political order:

> What I have so often said jokingly—that it does not make any difference what government I live under just so I get to know who it is, who is *Imprimatur*—it now occurs to me that this is really Christianity. For in the story about the tax coin Christ asks: Whose likeness is this, who is *Imprimatur*? Christ clearly means this: If you want to be a Christian, then snap your fingers first and foremost and above all at politics; whether the picture you see on the coin is named Peter or Paul, is a native or an alien—forget it—give him the tax and do not waste a single moment on such squabbling, you who as a Christian have enough to do giving God what is his due, for the emperor's image is on the tax coin, but the Christian bears God's image and therefore does with his whole person what he is commanded to do with the coin—gives himself wholly to the one whose image he bears.[1]

This entry seems to be saying that one condition for being a true Christian is to be entirely indifferent or even disdainful towards politics or the current political situation. With his reference to the picture on the coin being that of "Peter or Paul," he seems to deny the possibility of any religious community as well. Indeed, such a community seems to be lumped together with the political sphere. In another journal entry he contrasts what he takes to be the true Christianity of Christ with the later work of the apostles, which he takes to be a distortion:

---

[1]     *SKS* 21, 126, NB7:94 / *JP* 4, 4151.

In Christ Christianity is the single individual; here is the one and only single individual. In the apostle there is at once—community. But in this way Christianity is transposed into an entirely different conceptual sphere. This concept has been the ruination of Christendom. This concept is responsible for the confusion that whole states, countries, nations, kingdoms are Christian.[2]

The message is again that true Christianity solely concerns the individual and has nothing to do with the community or group.

Due to his insistent and urgent interest in religion, Kierkegaard has seemed to some not to be interested in politics since it simply leads away from true religious faith. For a time Kierkegaard took regular walks with the jurist J.L.A. Kolderup-Rosenvinge (1792–1850), and on these walks they discussed many subjects.[3] In a letter, Kierkegaard responds to Kolderup-Rosenvinge's statement that they had forgotten to discuss political events on their recent walk: " 'We did not get around to talking about politics,' you remark. No wonder!...No, politics is not for me."[4] Here Kierkegaard seems to confirm straightforwardly that he has no desire to get into discussions about politics. Given this, for many years there seemed to be no good reason for scholars to go in search of a Kierkegaardian political theory. Not only did he not have one, but he was even dismissive or hostile to the very idea of occupying himself with the subject.

This apolitical tendency was an issue during Kierkegaard's own lifetime and in the immediate reception of his thought. Kierkegaard carried on an animated polemic with the controversial Danish pastor and theologian N.F.S. Grundtvig (1783–1872) and his large group of loyal followers.[5] In contrast to Kierkegaard, Grundtvig placed great emphasis on the role of the Christian church and the community. It was no accident that Grundtvig was also active politically and became a member of the Danish parliament. Kierkegaard rebuked the Grundtvigians for misunderstanding the personal inward nature of Christian belief and for irresponsibly conflating religion with politics.

Although not a Grundtvigian, Hans Lassen Martensen (1808–84), the successor of Bishop Jakob Peter Mynster (1775–1854) as the head of the Danish State Church, was also attentive to the apparent apolitical nature of Kierkegaard's thought. In his memoirs Martensen writes: "He [Kierkegaard] did not want to found a congregation or establish any new society. He totally denied every notion of society or associations,

---

[2]      *SKS* 25, 398, NB30:19 / *JP* 2, 2056.
[3]      See J. Michael Tilley, "J.L.A. Kolderup-Rosenvinge: Kierkegaard on Walking Away from Politics," in *Kierkegaard and His Danish Contemporaries*, Tome I, *Philosophy, Politics and Social Theory*, ed. by Jon Stewart, Aldershot: Ashgate 2009 (*Kierkegaard Research: Sources, Reception and Resources*, vol. 7), pp. 77–83.
[4]      *B&A*, vol. 1, pp. 200–1 / *LD*, Letter 184, pp. 252–3.
[5]      See Anders Holm, "Nikolai Frederik Severin Grundtvig: The Matchless Giant," in *Kierkegaard and His Danish Contemporaries*, Tome II, *Theology*, ed. by Jon Stewart, Aldershot: Ashgate 2009 (*Kierkegaard Research: Sources, Reception and Resources*, vol. 7), pp. 95–151. This same volume also contains useful articles on Kierkegaard's varying relations to individual Grundtvigians such as Hans Frederik Helveg, Jacob Christian Lindberg, and his elder brother Peter Christian Kierkegaard.

and he looked only to individuals."[6] It was natural for Martensen to be attentive to this since he himself was keenly interested in social and political issues, penning an ethics and political theory in his *Outline to a System of Moral Philosophy*, in 1841.[7] Many years after Kierkegaard's death, Martensen also developed an extended theory of social-political philosophy in the context of his monumental work, *Christian Ethics*.[8]

If apathy were not enough, Kierkegaard was also reproached for being a hopeless political reactionary, and this has certainly also played a role in discouraging people from exploring his views in this area. For example, many of his statements make it clear that he was on the side of the conservatives in the Revolution of 1848, which saw the end of absolutism in Denmark and the establishment of the constitutional monarchy the following year. It is fairly easy to find passages in which Kierkegaard gives the clear impression that he was anything but a democrat.[9]

In Kierkegaard's assessment of the present age in his *Literary Review of Two Ages*, his comments on the contemporary movement toward democracy indicate that he was very suspicious and uncomfortable with the social changes that accompanied democracy. He criticizes the modern age for its tendency towards leveling in that it destroys differences between individuals and classes. He writes: "The dialectic of the present age is oriented to equality, and its most logical implementation…is leveling, the negative unity of the negative mutual reciprocity of individuals."[10] In his discussion here he is critical specifically of the modern movements of democracy and equality since he sees them as antithetical to the cultivation of the individual and to the individual's inward, subjective religiosity. Democracy and equality transform

---

6    Hans Lassen Martensen, *Af mit Levnet. Meddelelser*, vols. 1–3, Copenhagen: Gyldendal 1882–83, vol. 3, p. 19. (This passage is quoted at length in English in *Encounters with Kierkegaard*, ed. and trans. by Bruce H. Kirmmse, Princeton: Princeton University Press 1996, p. 203.)

7    Hans Lassen Martensen, *Grundrids til Moralphilosophiens System*, Copenhagen: C.A. Reitzel 1841. (English translation: *Outline to a System of Moral Philosophy*, in *Between Hegel and Kierkegaard: Hans L. Martensen's Philosophy of Religion*, trans. by Curtis L. Thompson and David J. Kangas, Atlanta: Scholars Press 1997, pp. 245–313.)

8    Hans Lassen Martensen, *Den christelige Ethik. Den almindelige Deel*, Copenhagen: Gyldendal 1871. *Den christelige Ethik. Den specielle Deel. Første Afdeling: Den individuelle Ethik*, Copenhagen: Gyldendal 1878. *Den christelige Ethik. Den specielle Deel. Anden Afdeling: Den sociale Ethik*, Copenhagen: Gyldendal 1878. (English translation: *Christian Ethics*, General Part, trans. by C. Spence, Edinburgh: T. & T. Clark 1873; *Christian Ethics*, Special Part, First Division: *Individual Ethics*, trans. by William Affleck, Edinburgh: T. & T. Clark 1881; *Christian Ethics*, Special Part, Second Division: *Social Ethics*, trans. by Sophia Taylor, Edinburgh: T. & T. Clark 1882.)

9    For example in a fragmentary journal entry he writes, "…cannot be formed according to the paradigm of balloting (balloting, balloting with discussion, balloting without discussion—O balloting, from, in, with, upon, by balloting) or be done according to the popular song: Let's a few of us get together, hurrah, hurrah, hurrah. Street-lighting and clothes and, with all due respect, the sanitation department can be reformed in this manner; but let us be men: Christianity does not lend itself to reformation in this way." *SKS* 24, 256, NB23:100 / *JP* 4, 4208.

10    *SKS* 8, 81 / *TA*, 84.

the individual into the group in the form of "the majority" or "the public." These modern movements level individuals into a homogeneous, anonymous mass. He writes: "The trend today is in the direction of mathematical equality, so that in all classes about so and so many uniformly make one individual."[11] Once again equality is criticized directly since it leads to uniformity and abstracts from individuality. Although he does not refer to the group as "the herd," as Nietzsche does, Kierkegaard clearly shares Nietzsche's suspicion that democracy and equality will lead to a sluggish homogeneity which can only be detrimental to the great spirits or the cause of individuality in general. On the contrary, Kierkegaard lauds the Greek world for its insistence on class distinction. Such a social order was full of passion, encouraged individuality, and did not run the danger of making the individual into the group. From these passages, Kierkegaard seems profoundly anti-democratic.

Similarly, many of his statements about social issues seem to betray a less than progressive attitude. He seemed wholly dismissive of the idea of equal rights for women, as can be seen in his criticism of the novel *Clara Raphael* by Denmark's first feminist writer Mathilde Fibiger (1830–72).[12] In his journals he gives a straightforward condemnation of the emancipation of women when he writes: "If girls were brought up the same way [sc. as boys]—then good night to the whole human race. And no doubt the emancipation of women, which tends toward this kind of upbringing is the invention of the devil."[13] In the following passage from the *Postscript*, misogyny is combined with anti-Semitism: "But if the dialectical is skipped, what then? Then it becomes woman-chatter and old wives blather, for, as is known Jews and women blather in a minute what a man is unable to do in a lifetime."[14] Finally, he claims in his journals, "Woman is personified egotism,"[15] and he adds, "an egotism of which man has no intimation."[16]

Likewise, like many others of his day, he seemed to have anti-Semitic tendencies that make many commentators uncomfortable given the subsequent history.[17] In his journals he writes, "Goethe notes…that when the Jews killed the Egyptians it was the reverse of the Sicilian Vespers. In the latter case the host murdered the guests, but in this case the guests murdered the host. But this is certainly the situation with respect to the Jews in Europe in our own time."[18] With an eerie anticipation of the scapegoating of the Jews in the twentieth century, Kierkegaard accuses the Jews of murdering their hosts, that is, the Europeans. True to traditional forms of anti-Semitism, Kierkegaard associates the Jews with the base activity of moneymaking: "The Jew generally

---

[11]      *SKS* 8, 81 / *TA*, 85.
[12]      See Katalin Nun, "Mathilde Fibiger: Kierkegaard and the Emancipation of Women," in *Kierkegaard and His Danish Contemporaries*, Tome III, *Literature, Drama and Aesthetics*, ed. by Jon Stewart, Aldershot: Ashgate 2009 (*Kierkegaard Research: Sources, Reception and Resources*, vol. 7), pp. 83–103.
[13]      *SKS* 22, 94, NB11:159 / *JP* 4, 4992.
[14]      *SKS* 7, 391 / *CUP1*, 430.
[15]      *SKS* 25, 421, NB30:49 / *JP* 4, 5000.
[16]      *SKS* 25, 350, NB29:92 / *JP* 4, 4998.
[17]      See Peter Tudvad, *Stadier på antisemitismens vej. Søren Kierkegaard og jøderne*, Copenhagen: Rosinante 2010.
[18]      *SKS* 21, 296, NB10:75.

lacks fantasy and sensibility, but he does have abstract understanding and numbers are his element. For the publicists, the battle for public opinion is neither more or less than stock exchange business."[19] In *A Literary Review*, he casually makes the Jews the scapegoats for economic difficulties in Denmark: "Just as Jews drained money out of the country by means of stocks and bonds, so too superficiality takes substance or significance out of literature."[20] Kierkegaard's dispute with the *Corsair* is well known. In the context of the controversy, his *ad hominem* criticism of the journal's Jewish editor Meïr Goldschmidt (1819–87) did not shrink from racism or anti-Semitism.[21] He writes in his journals: "For the *Corsair* is a revolt of the rabble, and what is more laughable than a revolt of Jews?"[22] In a similar vein, he writes: "For the *Corsair* is indeed a revolt of the Jews against the Christians...with the help of the *Corsair* a Jew wants to compel respect. Heretofore this has only been successful with money."[23] These passages speak for themselves, and it is difficult to see in them an advocacy of democracy, multiculturalism, and tolerance.

Given all this, it seemed prudent to many scholars with progressive political intuitions not to explore the issue of Kierkegaard's social-political thought any further. If he was a royalist, an antidemocrat, a sexist, and an anti-Semite, then it seemed doubtful that his views in this field could be regarded as useful or constructive today. For these commentators, given Kierkegaard's private sentiments regarding democracy, Jews, and women, it can hardly be seen as a great loss to posterity that he never developed a political theory. In this regard, one can invoke the conclusion of Bruce Kirmmse in his article "Kierkegaard, Jews and Judaism": "But to demand a pluralistic tolerance [sc. from Kierkegaard]—i.e., the sort of tolerance which our times views as genuine, authentic tolerance—is perhaps to demand too much, to demand something anachronistic."[24]

Critics have been quick to criticize Kierkegaard's apparent political apathy and his seemingly excessive emphasis on the individual in isolation, which, for many, seemed to undermine the concept of solidarity or community. This has often been pointed out as a shortcoming of Kierkegaard's thinking by otherwise sympathetic readers, such as the critical theorists Lukács (1885–1971), Theodor W. Adorno (1903–69), and Herbert Marcuse (1898–1979), who all criticize Kierkegaard on social and political grounds. For example, Marcuse explicitly identifies Kierkegaard as the champion of the "isolated individual" in contrast to Hegel's socially-

---

[19]   *SKS* 26, 196, NB32:108 / *JP* 3, 2985.

[20]   *SKS* 8, 25 / *TA*, 22–3.

[21]   See Johnny Kondrup, "Meïr Goldschmidt: The Cross-Eyed Hunchback," in *Kierkegaard and His Danish Contemporaries*, Tome III, *Literature, Drama and Aesthetics*, ed. by Jon Stewart, Aldershot : Ashgate 2009 (*Kierkegaard Research: Sources, Reception and Resources*, vol. 7), pp. 105–49.

[22]   *Pap.* VII–I B 18, p. 188.

[23]   *Pap.* VII–I B 13, p. 181.

[24]   Bruce H. Kirmmse, "Kierkegaard, Jews and Judaism," *Kierkegaardiana*, vol. 17, 1995, p. 95. See also his "Kierkegaard, jødedommen og jøderne," in *Kirkehistoriske Samlinger*, 1992, pp. 77–107.

constituted individual.[25] According to Marcuse, Hegel "demonstrated that the fullest existence of the individual is consummated in his social life," and that the "critical employment of the dialectical method tended to disclose that individual freedom presupposes a free society, and that the true liberation of the individual therefore requires the liberation of society."[26] But, by contrast, Kierkegaard's "fixation on the individual alone…amounts to adopting an abstract approach," which is antithetical to any social or cultural criticism.[27]

Likewise, many of the thinkers associated with the existentialist movement were quick to criticize Kierkegaard for his fixation on the individual at the expense of the community, even though some of them, such as the early Jean-Paul Sartre (1905–80), were reproached for exactly the same thing. For example, Karl Jaspers (1883–1969) argues that although an emphasis on individuality does not explicitly deny community, to interpret Kierkegaard's purpose as "the revival of the community spirit" is to appropriate his "concepts dishonestly" in a manner which is "alien to him."[28] Martin Buber (1878–1965) sees in Kierkegaard a theory of the isolated individual's special and unique relation to God without any reference to others. Buber claims: "This relation is an exclusive one, the exclusive one, and this means, according to Kierkegaard, that it is the excluding relation, excluding all others."[29] In the Kierkegaard secondary literature, this existentialist view was echoed in Mark Taylor's important work on Kierkegaard's relation to Hegel, where it is claimed that Kierkegaard's "journey to selfhood cannot culminate in spiritual community but must be a solitary sojourn that separates self from other."[30]

In time this picture of Kierkegaard's political apathy began to change, and scholars began the first tentative attempts to explore traces of a social or political thinking in his writings. Before this could be done, however, the picture of Kierkegaard as a champion of the isolated individual had to be challenged. This atomistic, asocial reading of Kierkegaard has been taken up in a critical manner by a number of recent commentators.[31] These works try to argue for a significant theory of the other and the importance of the community in Kierkegaard.

---

[25]     Herbert Marcuse, *Reason and Revolution: Hegel and the Rise of Social Theory*, London: Oxford University Press 1941, pp. 262–3.

[26]     Ibid., pp. 262–3.

[27]     Ibid., p. 263.

[28]     Karl Jaspers, *The Great Philosophers*, vols. 1–4, New York: Harcourt Brace and Company 1962–95, vol. 4, p. 289.

[29]     Martin Buber, *Between Man and Man*, trans. by Ronald Gregor Smith, London: Kegan Paul 1947, p. 50.

[30]     Mark Taylor, *Journeys to Selfhood: Hegel and Kierkegaard*, Berkeley: University of California Press 1980, p. 179.

[31]     See, for example, *Foundations of Kierkegaard's Vision of Community: Religion, Ethics, and Politics in Kierkegaard*, ed. by George Connell and C. Stephen Evans, Atlantic Highlands, New Jersey: Humanities Press 1992; *Kierkegaard: The Self in Society*, ed. by George Pattison and Steven Shakespeare, New York: St. Martin's Press 1998; Gregory R. Beabout and Brad Frazier, "A Challenge to the 'Solitary Self' Interpretation of Kierkegaard," *History of Philosophy Quarterly*, vol. 17, no. 1, 2000, pp. 75–98; *Kierkegaard After MacIntyre*, ed. by John Davenport and Anthony Rudd, Chicago: Open Court 2001; Merold

In time the way was cleared for other commentators to explore Kierkegaard's importance for social-political thought more directly.[32] Some recent scholars, notably Martin J. Matuštík and Jürgen Habermas, have moved beyond merely interpreting Kierkegaard's work and have developed some of the concepts in Kierkegaard's writings which can contribute, directly and indirectly, to contemporary discourses within social philosophy.[33] On the whole it can be said that this is a relatively new and unexplored branch of Kierkegaard studies.

Although Kierkegaard surely did not concentrate on the issue of political organization and structure, this is not to say that he had nothing to say about politics. On the contrary, his theory of the self-development of the individual is very relevant for the issue of how a political community nurtures participants in the political process who are going to be discerning and wise in exercising good judgment as citizens with power to lend their voice to the democratic discourse. It gradually became recognized that there are many elements in his philosophical anthropology and psychology that can be taken as an important point of departure for a wider political theory.

The present volume attempts to document the use of Kierkegaard by later thinkers in the context of social-political thought. It shows how his ideas have been employed by very different kinds of writers and activists with very different political goals and agendas. Many of the articles show that although Kierkegaard has been criticized for his reactionary views on some social and political questions, he has been appropriated as a source of insight and inspiration by a number of later thinkers with very progressive, indeed, visionary political views.

Given the history of the issue of social-political thought in Kierkegaard's writings, there is every reason to expect that this branch of Kierkegaard studies will continue to expand in the future. It is the hope of this series that the present volume will represent an important contribution to this expansion.

---

Westphal, *Kierkegaard's Critique of Reason and Society*, Macon, Georgia: Mercer University Press 1987; Salvatore Spera, *Kierkegaard politico*, Rome: Istituto di Studi Filosofici 1978.

[32] See, for example, Alison Assiter, *Kierkegaard, Metaphysics and Political Theory: Unfinished Selves*, New York: Continuum 2009; Alastair Hannay, *On the Public*, New York: Routledge 2005; J. Michael Tilley, *Interpersonal Relationships and Community in Kierkegaard's Thought*, Ph.D. Thesis, University of Kentucky, 2008.

[33] Martin J. Matuštík, *Postnational Identity: Critical Theory and Existential Philosophy in Habermas, Kierkegaard, and Havel*, New York and London: Guilford Press 1993; Jürgen Habermas, *The Future of Human Nature*, Oxford and Malden, Massachusetts: Blackwell 2003; and Jürgen Habermas, "Individuation through Socialization: On George Herbert Mead's Theory of Subjectivity," *Postmetaphysical Thinking*, Cambridge, Massachusetts: MIT Press 1992, pp. 164–70.

# Acknowledgements

Many highly qualified people have played an important role in the production of this volume. I would like to express my gratitude to the following individuals who helped with running down references and finding rare texts: Lee C. Barrett, Maria Binetti, Markus Kleinert, Peter Šajda, Jeanette Schindler-Wirth, Gerhard Schreiber, and Heiko Schulz. I am indebted to Michael Tilley generally for many very instructive conversations on the topic of Kierkegaard's political philosophy through the years and specifically for his selfless help with the Preface to the present volume. I would also like to thank Curtis Thompson for his constructive suggestions for the Preface. The outstanding preliminary work for the bibliographies that appear in this volume was done by Peter Šajda. I am also grateful to Katalin Nun who did the enormous editorial work in preparing the files electronically for publication. I am thankful for the invaluable assistance of Finn Gredal Jensen in the proofreading of this volume. Bjarne Still Laurberg has also rendered valuable services by attending to some of the administrative work involved in the series. I would also like to acknowledge the outstanding efforts of our friends and colleagues at Ashgate Publishing who have helped in the production of this volume: Philip Hillyer and Nicholas Wain. Finally, this volume would never have been possible if it were not for the selfless cooperation of the individual authors, who set aside their other obligations in order to write the articles that appear here. Their efforts and sacrifices are much appreciated.

# List of Abbreviations

BA      *The Book on Adler*, trans. by Howard V. Hong and Edna H. Hong, Princeton: Princeton University Press 1998.

C       *The Crisis and a Crisis in the Life of an Actress*, trans. by Howard V. Hong and Edna H. Hong, Princeton: Princeton University Press 1997.

CA      *The Concept of Anxiety*, trans. by Reidar Thomte in collaboration with Albert B. Anderson, Princeton: Princeton University Press 1980.

CD      *Christian Discourses*, trans. by Howard V. Hong and Edna H. Hong, Princeton: Princeton University Press 1997.

CI      *The Concept of Irony*, trans. by Howard V. Hong and Edna H. Hong, Princeton: Princeton University Press 1989.

CIC     *The Concept of Irony*, trans. with an Introduction and Notes by Lee M. Capel, London: Collins 1966.

COR     *The Corsair Affair; Articles Related to the Writings*, trans. by Howard V. Hong and Edna H. Hong, Princeton: Princeton University Press 1982.

CUP1    *Concluding Unscientific Postscript*, vol. 1, trans. by Howard V. Hong and Edna H. Hong, Princeton: Princeton University Press 1982.

CUP2    *Concluding Unscientific Postscript*, vol. 2, trans. by Howard V. Hong and Edna H. Hong, Princeton: Princeton University Press 1982.

CUPH    *Concluding Unscientific Postscript*, trans. by Alastair Hannay, Cambridge and New York: Cambridge University Press 2009.

EO1     *Either/Or*, Part I, trans. by Howard V. Hong and Edna H. Hong, Princeton: Princeton University Press 1987.

EO2     *Either/Or*, Part II, trans. by Howard V. Hong and Edna H. Hong, Princeton: Princeton University Press 1987.

EOP     *Either/Or*, trans. by Alastair Hannay, Harmondsworth: Penguin Books 1992.

EPW     *Early Polemical Writings*, among others: *From the Papers of One Still Living; Articles from Student Days; The Battle Between the Old and the New Soap-Cellars*, trans. by Julia Watkin, Princeton: Princeton University Press 1990.

EUD     *Eighteen Upbuilding Discourses*, trans. by Howard V. Hong and Edna H. Hong, Princeton: Princeton University Press 1990.

FSE     *For Self-Examination*, trans. by Howard V. Hong and Edna H. Hong, Princeton: Princeton University Press 1990.

FT     *Fear and Trembling*, trans. by Howard V. Hong and Edna H. Hong, Princeton: Princeton University Press 1983.

FTP     *Fear and Trembling*, trans. by Alastair Hannay, Harmondsworth: Penguin Books 1985.

JC     *Johannes Climacus, or De omnibus dubitandum est*, trans. by Howard V. Hong and Edna H. Hong, Princeton: Princeton University Press 1985.

JFY     *Judge for Yourself!*, trans. by Howard V. Hong and Edna H. Hong, Princeton: Princeton University Press 1990.

JP     *Søren Kierkegaard's Journals and Papers*, vols. 1–6, ed. and trans. by Howard V. Hong and Edna H. Hong, assisted by Gregor Malantschuk (vol. 7, Index and Composite Collation), Bloomington and London: Indiana University Press 1967–78.

KAC     *Kierkegaard's Attack upon "Christendom," 1854–1855*, trans. by Walter Lowrie, Princeton: Princeton University Press 1944.

KJN     *Kierkegaard's Journals and Notebooks*, vols. 1–11, ed. by Niels Jørgen Cappelørn, Alastair Hannay, David Kangas, Bruce H. Kirmmse, George Pattison, Vanessa Rumble, and K. Brian Söderquist, Princeton and Oxford: Princeton University Press 2007ff.

LD     *Letters and Documents*, trans. by Henrik Rosenmeier, Princeton: Princeton University Press 1978.

LR     *A Literary Review*, trans. by Alastair Hannay, Harmondsworth: Penguin Books 2001.

M     *The Moment and Late Writings*, trans. by Howard V. Hong and Edna H. Hong, Princeton: Princeton University Press 1998.

P     *Prefaces / Writing Sampler*, trans. by Todd W. Nichol, Princeton: Princeton University Press 1997.

PC     *Practice in Christianity*, trans. by Howard V. Hong and Edna H. Hong, Princeton: Princeton University Press 1991.

PF     *Philosophical Fragments*, trans. by Howard V. Hong and Edna H. Hong, Princeton: Princeton University Press 1985.

*Fridays*, trans. by Howard V. Hong and Edna H. Hong, Princeton: Princeton University Press 1997.

WL     *Works of Love*, trans. by Howard V. Hong and Edna H. Hong, Princeton: Princeton University Press 1995.

WS     *Writing Sampler*, trans. by Todd W. Nichol, Princeton: Princeton University Press 1997.

# Giorgio Agamben:

## State of Exception

### Leif Bork Hansen

*I. The Remainder—Incommensurability*

The Danish Kierkegaard scholar Gregor Malantschuk (1902–78) begins his lecture on *Political and Social Aspects of Kierkegaard's Thought* by emphasizing "an essential and important presupposition for all of Kierkegaard's activity both as a person and as an author: He perceived very early that he was an exception, something extraordinary, born at the beginning of a crisis period of unsuspected world-historical dimensions."[1] The Italian political philosopher Giorgio Agamben takes up just this dialectic in his works on *Homo sacer*.

Giorgio Agamben was born in Rome in 1942. He was educated at the University of Rome as a law student and is known today as a philologist, interpreter of literature and philosopher. He has constantly been occupied with caesuras, in particular the human "caesuras," "fractures," or "cuts." This occupation is not just with caesuras—but with caesuras of caesuras, divisions of divisions.[2] Agamben has become "the threshold's" dialectician *par excellence* against the background of the atrocities committed by the Nazis during World War II: the Nazis succeeded in stripping down people to such a degree that it was as if nothing human remained. The Nazis deprived the Jews of their citizenship and thus their civil rights. They treated human beings as if they had been pushed beyond the threshold, where they were no longer human, and then destroyed them. Was there anything remaining? Is the naked human being reduced to anything other than a human being—an animal? Is the naked human

---

[1]    Gregor Malantschuk, *The Controversial Kierkegaard*, trans. by Howard V. Hong and Edna H. Hong, Waterloo, Ontario: Wilfred Laurier University Press 1980, p. 1. According to Kierkegaard it is never possible for the individual to hide behind a collective identity but he points to the individual as the existentially naked human being. He notes in his journal: "Just as modesty forbids stripping oneself naked, so it is modesty which keeps one from forsaking privacy to be as the others and to be stripped as the single individual." He adds: "It is therefore a suffering to become the extraordinary, although it is still true that he must suffer if he is truly the extraordinary," *SKS* 25, 48, NB26:42 / *JP* 1, 1089.

[2]    Concerning Agamben's "caesuras"—and the meaning of the further divisions of divisions, culminating in the messianic caesura or division, one can observe a kind of parallel in Søren Kierkegaard's "stages"—presented by the pseudonym Johannes Climacus: the aesthetic—the ethical—and the religious stage: religiousness A—and the paradoxical religiousness, with the incarnation: religiousness B (that is, Christianity).

being commensurate with himself—or is there a caesura, a fracture, which creates a remainder that is eluded, a remainder that cannot be seen?

Is it the state which grants the individual human being his or her significance, and can it therefore take it back again? Does human life reach fulfillment in society or the state as the German philosopher G.W.F. Hegel (1770–1831) claimed?[3] Or is there— to use Søren Kierkegaard's terms—an "incommensurability" or "incongruence," such that human beings, without rights, become a part of or are absorbed in the state?[4]

The Nazis' experiments with concentration camp prisoners raise the question of whether it is still meaningful to speak of a human subject.[5] Nevertheless it can also mean, paradoxically enough, that after World War II one asks about the subject which the Nazis attempted to destroy. The Danish art and literary critic Jacob Lund Pedersen (b. 1971) writes thus with reference to Giorgio Agamben: "the occupation with the dehumanizing, depersonalizing, desubjectivizing, the neutrality and impersonalness, which stamps large parts of the post-war period's art and thought can be conceived as a testimony to or a reaction to the reduction and breaking down, the testing of the human subject that took place in the Nazi camps."[6]

This is what is at stake for Giorgio Agamben: the human being is not just an animal dressed like a citizen. The human being is not a political animal. The stripped down human being, who has been deprived of his significance as citizen in the city-state is not an animal. This appears in "the state of exception" in the "extreme situation" or "limit situation"[7]—especially as it appeared in the *Muselmann* in the concentration camp, who found himself on the threshold of being reduced to the non-human—

---

[3]     According to G.W.F. Hegel, the individual human being finds his τέλος—his goal, his determination in the universal, society, the state. Kierkegaard in *Fear and Trembling* refers to Hegel's position in the following manner: "As soon as the single individual asserts himself in his singularity before the universal, he sins, and only by acknowledging this [sc. the universal, society, the state] can he be reconciled again with the universal" (*SKS* 4, 148 / *FT*, 54). For this reason Hegel also regards the conscience of the individual as "a moral form of evil," when the individual wants to assert his conscience above society or the state. Kierkegaard later asks in *Practice in Christianity*: "Why has Hegel made conscience and the state of conscience in the single individual 'a form of evil' (see *Rechts-Philosophie*)? Why? Because he deified the established order" (*SKS* 12, 96 / *PC*, 87).

[4]     It is precisely the distinguishing characteristic of the existing order—which wants to make itself divine—that it does not want to know about any such "incommensurability" or "incongruence." Kierkegaard writes about the situation in the time of Jesus: "The outer and the inner had become entirely commensurable, so totally that the inner had dropped out. This commensurability and congruity are sure indications that an established order is in the process of deifying itself" (*SKS* 12, 97 / *PC*, 88).

[5]     People thus talk about a paradigm shift in Western thought after 1945, characterized by "the death of the subject." See Jacob Lund Pedersen, *Den subjektive rest. Udsigelse og (de)subjektivering i kunst og teori*, Århus: Aarhus Universitetsforlag 2008, p. 9.

[6]     Pedersen, *Den subjektive rest*, p. 17, cf. p. 11.

[7]     Giorgio Agamben, *Quel che resta di Auschwitz: l'archivio e il testimone: homo sacer III*, Turin: Bollati Boringhieri 1998, p. 43, cf. p. 48. (English translation: *Remnants of Auschwitz: The Witness and the Archive*, trans. by Daniel Heller Roazen, New York: Zone Books 1999, p. 48.)

without any longer being able to speak or understand anything. Although the Nazis wanted to reduce the concentration camp prisoner to a non-human—nevertheless the shame remained—just as Josef K. in Kafka's *The Trial* (1925) had a knife stabbed into his heart and turned around twice, while someone above him said: " 'Like a dog!'…it was as if the shame of it must outlive him."[8]

In this inverted and negative sense the human element is shown. "Is despair an excellence or a defect?" Kierkegaard asks in *The Sickness unto Death* (1849). He answers: "If only the abstract idea of despair is considered, without any thought of someone in despair, it must be regarded as a surpassing excellence. The possibility of this sickness is man's superiority over the animal, and this superiority distinguishes him in quite another way than does his erect walk."[9] Even if the realized possibility is regarded as higher than even the possibility itself, the relation here is just the opposite.[10] He continues:

> Consequently, to be able to despair is an infinite advantage, and yet to be in despair is not only the worst misfortune and misery—no, it is ruination. Generally this is not the case with the relation between possibility and actuality. If it is an excellence to be able to be this or that, then it is an even greater excellence to be that; in other words, to be is like an ascent when compared with being able to be. With respect to despair, however, to be is like a descent when compared with being able to be; the descent is as infinitely low as the excellence of possibility is high.

Kierkegaard adds: "Not to be in despair must signify the destroyed possibility of being able to be in despair; if a person is truly not to be in despair, he must every moment destroy the possibility."[11] Thus the possibility of despair presupposes a caesura, a fracture, or a cut in the human being.[12]

---

[8]     Franz Kafka, *The Trial*, trans. by Willa and Edwin Muir, revised and with additional material trans. by E.M. Butler, New York: Schocken Books 1970, p. 229. Agamben makes this reference to Kafka's *The Trial* in several places. See also Jacob Lund Pedersen, "Det skamfulde subjekt," *Tidsskriftet øjeblikket*, vol. 13, no. 47, 2006, pp. 18–20.

[9]     *SKS* 11, 130–1 / *SUD*, 14–15.

[10]     Compare a similar constellation of problems in Agamben in his interpretation of Herman Melville's *Bartleby. The Scrivener: A Story of Wall-Street* (1853). More precisely, see the remark, "I would prefer not to," in *Great Short Works of Herman Melville*, ed. by Warner Berthoff, New York: Perennial Classics 2004, pp. 47–8. Cf., for example, Giorgio Agamben, "Bartleby," in *La communità che viene*, Turin: Giulio 1990, p. 37 (English translation: *The Coming Community*, trans. by Michael Hardt, Minneapolis: University of Minnesota Press 1993, pp. 35–7) and Giorgio Agamben, *Homo Sacer I: Il potere sovrano e la nuda vita*, Turin: Einaudi 1995, p. 56 (English translation: *Homo Sacer: Sovereign Power and Bare Life*, trans. by Daniel Heller-Roazen, Stanford: Stanford University Press 1995, p. 48).

[11]     *SKS* 11, 131 / *SUD*, 15.

[12]     Cf. the German word for despair: *Verzweiflung*.

## II. Kierkegaard's "Syntheses"—Agamben's "Caesuras"

Kierkegaard begins his work *The Sickness unto Death* by giving an account of what he understands by the idea that the human being is a self or has the possibility of becoming one. He explains:

> A human being is spirit. But what is spirit? Spirit is the self. But what is the self? The self is a relation that relates itself to itself or is the relation's relating itself to itself in the relation; the self is not the relation but is the relation's relating itself to itself. A human being is a synthesis of the infinite and the finite, of the temporal and the eternal, of freedom and necessity, in short a synthesis. A synthesis is a relation between two. Considered in this way, a human being is still not a self. In the relation between two, the relation is the third as a negative unity.[13]

According to Kierkegaard, "the sickness unto death" or "despair" is the condition when a human being does not want to be himself but the self falls apart in despair.

In the introduction I have already pointed out that Giorgio Agamben's reference to "caesuras" and his bringing of the human subject into these caesuras—where the parts of the caesura are confronted "face to face" in the human subject—can be regarded as a new interpretation and concretization of Kierkegaard's claim that the human being is a synthesis, and as such it is the task of the human being to bring the parts together in his or her existence, indeed, that the human being only manages to be a subject, to be himself or herself, when this happens.

## III. "The Naked Life"—"The Exception"

According to Agamben, Western civilization culminates in the Auschwitz death camp with the destruction of what is different. This is not an accidental or erroneous development in the course of the history of civilization, but rather it has to do with the very foundation for civilization. Giorgio Agamben begins his revolutionary work, *Homo Sacer: Sovereign Power and Bare Life*, by explaining that in ancient Greece there were two words for life: first there was, according to Aristotle, the word ζωή, which designated life, be that plant, animal or human. In opposition to this, Aristotle used the word *βίος* about the kind of life qualified by the city state (πόλις), namely, the identity which the state gave to the individual as citizen, βίος πολιτικός.[14] According to Agamben, it is not by accident that Aristotle in his "*Politics* situates the proper place of the polis in the transition from voice to language"[15]—where the human being's own voice is excluded in the language spoken in the πόλις[16]

---

[13]　　SKS 11, 129 / SUD, 15.
[14]　　Agamben, *Homo Sacer I: Il potere sovrano e la nuda vita*, p. 3. (*Homo Sacer: Sovereign Power and Bare Life*, p. 1.)
[15]　　Agamben, *Homo Sacer I: Il potere sovrano e la nuda vita*, p. 11. (*Homo Sacer: Sovereign Power and Bare Life*, p. 7.)
[16]　　Agamben, *Homo Sacer I: Il potere sovrano e la nuda vita*, p. 11 (*Homo Sacer: Sovereign Power and Bare Life*, p. 8): "The question 'In what way does the living being have language?' corresponds exactly to the question 'In what way does bare life dwell in the *polis*?'"

The French philosopher and historian of ideas Michel Foucault (1926–84) in *The History of Sexuality* (1976–84) designates the threshold of the modern era as the place where "natural life begins to be included in the mechanisms and calculations of State power, and politics turns into *biopolitics*."[17] Giorgio Agamben is in agreement with Foucault's demonstration of governmental power, the sovereign's fatal disciplining of its inhabitants. State power grants the individual citizen his identity. But Agamben's objection to Foucault is that he has not taken into account the way in which sovereign power functioned in the concentration camps. According to Agamben, it is not the city but the concentration camp that reflects the modern political paradigm. Here arises the ancient distinction with its opposition between the life of the citizen with the rights that the state grants the individual citizen through citizenship and human rights, in opposition to the naked human being, who has been deprived of these rights. It has happened that the opposition between the citizen with the meaning and the rights that this gives, and the naked human being deprived of these rights has crept into the state itself. Thus law and lawlessness thrive under the same sovereign power which constitutes the state.[18]

The Jewish-German political thinker Hannah Arendt (1906–75) fled Germany in 1933—after the Reichstag fire—and came via France to the USA. For around twenty years Hannah Arendt had no citizenship. She experienced with her own body how the citizen without a state is without rights. This is a challenge that Giorgio Agamben takes up.

According to the German jurist and political theorist Carl Schmitt (1888–1985), the decisive political opposition is between friend and enemy. Agamben points to another set of opposites: "The fundamental categorial pair of Western politics is not that of friend/enemy but that of bare life/political existence, *zoê/bios*, exclusion/ inclusion."[19] Here the opposition has entered into the state itself, represented by the sovereign power, first as a condition of martial law, but martial law has a tendency to become the permanent rule. On February 28, 1933 Hitler issued his "Decree for the Protection of the People and the State," which suspended the articles of the Weimar

---

The living being has *logos* by taking away and conserving its own voice in it, even as it dwells in the *polis* by letting its own bare life be excluded, as an exception, within it." Agamben writes in the *Preface* to the English translation of *Infanzia e storia* (1978): "If for every author there exists a question which defines the *motivum* of his thought, then the precise scope of these questions coincides with the terrain towards which all my work is orientated....I have stubbornly pursued only one train of thought: what is the meaning of 'there is language'; what is the meaning of 'I speak'?" Giorgio Agamben, *Infanzia e storia: Distruzione dell'esperienza e origine della storia*, Turin: Giulio Einaudi Editore 1978. (English translation: *Infancy and History: The Destruction of Experience*, trans. by Liz Heron, London, New York: Verso 2007, p. 6.) Cf. Eva Geulen, *Giorgio Agamben. Zur Einführung*, Frankfurt am Main: Junius 2005, p. 26.

[17] Agamben, *Homo Sacer I: Il potere sovrano e la nuda vita*, p. 5. (*Homo Sacer: Sovereign Power and Bare Life*, p. 3.)

[18] Thus the distinction between democracy and totalitarian forms of government becomes fluid. The one develops out of the other.

[19] Agamben, *Homo Sacer I: Il potere sovrano e la nuda vita*, p. 11. (*Homo Sacer: Sovereign Power and Bare Life*, p. 8.)

Constitution concerning personal liberties.[20] The decree was never suspended but remained in force for 12 years until the fall of National Socialism with the defeat of 1945.

It was Carl Schmitt, with his book *Politische Theologie*, who drew attention to the precise connection between martial law and sovereign power.[21] It is with the help of martial law that the sovereign, paradoxical power shows his sovereignty. Agamben writes about this in *Homo Sacer: Sovereign Power and Bare Life*:

> The paradox of sovereignty consists in the fact the sovereign is, at the same time, outside and inside the juridical order. If the sovereign is truly the one to whom the juridical order grants the power of proclaiming a state of exception and, therefore, of suspending the order's own validity, then "the sovereign stands outside the juridical order and, nevertheless, belongs to it, since it is up to him to decide if the constitution is to be suspended *in toto*" (Schmitt, *Politische Theologie*, p. 13).[22]

Regarding the key point in Carl Schmitt's conception of the sovereign power, Agamben declares:

> The specification that the sovereign is "*at the same time* outside and inside the juridical order" is not insignificant: the sovereign, having the legal power to suspend the validity of the law, legally places himself outside the law. This means that the paradox can also be formulated this way: "the law is outside itself," or: "I, the sovereign, who am outside the law, declare that there is nothing outside the law" [*che non c'è un fuori legge*].[23]

It will only be possible—once and for all—to grasp the structure of this paradox from what Carl Schmitt presents as the structure of the exception (*Ausnahme*). Agamben quotes from Schmitt's *Politische Theologie*, where it is the sovereign power's "decision in absolute purity," which sovereignly determines the order of society. For this reason the sovereign needs the exception: "The exception is that which cannot be subsumed; it defies general codification, but it simultaneously reveals a specifically juridical formal element: the decision in absolute purity. The exception appears in its absolute form when it is a question of creating a situation in which juridical rules can be valid."[24] It is the exception, which according to Carl Schmitt confirms the rule: "The exception is more interesting than the regular case. The latter proves nothing; the exception proves everything. The exception does not

---

[20]     Giorgio Agamben, *Stato di eccezione, Homo Sacer*, II, p. 1, Turin: Bollati Boringhieri 2003, pp. 10–11. (English translation: *State of Exception*, trans. by Kevin Attello, Chicago and London: University of Chicago Press 2005, p. 2.)

[21]     Agamben, *Stato di eccezione*, p. 9. (*State of Exception*, p. 1.)

[22]     Agamben, *Homo Sacer I: Il potere sovrano e la nuda vita*, p. 19. (*Homo Sacer: Sovereign Power and Bare Life*, p. 15.)

[23]     Ibid. Emphasis added.

[24]     Agamben, *Homo Sacer I: Il potere sovrano e la nuda vita*, p. 19. (*Homo Sacer: Sovereign Power and Bare Life*, pp. 15–16.)

only confirm the rule, the rule as such lives off the exception alone."[25] Carl Schmitt
gives the following as a theological grounding for this:

> A Protestant theologian who demonstrated the vital intensity of which theological
> reflection was still capable in the nineteenth century said: "The exception explains
> the general and itself. And when one really wants to study the general, one need only
> look around for a real exception. It brings everything to light more clearly than the
> general itself. After a while, one becomes disgusted with the endless talk about the
> general—there are exceptions. If they cannot be explained, then neither can the general
> be explained. Usually the difficulty is not noticed, since the general is thought about not
> with passion but only with comfortable superficiality. The exception, on the other hand,
> thinks the general with intense passion." (*Politische Theologie*, pp. 19–22).[26]

Giorgio Agamben adds: "It is not by chance that in defining the exception Schmitt
refers to the work of a theologian (who is none other than Søren Kierkegaard)."[27]
The quotation is taken from a page in Kierkegaard's work *Repetition*.[28] According
to Agamben, it is not by accident that Schmitt refers to a theologian since the
fundamental political concepts, according to Schmitt, are in actuality secularized
theological concepts. Here Schmitt places Kierkegaard's conception of the dialectical
relation between the rule and the exception in a juristic context.

According to Schmitt, the sovereign power is manifested especially in the
condition of martial law, where the sovereign power both ensures that the law is
upheld and the same power is able to suspend the law. For Schmitt it was decisive
that the suspending of the law took place within the framework of the law. This
pretext to suspend the protection of the law for certain groups was rejected by the
Jewish art critic and philosopher Walter Benjamin (1892–1940). Just like Hannah
Arendt, he emigrated from Germany in 1933 to France. In 1940 he tried to flee from
France to the USA but was stopped at the Spanish border. He committed suicide in
order not to be delivered to the Gestapo.[29] Walter Benjamin wrote:

> The tradition of the oppressed teaches us that the "state of emergency" in which we
> live is not the exception but the rule. We must attain to a conception of history that is in
> keeping with this insight. Then we shall clearly realize that it is our task to bring about
> a real state of emergency, and this will improve our position in the struggle against
> Fascism.[30]

---

[25]     Agamben, *Homo Sacer I: Il potere sovrano e la nuda vita*, p. 20. *(Homo Sacer: Sovereign Power and Bare Life*, p. 16.)

[26]     Ibid.

[27]     Ibid.

[28]     *SKS* 4, 93 / *R*, 227.

[29]     Agamben was responsible for the publication of Walter Benjamin's collected works in Italian in the years 1979–94.

[30]     Walter Benjamin, *Illuminations*, ed. by Hannah Arendt, trans. by Harry Zohn, London: Fontana Press 1992, pp. 248–9, cf. Agamben, *Stato di eccezione*, pp. 74–5 (*State of Exception*, p. 57). Bülent Diken and Carsten Bagge Laustsen, *The Culture of Exception: Sociology Facing the Camp*, London and New York: Routledge 2005, p. 165.

For as conservative as Schmitt is, Walter Benjamin is revolutionary. Schmitt argues that the sovereign power can suspend the law in a condition of martial law and thus use violence. Here the violence takes place within the framework of the law. In opposition to this Benjamin speaks of a form of violence beyond the law, which he calls "pure violence." This is a violence that takes place outside the limits of the law and warns of something new.[31]

Giorgio Agamben refers by way of example to an outcast, a person without rights within the state, to a figure in the ancient Roman legal practice, namely, the "*homo sacer.*" Agamben writes:

> Let us now observe the life of *homo sacer*, or of the bandit, the *Friedlos*, the *aquae et igni interdictus*, which are in many ways similar. He has been excluded from the religious community and from all political life: he cannot participate in the rites of his *gens*,[32] nor (if he has been declared *infamis et intestabilis*[33]) can he perform any juridical valid act.[34]

With the legal declaration *aquae et igni interdictus* ("forbidden to access to water and fire") a person was condemned to go into voluntary exile. Agamben refers to the Greek ζωή, in the distinction between βίος and ζωή:

> What is more, his entire existence is reduced to a bare life stripped of every right by virtue of the fact that anybody can kill him without committing homicide; he can save himself only in perpetual flight or a foreign land. And yet he is in continuous relationship with the power that banished him, precisely insofar as he is at every instant exposed to an unconditioned threat of death. He is pure *zoê*, but his *zoê* is as such caught in the sovereign ban and must reckon with it at every moment finding the best way to elude or deceive it. In this sense, no life, as exiles and bandits know well, is more "political" than this.[35]

[31]    Giorgio Agamben writes about Walter Benjamin's essay "Critique of Violence" from 1921: "The aim of the essay is to ensure the possibility of a violence...that lies absolutely 'outside' (*ausserhalb*) and 'beyond' (*jenseits*) the law and that, as such, could shatter the dialectic between lawmaking violence and law-preserving violence (*rechtsetzende und rechtserhaltene Gewalt*). Benjamin calls this other figure of violence 'pure' (*reine Gewalt*) or 'divine,' and, in the human sphere, 'revolutionary.' The proper characteristic of this violence is that it neither makes nor preserves law, but deposes it (*Entsetzung des Rechtes*) and thus inaugurates a new historical epoch," Agamben, *Stato di eccezione*, pp. 69–70 (*State of Exception*, p. 53).

[32]    The Latin word *gens* means a tribe or people.

[33]    The Latin formulation *infamis et intestabilis* means "infamous and excluded from being able to bear witness in a trial."

[34]    Agamben, *Homo Sacer I: Il potere sovrano e la nuda vita*, p. 205. (*Homo Sacer: Sovereign Power and Bare Life*, p. 183.)

[35]    Agamben, *Homo Sacer I: Il potere sovrano e la nuda vita*, p. 205. (*Homo Sacer: Sovereign Power and Bare Life*, pp. 183–4.)

The *homo sacer* was thus a person, whom one certainly did not have to kill, but if one did, then one was not prosecuted for it.[36] The artist Veronica Juhl writes in *No-land*:

> With a quick sketch one can see the difference between the *homo sacer*, the outlaw, the accursed, the myth of the werewolf (who does not belong either among animals or human beings, in the city or in the forest), the Muslim (who is stripped of all of his human and cultural attributes), the refugee and the asylum seeker (driven from his native soil and assigned to a transient existence)."[37]

Those people who are interned find themselves in a no-man's-land, without recourse to human rights.

Agamben's main point is that society or the state needs a *homo sacer*: it is in relation to the outcast, the interned, that society defines itself. Agamben draws a direct line from the death camps during World War II to the interment camps for asylum seekers, to the American military base at Guantanamo, where prisoners are incarcerated without having any opportunity to defend themselves by legal means.

Agamben attempts "a rethinking of all categories of our political tradition in light of the relation between sovereign power and bare life."[38] His work *Homo Sacer* stands out as the first product of this new rethinking of all the political categories.[39]

## IV. *"Ethica more Auschwitz demonstrata"*

As noted, Giorgio Agamben was born in 1942 and thus did not himself experience World War II first-hand. Agamben asks who are the true witnesses to what happened at Auschwitz? He comments on the chemist and author Primo Levi (1919–87), who survived Auschwitz. Levi spoke of his deportation to, and stay at, Auschwitz in his book with the challenging title *If This Is a Man* (*Se questo è un uomo*, 1947). For the Nazis the prisoners at the camp were no longer human. Levi clearly plays on David's Psalm 8 from the Old Testament:

> O Lord, our Lord, how excellent is thy name in all earth! who hast set thy glory above the heavens. Out of the mouth of babes and sucklings hast thou ordained strength because of thine enemies, that thou mightest still the enemy and the avenger. When I consider thy heavens, the work of thy fingers, the moon and the stars, which thou hast ordained; What is a man, that thou art mindful of him?[40]

---

[36] Cf. Agamben, *Homo Sacer I: Il potere sovrano e la nuda vita*, p. 79 (*Homo Sacer: Sovereign Power and Bare Life*, p. 71), with reference to Pompeius Festus, *De verborum significatione* (*On the Significance of Words*).

[37] Veronica Juhl, *No-land*, Copenhagen: Introite! 2004, pp. 82–3.

[38] Giorgio Agamben, *Mezzi senza fine. Note sulla politica*, Turin: Bollati Boringhieri 1996, p. 10. (English translation: *Means without End*, trans. by Vincenzo Binetti and Cesare Casarino, Minneapolis and London: University of Minnesota Press 2000, p. x.)

[39] Ibid.

[40] Ps 8:1–4, King James version.

David thus asks in Psalm 8: "What is a man?" Primo Levi begins *If This Is a Man* with the following words:

> You who live safe
> In your warm houses,
> You who find, returning in the evening,
> Hot food and friendly faces:
> Consider if this is a man
> Who works in the mud
> Who does not know peace
> Who fights for a scrap of bread
> Who dies because of a yes or a no.
> Consider if this is a woman,
> Without hair and without name
> With no more strength to remember,
> Her eyes empty and her womb cold
> Like a frog in winter.
> Meditate that this came about:
> and commend these words to you.
> Carve them in your hearts
> At home, in the street,
> Going to bed, rising;
> Repeat them to your children,
> Or may your house fall apart,
> May illness impede you,
> May your children turn their faces from you.[41]

Were they still human beings? Is it not the state, which gives the individual his significance by investing him with citizenship and civil rights, and also can take these back again? If this has happened, how can we forget it? Levi writes in the chapter "On the Bottom":

> Imagine now a man who is deprived of everyone he loves, and at the same time of his house, his habits, his clothes, in short, of everything he possesses: he will be a hollow man, reduced to suffering and needs, forgetful of dignity and restraint, for he who loses all often easily loses himself. He will be a man whose life or death can be lightly decided with no sense of human affinity, in the most fortunate of cases, on the basis of a pure judgment of utility. It is in this way that one can understand the double sense of the term "extermination camp," and it is now clear what we seek to express with the phrase: "to lie on the bottom."[42]

---

[41]    Here quoted from Primo Levi, *Survival in Auschwitz: The Nazi Assault on Humanity*, trans. by Stuart Woolf, New York: Collier Books 1987 [1961], p. 8. *Survival in Auschwitz* originally appeared in English under the title *If This Is a Man*, trans. by Stuart Woolf, New York: Orion Press 1959.

[42]    Levi, *Survival in Auschwitz*, p. 23.

Levi survived the horrors of Auschwitz. Nevertheless he did not feel that he was the right person to bear witness to what went on there. He tells of the shame of the prisoners for having survived the concentration camp. On the other hand, there are only the survivors who can bear witness to what took place. The real witnesses were those who hit bottom, saw Gorgon and died. No one has returned from this and has been able to bear witness to what befell the prisoners of the concentration camp.[43] It is not just a question of registering in a historically precise manner what took place. It is not merely a question of remembering but of bearing witness to what took place. It is important that here the witness enters into the events about which he bears witness, into what happened.

Agamben takes up Levi's accounts of Auschwitz in his book with the title *Remnants of Auschwitz: The Witness and the Archive* (1999). It is only the survivors who can bear witness to what took place at Auschwitz. They are the remains after Auschwitz, what remained left over. There is a difference in the witnesses—and also in the archives, the historical archives. There are neutral reports where the reporter himself does not enter into the events. It was only by bearing witness to what they themselves were a part of—although they survived it—that it was meaningful to bear witness to what took place, thus to witness another person's nakedness, to the greatest degree in the concentration camp, namely in *the Muselmann*, and thus to be confronted with one's own human nakedness.[44]

Levi gives an account of what was worst in the concentration camp, what he called "the grey zone." Here the Nazis forced the prisoners of the camp to help with the gassing and cremation of their fellow prisoners, only later to themselves suffer the same gruesome fate. The prisoners of the camp were even deprived of their human innocence. The difference between executioner and victim was eliminated.

---

[43] Concerning Gorgon and the impossibility of witnessing, see Agamben, *Quel che resta di Auschwitz*, p. 31, cf. p. 49. (English translation: *Remnants of Auschwitz: The Witness and the Archive*, p. 33, cf. p. 54): "I [Primo Levi] must repeat: we, the survivors, are not the true witnesses....We survivors are not only an exiguous but also an anomalous minority: we are those who by their prevarications or abilities or good luck did not touch bottom. Those who did so, those who saw the Gorgon, have not returned to tell about it or have returned mute, but they are the Muslims, the submerged, the complete witnesses, the ones whose deposition would have a general significance. They are the rule, we are the exception....We who are favored by fate tried, with more or less wisdom, to recount not only our fate but also that of the others, indeed of the drowned; but this was a discourse 'on behalf of third parties,' the story of things seen at close hand, not experienced personally. The destruction brought to an end, the job completed, was not told by anyone, just as no one ever returned to describe his own death."

[44] The Hungarian Jewish political thinker Agnes Heller (b. 1929) in her book on Shakespeare, *The Time is Out of Joint: Shakespeare as Philosopher of History* (Lanham: Rowman & Littlefield 2002) treats Shakespeare's drama *King Lear*. King Lear has come into a storm in more than one sense of the word. During the stormy weather King Lear tears his clothes into pieces. Does he do this because he has become mad? Or is this an expression of the fact that King Lear has become aware of another Lear than the one who is wearing his clothes? In other words, is this due to the fact that King Lear has been confronted with himself—as he stands there in the stormy weather? According to Heller, his actions are explained by the fact that he has been confronted with his own human nakedness, an expression of "the *ultimate existential experience*," p. 52.

If one is to speak of an ethics in the future—it must be an ethics that is tested by the horrors that took place in Auschwitz. This is what Agamben calls an *ethica more Auschwitz demonstrata*,[45] that is, an ethics tested on the background of Auschwitz. Thus there is no talk of a "bourgeois" ethics or morality, but of an ethics based on the naked human being, and where human dignity[46] has broken down.[47] By being confronted with this making people inhuman, impersonal, one must ask whether there remains anything after Auschwitz, or if the Nazis have been so successful in carrying out their project of stripping down human beings that there is nothing left. According to the Nazis, if the individual had no citizenship and the rights attached to it as citizen, then they were no longer humans.[48] It is based on the Nazis' stripped-down human being that one must ask from the beginning what it is that makes us human. If there is a remainder after Auschwitz, what is it that the Nazis could not manage to destroy?

According to Levi, the real witness of what took place in the concentration camps is the *Muselmann*. This figure is the limit existence of the concentration camp. A figure which none of the other prisoners of the camp liked to be confronted with since they could see in the *Muselmänner* what was waiting for them themselves.[49]

---

[45] Agamben, *Quel che resta di Auschwitz: l'archivio e il testimone: homo sacer III*, p. 9. (*Remnants of Auschwitz: The Witness and the Archive*, p. 13.) Cf. below about Agamben's concluding remark in his essay, *Beyond Human Rights*.

[46] The paradoxical element involved in the fact that the new ethic begins only after human dignity has been lost after Auschwitz is expressed by Agamben thus: "The good that the survivors were able to save from the camp—if there is any sense of speaking of a 'good' here—is therefore not dignity. On the contrary, the atrocious news that the survivors carry from the camp to the land of human beings is precisely that it is possible to loose dignity and decency beyond imagination, that there is still life in the most extreme degradation. And this new knowledge now becomes the touchstone by which to judge and measure all morality and dignity. The *Muselmann*, who is its most extreme expression, is the guard on the threshold of a new ethics, an ethics of a form of life that begins where dignity ends," Agamben, *Quel che resta di Auschwitz: l'archivio e il testimone: homo sacer III*, p. 63 (*Remnants of Auschwitz: The Witness and the Archive*, p. 69).

[47] Agamben in *La communità che viene*, p. 10 (*The Coming Community*, p. 13): "The meaning of ethics becomes clear only when one understands that the good is not, and cannot be, a good thing or possibility beside or above every bad thing or possibility, that the authentic and the true are not real predicates of an object perfectly analogous (even if opposed) to the false and the inauthentic. Ethics begins only when the good is revealed to consist in nothing other than a grasping of evil and when the authentic and the proper have no other content than the inauthentic and the improper."

[48] Thus Agamben emphasizes: "One of the few rules the Nazis constantly obeyed throughout the course of the "final solution" was that Jews and Gypsies could be sent to extermination camps only after having been fully denationalized (that is, after they had been stripped of even that second-class citizenship to which they had been relegated after the Nuremberg Laws)," Agamben, *Mezzi senza fine. Note sulla politica*, p. 26 (*Means without End*, p. 22).

[49] The expression *Muselmann* or Muslim is presumably derived from the way in which they moved by being bent forward, which bears some similarity to the posture Muslims assume in prayer.

According to Agamben, the subject is placed in the caesuras, the fractures, or the cuts.[50] The subject or the self does not exist ahead of time—but only by becoming a witness: by speaking where there was no language.[51] Thus one can only bear witness to the human by witnessing the inhuman. There is a remainder after Auschwitz. The subject is this remainder and connection: "It is because there is testimony only where there is an impossibility of speaking, because there is a witness only where there has been desubjectification, that the *Muselmann* is the complete witness and that the survivor and the *Muselmann* cannot be split apart," Agamben writes.[52]

Agamben writes about this caesura or limit figure, which the *Muselmann* represented, about the various perspectives from which they could be regarded:

> At times a medical figure or an ethical category, at times a political limit or an anthropological concept, the *Muselmann* is an infinite being in whom not only humanity and non-humanity, but also vegetative existence and relation, physiology and ethics, medicine and politics, and life and death continuously pass through each other.[53]

The *Muselmann* represented, according to Agamben, "the perfect cipher of the camp, the non-place in which all disciplinary barriers are destroyed and all embankments flooded."[54] In continuation of this Agamben in *Remnants of Auschwitz* refers to Kierkegaard, since he has Kierkegaard's existential concept of "the exception" appear in the jurists' description of the condition of martial law.[55]

---

[50]     Cf. Agamben, *Quel che resta di Auschwitz: l'archivio e il testimone: homo sacer III*, p. 135 (*Remnants of Auschwitz: The Witness and the Archive*, p. 145).

[51]     Agamben calls "subjectivity as that which, in its very possibility of speech, bears witness to an impossibility of speech. This is why subjectivity appears as *witness*; this is why it can speak for those who cannot speak. Testimony is a potentiality that becomes actual through an impotentiality of speech; it is, moreover, an impossibility that gives itself existence through a possibility of speaking. These two movements cannot be identified either with a subject or with a consciousness; yet they cannot be divided into two communicable substances. Their inseparable intimacy is testimony," Agamben, *Quel che resta di Auschwitz: l'archivio e il testimone: homo sacer III*, p. 136 (*Remnants of Auschwitz: The Witness and the Archive*, p. 146). Cf. Kierkegaard's talk about the self as a synthesis in the introduction to *The Sickness unto Death* (*SKS* 11, 129 / *SUD*, 13). Concerning "the dialectic inherent in the self as a synthesis, and therefore each constituent is its opposite," see *SKS* 11, 146 / *SUD*, 30.

[52]     Agamben, *Quel che resta di Auschwitz: l'archivio e il testimone: homo sacer III*, p. 147. (*Remnants of Auschwitz. The Witness and the Archive*, p. 158.) (It would be impossible to make oneself understood with the help of the Nazis' language. It is another matter that the *Muselmann* literally no longer had language.)

[53]     Agamben, *Quel che resta di Auschwitz: l'archivio e il testimone: homo sacer III*, p. 43. (*Remnants of Auschwitz: The Witness and the Archive*, p. 48.)

[54]     Ibid.

[55]     One can primarily read the works *Homo Sacer: Sovereign Power and Bare Life*, *Remnants of Auschwitz: The Witness and the Archive*, and *The Time That Remains: A Commentary on the Letter to the Romans*, respectively, juridically, ethically, and messianically, in accordance with the manner in which the caesuras or cuts are made in, respectively, a juridical, ethical and messianic determination of the "state of exception."

It is with reference to the same quotation in *Repetition*, which Carl Schmitt used to describe the juristic-political condition of martial law in his *Politische Theologie*[56] that Agamben writes:

> Recently, philosophers and theologians alike have invoked the paradigm of the "extreme situation" or "limit situation." The function of this paradigm is analogous to the function ascribed by some jurists to the state of exception. Just as the state of exception allows for the foundation and definition of the normal legal order, so in the light of the extreme situation—which is at bottom, a kind of exception—it is possible to judge and decide on the normal situation. As Kierkegaard writes, "the exception explains the general as well as itself. And when one really wants to study the general, one need only look around for a real exception."[57]

It is not "the general," which explains itself and "the exception," but the other way around. Or is it?

### V. The Collective Identity—the Individual Human Being

In his work *Two Ages: The Age of Revolution and the Present Age, A Literary Review* (1846) Kierkegaard undertook a critical analysis of society. The external occasion for Kierkegaard's review was provided by the novel *Two Ages*, which was written by Madame Gyllembourg (1773–1856), although her name does not appear on the cover of the book which was published by her son, Johan Ludvig Heiberg (1791–1860). The two ages in question were the French Revolution of 1789 and its effects on life in Copenhagen,[58] and then one generation later, in Kierkegaard's own contemporary age. First there was the age of revolution with its immediate passion and then the next generation which represented a reflective age.

Kierkegaard presents in *A Literary Review* a characterization of the dialectic which was the distinguishing mark of, respectively, antiquity, the epoch of Christianity along with the present age, namely, the period after the French Revolution. Kierkegaard thus shows how the conception of the state and the self-consciousness of the individual—or lack thereof—correspond to each other:

> The dialectic of antiquity was oriented to the eminent (the great individual—and then the crowd; one free man, and then the slaves); at present the dialectic of Christianity is oriented to representation (the majority perceive themselves in the representative and are liberated by the awareness that he is representing them in a kind of self-consciousness). The dialectic of the present age is oriented to equality, and its most logical implementation, albeit abortive, is leveling, the negative unity of the negative unity of the negative mutual reciprocity of individuals.[59]

---

[56]      Cf. note 26 and note 28.

[57]      Agamben, *Quel che resta di Auschwitz: l'archivio e il testimone: homo sacer III*, p. 43. (*Remnants of Auschwitz: The Witness and the Archive*, p. 48.)

[58]      According to both Kierkegaard and Agamben, the French Revolution comes to play a decisive role in the understanding of the identity of the individual human being.

[59]      *SKS* 8, 81 / *TA*, 84.

What happens when passion is driven by the thought of equality (cf. age of the French Revolution as the age of passion in relation to the later age as that of reflection)? Then arises envy—that one person should not be greater than another. And when envy joins forces, it happens in what Kierkegaard designates as "the *negatively unifying principle*."[60] There is nothing positive for people to join forces about. Kierkegaard gives the following acute analysis:

> [T]he envy is therefore two-sided, a selfishness in the individual and then again the selfishness of associates toward him. Reflection's envy holds the will and energy in a kind of captivity. The individual must first of all break out of the prison in which his own reflection holds him, and if he succeeds, he still does not stand in the open but in the vast penitentiary built by the reflection of his associates, and to this he is again related through the reflection-relation in himself, and this can be broken only by religious inwardness, however much he sees through the falseness of the relation. But the fact that reflection is holding the individual and the age in a prison, the fact that it is reflection that does it and not tyrants and secret police, not the clergy and the aristocracy—reflection does everything in its power to thwart this discernment and maintains the flattering notion that the possibilities which reflection offers are much more magnificent than a paltry decision.[61]

It is the individual human being's relation to himself or lacking relation to himself and the meaning pressed from the surroundings that the individual receives, which Kierkegaard takes up. For Kierkegaard it is not just about being represented by others in existence—about being satisfied to exist second-hand:

> It will be no good to appeal to and summon a Holger the Dane[62] or a Martin Luther. Their age is past, and as a matter of fact it is indolence on the part of individuals to want such a one, it is a finite impatience that wants to have at cheap, second-hand prices the highest, which is dearly bought at first-hand.[63]

What Kierkegaard wrote in *Fear and Trembling* (1843)—written under the pseudonym Johannes de silentio—is informative:

> It is a simple matter to level all existence to the idea of the state or the idea of a society. If this is done, it is also simple to mediate, for one never comes to the paradox that the single individual is higher than the universal, something I can also express symbolically in a statement by Pythagoras to the effect that the odd number is more perfect than the even number.[64]

Kierkegaard does not wish to go back to antiquity or to the age of Christianity in the direction of the idea of representation, but in spite of everything he wishes to say yes to the leveling, which his contemporary age would have—and where the individual either must be destroyed by or leap over the sword of leveling—where there is

---

[60]  *SKS* 8, 78 / *TA*, 81.
[61]  *SKS* 8, 78 / *TA*, 81–2.
[62]  A Danish hero of legend, who will only awaken when Denmark is in grave peril.
[63]  *SKS* 8, 85 / *TA*, 89.
[64]  *SKS* 4,155 / *FT*, 62.

nothing remaining, no hierarchical system to stick to, but where the individual exists for God. Kierkegaard writes about the leap:

> Then it will be said: "Look, everything is ready; look, the cruelty of abstraction exposes the vanity of the finite in itself; look, the abyss of the infinite is opening up; look, the sharp scythe of leveling permits all, every single one, to leap over the blade—look, God is waiting! Leap, then, into the embrace of God."[65]

Thus leveling is a dialectic: it can either mean that the individual human being is destroyed or the opposite. This is Kierkegaard's real point. The entire emphasis is placed all the time on the decision of the individual—before God.

Agamben likewise does not wish to revert to earlier times:

> Of course, the task at hand is not to bring the state of exception back within its spatially and temporally defined boundaries in order to reaffirm the primacy of a norm and of rights that are themselves ultimately grounded in it. From the real state of exception in which we live, it is not possible to return to the state of law [*stato di diritto*], for at issue now are the very concepts of "state" and "law."[66]

Kierkegaard writes later in *The Sickness unto Death*:

> If order is to be maintained in existence—and God does want that, for he is not a God of confusion—then the first thing to keep in mind is that every human being is an individual human being and is to become conscious of being an individual human being. If men are first permitted to run together in what Aristotle calls the animal category—the crowd—then this abstraction, instead of being less than nothing, even less than the most insignificant individual human being, comes to be regarded as being something—then it does not take long before this abstraction becomes God.[67]

On the one hand, the individual takes on the identity of the mass, but at the same time is deprived of his own significance and thereby becomes "less than nothing, even less than the most insignificant individual human being."[68] Precisely by the human being running together and as the mass wanting to assert itself, it falls under Aristotle's "animal category"—just as also Agamben makes his criticism of Western civilization on precisely this point. He perceives a mistake which enters into the very foundation of civilization right from the beginning, and the fatal consequences of it have found their preliminary culmination in the death camps of the twentieth century.

[65]  *SKS* 8, 102–3 / *TA*, 108.
[66]  Agamben, *Stato di eccezione*, p. 111. (*State of Exception*, p. 87.)
[67]  *SKS* 11, 229 / *SUD*, 117–18. Cf. Aristotle, *Politics*, Book III, 11, 1281a 40–43. A collective identity reduces the human being to an "animal category," with "the predominance of the generation over the individual" (*SKS* 11, 229 / *SUD*, 118).
[68]  Ibid.

## VI. The Denationalized Human Being

In his dissertation *The Concept of Irony* (1841) Kierkegaard criticizes Socrates for the fact that his virtues—to use a Hegelian formulation—"lacked the deep earnestness that every virtue acquires only when it is ordered in a totality. But since the state had lost its significance for Socrates, his virtues are not civic virtues but personal virtues— indeed, to define them more sharply, they are imaginatively constructed virtues."[69] In line with this, Hegel had designated the conscience of the individual as belonging to "a moral form of evil." If the individual followed his conscience without allowing himself to be incorporated into the totality that the state constituted, it would lead to "arbitrariness."[70] Kierkegaard is upset about his statements about Socrates and notes in his journals under the heading, "A Passage in My Dissertation":

> Influenced as I was by Hegel and whatever was modern, without the maturity really to comprehend greatness, I could not resist pointing out somewhere in my dissertation that it was a defect on the part of Socrates to disregard the whole and only consider numerically the individuals. What a Hegelian fool I was! It is precisely this that powerfully demonstrates what a great ethicist Socrates was.[71]

In the second part of his work *For Self-Examination: Judge for Yourself!*, which was only published after his death,[72] Kierkegaard portrays Jesus as at once a reconciler and a model:

> He allows himself to be born in poverty and lowliness, and not only that, but in disrepute, of a betrothed virgin, to whom the upright man to whom she was betrothed showed the kindness of not quietly separating from her (which he had at first considered doing and which, humanly speaking, would have been an act of mercy). That is how he came into the world, as if he were outside the world, ostracized by the world immediately upon his arrival, "without father, without mother, without genealogy," attached by birth to no other human being.[73]

Kierkegaard expands on this: "birth itself, when the baby thereby comes to belong to a family, birth is a tie that immediately binds this human in closer alliance with other human beings."[74] Kierkegaard comments upon the continuation of the story with the flight into Egypt: "The family—if it may be called that, for it is no family—flees with the child. And now this child has no fatherland either…next to the alliance that binds the family together is the alliance that binds a people together."[75] Kierkegaard explains: "Therefore, he who is the prototype….He belonged to nothing and to no one, was in no alliance with anything or with anybody, was a stranger in this world,

---

[69]    *SKS* 1, 272 / *CI*, 239–40.
[70]    *SKS* 1, 270 / *CI*, 228.
[71]    *SKS* 24, 32, NB21:35 / *JP* 4, 4281.
[72]    Kierkegaard wrote this in the years 1851–52, but it was only published posthumously in 1876 by his brother Peter Christian Kierkegaard (1805–88).
[73]    *SV1* XII, 433 / *JFY*, 160.
[74]    Ibid.
[75]    *SV1* XII, 436 / *JFY*, 164.

in poverty and lowliness, without a nest, without a den, without a place where he could lay his head."[76] Jesus earned his living outside of the community. He was condemned to death as a rebel against the national unity. "Public safety" demanded it.[77]

## VII. Whatever Singularity

Agamben in *The Coming Community* raises a question about "the condition of belonging."[78] He asks, "What could be the politics of whatever singularity, that is, of a being whose community is mediated not by any condition of belonging (being red, being Italian, being communist)...?"[79] Agamben answers by referring to what happened at Tiananmen Square—the Square of Heavenly Peace in Beijing. Why did the Chinese authorities react by sending in tanks even if the demands of the students were so indefinable? Was it precisely because the authorities saw that there was more at stake here than the opposition between communism and democracy—namely, that the individual wanted to be able to be what he or she was as an individual? This is an issue that the leadership in China has in common with the Western states. Agamben explains: "Wherever these singularities peacefully demonstrate their being in common there will be a Tiananmen, and, sooner or later, the tanks will appear."[80] Agamben further explains:

> Whatever singularities cannot form a *societas* because they do not possess any identity to vindicate nor any bond of belonging for which to seek recognition. In the final instance the State can recognize any claim for identity—even that of a State identity within the State....What the state cannot tolerate in any way, however, is that the singularities form a community without affirming an identity, that humans co-belong without any representable condition of belonging.[81]

Agamben writes in the same context: "A being radically devoid of any representable identity would be absolutely irrelevant to the State."[82] It is what "the hypocritical dogma of the sacredness of human life and the vacuous declarations of human rights are meant to hide. *Sacred* here can only mean what the term meant in Roman Law:

---

[76] *SV1* XII, 439 / *JFY*, 167.
[77] *SV1* XII, 448 / *JFY*, 178.
[78] Agamben, *La comunità che viene*, p. 7. (*The Coming Community*, p. 9.)
[79] Agamben, *La comunità che viene*, p. 58. (*The Coming Community*, p. 85.)
[80] Agamben, *La comunità che viene*, p. 60. (*The Coming Community*, p. 87.)
[81] Agamben, *La comunità che viene*, p. 59. (*The Coming Community*, p. 86.) Agamben presents three theses as preliminary conclusions of his investigation, Agamben, *Homo Sacer I: Il potere sovrano e la nuda vita*, p. 202 (*Homo Sacer: Sovereign Power and Bare Life*, p. 181): "The first of these theses calls into question every theory of the contractual origin of state power and, along with it, every attempt to ground political communities in something like a 'belonging,' whether it be founded on popular, national, religious, or any other identity."
[82] Agamben, *La comunità che viene*, p. 59. (*The Coming Community*, p. 86.)

*Sacer* is the one who had been excluded from the human world and who, even though she or he could not be sacrificed, could be killed without committing homicide."[83]

Agamben dares to continue with this prophecy that "the coming politics will no longer be a struggle to conquer or to control the state on the part of either new or old social subjects, but rather a struggle between the state and the nonstate (humanity), that is, an irresolvable disjunction between whatever singularities and the state organization."[84] Kierkegaard expresses himself in line with this: "the established order will not put up with consisting of something as loose as a collection of millions of individuals....The established order wants to be a totality that recognizes nothing above itself but has every individual under it and judges every individual who subordinates himself to the established order."[85] This is the individual's "collision" with "the established order," and the existing order was upset about the fact "that the single individual wanted to withdraw from his relation to the established order."[86]

## VIII. Beyond Human Rights

In 1943 Hannah Arendt published the article "We Refugees."[87] Agamben takes up this essay precisely 50 years later in *Beyond Human Rights*. According to Arendt, the refugees who have been driven from their country are their people's avant garde.[88] Giorgio Agamben follows this up by stating that the refugee is perhaps the only imaginable figure for the people today against the background of the national state's unstoppable decline.[89] The national state more and more shows that it is unable to provide protection for the refugee. Hannah Arendt had drawn attention to how human rights showed themselves to be meaningless when there was really a need for them because they were only rights of citizens tied to the national state. Agamben comments on this:

> Hannah Arendt titled the chapter of her book *Imperialism* that concerns the refugee problem "The Decline of the Nation-State and the End of the Rights of Man." One should try to take seriously this formulation, which indissolubly links the fate of the Rights of Man with the fate of the modern nation-state in such a way that the waning

---

[83]    Agamben, *La communità che viene*, p. 59. (*The Coming Community*, pp. 86–7.)

[84]    Agamben, *Mezzi senza fine. Note sulla politica*, p. 72 (Agamben's prophecy is printed in italics in the Italian edition) (*Means without End*, p. 88).

[85]    *SKS* 12, 99–100 / *PC*, 91.

[86]    *SKS* 12, 101 / *PC*, 93. In his authorship prior to the *Concluding Unscientific Postscript* (1846), Kierkegaard emphasizes that the outer is not the inner and the inner is not the outer. This hidden innerness is turned in the last part of Kierkegaard's authorship into a "collision" in the outer with "the established order."

[87]    Hannah Arendt, "We Refugees," *The Menorah Journal*, vol. 31, no. 1, 1943, pp. 69–77. Referred to by Agamben, *Mezzi senza fine. Note sulla politica*, pp. 20–29. (*Means without End*, pp. 15–26.)

[88]    Agamben, *Mezzi senza fine. Note sulla politica*, p. 20 (*Means without End*, p. 16): "Refugees driven from country to country represent the vanguard of their peoples." Arendt, "We Refugees," p. 77.

[89]    Agamben, *Mezzi senza fine. Note sulla politica*, p. 21. (*Means without End*, p. 16.)

of the latter necessarily implies the obsolescence of the former. Here the paradox is that precisely the figure that should have embodied human rights more than any other—namely, the refugee—marked instead the radical crisis of the concept. The conception of human rights based on the supposed existence of human being as such, Arendt tells us, proves to be untenable as soon as those who profess it find themselves confronted for the first time with people who have really lost every quality and every specific relation except for the pure fact of being human.[90]

Agamben draws attention to the ambiguous title of the declaration from 1789: *Déclaration des droits de l'homme et du citoyen*. Are human rights in reality only tied to being a citizen? Agamben remarks about the impossible situation of the refugee merely to be what he or she is:

> That there is no autonomous space in the political order of the nation-state for something like the pure human in itself is evident at the very least from the fact that, even in the best of cases, the status of refugee has always been considered a temporary condition that ought to lead either to naturalization or to repatriation. A stable statute for the human in itself is inconceivable in the law of the nation-state.[91]

It is high time, Agamben claims, to stop regarding the human rights declaration of 1789—and what had been added subsequently of human rights declarations—as proclamations of "eternal, meta-juridical values,"[92] which have as their task to bind the legislator to respect such values. In reality human rights represent primarily

> the originary figure for the inscription of natural life in the political-juridical order of the nation-state. Naked life (the human being), which in antiquity belonged to God[93] and in the classical world was clearly distinct (as *zoê*) from political life (*bios*), comes to the forefront in the management of the state and becomes, so to speak, its earthly foundation. Nation-state means a state that makes nativity or birth [*nascita*] (that is, naked human life) the foundation of its own sovereignty.[94]

The sovereign power constitutes itself with the help of the naked human being. The one corresponds to the other. It is the naked human being who provides the body for the sovereign power. It is the naked human being who bears it.

---

[90]     Agamben, *Mezzi senza fine. Note sulla politica*, p. 23. (*Means without End*, p. 19.) Hannah Arendt, *Imperialism*, Part 2 of *The Origins of Totalitarianism*, New York: Hartcourt, Brace 1951, pp. 290–5.

[91]     Agamben, *Mezzi senza fine. Note sulla politica*, p. 24. (*Means without End*, p. 20.)

[92]     Ibid.

[93]     According to Agamben, *Homo Sacer I: Il potere sovrano e la nuda vita*, p. 141 (*Homo Sacer: Sovereign Power and Bare Life*, p. 128): "Declarations of rights must therefore be viewed as the place in which the passage from divinely authorized royal sovereignty to national sovereignty is accomplished. This passage assures the exception of life in the new state order that will succeed the collapse of the *ancien régime*. The fact that in this process the 'subject' is...transformed into a 'citizen' means that birth—which is to say, bare natural life as such—here for the first time becomes (thanks to a transformation whose biopolitical consequences we are only beginning to discern today) the immediate bearer of sovereignty."

[94]     Agamben, *Mezzi senza fine. Note sulla politica*, p. 24. (*Means without End*, pp. 20–1.)

"If the refugee represents such a disquieting element in the order of the nation-state, this is so primarily because, by breaking the identity between the human and the citizen and that between nativity and nationality, it brings the originary fiction of sovereign to crisis,"[95] writes Agamben. What is new is the increasing groups of people who are not able to be represented within the national state. "Inasmuch as the refugee, an apparently marginal figure, unhinges the old trinity of state-nation-territory, it deserves instead to be regarded as the central figure of our political history."[96] The refugee is, according to Agamben, "nothing less than a limit-concept that at once brings a radical crisis to the principles of the nation-state and clears the way for a renewal that can no longer be delayed."[97] Agamben concludes *Beyond Human Rights* by stating: "Only in a world in which the spaces of states have been thus perforated and topologically deformed and in which the citizen has been able to recognize the refugee he or she is—only in such a world is the political survival of humankind thinkable."[98]

## IX. Dialectics of Caesuras

Agamben has nowhere given a better account of the fundamental significance of the caesuras as the crucial point of his entire authorship than in his commentary on Paul's Letter to the Romans under the title *The Time That Remains*. The way that the caesuras are interpreted has nothing to do with the older view of Hegelian theses and antitheses, which are then sublated and mediated in syntheses. Agamben does, however, make use of Hegel in his account of the dialectic of the condition of the exception.[99] Agamben does not aim at a universalism above the caesuras, but, vice versa, he wishes that the divisions of the divisions be followed to their furthest extreme. The presupposition for caesuras—and also for the divisions of caesuras—Agamben finds in the law. Thus he writes in *The Time That Remains*:

> Paul actually starts by stating that the law operates primarily in instituting divisions and separations. In so doing, he seems to take the etymological meaning of the Greek term *nomos* seriously, since he uses the term to designate the Torah as well as laws in general, in that *nomos* derives from *nemô*, "to divide, to attribute parts."[100]

Agamben points to the fundamental division in Jewish law "between Jews and non-Jews, or in Paul's words, between *Ioudaioi* and *ethnê*. In the Bible, the concept of a "people" is in fact already divided between *am* and *goy* (plural *goyim*). *Am* is Israel,

---

[95]     Agamben, *Mezzi senza fine. Note sulla politica*, p. 25. (*Means without End*, p. 21.)
[96]     Agamben, *Mezzi senza fine. Note sulla politica*, p. 25. (*Means without End*, p. 22.)
[97]     Agamben, *Mezzi senza fine. Note sulla politica*, p. 26. (*Means without End*, pp. 22–3.)
[98]     Agamben, *Mezzi senza fine. Note sulla politica*, pp. 28–9. (*Means without End*, p. 26.)
[99]     Agamben, *Homo Sacer I: Il potere sovrano e la nuda vita*, pp. 25–6. (*Homo Sacer: Sovereign Power and Bare Life*, p. 21.)
[100]    Giorgio Agamben, *Il tempo che resta. Un commento alla Lettera ai Romani*, Turin: Bollati Boringhieri 2000, p. 49. (English translation: *The Time That Remains: A Commentary on the Letter to the Romans*, trans. by Patricia Dailey, Stanford: Stanford University Press 2005, p. 47.)

the elected people, with whom Yahweh formed a *berit*, a pact; the *goyim* are the other peoples."[101] This division between Jews and non-Jews is total, and it has led to ethnic conflicts.

Agamben, however, refers to Apelles, who with his cut undertook a division of the division lengthwise.[102] Thus Paul undertakes a division of the division by distinguishing between "Jews according to the breath" and "Jews according to the flesh." It is one thing to be a Jew in the external sense by being circumcised, but it is another to truly be one.[103] Thus Paul makes use of the opposition between σάρξ and πνεῦμα.[104] Paul makes this same distinction of Jews and non-Jews, even if he does not express it directly. This division is not total, but there is a remainder left behind, both among the Jewish people and the non-Jewish people. None of these peoples coincide with themselves.[105]

This is Agamben's original new interpretation—and what he uses in an existential-political context. The Jewish people should not try to make itself into something other than Jews by raising itself up above the differences. Likewise, other peoples should not make themselves something different from what they are: there is no people—there is no human being—which coincides with itself, but there is a caesura, a remainder, upon which everything rests.[106] This comes forth, as Agamben writes in *Remnants of Auschwitz*, in the "extreme situation" or "limit situation": "As Kierkegaard writes: 'the exception explains the general as well as itself. And when one really wants to study the general, one need only look around for a real

---

[101]     Agamben, *Il tempo che resta. Un commento alla Lettera ai Romani*, p. 50. (*The Time That Remains: A Commentary on the Letter to the Romans*, p. 47.)

[102]     Concerning Apelles' cut, see Agamben, *Il tempo che resta. Un commento alla Lettera ai Romani*, p. 52. (*The Time That Remains: A Commentary on the Letter to the Romans*, p. 50.)

[103]     Agamben, *Il tempo che resta. Un commento alla Lettera ai Romani*, p. 52 (*The Time That Remains: A Commentary on the Letter to the Romans*, p. 50) (see Rom 2:28–9).

[104]     Agamben translates the Greek word πνεῦμα with "breath."

[105]     Agamben writes in his commentary on the Letter to the Romans: "This means that 'the [true] Jew is not the apparent one and that [true] circumcision is not that of the flesh' (Rom. 2:28–29). Under the effect of the cut of Apelles, the partition of the law (Jew/non-Jew), is no longer clear or exhaustive, for there will be some Jews who are not Jews, and some non-Jews who are not non-Jews. Paul states it clearly: 'not all of those of Israel are Israel' (Rom. 9:6); and, further on, citing Hosea, 'I will call my own people a non-people' (Rom. 9:25). This means that messianic division introduces a remnant [*resto*] into the law's overall division of the people, and Jews and non-Jews are constitutively 'not all,'" Agamben, *Il tempo che resta. Un commento alla Lettera ai Romani*, pp. 52–3. (*The Time that Remains*, p. 50.) Agamben draws a parallel to Nicholas of Cusa, in that he explains that what is at issue is "a logic like that of Nicholas of Cusa in his *De non aliud*, in which the A/non-A opposition admits a third term which then takes on the form of a double negation: non non-A," Agamben, *Il tempo che resta. Un commento alla Lettera ai Romani*, p. 53. (*The Time that Remains*, p. 51.)

[106]     It was this remnant that the Nazis did not want to know about. It was Nazi Germany's "biopolitical plan to produce a people without fracture," Agamben, *Mezzi senza fine. Note sulla politica*, p. 33. (*Means without End*, p. 34.) It is paradoxical that this "remnant" is to save the entire people.

exception.'" [107] In Bettelheim,[108] the camp as the exemplary extreme situation, thus allows for the determination of what is inhuman and human and, in this way, for the separation of the *Muselmann* from the human being."[109]

## X. Dialectics of Remnants

Agamben introduces *Remnants of Auschwitz* with quotations from respectively the Old Testament and the New Testament. The first quotation is from the prophet Isaiah:

> And then it shall come to pass in that day, that the remnant of Israel, and such as are escaped of the house of Jacob, shall no more again stay upon him that smote them; but they shall stay upon the Lord, the Holy One of Israel, in truth. The remnant shall be saved, even the remnant of Jacob, unto the mighty God. [110]

The second quotation is from the Apostle Paul: "Even so then at this present time also there is a remnant according to the election of grace…and so all Israel shall be saved."[111] Agamben's caesuras, the divisions of divisions, belong together with the rest which remains. Agamben's emphasis on the rest at all the various planes is an inexhaustible vision!

Without these caesuras, without these remainders, which among other things, make it impossible to reduce the *Muselmann* to a non-human, an animal, there would be no hope. *Remnants of Auschwitz* has moved into a context with the remainder, which the prophets spoke of among the Jewish people, and the remainder, which remains with the Messiah, and it is the task of the individual human being to grasp this remainder in the present age—in ὁ νῦν καιρός.[112] Agamben calls this present age "operational time," and Kierkegaard speaks similarly about "the moment." It is not a question of an eternal return of all things as in Nietzsche (1844–1900),[113] but of a "repetition" or "retrieval" (*Gjentagelse*),[114] in which the subject becomes a witness

---

[107]    Agamben, *Quel che resta di Auschwitz: l'archivio e il testimone:homo sacer III*, p. 43. (*Remnants of Auschwitz: The Witness and the Archive*, p. 48.)

[108]    Bruno Bettelheim (1903–90), psychoanalyst and child psychologist, was an Austrian Jew in the concentration camps Dachau and Buchenwald for 11 months. He escaped in 1939 and went to America.

[109]    Agamben, *Quel che resta di Auschwitz: l'archivio e il testimone: homo sacer III*, p. 43. (*Remnants of Auschwitz: The Witness and the Archive*, p. 48.)

[110]    Isa 10:20–21.

[111]    Rom 11:5–26.

[112]    The Greek expression ὁ νῦν καιρός is "the technical expression of messianic time," cf. Agamben, *Il tempo che resta. Un commento alla Lettera ai Romani*, p. 55 (*The Time that Remains*, p. 53) (Rom 11:5).

[113]    Cf. Agamben, *Homo Sacer I: Il potere sovrano e la nuda vita*, p. 56. (*Homo Sacer: Sovereign Power and Bare Life*, p. 48.)

[114]    Agamben writes in *Il tempo che resta. Un commento alla Lettera ai Romani*, pp. 74–5 (*The Time That Remains: A Commentary on the Letter to the Romans*, p. 75): "Paul does not use the substantive *anakephalaiôsis*, but the corresponding verb *anakephalaiômai*, which literally means 'to recapitulate.' The determining passage is Ephesians 1:10. Having just laid out the divine project of messianic redemption (*apolytrôsis*), Paul writes, 'as for the

to this. Without this witness there would be nothing left. The salvation of a people is paradoxically tied to this remainder—the remainder which it does not want to know anything about.


## XI. Subject Transformed to Citizen

Paradoxically Agamben does not want to fight to prevent the sovereign power turning the human being into *homo sacer*, into the naked human being. In the *Politics* Aristotle points out that the human being only has meaning by being taken up in the state as a citizen. But for Agamben the naked human being has meaning in himself or herself in "whatever singularity."[115]

As is evident from *A Literary Review*, Kierkegaard likewise did not wish to return to a hierarchical sovereign power but pointed towards the possibility—with the equality or leveling that the people demanded—that the human being could become the individual before God, without appealing to the support of any further authority.[116]

A popular political demonstration in Copenhagen in March 1848 led to Denmark receiving a free constitution the following year with the ratification of the "Grundlov" on June 5, 1849, which signaled the beginning of democracy. Kierkegaard has been read as a reactionary thinker with reference to his criticism of democracy. This is the way he is read by the American political and legal philosopher Adam Sitze,[117] who says with reference to Kierkegaard's *The Sickness unto Death*:[118] "I read this text not as a work of existentialism, but as one of the primary yet occluded points of reference in relation to which Schmitt formulated his theorems of juridical-political decisionism."[119] Here one should emphasize that Kierkegaard is in fact the existential thinker who sees the danger in reducing the single human being to a citizen in the

---

economy of the *pleroma* of times, all things are recapitulated in him, things in heaven and things on earth [εἰς οἰκονομίαν τοῦ πληρώματος τῶν καιρῶν, ἀνακεφαλαιώσασθαι τὰ πάντα ἐν τῷ Χριστῷ, τὰ ἐπὶ τοῖς οὐρανοῖς καὶ τὰ ἐπὶ τῆς γῆς ἐν αὐτῷ].' This short verse is laden with meaning to the point that one could say that several fundamental texts of Western culture—such as...repetition or retrieval [*Gjentagelse*] in Kierkegaard; the eternal return in Nietzsche...—are the consequences of an explosion of the meaning harbored within."

[115]     Agamben, *La communità che viene*, p. 3. (*The Coming Community*, p. 2.)

[116]     It is not primarily the idea of equality that Kierkegaard (or for that matter Agamben) is concerned with but rather that of the single individual, that is, the single individual in his or her particularity—in opposition to an abstract equality of representation, cf. *SKS* 9, 270–1 / *WL*, 272.

[117]     In his reading of Kierkegaard, Adam Sitze relies on Theodor W. Adorno's book from 1933: *Kierkegaard: The Construction of the Aesthetic*, trans. by Robert Hullot-Kentor, Minneapolis: University of Minnesota Press 1989, cf. Adam Sitze, "At the Mercy Of," in *The Limits of Law*, ed. by Austin Sarat, Lawrence Douglas, and Martha Merrill Umphrey, Stanford: Stanford University Press 2005, p. 255. See also ibid., pp. 259–60; p. 263.

[118]     Cf. The Sin of Despairing of the Forgiveness of Sins (Offence); *SKS* 11, 225–36 / *SUD*, 113–24.

[119]     Adam Sitze, "At the Mercy Of," in *The Limits of Law*, ed. by Austin Sarat, et al., p. 247.

state—indeed who sees the horror of human beings running together as a crowd, and where the state is incarnated in the crowd and with "the mob" being compared with the "God-man." Kierkegaard points out this danger in *The Sickness unto Death* with reference to Aristotle's *Politics*:

> If order is to be maintained in existence—and God does want that, for he is not a God of confusion—then the first thing to keep in mind is that every human being is an individual human being and is to become conscious of being an individual human being. If men are first permitted to run together in what Aristotle calls the animal category—the crowd—then this abstraction, instead of being less than nothing, even less than the most insignificant human being—then it does not take long before this abstraction becomes God...that the mob is the God-man.[120]

Is it really the case that people as a crowd make themselves naked before the state so that the civilly liberated and sovereign human being[121] thereby becomes "less than nothing, even less than the most insignificant human being"?

## XII. Ethics of Incongruence and Incommensurability

Agamben combines the Jewish legal thinking in the Old Testament with the messianic remnant in the New Testament in Paul. It is in this context that *Remnants of Auschwitz* should be read. Agamben ends *Remnants of Auschwitz* by explaining who he conceives this remnant to be.[122] It is not about those who died in Auschwitz or those who survived, but about the bond between them.[123] In this bond the remnant of Israel, the messianic remnant, the remnants after Auschwitz, are not isolated, but become a hope for ὁ νῦν καιρός. The salvation of the people is tied to this remnant, to this *ethica more Auschwitz demonstrata*, precisely the remnant that Auschwitz destroyed.

Agamben points to an ethic of the exception, which is reminiscent of Kierkegaard, an ethics of incongruence and incommensurability. This corresponds to Kierkegaard's critical account of Hegel's social ethics, as the universal, the community or the state's ethics, in which Kierkegaard sees a modern version of ancient Greece's conception of the relation between the individual and the *polis*, and where the task of the individual is to enter into and fulfill his life in the *polis*.

Agamben opens up a new reading of Kierkegaard in a political context— especially against the background of Auschwitz, where the consequence of a totalizing of the political culminates in a way that had never been seen previously in

---

120     *SKS* 11, 229 / *SUD*, 117–18.
121     Cf. Agamben, *Mezzi senza fine. Note sulla politica*, pp. 24–5 (*Means without End*, pp. 20–1); Agamben, *Homo Sacer I: Il potere sovrano e la nuda vita*, pp. 141–3 (*Homo Sacer: Sovereign Power and Bare Life*, pp. 128–9).
122     Agamben, *Quel che resta di Auschwitz: l'archivio e il testimone: homo sacer III*, pp. 151–3. (*Remnants of Auschwitz: The Witness and the Archive*, pp. 162–4.)
123     Agamben, *Quel che resta di Auschwitz: l'archivio e il testimone: homo sacer III*, p. 153. (*Remnants of Auschwitz: The Witness and the Archive*, p. 164.)

history. The political is never an end in itself and can never be one except at the cost of the individual, the exception.[124]

*Translated by Jon Stewart*

---

[124] Agamben asks, "What do we owe to the dead?" He answers by referring to Kierkegaard's *Works of Love*: " 'The work of love in recollecting the one who is dead,' Kierkegaard writes, 'is the work of the most disinterested, free, and faithful love.' " Giorgio Agamben, *Nudità*, Rome: Nottetempo 2000, p. 61; English translation: *Nudities*, trans. by Kishik and Stefan Pedatella, Stanford: Stanford University Press 2011, p. 39. Agamben refers to the passage corresponding to *SKS* 9, 351 / *WL*, 358. Kierkegaard adds: "Therefore go out and practice it; recollect the one who is dead and just in this way learn to love the living unselfishly, freely, faithfully." *SKS* 9, 351 / *WL* 358.

# Bibliography

*I. References to or Uses of Kierkegaard in Agamben's Corpus*

*Homo Sacer I: Il potere sovrano e la nuda vita*, Turin: Einaudi 1995, p. 20. (English translation: *Homo Sacer: Sovereign Power and Bare Life*, trans. by Daniel Heller-Roazen, Stanford: Stanford University Press 1998, p. 16.)

*Categorie italiane: Studi di poetica e di letteratura, Postfazione di Andrea Cortellessa*, [Venice: Marsilio 1996] Rome-Bari: Laterza 2010, p. 11; p. 13. (English translation: *The End of the Poem*, trans. by Daniel Heller-Roazen, Stanford: Stanford University Press 1999, p. 10; p. 11.)

*Quel che resta di Auschwitz: l'archivio e il testimone: homo sacer III*, Turin: Bollati Boringhieri 1998, p. 43. (English translation: *Remnants of Auschwitz: The Witness and the Archive*, trans. by Daniel Heller Roazen, New York: Zone Books 1999, p. 48.)

*Il tempo che resta. Un commento alla Lettera ai Romani*, Turin: Bollati Boringhieri 2000, pp. 74–5. (English translation: *The Time That Remains: A Commentary on the Letter to the Romans*, trans. by Patricia Dailey, Stanford: Stanford University Press 2005, p. 75.)

*Nudità*, Rome: Nottetempo 2009, p. 61. (English translation: *Nudities*, trans. by David Kishik and Stefan Pedatella, Stanford: Stanford University Press 2011, p. 39.)


*II. Sources of Agamben's Knowledge of Kierkegaard*

Adorno, Theodor W., *Kierkegaard. Konstruktion des Ästhetischen*, Tübingen: J.C.B. Mohr 1933.

— *Dialektik der Aufklärung. Philosophische Fragmente* (co-authored with Max Horkheimer), Amsterdam: Querido Verlag N.V. 1947, p. 23; pp. 210–11.

— *The Authoritarian Personality* (co-authored with Else Frenkel-Brunswik et al.), New York: Harper & Brothers 1950, p. 728; pp. 731–2.

— *Minima moralia. Reflexionen aus dem beschädigten Leben*, Berlin and Frankfurt am Main: Suhrkamp 1951, p. 131; p. 157; p. 249; pp. 288–92; pp. 430–1

Arendt, Hannah, "What is Existenz Philosophy," *Partisan Review*, vol. 13, no. 1, 1946, pp. 34–56; see p. 38; pp. 42–5; p. 52.

— *The Human Condition*, Chicago: University of Chicago Press 1958, p. 275; p. 293; p. 313; p. 319, note.

— *Between Past and Future: Six Exercises in Political Thought*, New York: The Viking Press 1961, p. 25; p. 26; pp. 28–32; p. 35; pp. 38–9; p. 94.

— "Marx, Kierkegaard et Nietzsche," *Preuves*, no. 133, 1962, pp. 14–29.

Benjamin, Walter, *Ursprung des deutschen Trauerspiels*, Berlin: Rowohlt 1928, pp. 233–4.

— *Das Passagen-Werk*, in *Gesammelte Schriften*, vols. 1–6 in 12 tomes, ed. by Rolf Tiedemann and Hermann Schweppenhäuser with Theodor W. Adorno and Gershom Scholem, Frankfurt am Main: Suhrkamp 1971–99, vol. 5, pp. 429–31.

Derrida, Jacques, *L'écriture et la différence*, Paris: Seuil 1967, p. 51; p. 143; pp. 161–5.

— *Glas*, Paris: Galilée 1974, pp. 224–5; pp. 258–9.

— *Passions*, Paris: Galilée 1993, pp. 57–8; p. 84.

— *Adieu à Emmanuel Lévinas*, Paris: Galilée 1997, p. 24; pp. 166–7; p. 209.

— *Donner la mort*, Paris: Galilée 1999.

Heidegger, Martin, *Sein und Zeit*, Halle: Niemeyer 1927, pp. 175–96, see also p. 190, note 1; p. 235, note 1; and p. 338, note 1.

— "Nietzsches Wort *Gott ist tot*," in *Holzwege*, Frankfurt am Main: Klostermann 1950, p. 230 (in Martin Heidegger, *Gesamtausgabe*, Abteilungen 1–4, vols. 1–102, Frankfurt am Main: Klostermann 1975–, Abteilung 1 (*Veröffentlichte Schriften 1910–1976*), vol. 5, *Holzwege* (1977), p. 249.

Kafka, Franz, *Tagebücher*, vols. 1–3, ed. by Hans-Gerd Koch, Michael Müller, and Malcolm Pasley, Frankfurt am Main: Fischer 1990, vol. 1, p. 578; p. 803; p. 925.

Schmitt, Carl, *Politische Theologie, Vier Kapitel zur Lehre von der Souveränität*, Munich and Leipzig: Duncker und Humblot 1922, p. 22; p. 27; p. 69; p. 71.

### III. Secondary Literature on Agamben's Relation to Kierkegaard

Pedersen, Jacob Lund, "Det skamfulde subject," *Tidsskriftet øjeblikket*, vol. 13, no. 47, 2006, pp. 18–20.

Sitze, Adam, "At the Mercy Of," in *The Limits of Law*, ed. by Austin Sarat, Lawrence Douglas, and Martha Merrill Umphrey, Stanford: Stanford University Press 2005, pp. 246–308.

# Hannah Arendt:

## Religion, Politics and the Influence of Kierkegaard

### Marcio Gimenes de Paula

Hannah Arendt (1906–75), the woman, the Jew, and the thinker, was one of the most challenging figures of the twentieth century. Thanks to her broad knowledge of philosophy and theology, as well as her acute insight into the nature of totalitarianism, she gained respect and recognition from the academic and political milieus. There have been many and multifaceted interpretations of her work, and, until this very day, new research continues to follow up on many different aspects of her philosophy. However, the relation of Arendt's thought to that of Kierkegaard has rarely been explored. Our purpose is to evaluate this relation in five steps, which correspond to the parts of this article: (1) a brief overview of the life and works of Arendt; (2) an account of Arendt, as reader of Kierkegaard; (3) an account of the use of Kierkegaard by Arendt; (4) an analysis of modernity and doubt, two key terms for Arendt's understanding of Kierkegaard as the master of suspicion; (5) and finally some concluding remarks about the Arendt–Kierkegaard relation.

### I. A Brief Overview of the Life and Works of Hannah Arendt

Hannah Arendt was one of the most influential thinkers of the twentieth century. Her times were stamped by the immense challenges brought about by two world wars and totalitarianism. Born and raised in Germany, she lived in France for almost a decade, eventually leaving Europe to settle in New York in 1941, where she lived until her death and where she mostly worked during her life in the USA. From the beginning of the 1950s until her very last days, she published a string of leading works, among them, *The Origins of Totalitarianism* (1951),[1] a study of the nature and the historical foundations of totalitarian movements, and *The Human Condition* (1958),[2] where she carries out an analysis of the fundamental categories of the *vita activa*. Two works published in 1963 also deserve to be mentioned: *Eichmann in*

---

[1]     Hannah Arendt, *The Origins of Totalitarianism*, New York: Harcourt, Brace & Co. 1951.

[2]     Hannah Arendt, *The Human Condition*, Chicago: University of Chicago Press 1958.

*Jerusalem*[3] and *On Revolution*,[4] as well as the posthumous volume, *Life in Spirit*,[5] published in 1978, three years after her death. In addition to these titles, she also wrote a vast number of remarkable essays on topics that range from modernity and tradition, to authority and freedom, to the nature of revolution. Most of these essays were reprinted in *Between the Past and the Future* (1961)[6] and *Men in Dark Times* (1968).[7]

Arendt held a degree in philosophy and had substantial knowledge of theology and ancient Greek; she studied with some of the most important and influential thinkers of the twentieth century, namely, Romano Guardini (1885–1968), Martin Heidegger (1889–1976), Rudolf Bultmann (1884–1976), Karl Jaspers (1883–1969), and Edmund Husserl (1859–1938). Born on October 14, 1906, Hannah Arendt was the only daughter of Paul and Martha Cohn, of Jewish Russian ancestry. Her childhood was far from calm and peaceful; when she was three, her family moved to Königsberg, then the capital of Eastern Prussia. At the age of seven, she lost her father and would live with her mother until she re-married in 1920. Hannah Arendt attended Gymnasium or secondary school in Königsberg and enrolled at the University of Marburg in 1924, where she had the opportunity to study with Heidegger. Their love affair started the following year, and she carried on a philosophical correspondence with him. In 1926, she went to the University of Heidelberg, where she made her first contact with Jaspers, who would later be the advisor for her dissertation on the concept of love in Augustine—a work published in 1929.[8] Towards the end of 1926, she enrolled at the University of Heidelberg, where she met Husserl. When she married Günther Stern (1902–92) in 1929, she moved to Berlin. From 1933 onwards, Arendt joined the Zionist movement and travelled in Palestine between 1935 and 1938. During that period, in 1936, she met Heinrich Blücher (1899–1970), who would become her second husband in 1941, after her divorce from Stern in 1937. The peak of her academic production took place during the three decades of the 1940s, 1950s, and 1960s. Arendt held a chair at the New School for Social Research in New York from 1967, but even before that time she was intensely active in the academic world and intensely engaged in political issues in the prevailing debates of the twentieth century. This unrelenting activity continued until her death in 1975.

---

3       Hannah Arendt, *Eichmann in Jerusalem: A Report on the Banality of Evil*, New York: Viking Press 1963.

4       Hannah Arendt, *On Revolution*, New York: Viking Press 1963.

5       Hannah Arendt, *The Life of the Mind*, New York: Harcourt Brace Jovanovich 1978.

6       Hannah Arendt, *Between Past and Future: Six Exercises in Political Thought*, New York: Viking Press 1961.

7       Hannah Arendt, *Men in Dark Times*, New York: Harcourt, Brace & World 1968.

8       Hannah Arendt, *Der Liebesbegriff bei Augustin*, Berlin: Springer 1929. (English translation: *Love and St. Augustine*, trans. by E.B. Ashton, Chicago: Chicago University Press 1996.)

## *II. Hannah Arendt as a Reader of Kierkegaard*

Three authors were fundamental for Arendt's reading of Kierkegaard. The first is the translator Theodor Haecker (1879–1945), who made available a number of translations to German readers, and naturally to philosophers and thinkers, among them Theodor W. Adorno (1903–69), Georg Lukács (1885–1971), Walter Benjamin (1895–1942), Heidegger, Karl Löwith (1897–1973), and Jaspers, as well as Arendt herself. The second was Emanuel Hirsch (1886–1972), who also became famous for translating Kierkegaard.

The third was Jaspers. Arendt had studied with him, and Jaspers had supervised her dissertation *The Concept of Love in Augustine*,[9] and she was aware of Jaspers' remarks about Kierkegaard in his work *Man in the Modern Age*.[10] Jaspers was a profound admirer of Kierkegaard, and he knew his works well; several of Jaspers' works show the depth of his understanding of the Danish thinker and the important role he played for Jaspers. In fact, he believed that Kierkegaard had written the sharpest criticism of modern times that had ever been produced.[11] Jaspers' critical analyses of Kierkegaard came to be known not only to Arendt but also to Husserl, Heidegger, and Löwith. They were harshly criticized by Lukács in his well-known work *The Destruction of Reason*,[12] where the Hungarian philosopher stated his conviction that Löwith was wrong to put Kierkegaard and Karl Marx (1818–83) together under the same rubric, and to approach all the post-Hegelians as if they stood as a unified group.[13]

As for Arendt, who followed Augustine with regard to the relation between faith and reason, the leap of faith in Kierkegaard seems to be central to her interests from the time she started working under Jaspers' supervision. One should mention here a curious fact that proves that her interest in Kierkegaard dates back to an earlier period in her life. Arendt, who preferred to be known as a scholar in political theory, made an interesting claim in an interview conducted by Günther Gaus (1929–2004) and broadcast on television in 1964. In this interview she firmly stated that ever since she was 14 years of age, she had developed an interest in philosophical and theological issues. She told her interviewer that after reading Immanuel Kant and

---

[9]     Ibid.

[10]     Karl Jaspers, *Die geistige Situation der Zeit*, Berlin: Walter de Gruyter 1931. (English translation: *Man in the Modern Age*, trans. by Eden Paul and Cedar Paul, London: Routledge 1933.)

[11]     Jaspers, *Die geistige Situation der Zeit*, p. 11: "*Die erste umfassende, in ihrem Ernst von allen vorhergehenden unterschiedene Kritik seiner Zeit brachte Kierkegaard. Seine Kritik hören wir zum erstenmal wie eine Kritik auch unserer Zeit; es ist, als ob sie gestern geschrieben ware.*"

[12]     György Lukács, *Die Zerstörung der Vernunft*, Berlin: Hermann Luchterhand Verlag Darmstadt und Neuwied 1954. (English translation: *The Destruction of Reason*, trans. by Peter Palmer, London: Merlin Press 1980.)

[13]     Karl Löwith, *Von Hegel zu Nietzsche—Der Revolutionäre Bruch in Denken des neunzehnten Jahrhunderts*, Berlin: S. Fischer 1939. (English translation: *From Hegel to Nietzsche*, trans. by David E. Green, New York: Columbia University Press 1964.)

Jaspers' *Psychology of World Views*,[14] she started reading the Danish thinker: "Then I read Kierkegaard, and everything fell into place."[15]

Moreover, Arendt had no negative bias whatsoever towards theological issues, and always related them to philosophical issues. In doing so, she was following what she had learned from Bultmann, one of her former professors: "They fit together in such a way for me they both belong together. I had some misgivings only as to how one deals with this if one is Jewish...how one proceeds. I had no idea, you know. I had difficult problems that were then resolved by themselves."[16] As a result, in a beautiful text published in 1965, dedicated in full-length to the Christian, Angelo Giuseppe Roncalli, that is, Pope John XXIII (1881–1963), Arendt reinstates the importance of Kierkegaard and the challenges faced when correlating philosophy and theology: "Generations of modern intellectuals, insofar as they were not atheists—that is, fools who pretended to know what no man can know—have been taught by Kierkegaard, Dostoevsky, Nietzsche, and their countless followers inside and outside the existentialist camp, to find religion and theological questions 'interesting.' "[17]

In addition to the discussion between faith and reason, Arendt was also interested in the relevance given by Kierkegaard to the topic of the single individual. We can understand her criticism of the bourgeois world from this perspective. In a time of deep conformity, this was seen by her as something as important as the idea of destiny to Napoleon Bonaparte, or the idea of history to G.W.F. Hegel.[18] Accordingly, Kierkegaard was understood by Arendt as the initiator of the modern philosophy of existence, and his merits lie in his struggle against the great names of his day and in his proposal of an alternative to their philosophies:

> Modern existential philosophy begins with Kierkegaard. There is not a single existential philosopher who does not show evidence of his influence. As we know, Kierkegaard's point of departure was a critique of Hegel (and, we might add, a conscious neglect of Schelling, with whose late philosophy Kierkegaard was familiar from lectures). Against Hegel's system, which presumed to comprehend and explain the "whole," Kierkegaard set the "individual," the single human being, for whom there is neither place nor meaning

---

[14]     Karl Jaspers, *Psychologie der Weltanschauungen*, Berlin: Springer 1919.

[15]     Hannah Arendt, "Was bleibt? Es bleibt die Muttersprache" in Günther Gaus, *Zur Person: Porträts in Frage und Antwort*, Munich: dtv 1964, p. 21. (English translation: "'What Remains? The Language Remains': A Conversation with Günther Gaus," trans. by Joan Stambaugh in *Essays in Understanding, 1930–1954: Formation, Exile, and Totalitarianism*, ed. by Jerome Kohn, New York: Harcourt Brace & Co.. 1994, p. 9., translation modified)

[16]     Arendt, "Was bleibt? Es bleibt die Muttersprache" in Günther Gaus, *Zur Person: Porträts in Frage und Antwort*, p. 21. (" 'What Remains? The Language Remains': A Conversation with Günther Gaus," p. 9.)

[17]     Hannah Arendt, "Angelo Giuseppe Roncalli: A Christian on St. Peter's Chair from 1958 to 1963," in *Men in Dark Times*, New York: Harcourt, Brace & World 1968, p. 67.

[18]     Hannah Arendt, "Franz Kafka: A Revaluation" *Partisan Review*, vol. 11, no. 4, 1944, pp. 412–22. (Reprinted in *Essays in Understanding 1930–1954*, ed. by Jerome Kohn, pp. 69–80.)

in a totality controlled by world spirit. In other words, Kierkegaard's point of departure is the individual's sense of being lost in a world otherwise totally explained.[19]

Arendt indicates that Socrates is an inspiring and constant presence in the bulk of Kierkegaard's production. Socrates is in fact his great model, his guide in the search for truth in subjectivity. The conception of the single individual can be seen as in line with Socrates' thought. Based on the thesis of the importance of human subjectivity and on the understanding that at the same time, each human being can be, by himself, an exception when he hears God's call, Kierkegaard regains possession of the Socratic heritage and reads it now as a key to Christianity, thus bringing a new interpretation to the concept of the moment. For Kierkegaard, the consciousness of death and finitude becomes decisive for the very act of doing philosophy.

For Arendt, there is here a peculiar curiosity, namely, the possibility of comparing Kierkegaard and Marx. In her view, both take for granted that men, as singulars, give their answers in a determined instant of their existence. But Marx directs his explanation to politics, whereas Kierkegaard goes into psychology. As a result, Marx believes that man can change certain structures, and Kierkegaard once more states his belief in human subjectivity. The truth is that, in the eyes of Arendt, Marx apparently gets entangled in Hegelian philosophy and, even when he wants to reverse it, still takes refuge in it. Kierkegaard, by contrast, seems to challenge Hegelian philosophy more effectively, and, for Arendt, he has thus proved to be more audacious than Marx: "Kierkegaard became much more important than Marx for the later development of philosophy because he clung to his despair of philosophy."[20]

## III. Kierkegaard by Hannah Arendt

In "Søren Kierkegaard," a text originally published in the *Frankfurter Zeitung* and later included in English translation in the collection *Essays in Understanding 1930–1954*,[21] Arendt seems to single out two strands of reception of the Danish thinker. The first has been somewhat forgotten, and it comprehended the times when the author remained only known in Denmark, his words and fame taking a long time to reach the rest of Europe. The second is the reception that actually took place in Germany in the 1920s and 1930s, thanks to the translations first by Christoph Schrempf (1860–1944) and then by Haecker. This second reception typically presented Kierkegaard as a defender of authentic Christianity, in an open and fierce fight against Christendom.

---

[19]    Hannah Arendt, "What is Existenz Philosophy?" *Partisan Review*, vol. 13, no. 1, 1946, pp. 42–3. (Reprinted in "What is Existential Philosophy?" in *Essays in Understanding 1930–1954*, ed. by Jerome Kohn, p. 173.)

[20]    Arendt, "What is Existenz Philosophy?" p. 45. (Reprinted as "What is Existential Philosophy?" in *Essays in Understanding 1930–1954*, ed. by Jerome Kohn, p. 173.)

[21]    Hannah Arendt, "Sören Kierkegaard," *Frankfurter Zeitung*, nos. 75–7, January 29, 1932, p. 9. (English translation: "Søren Kierkegaard," in *Essays in Understanding, 1930–1954*, ed. by Jerome Kohn, pp. 44–9.)

Nonetheless, within the context of World War II, at a time when scientific knowledge was regarded as a kind of idea, Kierkegaard became an author of secondary interest. In this period people were reluctant to give credit to a master of *suspicion*. Arendt observes: "It was not until the post-war years, which brought a willingness to tear down outmoded intellectual structures that Germany would offer a soil in which Kierkegaardian thought could take root."[22] In fact, Arendt also believed that Friedrich Nietzsche might have prepared German soil so that Kierkegaard might flourish:

> Nietzsche and the so-called life philosophy (*Lebensphilosophie*), Bergson, Dilthey, and Simmel had prepared the way for Kierkegaard in Germany. In Nietzsche, systematic philosophy saw its fundamental tenets threatened for the first time, for Nietzsche's destruction of old psychological assumptions revealed the extra-philosophical, psychic, and vital energies that actually motivated philosophers to philosophize. This revolt of a philosopher against philosophy clarified the situation of philosophizing itself and insisted that philosophizing *was* philosophy. The meant the salvation of the individual's subjectivity.[23]

With these words, Kierkegaard clearly emerges as the critic of Christianity in his time and as the critic of the Hegelian system. The question of the individual, a modern issue *par excellence*, present in the best critics and polemicists of the time, is here recovered side by side with the profound research on interiority and subjectivity. These themes originate in distant traditions, namely, the Socratic and the Augustinian. The question raised by Arendt is directed at post-war Germany and concerns the capability of assimilating Kierkegaardian philosophy, specifically, the capability of inserting in the philosophical debate such notable issues and themes as the paradox, existence, and the criticism of the very concept of history.

In Arendt's view, Kierkegaard is also the *father* of a certain type of radical skepticism that afflicts both Catholics and Protestants. This feature is related not only to his writings but also to his personal life, all the more so since he lived in a society heading towards secularization, despite its being stamped and dominated by ecclesiastical rules. Arendt states: "Kierkegaard was the first thinker to live in a world constituted much like our own, that is, in a wholly secularized world stemming from the Enlightenment."[24] Kierkegaard's challenge in the face of secularization seems then even larger than the challenges faced in the early days of Christianity, when the religion was only followed by a minority. In the modern era, now that secularization and suspicion have settled in, one needs not only to stand for Christianity, but also to stand by Christianity when all the others negate it by means of well-constructed arguments and theses. Arendt concludes: "To be radically religious in such a world means to be alone not only in the sense that one stands alone before God but also

---

[22]     Arendt, "Sören Kierkegaard," *Frankfurter Zeitung*, p. 9. ("Søren Kierkegaard" in *Essays in Understanding 1930–1954*, ed. by Jerome Kohn, p. 45.)
[23]     Ibid.
[24]     Arendt, "Sören Kierkegaard," *Frankfurter Zeitung*, p. 9. ("Søren Kierkegaard" in *Essays in Understanding 1930–1954*, p. 46.)

in the sense that no one else stands before God."[25] In other words, the Christian community seems to have disappeared, leaving room for a few individuals who continue to keep the integrity of the Christian message. At the same time, this is not a form of egoism, however; it is instead a renouncing of the secular world, a form of turning to God. Existence is fully actualized in God: in God one can fulfill oneself or one can turn away from God, by the decision of one's will. There is a permanent tension here between the human wish and the submission of this wish to that of God. All this is present in Kierkegaard, surrounded as he is by his pseudonyms, their logic, and their strategies; his aesthetic themes and pseudonyms may seem, at first glance, to be strongly influenced by Romanticism, but, for Arendt, both Kierkegaard and Nietzsche represent an overcoming of Romanticism itself. In both authors, one can detect the transformation of simply aesthetic problems into ethical and existential problems, and she claims that "Kierkegaard paid back with his life the debts that Romanticism piled up with noncommittal abandon."[26]

### IV. Modernity and Doubt: Kierkegaard as Master of Suspicion

When Arendt analyzes the concept of tradition and modern times, she starts inevitably with Plato and Aristotle, but her main intent is to examine three of the main interpreters of modernity: Marx, Kierkegaard, and Nietzsche. It should be noted that, contrary to the canonical tradition that places Marx, Nietzsche, and Sigmund Freud (1856–1939) as *celebrated masters of suspicion*, Arendt seems to underscore the Danish thinker's place as worthy of being called the father of psychoanalysis. In Arendt's perspective, Marx is a modern author in the sense that he presents a special and peculiar articulation of the relation between philosophy and politics, something that had not been achieved since the ancient Greeks. According to Arendt, the German thinker's priority is to *transform* instead of *to interpret*, as one can see in the eleventh of the "Theses on Feuerbach": "The philosophers have only *interpreted* the world in various ways: the point, however, is to *change* it."[27] Accordingly, Arendt follows this clue to assess Kierkegaard, Marx, and Nietzsche, since they are authors who directly question the basic foundations of traditional religion:

> The end of a tradition does not necessarily mean that traditional concepts have lost their power over the minds of men. On the contrary, it sometimes seems that this power of well-worn notions and categories becomes more tyrannical as the tradition loses its living force and as the memory of its beginning recedes; it may even reveal its full coercive force only after its end has come and men no longer even rebel against it. This at least seems to be the lesson of the twentieth-century aftermath of formalistic and compulsory thinking, which came after Kierkegaard, Marx and Nietzsche had challenged the basic assumptions of traditional religion, traditional political thought, and

---

[25]     Arendt, "Sören Kierkegaard," *Frankfurter Zeitung*, p. 9. ("Søren Kierkegaard" in *Essays in Understanding 1930–1954*, p. 47.)
[26]     Arendt, "Sören Kierkegaard," *Frankfurter Zeitung*, p. 9. ("Søren Kierkegaard" in *Essays in Understanding 1930–1954*, p. 49.)
[27]     Karl Marx and Friedrich Engels, *The Marx–Engels Reader*, ed. by Robert C. Tucker, New York: W.W. Norton 1972, p. 145.

traditional metaphysics by consciously inverting the traditional hierarchy of concepts. However, neither the twentieth-century aftermath nor the nineteenth-century rebellion against tradition actually caused the break in our history. This sprang from a chaos of mass-perplexities on the political scene and of mass-opinions in the spiritual sphere, which the totalitarian movements, through terror and ideology, crystallized into a new form of government and domination. Totalitarian domination as an established fact, which in its unprecedentedness cannot be comprehended through the usual categories of political thought, and whose "crimes" cannot be judged by traditional moral standards or punished within the legal framework of our civilization, has broken the continuity of Occidental history. The break in our tradition is now an accomplished fact. It is neither the result of anyone's deliberate choice nor subject to further decision.[28]

Taking into consideration that the tradition is still firm in the minds of men, as Arendt suggests, what the twentieth century could at the utmost do is merely to question the tradition in thought:

> The rebellion against tradition in the nineteenth-century remained strictly within a traditional framework; and on the level of mere thought, which could hardly be concerned then with more than the essentially negative experiences of foreboding, apprehension, and ominous silence, only radicalization, not a new beginning and reconsideration of the past, was possible.[29]

This is the peculiar reason why Kierkegaard, Marx, and Nietzsche, each in his own way, are Hegelians. One can observe that even in Arendt's formulation Kierkegaard is primarily seen (just as in "What is *Existenz* Philosophy?") as an anti-Hegelian, and in this case, her interpretation brings Kierkegaard closer to Hegel. In all three of the analyzed philosophers, even in Kierkegaard and Nietzsche, despite the bulk of their criticism, the theme of universal history now occupies a central place:

> Kierkegaard, Marx, and Nietzsche remained Hegelians insofar as they saw the history of the past philosophy as one dialectically developed whole; their great merit was that they radicalized this new approach toward the past in the only way it could still be further developed, namely, in questioning the conceptual hierarchy which had ruled Western philosophy since Plato and which Hegel had still taken for granted.[30]

One might actually say that these three thinkers made a *leap* against tradition. Kierkegaard executes a leap from doubt to faith. In the meanwhile, more than merely performing that leap, Kierkegaard alters the traditional relation between faith and reason established by Descartes, while offering a criticism of the incredulous modernity of his day. Marx jumps, as one observes, from theory to action, from the interpretation of the world to its transformation. The Nietzschean leap is characterized by the inversion of Platonism, and of Christianity as popular Platonism, into the assertion of life and human potentiality.

Arendt is extremely clear when she points out that Kierkegaard's wish is only to assert the dignity of faith against reason and reasoning. It must be said that

---

28    Arendt, *Between Past and Future: Six Exercises in Political Thought*, p. 26.
29    Ibid., pp. 27–8.
30    Ibid., p. 28.

this is in no way a case of defending irrationalism or simplistic fideism. What the Danish thinker seems to be claiming is that our human reason is not capable of producing a complete explanation of things, and, for that very reason, faith can only be understood as absurd or paradoxical. On the other hand, Kierkegaard does not appear to be struggling on the same side of the theoretical debate as modern science and rationalism; rather his side is that of philosophy and the question of conscience. Therefore, one cannot regard him as *irrationalist*. His investigation takes place in the domain of human interiority; this is why, for Kierkegaard, any attempt by religion to assert itself rationally is mistaken, just as scientific rationalism does, intending to explain everything at any cost, indeed, at the cost of faith and of religion.

Arendt claims that the first point one should take into account is that when one leaps from doubt to faith, the Danish thinker brings doubt itself into the religious discussion. This trait allows one to draw parallels with great Christian authors like Pascal, for example. This is clearly stated in the following excerpt from *The Human Condition*:

> The outstanding characteristic of Cartesian doubt is its universality, that nothing, no thought and no experience, can escape it. No one perhaps explored its true dimensions more honestly than Kierkegaard when he leaped—not from reason, as he thought, but from doubt—into belief, thereby carrying doubt into the very heart of modern religion.[31]

Hence, Kierkegaard claims that at a time when modern science issues a strong criticism of religion, one should transfer the debate from the external domain of observation to the domain of interiority, the only sphere where belief may evolve and be nurtured. It should be stressed that this strategy, beginning with Augustine, was also represented in the literature of the day, as for example in the work of Dostoevsky (1821–81): "No clearer symptom of this modern religious situation can be found than the fact that Dostoevsky, perhaps the most experienced psychologist of modern religious beliefs, portrayed pure faith in the character of Myshkin 'the idiot,' or of Alyosha Karamazov, who is pure in heart because he is simple-minded."[32]

We should pay attention to Arendt's analysis of how Pascal and Kierkegaard, by introducing the theme of doubt into the religious debate, eventually destabilize structures that had remained untouched by eighteenth-century atheism, and nineteenth-century materialism. Here lies precisely the challenge posited by Kierkegaard's philosophy:

> For what undermined the Christian faith was not the atheism of the eighteenth century or the materialism of the nineteenth—their arguments are frequently vulgar and, for the most part, easily refutable by traditional theology—but rather the doubting concerning the salvation of genuinely religious men, in whose eyes the traditional Christian content and promise had become "absurd."[33]

---

[31]     Arendt, *The Human Condition*, p. 275.
[32]     Arendt, *Between Past and Future: Six Exercises in Political Thought*, p. 28.
[33]     Arendt, *The Human Condition*, p. 319.

*V. Final Remarks*

In this brief article, we intended to present an overview that makes clear how fundamental Kierkegaard's thought was for the development of Hannah Arendt's philosophy. More than pointing out affinities or biographical points of overlap, our aim was to illustrate the evidence of the presence of Kierkegaard in her writings, using Arendt's own writings and statements. The close reading of certain of her works has enabled us to see the constant and abundant presence of the Danish thinker and the remarkable role he plays in her own thought. Unfortunately, this presence has not always been clearly perceived. *The Cambridge Companion to Hannah Arendt*,[34] though a respectable collection of 14 essays by scholars specialized in the field, does not mention Kierkegaard's name at all; this can only be regarded as regrettable since the Danish thinker is an important figure in Arendt's works and in the structure of her thought. Arendt's combination of philosophy and theology is also at the core of Kierkegaard's pursuit, following the best heritage of modern philosophy, since the *Tractatus Theologico-Politicus* by Spinoza. Further, it has been fundamental for discussions of issues in the areas of politics, religion, and theology, as well as in research on the topic of secularization. Arendt's criticism of society, her political theory, which tries to understand the genesis of totalitarianism, and her continual concern with democratic values can also be observed in the political scenery of the nineteenth century and in the discussions on the far from peaceful interaction between religion and society. Now, Arendt was well acquainted with Kierkegaard's attack on the Danish Church, the cultural establishment and the state, and even taking into account the limits imposed by the age she lived in during her formative years, we judge that Arendt was well positioned to understand quite well the challenges raised by Kierkegaard concerning philosophy, politics, and religion.

*Translated by Elisabete M. de Sousa*

---

[34]    *The Cambridge Companion to Hannah Arendt*, ed. by Dana Vila, Cambridge: Cambridge University Press 2000.

# Bibliography

*I. References to or Uses of Kierkegaard in Arendt's Corpus*

"Sören Kierkegaard," *Frankfurter Zeitung*, nos. 75–7, January 29, 1932, p. 9. (English translation: "Søren Kierkegaard," trans. by Robert and Rita Kimber in *Essays in Understanding, 1930–1954: Formation, Exile, and Totalitarianism*, ed. by Jerome Kohn, New York: Harcourt, Brace and Co. 1994, pp. 44–9.)

"What is Existenz Philosophy," *Partisan Review*, vol. 13, no. 1, 1946, pp. 34–56; see p. 38; pp. 42–5; p. 52. (Reprinted in *Essays in Understanding, 1930–1954: Formation, Exile, and Totalitarianism*, ed. by Jerome Kohn, New York: Harcourt, Brace and Co. 1994, pp. 163–87; see p. 168; pp. 173–6; p. 182.)

"Tradition and the Modern Age," *Partisan Review*, vol. 21, no. 1, 1954, pp. 53–75. (Revised and enlarged version republished in her *Between Past and Future: Eight Exercises in Political Thought*, Harmondsworth: Penguin 1980, pp. 17–40.)

*The Human Condition*, Chicago: University of Chicago Press 1958, p. 275; p. 293; p. 313; p. 319, note.

*Between Past and Future: Six Exercises in Political Thought*, New York: Viking Press 1961, pp. 25–6; pp. 28–32; p. 35; pp. 38–9; p. 94.

"Marx, Kierkegaard et Nietzsche," *Preuves*, no. 133, 1962, pp. 14-29.

"Was bleibt? Es bleibt die Muttersprache" in Günther Gaus, *Zur Person: Porträts in Frage und Antwort*, Munich: dtv 1964, pp. 15–32; see p. 21. (English translation: "'What Remains? The Language Remains': A Conversation with Günther Gaus," trans. by Joan Stambaugh in *Essays in Understanding, 1930–1954: Formation, Exile, and Totalitarianism*, ed. by Jerome Kohn, New York: Harcourt, Brace and Co. 1994, pp. 1–23; see p. 9.)

*Men in Dark Times*, New York: Harcourt, Brace & World 1968, p. 67.


*II. Sources of Arendt's Knowledge of Kierkegaard*

Camus, Albert, *Le Mythe de Sisyphe*, Paris: Gallimard 1942, p. 39; pp. 42–3; p. 51; pp. 56–61; p. 65; pp. 69–72.

Guardini, Romano, *Das Ende der Neuzeit. Ein Versuch zur Orientierung*, Basel: Hess Verlag 1950, p. 31; pp. 125–6.

Heidegger, Martin, *Sein und Zeit*, Halle: Niemeyer 1927, pp. 175–96, see also p. 190, note 1; p. 235, note 1; and p. 338, note 1.

Jaspers, Karl, *Psychologie der Weltanschauungen*, Berlin: Springer 1919, p. 12; p. 61; p. 90; pp. 94–6; p. 99; pp. 217–18; pp. 238–9; pp. 245–7; pp. 255–6; p. 329; pp. 332–5; p. 339; p. 341; pp. 348–9; p. 351; pp. 354–5; p. 357; p. 359; pp. 370–81.

— *Die geistige Situation der Zeit*, Berlin and Leipzig: Walter de Gruyter 1931,
    pp. 10–11; pp. 13–14; pp. 35–6; pp. 43–5; p. 145; p. 163.
Kierkegaard, Søren, *Zur Kritik der Gegenwart*, trans. and ed. by Theodor Haecker,
    Innsbruck: Brenner Verlag 1922.
— *Gesammelte Werke*, vols. 1–36, trans. and ed. by Emanuel Hirsch et al., Düsseldorf:
    Eugen Diedrichs Verlag 1950–69.
Sartre, Jean-Paul, *L'être et le néant. Essai d'ontologie phénoménologique*, Paris:
    Gallimard 1943 (*Bibliothèque des Idées*), pp. 58–84; pp. 94–111; pp. 115–49;
    pp. 150–74; pp. 291–300; pp. 508–16; pp. 529–60; pp. 639–42; pp. 643–63;
    pp. 669–70; pp. 720ff.
— *L'existentialisme est un humanisme*, Paris: Nagel 1946, pp. 27–33.


*III. Secondary Literature on Arendt's Relation to Kierkegaard*


Gimenes de Paula, Marcio, "A temática da secularização: Hannah Arendt, leitora de
    Kierkegaard," in *Kierkegaard no nosso tempo*, ed. by Álvaro Valls and Jasson
    Martins, São Leopoldo: Nova Harmonia 2010, pp. 327–45.
Glöckner, Dorothea, *Das Versprechen. Studien zur Verbindlichkeit menschlichen
    Sagens in Søren Kierkegaards Werk Die Taten der Liebe*, Tübingen: Mohr
    Siebeck 2009, pp. 9–12; p. 92; pp. 101–2; pp. 117–23; pp. 141–4; p. 167;
    pp. 181–8; p. 191; pp. 194–5; p. 198; p. 207; p. 215.
Thomson, Iain, "Heidegger and National Socialism," in A Companion to Heidegger,
    ed. by Hubert L. Dreyfus and Mark A. Wrathall, New York: Blackwell 2007,
    pp. 32–48.

# Alain Badiou:

# Thinking the Subject after the Death of God

Michael O' Neill Burns

In the first decade of the twenty-first century, Alain Badiou has gone from being a philosopher relatively unknown to those working outside of France to the most influential living European philosopher in English-language scholarship. Writing in the wake of the post-structuralist and post-modernist movements that remained prominent through the end of the twentieth century, Badiou proposes a revival of categories such as truth, subjectivity, and universality; and rather than relying on a philosophical methodology that could be considered a sort of post-Heideggarian poetics, Badiou instead utilizes post-Cantorian set theory mathematics to once again attempt to think being-qua-being. Rather than celebrating the "end of metaphysics" and the "death of the subject," Badiou continues to work as if these events were mere mishaps in the continuing history of classical philosophical thought.

While this reliance on mathematics for the development of an axiomatic ontology and theory of subjectivity may seem to have no relationship to the religious anti-philosophy of Søren Kierkegaard, upon closer examination Badiou begins to bear a striking resemblance to Kierkegaard, one that may put Badiou in closer proximity to Kierkegaard than the deconstructive and phenomenological strands of thought he has recently been considered in relation to.[1]

To this end, it is the concern of the present chapter to briefly elucidate this yet to be explored relationship between Alain Badiou and Søren Kierkegaard. We will begin with a brief account of Badiou's project. We will then move on to examine the historical relationship between Kierkegaard and many of Badiou's primary philosophical influences, noting some of the recent secondary texts that have remarked upon this relationship. Next we will evaluate Badiou's brief direct engagement with Kierkegaard, focusing primarily on the chapter of Badiou's recent *Logics of Worlds* that engages specifically with Kierkegaard's thought. Finally, we will briefly outline some of the conceptual points of intersection between Badiou and Kierkegaard, and outline some questions for future research.

---

[1]     For examples of this reading of Kierkegaard see *The New Kierkegaard*, ed. by Elsebet Jegstrup, Bloomington, Indiana: Indiana University Press 2004 and *Kierkegaard in Post/Modernity*, ed. by Martin J. Matuštík and Merold Westphal, Bloomington, Indiana: Indiana University Press 1995.

## *I. Alain Badiou and the Return of Truth*

Alain Badiou was born in Rabat, Morocco in January 1937 to his mother, who studied literature and poetry, and his father, a mathematician. He was educated in philosophy and mathematics at the École Normale Supérieure in Paris. He began teaching at the University of Paris VIII in 1969 and in 1999 took up the chair of philosophy at the École Normale Supérieure.[2] While he is an accomplished author of philosophy, politics, literature, and theater, Badiou's philosophical project is contained in his three major works: *Theory of the Subject* (1982), *Being and Event* (1988), and *Logics of Worlds* (2006).[3] A fourth major work, entitled *Immanence of Truths*, is said to be currently under way.[4]

Throughout his major works Badiou develops an ontology centered on the categories of truth and subjectivity. While he affirms the existence of such things as universal truths, these truths are always non-philosophical, and instead occur under four conditions: art, politics, love, and science. In this sense, philosophy itself does not produce truths, but instead takes its material for thought from these four non-philosophical conditions, which he calls generic procedures. Of equal importance for Badiou's philosophy is the evental nature of truths. Truths always emerge like a flash and dramatically change the field of possibilities in the situation in which they emerge. It is important to note that, for Badiou, events never happen as such, but retroactively will-have-happened if the consequences of an event are faithfully worked out by a subjective body.

For example, in *Logics of Worlds* Badiou takes the Paris commune to exemplify an event of emancipatory politics.[5] The possibility for such an occurrence was not contained in the previous situation, so the emergence of the commune is an impossible possibility that changes the situation and brings with it a new set of possibilities and opportunities for subjective commitment.

In the wake of this event, individuals are offered the possibility of joining the subject-body created by this event, and must subsequently live in fidelity to the consequences of the event. This act of fidelity to an event thus leads to the creation of a new world, founded on this evental truth. So for example, an individual (or more often a group of individuals) experience an event, such as a radical political rupture. After witnessing this event they subsequently make a wager on the truth contained within this event; there is never a guarantee, and so the subject must make a leap of faith that if they participate in working out the consequences of this event then it

---

[2]     While there is little biographical information available on Badiou in print, a basic intellectual biography is contained in Oliver Feltham, *Alain Badiou: Live Theory*, London: Continuum 2008.

[3]     See Alain Badiou, *Theorie du sujet*, Paris: Seuil 1982 (English translation: *Theory of the Subject*, London: Continuum 2009); Alain Badiou, *L'Être et l'événement*, Paris: Seuil 1988 (English translation: *Being and Event*, London: Continuum 2006); and Alain Badiou, *Logiques des Mondes*, Paris: Seuil 2006 (English translation: *Logics of Worlds*, London: Continuum 2009).

[4]     According to Badiou's translator Bruno Bosteels, at "Subject and Appearance" workshop, Friday, November 20, 2009, London.

[5]     Badiou, *Logiques des Mondes*, pp. 377–402. (*Logics of Worlds*, pp. 363–80.)

will-have-occurred. If this subject-body is faithful to this eventual truth, then they can inaugurate the possibility of a new world with a new state of the situation that says what is and is not possible.

It must be said that this brief account of Badiou's philosophy does little justice to the depth and complexity of his system, but a full-scale explication falls outside the scope of the present article. Curious readers are encouraged to consult the bibliography for a more complete list of introductory sources for Badiou's work.

## II. Kierkegaard's Influence on Badiou

While we have limited resources by which we can construct an accurate intellectual biography of Badiou, we can briefly speculate on ways he may have encountered the work of Kierkegaard (or at least Kierkegaardian themes) in the works of some of his primary influences. In an article titled "Philosophy as Biography" Badiou states that his three great masters were Jean-Paul Sartre, Jacques Lacan, and Louis Althusser.[6] While there is no good reason to believe that Kierkegaard had any substantial influence on the scientific Marxism of Althusser, the influence of Kierkegaard on both Sartre and Lacan has been widely noted.[7] To name just one example, Badiou uses anxiety as a subjective affect in both *Theory of the Subject* and *Logics of Worlds*. He likely gleans this concept from the work of his masters Lacan and Sartre, but it is clear that this concept is one that finds its original grounds in Kierkegaard's *The Concept of Anxiety*, which was studied by both Lacan and Sartre. While there may surely be more to this hand-me-down influence of Kierkegaard on Badiou through his masters Lacan and Sartre, it would be difficult to demonstrate this with the necessary rigor.

While there exists no full-scale work in English exploring the relationship between Kierkegaard and Badiou, a number of recent texts have commented on this relationship with varying degrees of detail. Peter Hallward's landmark study of Badiou's philosophy, *Badiou: A Subject to Truth*, mentions Kierkegaard in the context of the influence of the anti-philosophical tradition on Badiou and speaks of the great importance of this tradition in the formation of Badiou's project, but does not go into any detail as to Kierkegaard's specific influence on Badiou.[8]

John Mullarkey, in his work *Post Continental Philosophy: An Outline*, discusses the similarity between Badiou and Kierkegaard's theories of subjectivity in relation to

---

[6]     See http://www.lacan.com/symptom9_articles/badiou19.html.

[7]     While there is no shortage of works commenting on the influence of Kierkegaard on Sartrean existentialism, there is a small but growing body of work dedicated to exploring the relationship between Kierkegaard and Lacan. Two recent texts of note, one in French the other in English are Rodolphe Adam, *Lacan et Kierkegaard*, Paris: Presses Universitaires de France 2005, and Marcus Pound, *Theology, Psychoanalysis and Trauma*, London: SCM Press 2007. This relationship has also been briefly alluded to in the work of Slavoj Žižek.

[8]     Peter Hallward, *Badiou: A Subject to Truth*, Minneapolis: University of Minnesota Press 2003, pp. 20–1; p. 203.

becoming and a constant striving for truth.[9] While brief, Mullarkey concisely points out the surprising structural similarities between these two theories of subjectivity, noting that Badiou's subject is "very Kierkegaardian."[10]

One of the most extensive engagements (relatively speaking) between Badiou and Kierkegaard takes place in John Milbank's article "The Return of Mediation, or the Ambivalence of Alain Badiou" in which Milbank argues for a reading of Badiou's theory of the event which is much more Kierkegaardian than Hegelian.[11] He argues this based on the fact that Badiou's dialectic between being and appearance takes the form of a Kierkegaardian positive mediation, rather than a Hegelian double negation. That said, Milbank does not indicate at any point whether or not the seeming influence of Kierkegaard on the ontology of Badiou is due to an explicit influence of the former on the later, or merely an incidental one.

While concise and scattered, the Slovenian Marxist-philosopher Slavoj Žižek has also briefly referenced the similarities between Kierkegaard and Badiou. He does this initially in a footnote to an article entitled "From Purification to Subtraction: Badiou and the Real," in which he posits the relationship between passionate commitments in Kierkegaard and generic procedures in Badiou. In a more recent work, *In Defense of Lost Causes*, Žižek briefly argues for the similarity between the triads of aesthetic–ethical–religious in Kierkegaard and being–event–world in Badiou. Once again, these references are always in passing and contain no further explication.

And most recently, French philosopher and writer Remy Bac has published a critical piece examining Badiou's reading of Kierkegaard in *Logics of Worlds* entitled "Kierkegaard selon Badiou" in which he explores the accuracy and efficacy of Badiou's use of Kierkegaard, eventually concluding that the interiority of the Kierkegaardian subject bears little resemblance to the Badiouian subject which is little more than a local configuration of a truth procedure.

### III. Badiou's Interaction with Kierkegaard

While his *corpus* is vast and still growing, Badiou only has two direct textual engagements with the work of Kierkegaard. One, in his *Briefings on Existence*,[12] is little more than a passing reference without much theoretical significance, and the other an entire chapter in *Logics of Worlds*.

The first mention takes place in the prologue to *Briefings*, entitled "God is Dead." In this prologue Badiou proclaims that he takes the formula "God is dead" literally.[13]

---

[9]     John Mullarkey, *Post Continental Philosophy: An Outline*, London: Continuum 2007, pp. 107–8.
[10]    Ibid., p. 107.
[11]    See "The Return of Mediation, or The Ambivalence of Alain Badiou," *Angelaki*, vol. 12, no. 1, 2007. pp. 127–43, see p. 130.
[12]    Alain Badiou, *Court Traité d'ontologie transitoire*, Paris: Seuil 1998. (English translation: *Briefings on Existence*, trans. by Norman Madarasz, Albany: State University of New York Press 2006).
[13]    Badiou, *Court Traité d'ontologie transitoire*, p. 12. (*Briefings on Existence*, p. 23.)

Badiou then goes on to interrogate the claim of Kierkegaard's formula for the self from *The Sickness unto Death*: "The self is a relation that relates itself to itself or is the relation's relating itself to itself in the relation; the self is not the relation but is the relation's relating itself to itself."[14] For Badiou, "God is dead means that he is no longer the living being who can be encountered when existence breaks the ice of its own transparency."[15] Thus, when there is no longer a living God to establish this mode of relation, there is no longer a way to purify the effect of subjective despair. This is problematic for Badiou, since for him the subject cannot be founded by something that resides "outside" existence, and for him the concept of God carries this sense of absolute and transcendent otherness. At this point, the appearance of Kierkegaard in Badiou's writing seems incidental at best, and fails to interact with his work in any profound or telling manner.

Badiou's other, and much more substantial, engagement with Kierkegaard takes place in *Logics of Worlds*, which serves as the sequel to *Being and Event*. Whereas *Being and Event* was primarily concerned with providing a mathematical ontology (based on axiomatic set theory) that could account for the being of the subject, *Logics of Worlds* attempts to supplement this with a mathematical phenomenology (this time based on category theory) that can account for the appearing of truths and their accompanying subject-bodies in evental worlds.

Badiou's chapter on Kierkegaard is in Book VI of *Logics of Worlds*, which bears the title "Theory of Points." Put simply, Badiou theorizes a point as an impasse in the subjective process which forces a decision, a "yes" or a "no" from a subject. Usually this point is one that forces the subject to either give up (denying the truth of an evental occurrence) or keep going (which serves to affirm the truth of the event). Badiou subsequently considers the thought of Kierkegaard as it pertains to this manner of absolute choice.

Badiou opens the chapter by situating Kierkegaard in the lineage of the anti-philosophical tradition, with Kierkegaard serving as the ultimate anti-philosopher who is for/against Hegel.[16] He goes on to note: "for Kierkegaard, the key to existence is none other than absolute choice, the alternative, disjunction without remainder."[17] Badiou once again brings up the famous formula of the relational self from *The Sickness unto Death*, this time calling the formula "very beautiful."[18] For Badiou, "the dispute between Hegel and Kierkegaard is in effect a dispute about Christianity, and it concerns the function of decision in the constitution of Christian subjectivity."[19]

For Kierkegaard, the important thing is that, for Christianity, the eternal itself appears in time, and thus the universal for a moment becomes singular. Badiou notes that this stands in opposition to Hegel, for whom time is the "being there of the concept."[20] But in opposition to this "spectacular fusion of time and eternity," Badiou

---

| | |
|---|---|
| 14 | *SKS* 11, 129 / *SUD*, 13. |
| 15 | Badiou, *Court Traité d'ontologie transitoire*, p. 12. (*Briefings on Existence*, p. 24.) |
| 16 | Badiou, *Logiques des Mondes*, p. 447. (*Logics of Worlds*, p. 425.) |
| 17 | Ibid. |
| 18 | Ibid. |
| 19 | Badiou, *Logiques des Mondes*, p. 448. (*Logics of Worlds*, p. 426.) |
| 20 | Ibid. |

notes that, for Kierkegaard, "the time that is at stake in Christianity is my time, and Christian truth is of the order of what happens to me, and not what I contemplate."[21]

Badiou goes on to write of Kierkegaard's "Christian paradox" in a way that sounds very similar to his own theory of event, in which something infinite emerges from within finite materiality. Badiou argues that this Christian paradox is: "A challenge addressed to the existence of each and everyone, and not a reflective theme that a deft use of dialectical mediations would externally enlist in the spectacular fusion of time and eternity."[22] Once again, Badiou's description of Kierkegaard's thought paints a picture quite similar to Badiou's own position. For Badiou, an event is something that necessitates a response from each person. There is little room for reflection on possibility in Badiou's subjective axiom, as one must always say "yes" or "no" to the event, and subsequently continue this process in the working out of the event's implications. Moving on to consider the *Concluding Unscientific Postscript*, Badiou argues that Kierkegaard has an entirely militant theory of truth, which places him in complete fidelity with the apostle Paul, who is another one of Badiou's favored non-philosophical sources.[23] He goes on to provide this quotation from the *Postscript*:

> Only the truth which *builds up* is a truth *for you*. This is an essential predicate relating to truth as inwardness; its decisive characterization as upbuilding *for you*, that is, for the subject, is its essential difference from all objective knowledge, inasmuch as the subjectivity itself becomes part of the mark of the truth.[24]

Badiou uses this passage to highlight what he sees as the essential difference between Hegel and Kierkegaard, and why for this reason his theory of the subject is more indebted to Kierkegaard's anti-philosophy. The crucial points are the *essential difference of the subject from all objective knowledge*, and the fact that *subjectivity itself becomes a part of the mark which signifies truth*. While for Hegel it is necessary that one have knowledge of the stages of becoming-subject of the absolute, Kierkegaard insists that knowing is useless, and that rather than knowing the absolute, one experiences it through a process of subjective inwardness.[25] Once again, Badiou is here providing a reading of Kierkegaard that aligns him with his own position, since the Badiouian subject can never *know* the truth of an event, but rather plays an experiential role in the *becoming* of this truth. Rather than attain any form of objective knowledge, Badiou's militant subject always participates in the process of becoming inherent to any truth. Badiou thus goes on to argue: "That is why, for Kierkegaard, there cannot exist a moment of knowledge ('absolute knowledge,' in Hegel's terms) where truth is complete or present as a result. Everything commences, or recommences, with each subjective singularity."[26] Shortly after, Badiou states: "In our own vocabulary, we could say that Kierkegaard

---

21      Ibid.

22      Ibid.

23      See Alain Badiou, *St. Paul: The Foundation of Universalism*, trans. by Ray Brassier, Stanford, Stanford University Press 2003.

24      *SKS* 7, 230 / *CUP1*, 252–3. Translation slightly modified by Badiou.

25      Badiou, *Logiques des Mondes*, pp. 448–9. (*Logics of Worlds*, pp. 426–7.)

26      Badiou, *Logiques des Mondes*, p. 449. (*Logics of Worlds*, p. 427.)

vigorously maintains that thought and truth must not simply account for their being, but also for their appearing, which is to say for their existence....Thinking must also be a form of commitment in the thought that thinks."[27]

Once again we see Badiou reading his own theory of subjectivity back into the work of Kierkegaard. Because truth is never something that can be complete, or present as a result, it is up to the militant subject of that truth to continually recommence the process of working out the implications of this truth, and each point of recommencement is what Badiou calls a point, in which the subject says "yes" or "no." For Badiou there can never simply be a thought of truth, but always a committed subjective response invigorated by the experience of a truth, and Badiou rightly reads Kierkegaard as having a similar theory.

Badiou moves on to structure the rest of his concise engagement with Kierkegaard around investigating the link between truth, subject, and point in Kierkegaard's work.[28] Badiou begins by focusing on the foundation for truth in the work of Kierkegaard, the Christian paradox. As we have already seen, the Christian paradox offers a conception of truth and of the subjective response to truth that, at least formally, mirrors that of Badiou. The crucial difference is, of course, that for Kierkegaard this paradox is dependent on God, and the human must exist in absolute relation to God, while for Badiou, on the other hand, God is long dead.

Badiou goes on to argue that "if 'truth' is the name of a subjective connection constructed between existence and eternity, Kierkegaard very clearly proposes a conception of truth as always generic or anonymous."[29] On Badiou's reading, and once again in line with his own system, this means that the experience of truth is available to anyone, regardless of who or where they are, the truth never discriminates or excludes. Badiou also remarks that Kierkegaard is especially close to the idea of incorporation, which for Badiou signifies the inclusion of the individual into a subject-body which collectively works out the implications of a truth.

Badiou then follows the reading of Slavoj Žižek[30] and notes the vast difference between the leap from the aesthetic to the ethical and the leap from the ethical to the religious. On Badiou's reading, this second leap is much more complex and obscure than the first because the religious sphere involves the abiding of subjectivity in the absolute paradox itself. Badiou here reads the religious stage of existence as the moment of incorporation of the subject into truth itself.[31] The religious, or Christian stage, is the one which requires the absolute choice of saying "yes" to the absurd in an absolute subjective commitment which refuses to hold to any objective certainty. Badiou goes on to argue "the moment of absolute choice, and it alone, reveals subjective energy."[32] At this point Badiou highlights one of the points of divergence between his own thought and that of Kierkegaard, and arguably this is a

---

27    Ibid.
28    Badiou, *Logiques des Mondes*, p. 450. (*Logics of Worlds*, p. 428.)
29    Badiou, *Logiques des Mondes*, p. 451. (*Logics of Worlds*, p. 429.)
30    See Slavoj Žižek, *In Defense of Lost Causes*, London: Verso 2008, pp. 396–7.
31    Badiou, *Logiques des Mondes,* p. 452. (*Logics of Worlds*, p. 430.)
32    Badiou, *Logiques des Mondes*, p. 453. (*Logics of Worlds*, p. 431.)

point at which Badiou could gain something through a further consideration of the Kierkegaardian framework, and its accompanying anthropology.

Badiou notes that it is a passion, a subjective energy, which "grounds the possibility for the subject to encounter reality in time."[33] This energy or passion, which Kierkegaard also refers to as will, is something that thoroughly humanizes the subject in his thought. This is problematic for Badiou because his theory of subjectivity goes to great lengths to avoid any form of humanism, and especially any emphasis on the subject as an individual human entity. Badiou then goes on to close his discussion of Kierkegaard by noting the specifically Christian limitation of his thought.[34] Badiou not only considers what he sees as the teleological character of Christian religion, but the limitation placed on the subject by the necessity of its relationship to God. If there is no God, then the subject is left in a situation of absolute despair with no absolute with which to relate. Badiou closes this chapter noting "this figure [of the Christian subject] only holds up if it is supported by God, to the extent that his own coming has taken place in time."[35] While he finds much in common with his formal theory of existence and subjectivity, the place of the divine in Kierkegaard's thought is what ultimately leaves it as no more than an anti-philosophical resource for Badiou.

### IV. Outlines for Future Research on the Kierkegaard–Badiou Relationship

While Badiou's recent engagement with Kierkegaard is brief, it is remarkably telling. While Badiou's ontology often bears the formalism of a Hegelian dialectic (*Theory of the Subject* has a substantial engagement with Hegel, and both of his subsequent major works also contain important chapters in which Badiou engages with Hegel), his theory of subjectivity reveals itself as much more indebted to the "Christian paradox" of Kierkegaard. While it is clear that Badiou has no regard for the inherent religiosity of Kierkegaard's anti-philosophical writings, he seems happy to (almost) fully endorse the formal structure of Kierkegaard's theory of subjectivity and the ontology underlying this theory. While this may seem heretical to some, it seems as if when the issue is approached formally that Badiou can be seen as Kierkegaard's most faithful follower, and just like the melancholy Dane, Badiou has once again brought the question of subjectivity and its relation to truth to bear on a generation of post-modern and post-structuralist thinkers for whom the subject was a dated and thoroughly modern philosophical concept.

Three issues thus seem to remain in the aftermath of this encounter between Badiou and Kierkegaard. First is the question of the individual subject. While for Kierkegaard it is always the single individual who must decide for herself and make a leap into the subjective uncertainty of the truth, for Badiou the subject is always a formal body, or collection of individuals. So while for Kierkegaard one must first be a subject to then enter into the body of the truth (or, the Church), for Badiou one cannot be a subject until that moment at which they join the collective body.

---

[33]    Ibid.
[34]    Badiou, *Logiques des Mondes*, p. 455. (*Logics of Worlds*, p. 433.)
[35]    Badiou, *Logiques des Mondes*, p. 457. (*Logics of Worlds*, p. 435.)

Next is the issue of humanity. It is clear that for Kierkegaard the subject is one marked by the passion and will of the particularly human, and clearly he has no desire to discuss the subjectivity of non-human entities. His is a thoroughly Christian humanism. Badiou, on the other hand, would follow his master Althusser and identify with his brand of scientific anti-humanism, in which the subject is an axiomatic formalism and by no means necessarily human. This becomes problematic, however, when we examine the nature of subjectivity in each of Badiou's generic procedures: politics, art, love, and science. In all of his works he has yet to show how the non-human can be affected by the event of truth, and how these non-human entities can subsequently join subjective bodies. Until Badiou can provide examples of how dogs, rocks, and trees can be taken up into a subjective body, the question of the human will continue to haunt his work.

Finally, there is the question of the religious. For Kierkegaard the religious is the form, or sphere, of truth, and the Christian paradox is the event that creates the possibility for his properly religious subjectivity, existence, and ethics. Badiou, by contrast, is an avowed atheist who nonetheless relies on the example of St. Paul to flesh out his theory of militant truth and subjectivity. Simon Critchley has noted this tension, stating, "for all his avowed atheism, might one not have the suspicion that although Badiou's account of the [ethical] subject is not substantially Christian in any metaphysical sense, it is still structurally Christian?"[36] Further consideration of this religious tension in the work of Badiou could potentially provide even more reason for us to consider him as one of the most important Kierkegaardians of the present century.

---

[36]     Simon Critchley, *Infinitely Demanding*, London: Verso 2007, p. 50.

# Bibliography

*I. References to or Uses of Kierkegaard in Badiou's Corpus*

*Court Traite d'ontologie transitoire*, Paris: Editions de Seuil 1998, pp. 12–15. (English translation: *Briefings on Existence: A Short Treatise on Transitory Ontology*, trans. by Norman Madarasz, Albany, New York: State University of New York Press 2006, pp. 24–5.)

*Logiques des Mondes*, Paris: Seuil 2006, pp. 447–57. (English translation: *Logics of Worlds*, trans. by Alberto Toscano, London: Continuum 2009, pp. 425–35.)

*II. Sources of Badiou's Knowledge of Kierkegaard*

Deleuze, Gilles, *Différence et répétition*, Paris: Presses Universitaires de France 1968, pp. 12–20; p. 38; p. 39, note 1; pp. 126–7; p. 289, note 1; pp. 347–8; p. 377; p. 397.

Heidegger, Martin, *Sein und Zeit*, Halle: Niemeyer 1927, pp. 175–96, see also p. 190, note 1; p. 235, note 1; and p. 338, note 1.

Kierkegaard, Søren, *Ou bien...ou bien*, trans. by F. Prior, O. Prior, and M.H. Guignot, Paris: Gallimard 1988 [1943].

— *Traité du désespoir. (La maladie mortelle)*, trans. by Knud Ferlov and Jean-Jacques Gateau, Paris: Gallimard 1990 [1932].

— *Post-scriptum aux Miettes philosophiques*, trans. by Paul Petit, Paris: Mesmil 2002 [1941].

Lacan, Jacques, "Le séminaire sur la 'Lettre vole,' " in his *Écrits*, Paris: Le Seuil 1966, pp. 45–6.

— "L'agressivité en psychanalyse," in his *Écrits*, Paris: Le Seuil 1966, p. 123.

— "Fonction et champ de la parole et du langage en psychanalyse," in his *Écrits*, Paris: Le Seuil 1966, p. 293.

— "D'un dessein," in his *Écrits*, Paris: Le Seuil 1966, p. 367.

— "D'une question préliminaire à tout traitement possible de la psychose," in his *Écrits*, Paris: Le Seuil 1966, p. 519.

— "A la mémoire d'Ernest Jones: Sur sa théorie du symbolisme," in his *Écrits*, Paris: Le Seuil 1966, pp. 716–17.

— *Le Séminaire. Livre II. Le Moi dans la théorie de Freud et dans la technique psychanalytique. 1954–1955*, Paris: Le Seuil 1978, p. 110; pp. 124–5.

— *Le Séminaire. Livre X. L'Angoisse. 1962–1963*, Paris: Éditions de Seuil 2004, p. 385.

— *Le Séminaire. Livre XI. Les Quatre Concepts fondamentaux de la psychanalyse*, Paris: Le Seuil 1974, p. 35; p. 59.

— *Le Séminaire. Livre XVII. L'envers de la psychanalyse*, Paris: Le Seuil 1991, pp. 51–2; pp. 168–9.

Sartre, Jean-Paul, *L'être et le néant. Essai d'ontologie phénoménologique*, Paris: Gallimard 1943 (*Bibliothèque des Idées*), pp. 58–84; pp. 94–111; pp. 115–49; pp. 150–74; pp. 291–300; pp. 508–16; pp. 529–60; pp. 639–42; pp. 643–63; pp. 669–70; pp. 720–2.

— *L'existentialisme est un humanisme*, Paris: Nagel 1946, pp. 27–33.

— "Un nouveau mystique," in his *Situations I*, Paris: Gallimard 1947, pp. 143–88, see pp. 154–5; pp. 162–3; pp. 168ff.

— "Questions de Methode," in *Critique de la raison dialectique*, vol. 1, *Théorie des ensembles pratiques*, Paris: Gallimard 1960, pp. 13–111, see pp. 15–32.

— *Critique de la raison dialectique*, vol. 1, *Théorie des ensembles pratiques*, Paris: Gallimard 1960, p. 117, note 1.

— "Kierkegaard: L'universal Singulier," in *Kierkegaard vivant. Colloque organisé par l'Unesco à Paris du 21 au 23 avril 1964*, Paris: Gallimard 1966, pp. 20–63.

— *Les carnets de la drôle de guerre. Novembre 1939–Mars 1940*, Paris: Gallimard 1983, pp. 333–7; pp. 342–7; pp. 348ff.; p. 352; pp. 382–3.

— *Lettres au Castor et à quelques autres*, vols. 1–2, ed. by Simone de Beauvoir, Paris: Gallimard 1983, vol. 1 (1926–39), p. 451; p. 491; p. 494; p. 496; p. 500; p. 518; vol. 2 (1940–63), p. 11; p. 16; pp. 38–9; pp. 40–1; p. 56; p. 111; p. 129; p. 197; p. 200; p. 215; p. 219; pp. 222–4; p. 264; p. 268; p. 279; pp. 285–6; pp. 289–90.

*III. Secondary Literature on Badiou's Relation to Kierkegaard*

Hallward, Peter, *Badiou: A Subject to Truth*, Minneapolis: University of Minnesota Press 2003, p. 20; p. 263.

Milbank, John, "The Return of Mediation, or The Ambivalence of Alain Badiou," *Angelaki*, vol. 12, no. 1, 2007, pp. 127–43.

Mullarkey, John, *Post-Continental Philosophy: An Outline*, London: Continuum 2006, pp. 107–9.

Žižek, Slavoj, "From Purification to Subtraction: Badiou and the Real," in *Think Again: Alain Badiou and the Future of Philosophy*, ed. by Peter Hallward, New York: Continuum 2004, p. 246, note 18.

— *The Parallax View*, Cambridge, Massachusetts: MIT Press 2006, p. 75.

— *In Defense of Lost Causes*, London: Verso 2008, pp. 396–7.

# Judith Butler:

## Kierkegaard as Her Early Teacher in Rhetoric and Parody

### Gerhard Thonhauser

In her essay "Can the 'Other' of Philosophy Speak?" Judith Butler tells the story of a "young teenager hiding out from painful family dynamics in the basement of her house where her mother's college books were stored."[1] The two books that stood out to the teenager, somehow attracting her attention and sparking her interest for philosophy, were Spinoza's *Ethics* and Kierkegaard's *Either/Or*. The story of the teenage girl is the narration of Butler's own adolescence and the description of her early introduction to philosophy. When investigating Butler's reception of Kierkegaard, we have to take into account the story of the teenager in the basement, a story that describes the role of Kierkegaard in her early introduction to philosophy. We have to consider that Kierkegaard's influence on Butler might not be found—at least not in the first place—in a scholarly reception, but that it has to be traced back to the teenager in the basement and to a certain sensibility, a certain cautious attitude towards any kind of text or argument, which emerged in these early years and which was decisively influenced by the reading of Kierkegaard. This sensibility, which would eventually become important for Butler's academic work and her political commitment, has something to do with the rhetorical dimension of a text, with the mode in which an argument is presented, a dimension that is usually overlooked, but which Kierkegaard and Butler force us to take into consideration.

### I. Short Overview of Butler's Life and Work

Butler was born on February 24, 1956, to a Jewish family of Hungarian and Russian ancestry and grew up in Cleveland, Ohio. She studied philosophy at Yale University, receiving her Ph.D. in 1984. She was trained in the tradition of continental philosophy, studying its main traditions: German Idealism, phenomenology, existentialism, hermeneutics, and the Frankfurt School. She also spent one year at Heidelberg University as a Fulbright Scholar to study German Idealism, attending the courses of Hans-Georg Gadamer and Dieter Henrich. Her dissertation advisor was the

---

[1]  Judith Butler, "Can the 'Other' of Philosophy Speak?" in *Undoing Gender*, New York and London: Routledge 2004, p. 235.

phenomenologist Maurice Natanson. Her dissertation dealt with the reception of Hegel's *Phenomenology of Spirit* in France and was subsequently published in an extended version as *Subjects of Desire: Hegelian Reflections in Twentieth-Century France*.[2]

Butler is usually associated with poststructuralist thought, and it might be a surprise to some that she, in fact, began to encounter poststructuralism only after she had finished her university education. She was first confronted with the works of Michel Foucault in the context of a women's studies faculty seminar, and it was not until her time as a postdoctoral fellow at Wesleyan University from 1983 to 1986 that she began to open up to so-called French theory.[3] Butler became a professor at Johns Hopkins University in 1991, before joining the University of California, Berkeley in 1993. She is currently the Maxine Elliott professor in the Rhetoric and Comparative Literature departments at the University of California, Berkeley and also co-director of the Program of Critical Theory. In addition, Butler is Hannah Arendt Chair at the European Graduate School in Saas-Fee, Switzerland.

In 1990 *Gender Trouble* was published, which brought Butler immediate world-wide fame as a leading figure of the third generation of feminism and as one of the founders of the upcoming queer theory.[4] *Gender Trouble* developed a deconstruction of the history of feminism, a challenge of the sex–gender distinction and the stability of the category of "women," and offers new possibilities to think about political agency beyond identity politics.

In the past twenty years since the publication of *Gender Trouble*, Butler has been highly productive, publishing more than ten books and a vast number of articles. In *Bodies that Matter*,[5] published in 1993, Butler offers a close examination of the notion of "sex" in the sex–gender distinction and of the materiality of the body, two closely related matters that were major concerns for many scholars after reading *Gender Trouble*. The questions of the constitution of the subject through a certain subordination and the performative[6] character of such constitution processes, which both had already been important issues in *Gender Trouble*, found further elaboration

---

[2]      Judith Butler, *Subjects of Desire: Hegelian Reflections in Twentieth-Century France*, New York: Columbia University Press 1987. See further Sarah Salih, *Judith Butler*, London and New York: Routledge 2002. In comparison to other introductions to Butler's thought, Salih's book has the advantage that it does not begin with *Gender Trouble*, thereby ignoring Butler's developments prior to this epoch-making work, but with an extended discussion of Butler's dissertation *Subjects of Desire* and her early developments as a scholar of Hegel.

[3]      See Butler's "Preface to the Paperback Edition" in *Subjects of Desire* (pp. vii–xvii) published in 1999, where she gives a brief account of her intellectual development in the 1980s. This edition is an identical reprint of the first edition from 1987.

[4]      Judith Butler, *Gender Trouble: Feminism and the Subversion of Identity*, New York and London: Routledge 1990.

[5]      Judith Butler, *Bodies that Matter: On the Discursive Limits of "Sex,"* New York and London: Routledge 1993.

[6]      For Butler, identities are not fixed and pregiven, but constituted through performative processes of reiteration. Performativity is the name for the possibility and necessity of these processes of performative construction of identity.

in *The Psychic Life of Power* and *Excitable Speech*, both published in 1997.[7] *Antigone's Claim*, published in 2000, offers not only an interpretation of Sophocles' tragedy, but also a controversial discussion of contemporary kinship structures.[8] Butler revised several of her positions on gender, sex, sexuality, kinship and other related issues in several essays that are collected in *Undoing Gender*.[9]

In recent years, a certain shift has taken place in Butler's work. One important feature of this shift is her new tendency to employ the language of moral philosophy as well as of ontology. This is especially the case in *Giving An Account of Oneself*, where Butler, in addition to her common references to Nietzsche and Foucault, offers readings of Adorno and Lévinas.[10] In her most recent writings, Butler is particularly concerned about questions of war and violence. This new focus of her work found its first expression in *Precarious Life* and continues in her most recent publication, *Frames of War*.[11]

The extent of Butler's fame, and the heated discussion that her works caused, have hindered a sober and pragmatic encounter with her work. This situation, however, seems to be changing in recent years and the discussion of Butler's work appears to become less heated and more productive, particularly in the context of questions of political theory.[12]

## II. Back to the Teenager in the Basement

In the narration of her teenage experience Butler reports that her "first introduction to philosophy was a radically deinstitutionalized one, autodidactic and premature":[13]

---

[7]     Judith Butler, *The Psychic Life of Power: Theories in Subjection*, Stanford: Stanford University Press 1997 and Judith Butler, *Excitable Speech: A Politics of the Performative*, New York and London: Routledge 1997.

[8]     Judith Butler, *Antigone's Claim: Kinship Between Life and Death*, New York: Columbia University Press 2000.

[9]     Judith Butler, *Undoing Gender*, New York and London: Routledge 2004.

[10]     Judith Butler, *Giving An Account of Oneself*, New York: Fordham University Press 2005.

[11]     Judith Butler, *Precarious Life: The Power of Mourning and Violence*, London and New York: Verso 2004 and Judith Butler, *Frames of War: When is Life Grievable?*, London and New York: Verso 2009.

[12]     For productive discussions of Butler's work in the context of political theory see Moya Lloyd, *Beyond Identity Politics: Feminism, Power and Politics*, London: Sage 2005; Samuel A. Chambers and Terrell Carver, *Judith Butler and Political Theory: Troubling Politics*, London and New York: Routledge 2008; Annika Thiem, *Unbecoming Subjects: Judith Butler, Moral Philosophy, and Critical Responsibility*, New York: Fordham University Press 2008; and Birgit Sauer, " 'Troubling Politics.' Der Beitrag Judith Butlers zu einer feministischen Theoretisierung von Staat, Demokratie und Geschlecht," in *Der Staat in der Postdemokratie. Staat, Politik, Demokratie und Recht in neueren französischen Denken*, ed. by Michael Hirsch and Rüdiger Voigt, Stuttgart: Franz Steiner 2009, pp. 145–68.

[13]     Butler, "Can the 'Other' of Philosophy Speak?," p. 235.

I sat in that basement, sullen and despondent, having locked the door so that no one else could enter, having listened to enough music. And somehow I looked up through the smoke of my cigarette in that darkened and airless room and saw a title that aroused in me the desire to read, to read philosophy.[14]

The first book that drew her attention was Spinoza's *Ethics*. In particular, it was the idea of the persistence of the *conatus*, that every being has the desire to persist in its own being that fascinated and inspired her.[15] This doctrine of a primary desire to be, a desire to life, would eventually be transformed to the notion of "the desire of desire"[16] and prove essential for Butler's scholarly work on Hegel in her dissertation.[17]

The second book that Butler took notice of was Kierkegaard's *Either/Or*, and she was immediately attracted by the intriguing modalities of Kierkegaard's pseudonymous authorship. She was fascinated and confused by *Either/Or*, this book that lacks the unity of one identifiable author, because whoever this author is, he does not speak with a single, unified voice. On the contrary, the book offers at least two voices, spoken from different perspectives, arguing against each other and contradicting each other: "There was no way to begin to understand this work without understanding the rhetorical and generic dimensions of Kierkegaard's writings...there was no way to extricate the philosophical point...without being brought through the language to the moment of its own foundering, where language shows its own limitation."[18]

Butler is convinced that *Either/Or* cannot be understood beyond the difficulty of interpretation, that it forces the reader to take the whole complexity of a pseudonymous authorship into consideration. When reading this text, one is confronted with a variety of written voices in the text that do not reveal, at least not in a direct manner, what the author intends to say. Instead, they continuously refer to the unspoken, to a dimension of the text beyond the text that presents itself as not communicable in language. Hence, Butler points out the fact that one of her first "confrontations with a philosophical text posed the question of reading, and drew attention to its rhetorical structure as a text."[19] This question of rhetoric would remain a focal point of all her subsequent scholarly and political work.

---

[14]    Ibid., p. 237.

[15]    Ibid., pp. 235–6.

[16]    Judith Butler borrows this notion from Jean Hyppolite's commentary on Hegel's *Phenomenology of Spirit*. See Judith Butler, "Longing for Recognition," in *Undoing Gender*, p. 137. See also Butler, *Giving an Account of Oneself*, pp. 43–4.

[17]    Butler, *Subjects of Desire*, pp. 17–60 and 79–92. In this book, Butler suggests that "Hyppolite's interpretation of the absolute knowledge as the 'disquiet of life' aligns Hegel more closely with Kierkegaard." Butler, *Subjects of Desire*, p. 83. Additionally, she states in the case of Sartre that it was a "Kierkegaardian filter" through which he appropriated Hegel. Butler, *Subjects of Desire*, p. 157. In other words, the French reception of Hegel opened up a way of approaching Hegel that makes the differences between him and Kierkegaard appear less significant than they otherwise would.

[18]    Butler, "Can the 'Other' of Philosophy Speak?," p. 236.

[19]    Ibid.

For the young teenager in the basement, Kierkegaard and Spinoza were philosophy.[20] But they were not the only sources for her early introduction to philosophical thought. Another important means for this introduction was her Jewish background. Butler not only attended Hebrew school, but because she was considered as a kind of problem child (too talkative in class, not behaving well and talking back at the teacher) she had to take a special tutorial with the rabbi. That was meant as a sort of punishment, but Butler reports that she had actually been thrilled about it. Butler also reports that when she was 12 she said in an interview that she "wanted either to be a philosopher or a clown" and the decision between the two "depended on whether or not I found the world worth philosophizing about, and what the price of seriousness might be. I was not sure I wanted to be a philosopher, and I confess that I have never quite overcome that doubt."[21]

A consequence of Butler's early introduction to philosophy in this de-institutionalized and autodidactic way was that she has always struggled with the institution of philosophy. To be more precise, she has struggled with a certain seriousness that constitutes the foundation of philosophy in the eyes of those that decide about the academic institutionalization of the discipline. It is a seriousness that forbids asking questions about the rhetoric of a text. Maybe Butler could identify herself with Kierkegaard in this respect, with his struggle about becoming an author; and the question about the price he had to pay to be an author, and what alternatives there were to this struggle. I will come back to this aspect in the following section.

During her years at Yale, Butler thought of herself as a serious philosopher and tried as hard as she could to act like one and eventually become one. During her undergraduate years she went to listen to a class of Paul de Man, but she left the class and "arrogantly decided," as she interprets today from the perspective of the mature professor, "that those who attended his seminars were not really philosophers," and she "returned to the more conservative wing of continental philosophy" claiming that the distance that divided what she did from what happened in the comparative literature department "was much greater than it could possibly be."[22] At that time, she was scandalized for the first time by Kierkegaard's remark in *Fear and Trembling*: "If philosophy among other vagaries were also to have the notion that it could occur to a man to act in accordance with its teaching, one might make out of that a queer comedy."[23] And she was scandalized for a second time when she heard the anecdote about Max Scheler, a German philosopher and supporter of a value ethics, who reportedly responded to questions about his own way of living that did not follow the high ethical standards he demanded in his writings: you do not expect from a signpost either for it to go in the direction it points to.[24] Through these

---

[20]     Ibid., p. 237.

[21]     Ibid., p. 234.

[22]     Ibid., p. 238.

[23]     *SKS* 4, 188 / *FT*, 98. The passage is freely cited in Butler, "Can the 'Other' of Philosophy Speak?," p. 239.

[24]     Butler recalls the anecdote the following way: "[T]hat the sign that points the way to Berlin does not need to go there to offer the right direction." Butler, "Can the 'Other' of Philosophy Speak?," p. 239.

scandalizing experiences, the frightening and painful insight slowly grew in Butler that "philosophy might be divorced from life, that life might not be fully ordered by philosophy" and it was only several years later and "with some sadness and loss that I came to reconcile myself to this post-idealist insight."[25]

While at Yale, Butler was also confronted with Kierkegaard in an academic setting. She took courses with Paul Holmer at Yale Divinity School, where Kierkegaard was taught, and she was a teaching assistant for Maurice Natanson, who gave a lecture course on existential philosophy, in which Kierkegaard's *Fear and Trembling* was read. Additionally, Butler reports that she also found several instances that reminded her of Kierkegaard in her early Jewish education. Thus, one has to see Butler's reception of Kierkegaard in connection with her own Jewish background, a background in which Kierkegaard, paradoxically, seems to play an important role for her. She mentions especially instances "where a certain silence informed the writing that was offered, where writing could not quite deliver or convey what it sought to communicate, but where the mark of its own foundering illuminated a reality that language could not directly represent."[26] But Butler also noticed that this is not only a question of rhetoric or a mere rhetorical problem. She claims that it was again her Jewish background, especially her education in Jewish ethics, that made her understand that this rhetorical problem was tightly linked "to questions of individual and collective suffering and what transformations were possible."[27] Thus, Butler's sensibility for the rhetorical dimension of a text corresponds not only with her struggle with philosophy as an academic discipline, but also with her concern about political matters, especially instances of violence and the question of possible change.

### III. Butler's Interpretation of Kierkegaard

Butler wrote an article about Søren Kierkegaard for the volume on *The Age of German Idealism* of the *Routledge History of Philosophy* in 1993.[28] This article is crucial for an investigation into Butler's reception of Kierkegaard because it is the only source in which Butler offers direct insight into her reading of Kierkegaard. In general, the article shows that Butler is well informed about Kierkegaard's authorship, and that she carefully read a variety of pseudonymous works in common English

---

[25]     Butler, "Can the 'Other' of Philosophy Speak?," p. 239.

[26]     Ibid., p. 238.

[27]     Ibid.

[28]     Judith Butler, "Kierkegaard's Speculative Despair," in *The Age of German Idealism*, ed. by Robert C. Solomon and Kathleen Marie Higgins, London: Routledge 1993, pp. 363–92. Appended to Butler's article is a bibliography with a selection of Kierkegaard's works in English translation and a selection of literature on Kierkegaard. I have included the texts on that list into the bibliography of sources of Judith Butler's knowledge of Kierkegaard, which is annexed to the present article, as the bibliography of Butler's article at least provides evidence about her knowledge of these sources, even though it cannot prove if Butler has actually read a specific text. Several obvious mistakes in the bibliographic information provided in Butler's article have been tacitly corrected.

translations. Butler offers a number of interesting interpretations, which would be worth further discussion. The article can generally be characterized by its affirmative tone and Butler's surprisingly high estimation of Kierkegaard. The article falls into the period of Butler's beginning fame, when she had already established herself as a well-known theorist in her own right, which makes her article on Kierkegaard in a companion even more remarkable.

## A. A Hegelian Parody

Butler begins her article with a general summary of Kierkegaard's critique of Hegel, which in her view "concerns primarily the failure of a philosophy of reflection to take account of that which exceeds reflection itself: passion, existence, faith."[29] The main question that Kierkegaard raises is where "Hegel, the existing individual, stands in relation to the systematic totality that Hegel elucidates?"[30] One is reminded of Kierkegaard's remark that "most systematizers in relation to their systems are like a man who builds an enormous castle and himself lives alongside it in a shed."[31] The point is that if Hegel's system cannot include Hegel, the existing individual, then there is an outside to the system and the system is not as complete and explanatory as it claims to be.[32] "Paradoxically, the very existence of Hegel, the existing philosopher, effectively—one might say *rhetorically*—undermines what appears to be the most important claim in that philosophy, the claim to provide a comprehensive account of knowledge and reality."[33]

That Kierkegaard demands to consider the existing individual does not mean that he supports an irrational philosophy or that he maintains a nonsystematic point of view about the individual. On the contrary, Kierkegaard makes extensive use of the speculative terminology of Hegelianism, but when he does so, "he appears to parody that discourse in order to reveal its constitutive contradictions."[34] Butler uses the opening page of *The Sickness unto Death* to highlight this Kierkegaardian parody.[35] In this passage, Butler explains, Kierkegaard is clearly employing Hegelian terminology, using several familiar Hegelian concepts, but, at the same

---

[29]     Butler, "Kierkegaard's Speculative Despair," p. 363.

[30]     Ibid.

[31]     *SKS* 18, 303, JJ:490 / *KJN* 2, 279.

[32]     It is interesting to note Butler's suggestion in *Subjects of Desire* that Hegel anticipated this Kierkegaardian critique in his own critique of Spinoza, who he claims fails to take the role of the knowing subject into account; Butler, *Subjects of Desire*, pp. 12–13. As we will see, this is in a way a general pattern of Butler's reading of Kierkegaard and Hegel.

[33]     Butler, "Kierkegaard's Speculative Despair," p. 363.

[34]     Ibid., p. 364.

[35]     She refers to the famous passage at the beginning of A.A: "A human being is spirit. But what is spirit? Spirit is the self. But what is the self? The self is a relation that relates itself to itself or is the relation's relating itself to itself in the relation; the self is not the relation but is the relation's relating itself to itself: A human being is a synthesis of the infinite and the finite, of the temporal and the eternal, of freedom and necessity, in short, a synthesis. A synthesis is a relation between two. Considered in this way, a human being is still not a self." *SKS* 11, 129 / *SUD*, 13.

time, it becomes also apparent that he is parodying this Hegelian language, in other words he makes use of it "for an analysis that both extends and exceeds the properly Hegelian purview."[36] Kierkegaard's parody is not a clear-cut rejection of Hegel; it preserves certain aspects of the original, even when converting its essence. Butler compares this parody to the Hegelian operation of *Aufhebung*, but it is an *Aufhebung* that lacks the final *synthesis* which was crucial for Hegel, but is absent from this Kierkegaardian reemployment of this operation: "Parody functions for Kierkegaard as an *Aufhebung* that leads not to synthesis between his position and Hegel's, but to a decisive break. Kierkegaard does not lay out his arguments against Hegel in propositional form. He re-enacts those arguments through the rhetorical construction of his text."[37]

Butler also offers an explanation of why Kierkegaard has to set forth his arguments in this way. She states that "if the issue he has with Hegel could be *rationally* decided, then Hegel would have won from the start" and, therefore, Kierkegaard has to change his strategy and, accordingly, his texts "counter Hegel most effectively on the level of style."[38] For the reader it is, hence, crucial to consider the rhetorical dimension of Kierkegaard's texts, the way in which his arguments are "performed through the parodic reiteration of Hegel."[39]

This is what Butler wants to exemplarily do with her interpretation of the opening page of *The Sickness unto Death*. I do not want to go into the details of Butler's interpretation, but it seems to me that she is exaggeratedly emphasizing this parodic dimension of the text, which leads her to underestimate the comprehensiveness and coherence of the notion of the self that Kierkegaard developed in this book.[40]

With regard to its content, the most important aspect that Butler retains from the book is that the self is constituted by a paradox. The task of the self is twofold from the beginning, having the task of self-constitution, but yet being derived. That the self "has been established by another" and that it "relates itself to that which established the entire relation,"[41] is interpreted by Butler in the way that "insofar as 'another' is infinite, and this prior infinity constitutes the self, the self partakes of infinity as well."[42] On the other hand, the self is also determined, being the embodied self it is, and hence the self is also finite. In conclusion Butler can write:

---

[36]    Butler, "Kierkegaard's Speculative Despair," p. 364.

[37]    Ibid., p. 366.

[38]    Ibid.

[39]    Ibid.

[40]    The opening passage of *The Sickness unto Death* has likely been cited more often than any other passage from Kierkegaard's body of work and was the cause for many discussions in Kierkegaard scholarship as well as an important source of inspiration for several subsequent investigations into the self. It appears that Butler is not familiar with these discussions; at least, she does not take them into consideration. In her defense, however, one has to add that the most prolific discussions about *The Sickness unto Death* took place after Butler had written her article. See especially the contributions in *Kierkegaard Studies Yearbook*, 1996.

[41]    *SKS* 11, 129 / *SUD*, 13.

[42]    Butler, "Kierkegaard's Speculative Despair," p. 370.

The self is inevitably both finitude and infinitude which the self lives, not as a synthesis, and not as the transcendence of the one over the other, but as a perpetual paradox. Inasmuch as the self is self-constituting, that is, has as its task the becoming of itself, it is finite; it is *this* self, and not some other. Inasmuch as the self is derived, a possibility actualized from an infinite source of possibility, and retains that infinity within itself as the passionate inwardness of faith, then that self is infinite.[43]

This notion has striking similarities to Hegel, as Butler points out. For Hegel as well as for Kierkegaard, the self is constituted by infinitude and finitude, but the difference is the "Hegelian ideal of becoming at one with oneself," a self-identity and coherency that is supposed to be achievable by the self's own effort.[44] The main point is:

If Hegel thought that the subject might be a synthesis of finite and infinite, he failed to consider that that subject, reconceived as a self with inwardness, can never mediate the absolutely qualitative difference between what is finite in that self and what is infinite. This failure of mediation is what underscores the paradoxical character of existence.[45]

In Butler's interpretation,[46] Hegel's *Phenomenology of Spirit* is a narration of the various ways in which the mediation of the subject fails and must fail. She calls this "the permanent irony of the Hegelian subject."[47] Precisely in this respect she can write that "Kierkegaard's own philosophical exercise is implied in the tradition of German Idealism."[48] But the difference is that Hegel insisted on the principal possibility that the mediation can be successful, that the self can come back to itself through the relation to others and the relation to the outside world. In the *Phenomenology of Spirit* "there is no final or constitutive failure to mediate. Every failure delineates a new and more synthetic task for the emerging subject of reflection."[49] But this is where Kierkegaard's enters the scene at the end of the *Phenomenology*, because

if Hegel thought that the subject of the *Phenomenology* had taken into account of everything along the way…then the last laugh is on Hegel's subject. In its mania for synthesis, the subject has forgotten to include that which can never be systematized, that which thwarts and resists reflection, namely, its very existence and its constitutive and mutually exclusive passions: faith and despair.[50]

---

[43]     Ibid., p. 371.

[44]     Ibid., p. 373.

[45]     Ibid., p. 372.

[46]     In this article, I cannot discuss Butler's controversial reception of Hegel, which focuses on the *Phenomenology of Spirit* and is importantly informed by the twentieth-century reception of Hegel in France. See especially Butler, *Subjects of Desire*, pp. 17–59.

[47]     Butler, *Subjects of Desire*, p. 7. Butler goes on to describe this permanent irony the following way: "it requires mediation to know itself, and knows itself only as the very structure of mediation; in effect, what is reflexively grasped when the subject finds itself 'outside' itself, reflected there, is this very fact itself, that the subject is a reflexive structure, and the movement out of itself is necessary in order for it to know itself at all." Ibid.

[48]     Butler, "Kierkegaard's Speculative Despair," p. 364.

[49]     Ibid., p. 365.

[50]     Ibid.

Butler refers to Kierkegaard's challenge, whether such a subject, as described in the *Phenomenology*, "might really be said to exist."[51] She links this challenge to the also Kierkegaardian question, what the actual motivation of the transitions in the *Phenomenology* is.[52] Additionally, she identifies despair and faith as the two main characteristics of the subject that—following Kierkegaard—make it impossible for this subject to perform a complete and final mediation of its paradoxical constitution. Thus, it is required to take a closer look at Butler's interpretation of Kierkegaard's notion of despair and faith.

## B. Kierkegaardian Despair and Faith

Again drawing from the opening page of *The Sickness unto Death*, Butler concludes that "despair is the result of the effort to overcome or solve the paradox of human existence."[53] The main point, in Butler's opinion, is that there is no solution to this paradox of human existence, in other words, the self can never overcome its paradoxical constitution. On the contrary, whenever it tries to solve this paradox it will fall into despair, and whenever it intends to overcome its despair by its own means, it will fall even deeper into despair. There is no solution to the paradox of human existence, at least not within the realm of the ability of the self, and every effort of the self to ignore or refuse this fact is another modality of despair.

Faith, on the contrary, can be defined as "the passionate and non-rational affirmation of that paradox, an affirmation that must be infinitely repeated."[54] Every individual must be either in despair or faith, *tertium non datur*. If an individual thinks that it is not in despair or does not know about its despair, this is only another sign of despair. For Butler, hence, it is crucial to notice that despair and faith do correspond in one aspect, namely, that both do "not provide a solution for the paradox of the self. Indeed, nothing provides such a solution."[55] To sum up Butler's reading, the difference between despair and faith is that whereas despair intends to ignore or refuse the paradox of human existence, faith tries to emphatically affirm it.

This is the context in which Butler turns to Kierkegaard's *Fear and Trembling*. The main line of her interpretation is that "in the story of Abraham we receive from Kierkegaard something like an allegory of the paradoxical self."[56] It is well known that it is one of the main aspects of Kierkegaard's Abraham that he cannot offer an explanation for his action; that he cannot justify his decision to sacrifice his beloved son, but that he is beyond the sphere of possible explanations, where only silence remains. The pseudonym Johannes de silentio rhetorically emphasizes this fact in the text, stating numerous times that he cannot possibly understand Abraham, but can only follow his steps and be astonished by his faith. Butler highlights that there are two aspects of the story that both seem to fascinate Kierkegaard: on the one

---

[51]     Butler, *Subjects of Desire*, p. 12.
[52]     Ibid., p. 135.
[53]     Ibid., p. 372.
[54]     Ibid.
[55]     Ibid., p. 373.
[56]     Ibid., p. 377.

hand, he is horrified by the fact that Abraham's faith leads him to actually sacrifice his own and only son; but on the other hand, "he is also appalled by the fact that Abraham appears to get Isaac back, that God not only asks for a sacrifice, but returns what has been lost, and all this *without reason*."[57] We cannot understand Abraham, as Johannes de silentio says, but we can understand and appreciate that Abraham is a true "knight of faith": "He turns against neither the finite (Isaac) nor the infinite (God), but prepares for the paradoxical affirmation of both."[58] This is what true faith is according to Butler's reading of Kierkegaard: the paradoxical affirmation of the paradox.

## C. Hegelian Rejoinder

In the context of Abraham's faith, it is important for Butler to point out that the often discussed "teleological suspension of the ethical"[59] is "not the denial of ethics," but the "postponement of the ethical domain in the name of what is higher" and that "this suspension of the ethical entails anxiety, and faith does not resolve anxiety, but exists with it."[60]

Butler compares this with Hegel's view of the ethical and his understanding of the relation that God has to the ethical sphere: "Hegel would believe that God is present in the ethical law, and that individuals, by submitting to the ethical law, come into a mediated relationship to God. This happy reconciliation of the ethical (called "the universal") and the religious (called "the absolute") is one that Kierkegaard firmly rejects."[61] Abraham takes distance from the ethical law, which considers him as a murderer, and by that move he becomes an individual. This departure from the ethical law is the modality of his individualization, and Kierkegaard seems to value this individuality, which in Hegel's point of view is sin. However, Butler highlights also another dimension of Hegel's account: "Although Hegel appears to worry about such a moment in which the individual stands apart from the ethical community, suspending the power of its laws to govern his or her life, Hegel also appreciates fear and trembling as necessary moments in the development of the human subject."[62]

For Butler, it is significant that "Kierkegaard does not acknowledge that moment in Hegel in which fear and trembling are considered to be necessary experiences in the acquisition of human freedom,"[63] and she can conclude, accordingly, that "Kierkegaard's characterization of Hegel is not always fair."[64] In this context, Butler refers to the bondsman in the *Phenomonology of Spirit*, who, after having overcome his enslavement at the end of the chapter on "Lordship and Bondage," cannot celebrate his liberation, but is rather frightened of his newly achieved freedom, a freedom

---

| | |
|---|---|
| 57 | Ibid., pp. 377–8. |
| 58 | Ibid., p. 378. |
| 59 | *SKS* 4, 148 / *FT*, 54. |
| 60 | Butler, "Kierkegaard's Speculative Despair," pp. 378–9. |
| 61 | Ibid., p. 381. |
| 62 | Ibid., p. 382. |
| 63 | Ibid. |
| 64 | Ibid., p. 383. |

without guidance from an authority that is "an unbearable situation which leads to the development, in the following chapter on the 'Unhappy Consciousness,' of a *conscience*, the self-imposition of the ethical law, what Hegel himself understands as a form of self-enslavement."[65] In *The Psychic Life of Power*, Butler closely examines the development of conscience in the *Phenomonology of Spirit*, and in this context she suggests that the chapter on the "Unhappy Consciousness" seems in a way to prefigure Kierkegaard's critique of the system of Hegelianism.[66] Already in *Subjects of Desire* she stated that "the 'trembling' of the bondsman highlights a different aspect of Hegel's thought" which "aligns him more closely with the fear and trembling of Kierkegaard."[67]

### D. Philosophical Implications

In her attempt to investigate the more general philosophical implications of the story of Abraham, Butler compares the encounter with Abraham with the famous claim by Aristotle "that philosophy begins with a sense of wonder, the wonder that there are things rather than no things."[68] The comparison is somewhat odd, because it misses or ignores a main point of the wonder Aristotle wrote about. In the first book of his *Metaphysics* Aristotle does, indeed, identify wonder or θαυμάζειν as the origin of philosophy.[69] The Aristotelian wonder, however, is, firstly, not caused by the fact that there are things rather than no things, but by the experience of the wondering individual that it cannot grasp why things are the way they are. Secondly, this wonder does not form a permanent condition of philosophy. On the contrary, it is precisely the aim of philosophy to overcome this initial state of wonder. For Aristotle, one wonders only because one does not know about the reasons, and philosophy is the way to find out about the reasons, and, hence, the goal of philosophy is to eventually overcome the initial state of wonder and to substitute it with knowledge about the reasons. The wonder Butler invokes here seems better to correspond with Heidegger's notion of the "wonder of all wonder: that beings are."[70] In contrast to the Aristotelian wonder, this wonder of all wonder is precisely one that cannot be resolved by knowledge, but precedes all knowing.[71]

   For the purpose of this article on Butler's reception of Kierkegaard, however, I suggest to ignore these difficulties and follow Butler's remarks. In her view, the main philosophical insight we can learn from Kierkegaard is: "There appears to be no

---

[65]    Ibid.

[66]    Butler, *The Psychic Life of Power*, p. 48.

[67]    Butler, *Subjects of Desire*, p. 91.

[68]    That is the way in which Butler formulates it. Butler, "Kierkegaard's Speculative Despair," p. 379.

[69]    *Metaphysics*, I 2, 982 b 11ff.

[70]    Martin Heidegger, "Postscript to 'What is Metaphysics,' " in *Pathmarks*, Cambridge: Cambridge University Press 1998, p. 234.

[71]    For Heidegger's discussion of the Aristotelian θαυμάζειν see Martin Heidegger, *Grundfragen der Philosophie. Ausgewählte "Probleme" der "Logik,"* in his *Gesamtausgabe*, Abteilungen 1–4, vols. 1–102, Frankfurt am Main: Klostermann 1975–, Abteilung 2 (*Vorlesungen 1919–1944*), vol. 45, pp. 157–72.

necessity that *these* beings came into existence, and that other did not, if we consider that the source or origin of all things is infinite possibility, another name for God."[72] Butler does not explicitly refer to Kierkegaard's text here, but we are reminded of the statement in *The Sickness unto Death*, where we can read: "since everything is possible for God, then God is this—that everything is possible."[73] Butler seems to notice—as I think rightfully—that this "definition" of God—if we can speak at all of a definition in the common sense of the word—is not a reduction of God's being, on the contrary, it is Kierkegaard's attempt to find an adequate expression for God's incomprehensible transcendence. That God is "infinite possibility," or that "God is this—that everything is possible," leaves us with at least two forms of wonder, as Butler explains. Firstly, we have to wonder why there is anything at all, because "not only is there no necessity for the infinite, God, to create the finite, the human world, but it is perfectly absurd that he did at all."[74] Secondly, we not only have to wonder that there are things at all, but we also have to wonder why there are precisely these things, because there is no reason why these things and not others "made the passage from infinite possibility into that which exists in the finite world."[75]

In this light, "the story of Abraham suggests that whatever exists in this world does so by virtue of a kind of grace, an arbitrary, and irrational act."[76] Butler focuses in particular on this last source of all despair: not to accept ones *groundedness* in the infinite, not to accept the contingency of one's own existence and the arbitrariness that surrounds one's emergence. In contrast to this state of despair, "to have faith means to affirm contingency, this absurd coming-into-being of existence, regardless of the suffering that recognition of absurdity causes."[77] In this light, Butler tries to understand the movement that Abraham represents:

> We might then understand the movement from the ethical domain to that of faith as the transformation of terror into a sense of grace. The difficulty with making this movement, however, is that the prospect of losing one's worldly attachments, indeed, one's own finite existence for no necessary reason, is not easy to face with anything other than terror.[78]

To be truly faithful one has to lose one's worldly attachments, in other words, no worldly being—also no existing individual—is allowed to become the fundamental reason for one to live, the ultimate source of meaning in life. This is especially true in the case of a beloved individual that gets elevated to this rank of the ultimate source of meaning for one's existence.

Butler goes on to compare the story of Abraham with the story of the young man in *Repetition*. Both are much alike in the sense that both have to sacrifice their most beloved one, but the difference is that whereas Abraham receives Isaac back, the

---

72      Butler, "Kierkegaard's Speculative Despair," p. 379.
73      *SKS* 11, 156 / *SUD*, 40.
74      Butler, "Kierkegaard's Speculative Despair," p. 380.
75      Ibid., pp. 379–80.
76      Ibid, p. 380.
77      Ibid.
78      Ibid.

young man seems to suffer an irretrievable loss.[79] This is not without significance, because this difference between Abraham and the young man marks precisely the difference between a "knight of faith" and a "knight of resignation."[80] The general insight that we can draw from the story of Abraham is the following:

> For Kierkegaard, it is only once we affirm the transience and contingency (nonnecessity) of that which we love in this world that we are free to love it at all....It is in this sense that Isaac was *always* a gift from God; one's own existence is a gift, and that of every other existing thing.[81]

In order to prove one's willingness to affirm this contingency, one has to let go of all worldly attachments. Butler suggests that this is also the reason why Kierkegaard had to break the engagement with Regine Olsen, because she was his ultimate worldly attachment that he needed to sacrifice for the sake of his own faith.[82]

### E. Consequences for Kierkegaard as a Writer

For Butler, one crucial thing we can learn from Kierkegaard is that the concept of faith is in a radical way not communicable, "that faith cannot be expressed in language."[83] But that insight forces us to ask the crucial question about the status of Kierkegaard's own texts. Butler detects a sort of irony that haunts Kierkegaard's own texts.[84] We have to wonder: How can Kierkegaard be a writer? What is the status of his authorship? How do we need to think about his existence as a writer in relation to his own faith?

That "faith cannot be communicated" implies that

> any effort to write a book that communicates faith will, by definition, have to fail. In this way, then, Kierkegaard must write a book which constantly fails to communicate faith, a book which insistently renounces its own authority to state what faith is, a text which turns back upon itself and effectively wills its own failure.[85]

One consequence is that "Kierkegaard's text must, then, perform the paradoxical task of enacting the limits of language itself."[86] But we have to be clear about the fact that the limits of language cannot be declared directly. The limits of language are no possible object of an explicit assertion. This is one of the things Butler claims to have

---

[79]   Butler writes about the young man in *Repetition*: "If the girl has become the ultimate reason for living, the source of all affirmation, then the young man has transferred and invested the boundlessness of his passion onto an existing individual; this is, for Kierkegaard, a kind of despair and a failure of faith. Precisely because she has become an object he is not willing to lose, he must demonstrate his willingness to lose her altogether." Ibid., p. 384.

[80]   Ibid.

[81]   Ibid., p. 385.

[82]   Ibid., p. 381.

[83]   Ibid., p. 387.

[84]   Ibid., p. 363.

[85]   Ibid., p. 389.

[86]   Ibid.

learned from Kierkegaard: "For Kierkegaard, the direct declaration of the limits of language is not to be believed; nothing less than the undoing of the declarative mode itself will do."[87]

But what does that mean when speaking about Kierkegaard's texts and Kierkegaard as an author? Butler suggests that in the diagnosis of the "demonic despair," which "really appear only in the poets"[88] at the end of the first part of *The Sickness unto Death*, we can find "a thinly veiled autobiographical confession."[89] Butler goes on to characterize this confession:

> The one in demonic despair can acknowledge the divine authorship that enables his own fiction, his pseudonymous work, only by admitting that what he produced is a necessary fraud. At the end of Part One of *Sickness unto Death*, Kierkegaard appears to begin this disavowal of his own production, clearing the way for an appreciation of God as the only "first-rate author" in town.[90]

Thus, we have to ask if a certain mode of despair was the precondition for Kierkegaard's authorship, as Butler seems to suggest at the end of her article. And she interprets the entry in Kierkegaard's journal from January 1846, in which he expresses his wish to quit being an author and to prepare to become a pastor instead,[91] in line with this confession about the desperate conditions of his authorship, suggesting that in *The Sickness unto Death* we can see "the fruition of Kierkegaard's intention to resist the seduction of authorship."[92] Finally, Butler suggests that this is why it seems that "Kierkegaard gave up his career as a literary and philosophical author after *The Sickness unto Death*, and persevered in writing purely religious tracts."[93]

### F. Conclusion

Butler's article shows that she is surprisingly well informed about Kierkegaard's authorship and that she has studied closely several of his major pseudonymous works, such as *The Sickness unto Death*, *Either/Or*, *Fear and Trembling*, *Repetition*, *Philosophical Fragments*, and *Concluding Unscientific Postscript*. Furthermore, the article makes extensive use of Butler's early scholarly work on Hegel, which allows her to closely follow Kierkegaard's criticism but also appropriation of Hegelian concepts and terminology.

It has to be noticed, however, that Butler seems to exclusively refer to Kierkegaard's pseudonymous works, thereby effectively reducing the complexity of his authorship to its pseudonymous parts. She does not consider Kierkegaard's discourses at all, therewith reproducing typical patterns of the reception of Kierkegaard, and the few journal entries she cites are taken from the several introductions to the English

---

[87]   Butler, "Can the 'Other' of Philosophy Speak?," p. 237.
[88]   *SKS* 11, 186 / *SUD*, 72.
[89]   Butler, "Kierkegaard's Speculative Despair," p. 389.
[90]   Ibid., p. 390.
[91]   *SKS* 20, 81, NB:107 / *JP* 5, 5961.
[92]   Butler, "Kierkegaard's Speculative Despair," p. 391.
[93]   Ibid.

translations of Kierkegaard's pseudonymous works, which is why it is doubtful that Butler has ever studied them independently.

This limited approach to the reading of Kierkegaard's text seems to also entail a one-sided view on his authorship. This becomes apparent at the end of Butler's article, where she suggests that Kierkegaard effectively gave up his career as an author after *The Sickness unto Death*, continuing with writing only purely religious tracts. Firstly, this shows that she is certainly holding Kierkegaard's religious writings in low esteem, implicitly claiming that they are of no intellectual value. Secondly, Butler seems to ignore the fact that, on the one hand, the publication of *The Sickness unto Death* does not mark a sharp end to Kierkegaard's pseudonymous authorship, and, on the other hand, that the pseudonymous authorship has been accompanied by the parallel publication of discourses from the beginning, so that a separation of Kierkegaard's pseudonymous and religious authorship will never hold up in its rigidity.

Nevertheless, these shortcomings of Butler's view of the complexity of Kierkegaard's authorship do not derogate Butler's insightful remarks about the rhetoric dimensions of Kierkegaard's texts and the role that style and parody play in his writing. In the final section, I will give a brief outline of the role that these matters play in Butler's writings.

## *IV. Rhetoric, Parody, Politics*

In her article on Kierkegaard, Butler shows that Kierkegaard's argumentation against Hegel does not take a propositional form. Rather, it is enacted through the rhetorical construction of the text and is—essentially, not only secondarily—located on the level of style. In general, the question of rhetoric is crucial for Kierkegaard's whole authorship, since what his authorship is all about seems to be something that cannot be put into a propositional form, something that cannot be said directly in language. The role of rhetoric is not reducible in Kierkegaard's texts, it is not a secondary addition that does not affect the content, but, on the contrary, it is constitutive for the very content itself.

Hence, a certain sensibility for matters of the rhetoric construction of the text is crucial for Kierkegaard as an author. In a journal entry, Kierkegaard called himself a "dialectician with an unusual sense for rhetoric."[94] This sense is clearly one of the major aspects that distinguishes Kierkegaard from other writers. But it also poses certain question about Kierkegaard's own status as a writer. What does it mean to be a writer under such conditions? How can writers consistently produce texts that must fail to communicate directly what they are supposed to communicate in order to be able to communicate it in an indirect manner? What consequence does this have for the status of an authorship?

But more importantly, this insistence on the irreducible and primordial status of the rhetoric of a text poses also a significant challenge to a certain version of rationality, a rationality that is constituted through and by an exclusion and

---

[94]     *SKS* 20, 98, NB:146 / *JP* 5, 5981.

condemnation of rhetoric. In the reading Butler suggested, this rationality, which is supposed to be purified from its rhetoric contamination, functions precisely as the foundation of philosophy in its traditional form.[95] Hence, to call for the recognition of the irreducibility of the rhetoric of a text means to challenge the foundations of philosophy in its predominant appearance.[96] It is important to point out, however, that this rhetorical challenge of philosophy does not mean an escape into irrationality. Kierkegaard was certainly not speaking in the name of irrationality, and Butler is not doing so either. It cannot seriously—in the name of the seriousness that forms the foundation of philosophy—be disputed that the works of Kierkegaard and Butler still remain a kind of philosophy, even though they might not be pure philosophy, might not fulfill the criteria of purity of the philosophical discourse. In this light, it does not seem surprising that neither Kierkegaard nor Butler were in the philosophical (or, for that matter, theological) academia,[97] but that both remained at a certain distance that nevertheless did not detach them entirely. In Butler's view, this position has its advantages:

> Much of the philosophical work that takes place outside of philosophy is free to consider the rhetorical and literary aspects of philosophical texts and to ask, specifically, what particular philosophical value is carried or enacted by those rhetorical and linguistic features. The rhetorical aspects of a philosophical text include its genre, which can be varied, the way of making the arguments that it does, and how its mode of presentation informs the argument itself, sometimes enacting that argument implicitly, sometimes enacting an argument that is quite to the contrary of what the philosophical text explicitly declares.[98]

This duplication of philosophy outside of the defined domains of philosophy—a kind of philosophy that is not entirely philosophy, but nevertheless not entirely excluded from it either—has the distinct advantage that it does allow one to ask those questions about the relation of rhetoric and philosophy which philosophy had to exclude from itself.

In the context of this revision of the relation of rhetoric and philosophy, we can also examine the role of parody. Parody is in this regard not only considered as a matter of acting, but also as a philosophical and political concern. For Butler a

---

[95]     We can already see this tendency in Plato, where the philosophical dialectic had to disregard the sophistic rhetoric. In this line of thought traced back to Plato, philosophy must necessarily exclude every rhetorical element, because rhetoric is concerned with emotions (*pathos*)—see, for instance, the Aristotelian *Rhetoric* that includes a long treaty about emotions—and emotionality disturbs the clarity of the rational, philosophical thought.

[96]     That I am formulating this argument with reference to philosophy is due to Butler's education. It is unrelated to the question if it is more adequate to characterize Kierkegaard as a theologian, a philosopher, a poet, etc. In the case of Kierkegaard, the argument could be reformulated to suit his relation to the academic theology of his time.

[97]     Butler, of course, is part of academia insofar as she is a professor connected to a University. However, even though she has received a rather traditional training in philosophy, she is not employed at a department of Philosophy, but at a department of Rhetoric and Comparative Literature, and in that sense she is outside of the *philosophical* academia.

[98]     Butler, "Can the 'Other' of Philosophy Speak?," pp. 234–5.

successful parody functions not only as an imitation of the original, rather, what a successful parody can expose is that already the imitated original is not as original as it is supposed to be, but already itself an imitation of this originality. In the case of Kierkegaard, that means that his parody of Hegelianism at the beginning of *The Sickness unto Death* does not only intend to make fun of Hegel through an imitation of his language, but that the parodistic definition of the self that reveals it in its constitutive paradoxicality ultimately exposes the possibility that already the Hegelian original has never been as self-identical as was assumed in the first place. In other words, Butler suggests accepting Kierkegaard's critique of Hegel, but she claims that this critique does not entail a refusal of Hegel, but that it forms a possible way of reading Hegel himself: a way that reveals something about Hegel's work that might have been the case all along.

The conclusion of Butler's *Gender Trouble* has the bewildering title "From Parody to Politics."[99] To understand this title and to anticipate the connection of this elaboration with politics, one has to remember that parody has the ultimate task of revealing the non-originality of the original. To parody an identity means to reveal that it has never been original and self-identical in the first place, just as Kierkegaard's parody of Hegel's conception of the self reveals that already the self in Hegel's *Phenomenology* was confronted with the same paradox as the self in Kierkegaard's *The Sickness unto Death*. In the conclusion of *Gender Trouble*, Butler locates politics itself in this frightening sphere, where subjects have to put their own identity into jeopardy, because they were never in full command of it to begin with.[100] This relocation of the political sphere puts the notion of politics itself into question, leading to Butler's concluding outlook that if the identity of the subject was no longer fixed as the foundation of politics "a new configuration of politics would surely emerge from the ruins of the old."[101]

---

[99]     Butler, *Gender Trouble*, p. 142.
[100]    Butler writes about the purpose of *Gender Trouble*: "This theoretical inquiry has attempted to locate the political in the very signifying practices that establish, regulate, and deregulate identity." Butler, *Gender Trouble*, p. 147.
[101]    Ibid., p. 149.

# Bibliography

*I. References to or Uses of Kierkegaard in Butler's Corpus*

*Gender Trouble: Feminism and the Subversion of Identity*, New York and London: Routledge 1990, p. 106.
"Kierkegaard's Speculative Despair," in *The Age of German Idealism*, ed. by Robert C. Solomon and Kathleen Marie Higgins, London: Routledge 1993, pp. 363–92.
*The Psychic Life of Power: Theories in Subjection*, Stanford: Stanford University Press 1997, p. 48.
*Subjects of Desire: Hegelian Reflections in Twentieth-Century France*, New York: Columbia University Press 1987, pp. 12–13; p. 22; p. 54; p. 55, note 21; p. 83; p. 91; p. 135 and p. 157.
"Can the 'Other' of Philosophy Speak?" in *Undoing Gender*, New York and London: Routledge 2004, pp. 232–50.
*Giving An Account of Oneself*, New York: Fordham University Press 2005, p. 7.
Pierpaolo Antonello and Roberto Farneti, "Antigone's Claim: A Conversation with Judith Butler," *Theory & Event*, vol. 12, no. 1, 2009 [online journal].


*II. Sources of Butler's Knowledge of Kierkegaard*

Adorno, Theodor, *Kierkegaard: Construction of the Aesthetic*, trans. by R. Hullot Kentor, Minneapolis: University of Minneapolis Press 1989.
Agacinski, Sylviane, *Aparté: Conceptions and Deaths of Søren Kierkegaard*, trans. by Kevin Newmark, Gainesville: University of Florida Press 1988.
Collins, James, *The Mind of Kierkegaard*, Chicago: Henry Regnery 1953.
Crites, Stephen, *In the Twilight of Christendom: Hegel vs. Kierkegaard on Faith and History*, Chambersburg: American Academy of Religion 1972 (*AAR Studies in Religion*).
Dupré, Louis, *Dubious Heritage: Studies in the Philosophy of Religion after Kant*, New York: Paulist Press 1977.
Fenves, Peter, *"Chatter": Language and History in Kierkegaard*, Stanford: Stanford University Press 1993.
Heiss, Robert, *Hegel, Kierkegaard, Marx: Three Great Philosophers whose Ideas Changed the Course of Civilization*, trans. by E.B. Garside, New York: Delta 1975.
Holmer, Paul L., *The Grammar of Faith*, San Francisco: Harper & Row 1978.
Kroner, Richard, "Kierkegaard or Hegel?" *Revue International de Philosophie*, vol. 6, no. 1, 1952, pp. 79–96.

Laclau, Ernesto, "Identity and Hegemony: The Role of Universality in the Constitution of Politial Logics," in Judith Butler, Ernesto Laclau, and Slavoj Žižek, *Contingency, Hegemony, Universality: Contemporary Dialogues on the Left*, London and New York: Verso 2000, p. 62; p. 79.

Lebowitz, Naomi, *Kierkegaard: A Life of Allegory*, Baton Rouge: Louisiana State University Press 1985.

Löwith, Karl, *From Hegel to Nietzsche: The Revolution in Nineteenth-Century Thought*, trans. by David E. Green, New York: Holt, Rinehart & Winston 1964.

Mackey, Louis, *Kierkegaard: A Kind of Poet*, Philadelphia: University of Pennsylvania Press 1971.

Malantschuk, Gregor, *Kierkegaard's Thought*, trans. by Howard V. Hong and Edna N. Hong, Princeton: Princeton University Press 1971.

Perkins, Robert L. (ed.), *Kierkegaard's "Fear and Trembling": Critical Appraisals*, Birmingham, Alabama: University of Alabama Press 1980.

Smith, Joseph H. (ed.), *Kierkegaard's Truth: The Disclosure of Self*, New Haven: Yale University Press 1981 (*Psychiatry and the Humanities Series*, vol. 5).

Taylor, Mark C., *Journeys to Selfhood: Hegel and Kierkegaard*, Berkeley: University of California Press 1980.

Theunissen, Michael, *The Other*, trans. by Christopher MacCann Boston: MIT Press 1987.

Thompson, Josiah (ed.), *Kierkegaard: A Collection of Critical Essays*, Garden City: Doubleday Anchor 1972.

Thompson, Josiah, *The Lonely Labyrinth: Kierkegaard's Pseudonymous Works*, Carbondale: Southern Illinois University Press 1967.

Thulstrup, Niels, *Kierkegaard's Relation to Hegel*, trans. by George L. Strengen, Princeton: Princeton University Press 1980.

Wahl, Jean, *Études kierkegaardiennes*, 4th ed., Paris: J. Vrin 1974.

Wyschogrod, Michael, *Kierkegaard and Heidegger*, The Hague: Nijhoff 1976.

Žižek, Slavoj, "Class Struggle of Postmodernism? Yes, Please!" in Judith Butler, Ernesto Laclau, and Slavoj Žižek, *Contingency, Hegemony, Universality: Contemporary Dialogues on the Left*, London and New York: Verso 2000, p. 102.

— "Da Capo senza Fine," in Judith Butler, Ernesto Laclau, and Slavoj Žižek, *Contingency, Hegemony, Universality: Contemporary Dialogues on the Left*, London: Verso 2000, p. 226; p. 258.

*III. Secondary Literature on Butler's Relation to Kierkegaard*

Rancher, Shoni, "Suffering Tragedy: Hegel, Kierkegaard, and Butler on the Tragedy of Antigone," *Mosaic: A Journal for the Interdisciplinary Study of Literature*, vol. 41, no. 3, 2008, pp. 63–78.

Thiem, Annika, "*Unbecoming Subjects: Subject Formation and Responsibility in the Context of Judith Butler's Thinking*," Ph.D. Thesis, Eberhard-Karls-Universität, Tübingen 2004, pp. 254–92.

# Jürgen Habermas:

# Social Selfhood, Religion, and Kierkegaard

## J. Michael Tilley

Jürgen Habermas (b. 1929) is often regarded as Germany's most influential living philosopher, and his work has been extremely influential in academic as well as social and political arenas. Although Habermas was familiar with Kierkegaard as a graduate student, his rediscovery of him on the occasion of a lecture delivered in Copenhagen in 1987 prepared the way for Habermas to rearticulate his central views on political liberalism and communicative action while developing new views on the nature of the self and the role of religion in philosophy and politics. I examine these themes in this article which is divided into three sections: (1) a brief overview of Habermas' life with particular attention to those events and works that are most significant for understanding his relation to Kierkegaard; (2) an account of Habermas' use of Kierkegaardian themes and texts; and (3) a treatment of how his use shapes Habermas' philosophy of religion as well as his overall philosophical project.

## I. Overview of Habermas' Life and Works

Habermas is the quintessential public intellectual and a prominent European philosopher and social theorist.[1] His academic work has been immensely influential for German and European culture and politics in the late twentieth and early twenty-first centuries; he regularly writes newspaper articles and other popular works on contemporary social and political issues. Born to a German bureaucrat and the grandson of a Protestant minister, he was four years old when the Nazis came to power in 1933. The Nazis were defeated in 1945 when Habermas was 15 years old, but he had joined the Hitler Youth and was required to assist the war efforts on the western defense. Up until this point, Habermas' world "still seem[ed] quite normal."[2] These adolescent events and the subsequent revelations about the Nazi

---

[1]     For further biographical information on Habermas, see Martin J. Matuštík, *Jürgen Habermas: A Philosophical-Political Profile*, Lanham, Maryland: Rowman & Littlefield Publishers 2001. For relevant autobiographical comments see the first chapter in Jürgen Habermas, *Zwischen Naturalismus und Religion. Philosophische Aufsätze*, Frankfurt am Main: Suhrkamp 2005. (English translation: *Between Naturalism and Religion*, trans. by Ciaran Cronin, Malden, Massachusetts: Polity Press 2008.)

[2]     Matuštík, *Jürgen Habermas*, p. 9.

regime profoundly changed Habermas. It culminated in a public denouncement of Heidegger in 1953 after Heidegger had published a lecture delivered in 1935. The lecture was unchanged, and it contained a reference to his philosophy as the "inner truth and greatness of the Nazi movement."[3] From this point forward, Habermas often criticized those scholars and academics whose work appeared as an apology for Germans and their role in National Socialism. The most notable instance is found in the so-called "Historians' Dispute."[4] For Habermas, it appeared as if German philosophy and scholarship itself were incapable of explaining or offering a normative critique of National Socialism.

Although Habermas sees himself as a political liberal, he was also a second-generation member of the Frankfurt School following Adorno and Horkheimer. He became a leader of the student movement in the 1960s in Germany and has also supported a number of other political positions concerning, for example, universal recognition of human rights, the European Union, and human cloning. Habermas sees his critical engagement in political activity as intimately related to his work as a scholar and an academic.

Habermas' primary project, as suggested by his political activities and his critique of Heidegger, has been to connect sociological explanations of phenomena with a philosophical account capable of normatively justifying social and political critique. He thus can be seen as reacting against the failure of German philosophy, represented in Heidegger's 1953 reintroduction of Nazi ideals. Habermas' first prominent work as an academic was his Habilitation in 1962, *The Structural Transformation of the Public Sphere*,[5] where he described the development of the public from its manifestation in eighteenth-century salons to the way it is constructed and maintained by the mass media in late bourgeoisie capitalism. The value of public deliberation, communication and argumentation are already partially contained within his account of the salons and his critique of contemporary portrayals of the public. His subsequent work, including *Knowledge and Human Interests* published in 1968,[6] developed a theoretical basis for his project. In 1981, he published his systematic treatise, *A Theory of Communicative Action*,[7] which lays the theoretical

---

[3]      Martin Heidegger, *Einführung in die Metaphysik*, Tubingen: Max Niemeyer 1953.

[4]      The Historian's Dispute was a debate among German academics—initiated by Habermas—that addressed what Habermas saw as the apologetic character of German historians about national socialism and its place in German history. Habermas' reintroduction of Kierkegaard's thought occurs in the midst of the dispute.

[5]      Jürgen Habermas, *Strukturwandel der Öffentlichkeit. Untersuchungen zu einer Kategorie der bürgerlichen Gesellschaft*, Neuwied: Luchterhand 1962 (*Politica*, vol. 4). (English translation: *The Structural Transformation of the Public Sphere: An Inquiry into a Category of Bourgeois Society*, trans. by Thomas Burger with Frederick Lawrence, Cambridge, Massachusetts: MIT Press 1989.)

[6]      Jürgen Habermas, *Erkenntnis und Interesse*, Frankfurt am Main: Suhrkamp 1968. (English translation: *Knowledge and Human Interests*, trans. by Jeremy J. Shapiro, Boston: Beacon Press 1971.)

[7]      Jürgen Habermas, *Theorie des kommunikativen Handelns*, vols. 1–2, Frankfurt am Main: Suhrkamp 1981. (English translation: *The Theory of Communicative Action*, vols. 1–2, trans. by Thomas McCarthy, Boston: Beacon Press 1987.)

groundwork for his social and political criticism and his future works on discourse ethics, deliberative democracy, and contemporary religious life.

## II. Habermas' References to Kierkegaard

Other than Habermas' newspaper article on the centennial of Kierkegaard's death,[8] there are very few published references to Kierkegaard until after his 1987 Copenhagen lecture. The absence of any significant references[9] to Kierkegaard during this period of time suggests that Habermas had little interest in Kierkegaard prior to 1987, although he initially read *Being and Time* in the 1950s "through Kierkegaard's eyes,"[10] that is, he read Kierkegaard as a student at Bonn because he was interested in Heidegger's reception of Kierkegaard in *Being and Time*. Habermas came back to Kierkegaard's texts upon the occasion of his 1987 Copenhagen lecture.[11] Minor points about Kierkegaard's place in the history of philosophy and religious thought occur frequently in a number of interviews and works after 1987.[12] These references, along with more substantive claims about Kierkegaard, have proliferated since that time. His more substantive use of Kierkegaard has taken two basic forms, and each form moves beyond an exegetical elaboration of Kierkegaard's views and instead develops a particular concept in Kierkegaard's writings which contributes to Habermas' own project. In the first form, Habermas describes a Kierkegaardian account of self largely derived from *The Sickness unto Death* that points toward the a post-conventional theory of identity presupposed in his theory of communicative action. In the second, he portrays Kierkegaard's religious thought as a contribution to

---

8       Jürgen Habermas, "Der Pfahl im Fleische...Eine verlegene Bemerkung zu Kierkegaards 100. Todestag," *Frankfurter Allgemeine Zeitung*, November 12, 1955.
9       There is one reference to Kierkegaard during this time period. Habermas claimed that Franz Rosenzweig was "one of the first [Jewish Philosophers] to establish links with Kierkegaard." Jürgen Habermas, *Philosophisch-politische Profile*, enlarged ed., Frankfurt am Main: Suhrkamp 1981, p. 40. (English translation: *Religion and Rationality*, trans. by Frederick G. Lawrence, ed. by Eduardo Mendieta, Cambridge, Massachusetts: MIT Press 2002, p. 39.)
10      Habermas, *Zwischen Naturalismus und Religion*, p. 23. (*Between Naturalism and Religion*, p. 19.)
11      Martin J. Matuštík, "Habermas's Reading of Kierkegaard: Notes from a Conversation," *Philosophy and Social Criticism*, vol. 17, no. 4, 1992, p. 315.
12      See Jürgen Habermas, *Faktizität und Geltung. Beiträge zur Diskurstheorie des Rechts und des demokratischen Rechtsstaats*, Frankfurt am Main: Suhrkamp 1992, p. 125 (English translation: *Between Facts and Norms*, trans. by William Rehg, Cambridge, Massachusetts: MIT Press 1996, p. 96); Habermas, *Religion and Rationality*, p. 157; Jürgen Habermas, *Nachmetaphysisches Denken. Philosophische Aufsätze*, Frankfurt am Main: Suhrkamp 1992, p. 47 (English translation: *Postmetaphysical Thinking*, trans. by William Mark Hohengarten, Cambridge, Massachusetts: MIT Press 1992, p. 39); Habermas, *Zwischen Naturalismus und Religion*, p. 114 (*Between Naturalism and Religion*, p. 109); Jürgen Habermas, *Wahrheit und Rechtfertigung. Philosophische Aufsätze*, Frankfurt am Main: Suhrkamp 1999, p. 100; p. 170; p. 321 (English translation: *Truth and Justification*, trans. by Barbara Fultner, Cambridge, Massachusetts: MIT Press 1993, p. 80; p. 159; p. 280).

his own work on religion. As I mentioned above, Habermas is a well-known public intellectual who often writes on pressing political or cultural issues in newspapers or other popular formats. His writing and arguments are noticeably different in these contexts, and I will note when a particular reference to Kierkegaard is made in one of the popular formats.

## A. Kierkegaard's Conception of Self and Sociality

In an article based on Habermas' Sonning Prize acceptance speech in Copenhagen on May 14, 1987, Habermas brought Kierkegaard's thought to bear on the Historians' Dispute as a way to describe post-conventional identity. Kierkegaard, he says, "who…has inspired our thinking far beyond the bounds of existential philosophy, was a contemporary of the national movements. But he did not speak of collective identities at all; he spoke only of the identity of the individual person."[13] He elaborates on this claim by appealing to one of the more paradoxical passages in *Either/Or*. "In *Either/Or* he focuses on the decision, taken in solitude, through which the moral individual assumes responsibility for his life history and 'makes himself the man he is.' "[14] The self is not created, but it is chosen among a host of other possibilities; the identity of an individual is developed by taking up a particular understanding of the history of the individual and directing one's life according to this historical portrait: "Every individual first encounters himself as the historical product of contingent life circumstances, but in 'choosing' himself as this product he constitutes a self to which the rich concreteness of the life history in which he merely found himself is attributed as something for which he will account retrospectively."[15] For Habermas, the implication is that the self is simultaneously distanced from and takes responsibility for his or her own conventional (or traditional) identity, that is, one's national, political, occupational, or religious affiliation. Although Habermas acknowledges that Kierkegaard was primarily concerned with Christian themes regarding the self, he maintains that "the reconstruction of one's own life history in light of an absolute responsibility for oneself can also be read in a somewhat more secular way."[16] The Kierkegaardian portrait of selfhood is much more amenable to post-traditional questions of identity, and this conception of identity provides a framework for articulating Habermas' criticism of the historians who "attempt[ed] to historicize the Nazi period for the public in such a way that it is normalized and distanced."[17]

Habermas sees in Kierkegaard a way to unite sociological explanation and normative critique. He sees in him a way to recognize the facticity inherent in human

---

[13]    Jürgen Habermas, *Eine Art Schadensabwicklung*, Frankfurt am Main: Suhrkamp 1987, p. 171 (*Kleine politische Schriften*, vol. 6). (English translation: *The New Conservativism*, Cambridge, Massachusetts: MIT Press 1991, pp. 259–60.)

[14]    Habermas, *Eine Art Schadensabwicklung*, p. 171. (*The New Conservativism*, p. 260.) See *SKS* 3, 206 / *EO2*, 215.

[15]    Habermas, *Eine Art Schadensabwicklung*, p. 172. (*The New Conservativism*, p. 260.)

[16]    Ibid.

[17]    Habermas, *Eine Art Schadensabwicklung*, p. 178. (*The New Conservativism*, p. 266.)

life and the ability of the individual both to transcend and take "responsibility for one's own life history."[18] In *Postmetaphysical Thinking*, Habermas supplements the basic picture of the Kierkegaardian self developed in his Copenhagen lecture with the work of George Herbert Mead (1863–1931). Although in this work, he appeals to *The Sickness unto Death* rather than *Either/Or*. He, once again, articulates a conception of the human self where one's own life history, which is not chosen, is encountered by a spontaneously acting subject who becomes conscious of being the very one who made this life history.[19] Taking responsibility for oneself is a rational reconstruction of one's life in such a way that one also takes responsibility for the direction of one's life. The self is constituted in the paradoxical choice to be who I am and who I want to be. The life history of a person makes an individual distinct from others when one's life history is taken up as one's own.

Kierkegaard, Habermas claims, lays the foundation for articulating how socialization can individuate a person. Prior to Kierkegaard, the individual could only be described in terms of the particularities through which the individual deviates from the universal or the more general social milieu; but Kierkegaard's understanding of the self as a task that is achieved when one is historically constituted and also takes responsibility for one's life history allows for an alternative conception of post-traditional identity. Ultimately, however, Habermas maintains that Kierkegaard's account is limited insofar as the constitution of the self is primarily described in terms of the God-relation.[20] This limitation is overcome when the process of historical constitution is supplemented and understood in a broader social context and the contingent circumstances of a person's life history are understood in terms of the traditional familial and social roles that a person occupies (cf. Mead's social psychology).

According to Habermas, Kierkegaard's conception of the self prepares for the development of a robust communicative theory of self where an individual is at the same time socially constituted in relation to others and responsible for the particular direction of one's own life.[21] His Kierkegaardian-inspired theory of identity provides a justification for the project of rationally reconstructing a historical position in order to justify it. Habermas had used the framework provided by his analysis of the Kierkegaardian self to elucidate his position concerning the "Historians' Dispute," and more recently he has used it in his work on biotechnology and human nature.

This latter work is based on a lecture, and although it contains lengthy sections that address Kierkegaard's thought and apply his ideas to advances in biotechnology and the sciences, few, if any, substantive positions about Kierkegaard are developed that were not contained in a more robust form earlier. The only significant addition

---

[18]     Habermas, *Nachmetaphysisches Denken*, p. 200. (*Postmetaphysical Thinking*, p. 162.)
[19]     Habermas, *Nachmetaphysisches Denken*, p. 203. (*Postmetaphysical Thinking*, p. 164.)
[20]     Habermas, *Nachmetaphysisches Denken*, pp. 200–6. (*Postmetaphysical Thinking*, pp. 162–7.)
[21]     Matuštík's interview with Habermas further develops these themes. See Matuštík, "Habermas's Reading of Kierkegaard: Notes from a Conversation," pp. 313–23.

to his prior development of Kierkegaard's thought is that Habermas is much more explicit about why it is appropriate to secularize Kierkegaard's insight into the nature of the human self. He argues that Kierkegaard's characterization of the self is "formal—that is, they are not *thick* descriptions—but…[b]ecause this ethics judges the existential mode, but not the specific orientation of individual life-projects and particular forms of life, it satisfies the conditions of a pluralism of worldviews."[22] In the end, Habermas takes Kierkegaard to express a characteristic of utmost importance in post-traditional societies—that is, he sees in Kierkegaard an account of the self that allows for an individual to both be within a tradition and step back from it without disengaging from it.

## B. Kierkegaard and Religious Thought

Habermas' use of Kierkegaard in his development of a post-traditional conception of identity plays a role in his work on religion, but Kierkegaard is also a foil for Habermas' own work dealing with the subject. There are two places where Habermas' work on religious topics intersect with his interest in Kierkegaard: the essay "Communicative Freedom and Negative Theology,"[23] and his book *Religion and Naturalism*. In the first essay, Habermas is offering an account and criticism of Michael Theunissen's work which seeks to appropriate the work of both Kierkegaard and Marx in a novel account of philosophy, religion, and the self. In doing so, Habermas, for the most part, adopts Theunissen's understanding of Kierkegaard. Habermas appreciates the dialogical character of both Theunissen's account of communicative freedom and the concept of self presented in *The Sickness unto Death*.[24] In particular, both Habermas and Theunissen appreciate the way in which the self in *The Sickness Unto Death* is only genuinely itself when "in its self-positing it relates to another through which it has itself been posited."[25] Both scholars appreciate how the self can only be formed and understood when formed by another. The individual is both historically constituted by another, but it also has a role in its own development.

Both Theunissen and Habermas, however, are critical of Kierkegaard for describing the positing arising from the other as a divine act. Following Theunissen, Habermas claims that Kierkegaard's explanation of the process by which the self is formed is, at best, incomplete. It ignores the ordinary ways in which people are

---

[22]    Jürgen Habermas, *Die Zukunft der menschlichen Natur. Auf dem Weg zu einer liberalen Eugenik?* Frankfurt am Main: Suhrkamp 2001, p. 27. (English translation: *The Future of Human Nature*, Oxford: Polity Press 2003, p. 11.)

[23]    Jürgen Habermas, "Kommunikative Freiheit und Negative Theologie," in *Dialektischer Negativismus. Michael Theunissen zum 60. Geburtstag*, ed. by Emil Angehrn et al., Frankfurt am Main: Suhrkamp 1992, pp. 15–34. (English translation: "Communicative Freedom and Negative Theology," in *Kierkegaard in Post/Modernity*, trans. by Martin J. Matuštík and Patricia Huntington, ed. by Martin J. Matuštík and Merold Westphal, Bloomington, Indiana: Indiana University Press 1995, pp. 182–98.)

[24]    Habermas, "Kommunikative Freiheit und Negative Theologie," pp. 15–16. ("Communicative Freedom and Negative Theology," p. 182; p. 188.)

[25]    Habermas, "Kommunikative Freiheit und Negative Theologie," p. 26. ("Communicative Freedom and Negative Theology," p. 189.)

shaped and formed in ordinary human relationships. Habermas affirms Theunissen's complaint that, for Kierkegaard, "the other is ultimately God and no longer the world."[26]

In *Religion and Naturalism*, Habermas discusses Kierkegaard's place in post-Kantian philosophy of religion. He contrasts Kierkegaard with both Schleiermacher and Marx. He claims that Schleiermacher sees the Christian religion revealed when the "subject is overcome by a feeling of utter dependence as it becomes aware of the spontaneity of its own conscious life….[Schleiermacher's] transcendental analysis of the feeling of piety equips religious experience with a general basis independent of both theoretical and practical reason…[as an] alternative to the Enlightenment."[27] Schleiermacher, according to Habermas, is concerned not with the content of religious faith but with the performative sense of having faith.[28] Nevertheless, he adopts the general anthropology given in the Enlightenment, which treats the self as an autonomous, rational agent who posits itself.

Marx and Kierkegaard, however, both offer alternative anthropologies to the Enlightenment. Marx inverts the relationship between theory and practice and Kierkegaard attempts to break out of speculative thought and the corruption of bourgeois society "through an existential response to the Lutheran question concerning the merciful God that plagued him."[29] Habermas draws a connection between Kierkegaard's approach and neo-orthodoxy, and in doing so, he re-evaluates Christian anthropology in contrast to the modern Enlightenment conception of the autonomous, reason-governed individual. The task for Kierkegaard is to convince his interlocutor "that the post-conventional morality of conscience can become the point of crystallization of a conscious life conduct only when it is embedded in a religious self-understanding."[30] For Habermas, Kierkegaard's critique of the Enlightenment conception of the self requires a post-traditional and postmetaphysical approach to philosophical questions. Kierkegaard's proposed solution, however, is presented only from the standpoint of the Kierkegaard's own religious standpoint. That is, Kierkegaard's analysis of the postmetaphysical predicament is accurate, but his solution is unacceptable for philosophy. Habermas explains:

> Kierkegaard was the first to confront postmetaphysical thought with the irreducible heterogeneity of a religious faith that unreservedly rejects the anthropocentricity of a form of philosophical thought that takes its point of departure from within the world. Philosophy first receives a serious dialectical relation to the domain of religious experience through this challenge. The core of this experience resists the secularizing

---

26     Habermas, "Kommunikative Freiheit und Negative Theologie," p. 27. ("Communicative Freedom and Negative Theology," p. 190.)

27     Habermas, *Zwischen Naturalismus und Religion*, p. 242. (*Between Naturalism and Religion*, p. 233.)

28     Habermas, *Zwischen Naturalismus und Religion*, p. 241. (*Between Naturalism and Religion*, p. 232.)

29     Habermas, *Zwischen Naturalismus und Religion*, p. 244. (*Between Naturalism and Religion*, p. 235.)

30     Habermas, *Zwischen Naturalismus und Religion*, p. 244. (*Between Naturalism and Religion*, p. 236.)

appropriation of philosophical analysis just as aesthetic experience resists rationalizing appropriation.[31]

This conception of different spheres of philosophy and religious discourse lays the foundation for Habermas' philosophy of religion. For Habermas, "Philosophy can draw *rational* sustenance from the religious heritage only as long as the source of revelation that orthodoxy counterposes to philosophy remains a cognitively unacceptable imposition for the latter."[32]

### III. Social Selfhood and Religion in Habermas

Habermas conceives of the Kierkegaardian conception of the self as a key development in the history of philosophy. It simultaneously frees the individual from his or her history and background while at the same time it places the self in an intimate relation to that same history. In his *Philosophical-Political Profile of Habermas*, Matuštík has used this framework for understanding Habermas' biography. He was formed by experiences in post-World War II Germany, and his life was profoundly influenced by his experiences in the aftermath of Auschwitz. His break with Heidegger and the Historians' Dispute arise out of this context, and they are illustrations of how one can adopt a critical perspective regarding one's historical setting while at the same time remaining within it. Habermas' reintroduction of Kierkegaardian themes occurs in the midst of the Historians' Dispute, and his work on the subject is illuminating on both philosophical and social-theoretic levels. It provides a mechanism for providing an explanatory hypothesis for a given phenomenon while at the same time providing grounds for a normative critique of it.

The dual character of Habermas' project in relation to Kierkegaard is seen most clearly in Habermas' philosophy of religion. For Habermas there are two different ways of viewing religion and religious discourse. On the one hand, Habermas seeks to appropriate the insights of religious world-views under the less cumbersome auspices of postmetaphysical thought through a process of secularization. This is illustrated most clearly in his *Theory of Communicative Action* where values that were once, and perhaps still are, accepted because of religious beliefs are generalized so that a social consensus among various groups of religious and non-religious people can be reached despite vast differences between each of these groups.[33] The notion of respecting individual persons, for example, is expressed religiously by saying that individuals are created in the image of God. This notion is secularized in contemporary society so that one maintains that individuals deserve respect, but this is done independently of any particular religious doctrine.

---

[31]     Habermas, *Zwischen Naturalismus und Religion*, p. 251. (*Between Naturalism and Religion*, p. 242.)

[32]     Habermas, *Zwischen Naturalismus und Religion*, p. 252. (*Between Naturalism and Religion*, p. 242.)

[33]     Habermas, *Theorie des kommunikativen Handelns*, vol. 2, pp. 428–30. (*The Theory of Communicative Action*, vol. 2, pp. 289–90.)

In the following passage, Habermas describes the concept of secularization more specifically:

> The concept of secularization is connected with the generalization of values at the level of the general action system. Parsons does not understand the secularization of religious values and ideas as the loss of their binding character. As the religious ethics of conviction take root in the world, their moral-practical contents do not get uprooted. Secularized value orientations do not necessarily detach themselves from their religious ground; more typically, a confessional faith exercising tolerance arranges itself ecumenically in the circle of other confessions (including the radically secularized, nonreligious variants of humanistically based ethics).[34]

Habermas says that Parsons does not understand secularization as the elimination of anything which is religious. Rather, the practical effect of religious commitments and values remains despite being generalized on a more reflexive level. Sociologically, secularization does not take place by simply rejecting religions, but it is usually the result of religiously based ecumenical movements. In other words, religions will voluntarily try to build interfaith relationships in order to achieve some common purpose such as the elimination of violence or the advancement of a common political agenda.

Not only does Habermas think secularization is occurring, but he also thinks that every religious doctrine faces the challenge of pluralism and secularization. He explains: "Every religious doctrine today encounters the pluralism of different forms of religious truth—as well as the skepticism of a secular, scientific mode of knowing that owes its social authority to a confessed fallibility and a learning process based on long-term revision."[35] Religious pluralism has a hand in secularization, but so do scientific forms of inquiry. Religious pluralism calls the universal scope of religious claims into question and calls for a reflexive attitude toward the particular claims of a religious tradition. Scientific forms of inquiry test all truth claims in that they require independent and publicly acceptable justification. Ultimately, for Habermas, secularization does not necessarily lead to the abandonment of religion, but it does require that it be justified by publicly accessible reasons if religion's claims are to have any universal applicability.

One the other hand, Habermas thinks that there is a recalcitrant character to religious language and experience such that no postmetaphysical account will be able to capture the full content of these insights. Philosophy is to generalize the insight so that it is acceptable to all, but this is purchased at the expense of some of the content and precision found in religious language. Although it is well known that Habermas trumpets the importance of secularization, this second theme is not often emphasized. In "Themes in Postmetaphysical Thinking," Habermas writes:

> Viewed from without, religion, which has largely been deprived of its world-view functions, is still indispensable in ordinary life for normalizing intercourse with the

---

[34]     Habermas, *Theorie des kommunikativen Handelns*, vol. 2, pp. 428–9. (*The Theory of Communicative Action*, vol. 2, p. 289.)

[35]     Habermas, *Religion and Rationality*, p. 150.

extraordinary. For this reason, even postmetaphysical thinking continues to coexist with religious practice—and not merely in the sense of the contemporaneity of the noncontemporareous. This ongoing coexistence even throws light on a curious dependence of a philosophy that has forfeited its contact with the extraordinary. Philosophy, even in its postmetaphysical form, will be able neither to replace nor to repress religion as long as religious language is the bearer of a semantic content that is inspiring and even indispensable, for this content eludes (for the time being?) the explanatory force of philosophical language and continues to resist translation into reasoning discourses.[36]

Even though religion no longer serves as a unifying world-view, it is still an important component of contemporary life. Habermas goes so far as to say that philosophy is dependent on religion in that religion allows for an infusion of meaning and content that is lacking in postmetaphysical philosophy. In some comments about this particular passage, Habermas says that this quotation "expresses the conviction that indispensable potentials for meaning are preserved in religious language, potentials that philosophy has not yet fully exhausted, has not yet translated into the language of the public, that is, of presumptively generally convincing, reasons."[37] Habermas explains, for example, that the concept of the individual person has been "articulated from the very beginning with all precision one could wish for" in the language of monotheistic doctrines.[38] Religious doctrines and practices are entrenched in the lifeworld of the people. Thus, even though the role of religion is vastly different from the role of philosophy—religion is still indispensable.

Despite the indispensable character of religious experience and language, religion must be scrutinized in a general and publicly acceptable way so that it will undermine communal solidarity. That is why "discourse ethics attempts a translation of the categorical imperative into a language that also lets us do justice to another intuition—I mean the feeling of 'solidarity,' the bond of a member of a community to her fellow members."[39] This explains why Habermas defends "methodological atheism" as the only proper philosophical method. Habermas says:

> [T]he evidence of my relation to a theological heritage does not bother me, as long as one recognizes the methodological difference of the discourses; that is, as long as the philosophical discourse conforms to the distinctive demands of justificatory speech. In my view, a philosophy that oversteps the bounds of methodological atheism loses its philosophical seriousness.[40]

Habermas does not explicitly defend his claim here, but he clearly affirms that methodological atheism is the only respectable mode of philosophical inquiry. In other places, however, Habermas distinguishes his methodological atheism from metaphysical atheism. For Habermas, like Kant and Hegel before him, reason is the final court of appeals for religious positions. The practical components of Christianity

---

36   Habermas, *Nachmetaphysisches Denken*, p. 60. (*Postmetaphysical Thinking*, p. 51.)
37   Habermas, *Religion and Rationality*, p. 162.
38   Ibid.
39   Ibid.
40   Ibid., p. 160.

are developed only in conformity with argumentative justification. This is distinct from the metaphysical atheism of the young Hegelians, for instance, since Habermas does not abandon religion for metaphysical reasons. Rather, religious positions are maintained insofar as they are justified through argumentation.[41]

But this method tends to water down some of the more important content and meaning within religious life. Habermas explicitly mentions this tendency in at least one passage,[42] and he illustrates it in other places. For instance, he claims that philosophy can never "entirely 'recover' or 'exhaust' the performative meaning of living faith."[43] Some religious concepts can be examined, criticized, and generalized, but much of the meaningful content will be lost in the translation of religious experience—of the living faith—into the publicly criticizable claims of philosophy. Although there is no contradiction, there is a tension (although perhaps a productive one) between Habermas' two attitudes towards religion. Religion and religious language are important in the procurement of meaning, and philosophy is unable to eclipse it; but the religious expression should be secularized and expressed in postmetaphysical terms for the sake of social and moral solidarity.

Habermas sees Kierkegaard's thought as a way to understand the relationship between philosophy and religion. He says:

> [Philosophy] receives innovative impulses when it succeeds in freeing cognitive contents from their dogmatic encapsulation in the crucible of rational discourse. Kant and Hegel are the most influential examples of this. The encounters of many twentieth-century philosophers with a religious writer such as Kierkegaard, who thinks in postmetaphysical, but not post-Christian, terms, are also exemplary in this regard.[44]

Habermas distinguishes between rationalist approaches (exemplified by Hegel) and dialogical approaches (exemplified by Jaspers). The former "subsume[s] the substance of faith into a philosophical concept" while the latter, "adopt[s] a critical attitude toward religious traditions while at the same time being open to *learning* from them."[45] Habermas takes the latter approach to revealed religious traditions, and he claims that the role of philosophy is not to determine the validity or normative status of a particular religious tradition but is solely concerned to salvage the cognitive contents from religious traditions. All semantic contents count as "cognitive" in this sense which can be translated into a form of discourse decoupled from the ratcheting effects of truths of revelation. In this discourse, only "public" reasons count, hence reasons that have the power to convince also beyond the boundaries of a particular religious community. The methodological separation between the two universes of discourse is compatible with the openness of philosophy to possible

---

[41] Jürgen Habermas, *Texte und Kontexte*, Frankfurt am Main: Suhrkamp 1991, p. 128. (*Religion and Rationality*, p. 68.)

[42] Habermas, *Religion and Rationality*, p. 154.

[43] Ibid., p. 163.

[44] Habermas, *Zwischen Naturalismus und Religion*, p. 149. (*Between Naturalism and Religion*, p. 142.)

[45] Habermas, *Zwischen Naturalismus und Religion*, p. 255. (*Between Naturalism and Religion*, p. 245.)

cognitive contents of religion. This "appropriation" is free from any intention to interfere or to launch "a hostile takeover."[46] Philosophy is too limited to answer ultimate questions about the validity of a particular religious tradition, yet it can be and often has been enhanced because of the content contained in those traditions. The Kierkegaardian characterization of the self as both historical and self-positing is central for Habermas' philosophy of religion.

## IV. Conclusion

Habermas became reacquainted with Kierkegaardian themes in 1987, and his work has taken new directions because of this influence. In Kierkegaard, Habermas sees the redemption of the important philosophical contributions that he previously saw in Heidegger, yet Kierkegaard also provides a foundation for a critique (if not an explicit rejection) of what Habermas finds objectionable in Heidegger. This renewed interest in Kierkegaard also seems to have spurred the growth and development of Habermas' own philosophy of religion. Prior to 1987, Habermas had only treated religion from a sociological standpoint with little attention paid to the positive and formative role of religion in both public and private realms. The Kierkegaardian-inspired theory of self developed after 1987 opens up critical distance regarding one's own tradition and background and, therefore, allows for rational reflection and deliberation on one's own faith tradition. In one sense, a person is supposed to move beyond the limitations of a religious world-view, and yet the faith tradition itself can enrich a person's life and self in profound ways that are unable to be fully captured outside the bounds of faith traditions. Additionally, Habermas' Kierkegaardian-inspired theory of self also has important implications for contemporary discussions of identity and selfhood. In particular, it suggests a novel way of understanding the relationship between a person's history and identity.

---

[46]      Ibid.

# Bibliography

*I. References to or Uses of Kierkegaard in Habermas' Corpus*

"A Conversation About God and the World," in *Religion and Rationality: Essays on Reason, God, and Modernity*, ed. by Eduardo Mendieta, Cambridge, Massachusetts: MIT Press 2002, p. 157.

"Begründete Enthaltsamkeit. Gibt es postmetaphysische Antworten auf die Frage nach dem 'richtigen Leben'?" in his *Die Zukunft der menschlichen Natur. Auf dem Weg zu einer liberalen Eugenik?* Frankfurt am Main: Suhrkamp 2001, pp. 11–33. (English translation: "Are There Postmetaphysical Answers to the Question: What is the 'Good Life'?," in his *The Future of Human Nature*, trans. by William Rehg, Oxford: Polity Press 2003, pp. 1–15.)

"Der Pfahl im Fleische...Eine verlegene Bemerkung zu Kierkegaards 100. Todestag," *Frankfurter Allgemeine Zeitung*, November 12, 1955.

*Eine Art Schadensabwicklung*, Frankfurt am Main: Suhrkamp 1987 (*Kleine Politische Schriften*, vol. 6), pp. 171–5 (English translation: *The New Conservativism*, ed. and trans. by Shierry Weber Nicholsen, Cambridge, Massachusetts: MIT Press 1991, pp. 259–63.)

*Faktizität und Geltung. Beiträge zur Diskurstheorie des Rechts und des demokratischen Rechtsstaats*, Frankfurt am Main: Suhrkamp 1992, p. 125. (English translation: *Between Facts and Norms*, trans. by William Rehg, Cambridge, Massachusetts: MIT Press 1996, p. 96.)

"Kommunikative Freiheit und Negative Theologie," in *Dialektischer Negativismus. Michael Theunissen zum 60. Geburtstag*, ed. by Emil Angehrn et al., Frankfurt am Main: Suhrkamp 1992, pp. 15–34. (Reprinted in *Vom sinnlichen Eindruck zum symbolischen Ausdruck*, Frankfurt am Main: Suhrkamp 1997, pp. 112–35; English translations: "Communicative Freedom and Negative Theology," in *Kierkegaard in Post/Modernity*, trans. by Martin J. Matuštík and Patricia Huntington, ed. by Martin J. Matuštík and Merold Westphal, Bloomington, Indiana: Indiana University Press 1995, pp. 182–98; and "Communicative Freedom and Negative Theology," in *The Liberating Power of Symbols*, trans. by Peter Dews, Cambridge, Massachusetts: MIT Press 2001, pp. 90–111 (reprinted in *Religion and Rationality: Essays on Reason, God, and Modernity*, trans. by Max Pensky, ed. by Eduardo Mendieta, Cambridge, Massachusetts: MIT Press 2002, pp. 110–28).)

*Nachmetaphysisches Denken. Philosophische Aufsätze*, Frankfurt am Main: Suhrkamp 1988, p. 33; p. 47; p. 155; p. 183; pp. 191–209. (English translation:

*Postmetaphysical Thinking*, trans. by William Mark Hohengarten, Cambridge,
   Massachusetts: MIT Press 1992, pp. 24–5; p. 39; p. 131; p. 143; pp. 152–70.)
*Philosophisch-politische Profile*, enlarged ed., Frankfurt am Main: Suhrkamp 1981,
   p. 40. (English translation: *Philosophical-Political Profiles*, ed. and trans. by
   Frederick G. Lawrence, Cambridge, Massachusetts: MIT Press 1983, p. 23;
   reprinted in *Religion and Rationality: Essays on Reason, God, and Modernity*,
   trans. by Max Pensky, ed. by Eduardo Mendieta, Cambridge, Massachusetts:
   MIT Press 2002, p. 39.)
*Texte und Kontexte*, Frankfurt am Main: Suhrkamp 1991, p. 128. (English translation:
   *Religion and Rationality: Essays on Reason, God, and Modernity*, trans. by Max
   Pensky, ed. by Eduardo Mendieta, Cambridge, Massachusetts: MIT Press 2002,
   p. 68.)
*Wahrheit und Rechtfertigung. Philosophische Aufsätze*, Frankfurt am Main: Suhrkamp 1999, p. 100; p. 170; p. 321. (English translation: *Truth and Justification*,
   trans. by Barbara Fultner, Cambridge, Massachusetts: MIT Press 1993, p. 80; p.
   159; p. 280.)
*Zwischen Naturalismus und Religion*, Frankfurt am Main: Suhrkamp 2005, p. 23;
   p. 114; p. 149; pp. 237–51. (English translation: *Between Naturalism and
   Religion*, trans. by Ciaran Cronin, Malden, Massachusetts: Polity Press 2008, p.
   19; p. 109; p. 142; pp. 229–42.)

## II. Sources of Habermas' Knowledge of Kierkegaard

Bultmann, Rudolf, *Theologische Enzyklopädie*, Tübingen: Mohr 1984, pp. 8–10;
   pp. 74–5.
Jaspers, Karl, *Der philosophische Glaube*, Munich: Piper 1948, p. 15; p. 22; p. 28;
   pp. 32–5; pp. 56–7; p. 84; pp. 86–7; pp. 95–7; pp. 127–8.
Theunissen, Michael, *Der Andere. Studien zur Sozialontologie der Gegenwart*, 2nd
   ed., Berlin: Walter de Gruyter 1977, p. 181; p. 249; p. 279; p. 360; p. 497.
— *Sein and Schein*, Frankfurt am Main: Suhrkamp 1978, p. 208; p. 378.
— *Das Selbst auf dem Grund des Verzweiflung. Kierkegaards negativistische
   Methode*, Frankfurt am Main: Suhrkamp 1991.
— *Negative Theologie der Zeit*, Frankfurt am Main: Suhrkamp 1991, p. 30;
   pp. 349–50; p. 359.
— *Selbstverwirklichung und Allgemeinheit*. Frankfurt am Main: Suhrkamp 1991,
   p. 2; p. 10; p. 18.
— *Der Begriff Verzweiflung. Korrekturn an Kierkegaard*, Frankfurt am Main:
   Suhrkamp 1993.
Theunissen, Michael and Wilfred Greve (eds.), *Materialien zur Philosophie Sören
   Kierkegaards*, Frankfurt am Main: Suhrkamp 1979.

## III. Secondary Literature on Habermas' Relation to Kierkegaard

Adams, Nicholas, *Habermas and Theology*, Cambridge: Cambridge University
   Press 2006, p. 101; p. 125; p. 162; pp. 192–3; p. 206.

Beck, Elke, *Identität der Person. Sozialphilosophische Studien zu Kierkegaard, Adorno und Habermas*, Würzburg: Königshausen & Neumann 1991.

Hoffman, Kevin, "Suffering and Discourse Ethics in Kierkegaard's Religious Stage," *Journal of Religion*, vol. 82, no. 3, 2002, pp. 393–410.

Matuštík, Martin J., *Habermas and Kierkegaard on Post-Traditional Identity: A Study in Communicative and Existential Ethics*, Ph.D. Thesis, Fordham University, New York 1991.

— "Habermas's Reading of Kierkegaard: Notes from a Conversation," *Philosophy and Social Criticism*, vol. 17, no. 4, 1992, pp. 313–23.

— *Postnational Identity: Critical Theory and Existential Philosophy in Habermas, Kierkegaard, and Havel*, New York and London: Guilford Press 1993.

— "Kierkegaard as Socio-political Thinker and Activist," *Man and World*, vol. 27, no. 2, 1994, p. 218.

— *Jürgen Habermas: A Philosophical-Political Profile*, Lanham, Maryland: Rowman & Littlefield Publishers 2001, p. 150.

— "The Scarcity of Singular Individuals in the Age of Globalization: A Kierkegaardian Response to Fundamentalism," in *Kierkegaard and Great Philosophers*, ed. by Roman Králik et al., Šaľa: Sociedad Iberoamericana de Estudios Kierkegaardianos 2007 (*Acta Kierkegaardiana*, vol. 2), pp. 141–60.

Perkins, Robert L., "Habermas and Kierkegaard: Religious Subjectivity, Multiculturalism, and Historical Revisionism," *International Philosophical Quarterly*, vol. 44, 2004, pp. 481–96.

Rosati, M., "Poter-essere-se-stessi e essere soggetti morali. J. Habermas tra Kierkegaard e Kant," *Rassegna Italiana di Sociologia*, vol. 44, no. 4, 2003, pp. 493–513.

Westphal, Merold, "Commanded Love and Moral Autonomy: The Kierkegaard–Habermas Debate," *Kierkegaard Studies Yearbook*, 1998, pp. 1–22.

Wind, H.C., *Religion og kommunikation. Teologisk hermeneutik*, Århus: Aarhus Universitetsforlag 1987.

# Martin Luther King, Jr.:

## Kierkegaard's *Works of Love*, King's *Strength to Love*

### Nigel Hatton

Martin Luther King, Jr. (1929–68), iconic civil rights leader, 1964 Nobel Peace Prize Laureate, and a dynamic Baptist preacher informed by the traditions of the African-American church, had a profound knowledge of ancient and modern religions, world literature, and Western philosophy cultivated during his undergraduate years at Morehouse College, religious study at Crozer Theological Seminary, and doctoral training at Boston University. His sermons and speeches, noted for King's powerful delivery at the lectern, in the pulpit, or during marches or street demonstrations, are equally remarkable for their rhetorical structure, symbolism and dialectical synthesis of competing social, religious, and philosophical discourses.

As one of the first African-American licensed preachers to have an earned university doctorate in theology, he brought philosophical inquiry into the pews, mixing together Christian parables and scripture, stories of African-American struggles taken from the oral tradition, and analyses or allusions to the likes of Plato, Hegel, or Nietzsche. In his pursuit of social justice, global peace, and equal rights, he met no intellectual boundary, expounding on the history of Mithraism one moment, the merits of Mohandas Gandhi (1869–1948) and peaceful nonviolence the next.[1]

King encountered the name Søren Aabye Kierkegaard as early as age 19, and his awareness of Kierkegaardian thought emerges in his writings up until his assassination on April 4, 1968, at the age of 39. Whether writing seminar papers on Reinhold Niebuhr (1892–1971), composing outlines of Kierkegaard's texts, completing his dissertation on Paul Tillich (1886–1965) and Henry Nelson Wieman (1884–1975), or plotting the philosophical roots that underpinned his religious convictions and activism, King found in the writings of Kierkegaard a spiritual ancestor, one he could rely on for negotiating ongoing inward battles between philosophy and religion, and within religion itself, particularly as they related to social action. Whereas King's teachers and the secondary texts that he read on Kierkegaard can be viewed as offering interpretations of Kierkegaard's ideas guided

---

[1]     For a discussion of the significance of King's doctoral study as an African-American preacher, see Vincent Harding's introduction to the text of King's March 3, 1968, sermon, "Unfulfilled Dreams," in *A Knock at Midnight: Inspiration from the Great Sermons of Reverend Martin Luther King, Jr.*, New York: Warner Books 1998.

by their own theological interests and positions, King's knowledge of and interest in Kierkegaard was not acquired solely as an exercise in intellectual thought or ivory tower polemics.[2] King derived from Kierkegaard, as he did from most of his examinations or readings of canonical philosophers, theologians, and writers within the Western intellectual tradition, further material for developing his own theory and praxis for social action and pursuit of freedom in a divided nation and world. As King scholar Clayborne Carson points out: "although [King] sought scholarly understanding of religion, his writings at Crozer consisted of an eclectic body of ideas that was rendered coherent not by his academic training but by his inherited values."[3] His work in universities greatly expanded his knowledge of the world, yet he remained informed by his experience as a black preacher, and the son, grandson and great-grandson of black preachers, working and living in black communities in the throes of movements for equality and justice.[4]

Though they came of age in different centuries, the personal and Christian experiences of King and Kierkegaard are somewhat comparable, from the relatively short but productive lives they lived (King until he was 39, Kierkegaard until the age of 43) to their relationships to influential fathers, from their struggles with and ultimate allegiances to Christianity, to the personal examinations surrounding their decisions to enter (King) or not to enter (Kierkegaard) the pulpit and into marriage.[5]

---

[2]     In *The Preacher King: Martin Luther King, Jr. and the Word that Moved America* (Oxford and New York: Oxford University Press 1997, p. 61), Richard Lischer makes a similar argument about King's knowledge and use of Hegel: "At Boston King had studied the philosopher Hegel in great detail, but the only piece of Hegel he ever displayed in public was his thesis-antithesis-synthesis scheme known to most beginners. The Hegelian triad not only was congenial to King's political goal to clarify both sides of an issue in order to reach a resolution but also activated his personal need to avoid frontal conflict and to please others if at all possible."

[3]     Clayborne Carson, "Introduction," *The Papers of Martin Luther King, Jr.*, vols. 1–6, ed. by Clayborne Carson et al., Berkeley: University of California Press 1992–2007, vol. 1, *Called to Serve, January 1929–June 1951*, p. 57.

[4]     See Keith D. Miller, *Voice of Deliverance: the Language of Martin Luther King, Jr., and its Sources*, Athens, Georgia: University of Georgia Press 1998. Carson also makes the point clear in his essay, "Martin Luther King, Jr. and the African-American Social Gospel": "King's rapid rise to prominence resulted from his ability to combine the insights of European-American theological scholarship with those of African-American homiletics. Although his published descriptions of his 'pilgrimage to non-violence' generally emphasized the impact of his academic training, in more personal statements he acknowledged his black Baptist roots. 'I am many things to many people,' King acknowledged in 1965, 'but in the quiet recess of my heart, I am fundamentally a clergyman, a Baptist preacher. This is my being and my heritage for I am also the son of a Baptist preacher, the grandson of a Baptist preacher and the great-grandson of a Baptist preacher." Clayborne Carson, "Martin Luther King, Jr. and the African-American Social Gospel," in *African American Religious Thought: An Anthology*, ed. by Cornel West and Eddie S. Glaude, Louisville, Kentucky and Westminster: Westminster John Knox Press 2003, p. 711.

[5]     King initially wanted to be a doctor, lawyer, or academic. He chose to become a preacher, he says, because he wanted to help humanity. Both King and Kierkegaard weighed their respective early-life decisions against the desires of their fathers. An understanding of

Both placed great importance on the concept of love: King called love "the greatest force in all the world,"[6] and Kierkegaard wrote that love "is a change, the most remarkable of all, but the most desirable."[7] King and Kierkegaard were religious human beings who placed their ultimate faith in God, yet both provided poignant and unapologetic critiques of the Christianities of their respective times, nineteenth-century Denmark in religious and political transition for Kierkegaard and the twentieth-century United States in the midst of war abroad and freedom struggles at home for King.[8]

Both can be viewed as iconoclasts in the academic world, Western intellectual tradition, and history of Christian thought, refusing to sacrifice their own ideas and convictions for the sake of normative scholarship and method, and Christian conformity. Thus, their respective bodies of work are notable for both content and form: Kierkegaard's novels, discourses and pseudonyms, and King's dynamic sermons, compelling letters from exile, and historic public speeches.

This article traces King's introduction to Kierkegaard, a relationship yet to be explored beyond anecdote in scholarship on either thinker. First I focus on his academic introduction to Kierkegaard and then posit ways in which we can explore the presence of Kierkegaard in King's speeches and sermons. Coretta Scott King (1927–2006) said her husband "was influenced by Hegel and hated Nietzsche, whose *Will to Power* almost brought Martin to despair of his hope of influencing the world through the power of love, though it served as an antidote for Hegel's easy idealism."[9] King also read Kierkegaard during this period. Writing months after King's death, Mohan Lal Sharma divided King's scholarly influences into four movements that

---

Coretta Scott King strengthens any analysis of King's work and life. Kierkegaard's broken engagement with Regine Olsen figures greatly in his writings. For biographical material on King, see Clayborne Carson's introductions to *The Papers of Martin Luther King, Jr.*, vols. 1–6, as well as *The Autobiography of Martin Luther King, Jr.*, ed. by Clayborne Carson, New York: Grand Central Publishing 1988.

[6]    King made the remark in a sermon titled, "Levels of Love," delivered at Ebenezer Baptist Church on September 16, 1962. The sermon is printed in *The Papers of Martin Luther King, Jr.*, vols. 1–6, ed. by Clayborne Carson, vol. 6, *Advocate of the Social Gospel, September 1948–March 1963*, p. 444.

[7]    Kierkegaard's statement can be found in *Works of Love*, published in 1847. See *SKS* 9, 264–5 / *WL*, 248. Many parallels can be found in King and Kierkegaard's philosophies of love through a comparison of Kierkegaard's *Works of Love* and King's *Strength to Love* (New York: Harper & Row 1963), a collection of King sermons.

[8]    Kierkegaard, in his journals, and King, in his autobiographical writings, express similar ideas about growing up in orthodox religious households. King writes: "my college training, especially the first two years, brought many doubts in my mind. It was then that the shackles of fundamentalism were removed from my body," King, *The Autobiography of Martin Luther King, Jr.*, ed. by Clayborne Carson, p. 15. Kierkegaard writes: "As you know, I grew up so to speak in orthodoxy, but as I began to think for myself the huge colossus gradually began to totter," *Pap.* I A 72 / *PJ*, 30. For a discussion of politics and religion at the time Kierkegaard came of age, see, for example, Bruce H. Kirmmse, *Kierkegaard in Golden Age Denmark*, Bloomington and Indianapolis: Indiana University Press 1990.

[9]    Coretta Scott King, *My Life with Martin Luther King*, New York: Holt, Rinehart and Winston 1969, p. 71.

Coretta Scott King and King's biographers also highlight: his introduction to Walter Rauschenbusch's social gospel and *Christianity and the Social Crisis* at Crozer; Reinhold Niebuhr and Paul Tillich's Neo-Orthodox Protestantism; Personalism, with which he became familiar with while studying at Boston University; and the philosophy of Mohandas Gandhi. The Niebuhr and Tillich period included extensive reading in the area of existentialism, "first in Kierkegaard and Nietzsche, later Jaspers, Heidegger, and Sartre."[10] The documentation of King's study of Kierkegaard and awareness of his texts suggest that the parallels to or resonances of Kierkegaardian ideas in King's speeches are more than mere coincidence. King was aware of the Kierkegaardian echoes in his rhetoric.

## *I. Reading Kierkegaard at Crozer*

After entering Morehouse College at the age of 15 and graduating with a sociology degree, King entered Crozer Theological Seminary, a Baptist institution in Chester, Pennsylvania. The Crozer admissions committee noted that King had limited training in philosophy, since he only took an Introduction to Philosophy course at Morehouse. In addition to his ministerial studies at Crozer, King attended courses on "Greek Religion," "Great Theologians," "Philosophy of Religion," and "Advanced Philosophy of Religion." His transcript also shows two courses taken at the University of Pennsylvania—"Kant," and "Problems of Esthetics." In his first year, King wrote a paper titled "What the Mystics Say," looking at the ideas of Kierkegaard, Meister Eckhart, Rufus Matthew Jones, St. Teresa of Avila, and St. Francis of Assisi. From September 13 to November 19, 1949, King completed a paper titled, "The Place of Reason and Experience in Finding God," for a course on "Christian Theology Today." The paper is among the first in which King uses Kierkegaard as well as the scholarship of contemporary theologians who had written about Kierkegaard, namely, Karl Barth, Reinhold Niebuhr, Henry Nelson Wieman, Edwin E. Aubrey, and especially Edgar Sheffield Brightman (1884–1953), whom King would go on to study with at Boston University. In the paper, King rejects Barth's interpretation of the Fall as the undoing of man and writes that the "Barthian attempt to undermind [*sic*] the rational in religion is one of the perils of our time."[11] Whereas Barth believes man cannot rely on reason and experience to know God,[12] King draws on William James, Brightman, and Spinoza to refute the Barthian claim. The paper positions Kierkegaard as a predecessor to Barth:

> We have already stated above the Barthian objection to this method. Briefly we might discuss the objections which in earlier theologians give to the validity of reason in finding God, viz., Kierkegaard. He reverses the Hegelian dialectic in such a way as to

---

[10]     Mohan Lal Sharma, "Martin Luther King: Modern America's Greatest Theologian of Social Action," *The Journal of Negro History*, vol. 53, no. 3, 1968, p. 258.

[11]     King, "The Place of Reason and Experience in Finding God," *The Papers of Martin Luther King, Jr.*, vol. 1, p. 232.

[12]     Ibid., p. 232: "Following the Hegelian dialectic they see God as the synthesis between every thesis and antithesis. We may know the thesis and antithesis, but never the synthesis."

place the unity (synthesis) prior to the diversity (thesis and antithesis); and he goes on to attribute the diversity to the inevitable limitation of human thought. In other words, the Divine synthesis manifests itself to reason as a contradiction. Therefore, he argues, reason can never lead to God because it is by nature self-contradictory.[13]

In the margins of his paper, King attributes his reading of Kierkegaard to E.E. Aubrey, author of *Present Theological Tendencies.* In fact, the statement comes directly from Aubrey's text: "Kierkegaard as we saw, reversed the Hegelian dialectic in such a way as to place the unity prior to diversity; and attributed the diversity to the inevitable limitation of human thought."[14] It is not the first time King situates Barth as using ideas that come from Kierkegaard. In a later Crozer assignment, King calls one of Barth's sermons "boring" and again questions the views of a theologian whose "ancestral line runs back through [*Søren*] Kierkegaard to [*Martin*] Luther and [*John*] Calvin and so to Paul and Jeremiah."[15]

King's work at Crozer relies heavily on the scholars whose work he consults or writes about, though he occasionally makes strong assertions and arguments that foreshadow his later thinking. The interaction with Kierkegaard at this point appears to mimic the reception of Kierkegaard in religious scholarship in the United States in the mid-twentieth century. In other words, the allusions or references to Kierkegaard are best described as King's parroting the opinions of others. Editors of the Martin Luther King, Jr., Papers Project have posited myriad explanations for the instances of plagiarism, uncritical appropriation, and over-summarization in King's writings. According to the series editor Clayborne Carson:

> Even as we became more and more aware of the extent to which King relied upon the words of others, we also came to the somewhat paradoxical conclusion that King's academic writings—and certainly his later writings and speeches as a public figure— were reliable expressions of his public persona. Writings that were flawed by plagiaries were nevertheless revealing in that they expressed views that were consistent internally and over time. This consistency helps to explain why King's professors and later readers of his papers did not notice the extensive textual appropriations. We also suggested that the compositional practices that raised ethical issues during King's graduate-school days were closely related to the positive qualities that later made him an influential public figure. Rather than youthful lapses in judgment, King's appropriations reflected a deeply ingrained attitude regarding the use of erudite language to achieve personal and social ends. Our findings suggest that, once he entered public life, King's theological training became an asset, distinguishing him from other black leaders and providing him with

---

[13]    King, "The Place of Reason and Experience in Finding God," *The Papers of Martin Luther King, Jr.*, vol. 1, pp. 234–35.

[14]    Ibid., p. 235, note 11. Editors of *The Papers of Martin Luther King, Jr.* point out that the passage appears in Edwin Ewart Aubrey, *Present Theological Tendencies*, New York: Harper & Brothers 1936, p. 83.

[15]    King, "Karl Barth," *The Papers of Martin Luther King, Jr.*, vol. 6, *Advocate of the Social Gospel, September 1948–March 1963*, p. 101.

intellectual resources that enhanced his ability to influence white middleclass public opinion.[16]

Thus, while it is useful to trace King's introduction to primary and secondary Kierkegaard sources, as well as those moments where King mentions Kierkegaard directly in his writings, it is equally important to notice the allusions to Kierkegaard that are woven seamlessly into King's sermons and speeches. What Kierkegaard perhaps achieved with his pseudonyms, King attempted to accomplish through a variety of rhetorical strategies that scholars continue to debate and investigate. King, for example, appreciated the theological concepts of a Barth sermon, but questioned Barth's use of "an obstruse [*sic*] mode of expression which only the learned can understand. He leaven [*sic*] the average mind lost in the fog of theological abstractions."[17] Carson argues that

> King's deep roots in African-American culture undoubtedly affected his ability and willingness to communicate his thoughts in writing. Perhaps the most challenging questions that were raised by our discovery of King's plagiarism relate to the issue of determining King's level of comfort with academic writing as a vehicle for self-revelation. What was the relationship between his academic persona as presented in his academic papers and his evolving persona as an African-American religious leader? Although there is a consistency in the views expressed in his academic papers and those expressed in his sermons, King gradually became more willing to use the emotionally charged language of the black church rather than the emotionally arid language of the academy to express his views. His writings suggest that his academic training may have given him the ability to conceal or repress his emotions and his African-American cultural roots.[18]

If the relationship between the two is governed by mainstream discourses and an immediacy that both men spent their lifetimes attempting to escape, how then are we to detect any authentic use of Kierkegaard in the work of King? I have suggested that this requires close examination of King's speeches, sermons, and non-academic writings, where he is often drawing on the same parables as Kierkegaard and attempting to articulate his thinking on the anxiety and despair faced by human beings in an unjust world. The African-American preaching tradition has always included the phenomenon of a preacher from one church or community hearing the sermon of another preacher in a neighboring community and incorporating those ideas into his or her own without attribution. King may have studied Kierkegaard on an academic level, but perhaps his greatest use of Kierkegaard comes in this unattributed form, which allows King to maintain agency and authentic voice in the pulpit while preaching to his African-American audience.

---

[16]        Clayborne Carson, "Editing Martin Luther King, Jr.: Political and Scholarly Issues," in *Palimpsest: Editorial Theory in the Humanities*, ed. by George Bornstein and Ralph G. Williams, Ann Arbor: University of Michigan Press 1993, p. 309.

[17]        King, "Karl Barth," *The Papers of Martin Luther King, Jr.*, vol. 6, p. 103.

[18]        Carson, "Editing Martin Luther King, Jr.: Political and Scholarly Issues," p. 312.

## II. Boston University

King read most of his Kierkegaard while a student at Boston University School of Divinity. Several factors led King to choose Boston University for doctoral studies. Both Boston and the University of Edinburgh had accepted his application for admission. He was denied by Yale, his first choice. As a Methodist institution that valued egalitarianism, The Boston University School of Divinity admitted African Americans and women to all of its programs from the day it opened its doors in 1871. By the time King enrolled at Boston on September 13, 1951, a number of African-American scholars and preachers had preceded him, including the noted African-American theologian Samuel Dewitt Proctor (1921–97). Boston was also the center of activity for personalist theology, which King had been introduced to at Crozer. Eager to increase the intensity of his studies, King found in Boston an ideal intellectual space with a large community of African-American students both at Boston University and within the greater Boston area, and a faculty that included leading proponents of personalism, most notably Edgar Brightman, and Brightman's protégé, L. Harold DeWolf (1905–86).

King kept detailed notes of material he studied at both Crozier and Boston. He arranged personal note cards in alphabetical order, and the topics listed under "K" from 1948 to 1954 included notations on Kierkegaard. King also took notes on Kierkegaard for courses on "Religious Teachings of the New Testament" and "Seminar in Systematic Theology" during spring semester 1952, and "History of Recent Philosophy" in the fall of 1952. During this time King registered for philosophy courses at Harvard University: "History of Modern Philosophy" and "Philosophy of Plato," both with Raphael Demos, and "Philosophy of Whitehead" with Nathaniel Lawrence. Even away from the classroom, King recalls reading unassigned philosophical texts. King organized and led meetings of the Dialectical Society, a gathering of theology students who focused on a paper presented by one member of the group each month. King's notes from May 5, 1954, indicate that Kierkegaard was part of the Dialectical Society discussion.

King managed to pursue his doctoral coursework while preaching up and down the east coast to adoring congregations between Boston and his home in Atlanta, where he remained affiliated with Ebenezer Baptist Church.[19] Word spread of his dynamism and led to several invitations to preach. He was also in a relationship with Coretta Scott, then a student at the New England Conservatory of Music. They married on June 18, 1953. The demands of graduate school, courtship, preaching, and trips between Atlanta and Boston, took their toll on the quality of King's work. According to Carson, King's second year included an oversubscribed term, which included two lecture courses, a seminar, a two-semester course on Hegel with Brightman, and the Plato course with Demos at Harvard. The Brightman course focused on Hegel's *Phenomenology of Spirit*, and King said that he chose to read *Philosophy of Right* and *Philosophy of History* in his spare time. However,

---

[19]    King was baptized at Ebenezer and ordained as a minister there at the age of 19. In 1960, he was named co-pastor of the church along with his father.

[T]he first sign of a troubled term came when King stumbled through an exploratory quiz for the Hegel seminar, missing such basic definitions as "logos" and "naturalism." King had studied Hegel in other courses at Boston University, including Richard Millard's History of Recent Philosophy, but the seminar with Brightman constituted King's first prolonged exposure to Hegel's thought. A less than thorough knowledge of German heightened King's difficulty with the course, and—perhaps an indication of his frustration with the philosopher's abstruse language—his essays for the seminar were appropriated largely from a synopsis of Hegel's philosophy. The loss of his mentor's guidance added to King's difficulties. Two weeks after the beginning of the semester a cerebral hemorrhage disabled Brightman, who was replaced by Peter Bertocci as leader of the seminar. Following Brightman's death several months later, King chose DeWolf as his advisor.[20]

For King, Boston represented the place that he became immersed in the philosophy of personalism under Brightman and DeWolf. According to King:

It was mainly under these teachers that I studied Personalistic philosophy—the theory that the clue to the meaning of ultimate reality is found in personality. This personal idealism remains today my basic philosophical position. Personalism's insistence that only personality—finite and infinite—is ultimately real strengthened me in two convictions: it gave me metaphysical and philosophical grounding for the idea of a personal God, and it gave me a metaphysical basis for the dignity and work of all human personality.[21]

Just as King's teachers like Brightman and DeWolf influenced his thinking on personalism, they also steered the direction of his understanding of existentialism, in general, and Kierkegaard, in particular. In an exam for DeWolf's "History of Christian Doctrine" course in spring 1953, for example, students were asked to "Show the place of philosophy in relation to the theology of Duns Scotus, Edwards, Ritschl and Kierkegaard." King responded in his own handwriting that

Kierkegaard had no use for philosophy. System making was at best a game. Philosophy is based on the false premise that one can be objective. But in the realm of Christianity one is called upon to make a choice which has ultimate significance. To make such a choice the individual must give his whole self to God or reality rather than wait for all the answers. Knowledge of existence is individual subjective and [*strikeout illegible*] existential. Universals do not give us knowledge because universals do not exist. So Kierkegaard ends up affirming that the chief instrument of philosophy, viz., reason must be crucified.[22]

The question is followed by a query on Barth: "How appropriate is the designation of Barth's theology as a 'new orthodoxy'?" King's disagreement with Barth's theology becomes evident in his response, which also aligns Barth with Kierkegaard, a connection King had accepted earlier in his studies at Crozer. King writes:

---

[20]     Carson, "Introduction," *The Papers of Martin Luther King, Jr.*, vol. 1, p. 15.

[21]     King, *The Autobiography of Martin Luther King, Jr.*, pp. 31–2.

[22]     King, *The Papers of Martin Luther King, Jr.*, vol. 2, *Rediscovering Precious Values, July 1951–November 1955*, p. 194.

For an instance [Barth's] insistence on the unknowability and the incomprehensibility of God is not only unorthodox, but also unbiblical. His affirmation that God is the "Wholly Other" is much more Kierkegaardian that [*sic*] Biblical. His scorn for history seems to me to be also a quite unorthodox position. In fact Barth's whole doctrine of God is much more unorthodox and radical than he thinks it is. His God who is so transcendent that he can never come in touch with the [*strikeout illegible*] without a mediator is much more Greek than Christian orthodox.[23]

King's references to Kierkegaard can both be traced to his mentor Brightman, who influenced King's viewpoint on the relation of Hegel to Kierkegaard, and Hegel to Barth. In his book, *A Philosophy of Religion*, Brightman writes:

> Those who assert the uniqueness of religious values to the exclusion of their coalescence with other values, and who believe that religion is wholly incommensurable with any other dimension of life (such men as Sören Kierkegaard) are able to declare that religion is independent of philosophy. They rely on some divine revelation or mystical moment to impart an absolute quality to the whole of experience. But they do it at a very high price. The price they have to pay is either extreme subjectivism or objective irrationalism.[24]

Brightman's view is an outdated one, evidenced by recent scholarship on the sociality of Kierkegaard's thought, particularly through analyses of his *Works of Love* as well as biographical material detailing his activities in his native Denmark and his interaction in the streets of Copenhagen. Brightman attempted to quantify and conceptualize Kierkegaard in relation to alternate threads of thought, and, in doing so, simplified Kierkegaard's religious convictions, which require an analysis that is part theological, philosophical, biographical, and aesthetic, in order to follow lines of argument complicated by Kierkegaard's varying choices of form (discourse, deliberation, novel, parody, satire), authorship (pseudonym, Kierkegaard), and audience (the single individual, reader). Brightman attempts to justify the principles of personalism against what he views as a

> marked revolt against humanism and in favor of a radically objective attitude toward God. Sören Kierkegaard (1813–1855), a Danish theologian, was largely responsible for initiating this line of thought in the nineteenth century, although it also has much in common with the system of John Calvin (1509–1564), as well as with some of the beliefs of Martin Luther (1483–1546).[25]

Brightman similarly leads King down the road of oversimplifying the relationship between Hegel and Kierkegaard as one in which the latter rebels against the absolutism of the former.[26] King limited his repetition of this kind of thinking to the academic

---

[23]    Ibid., p. 195.

[24]    Edgar Sheffield Brightman, *A Philosophy of Religion*, New York: Prentice Hall 1940, p. 110.

[25]    Ibid., p. 145.

[26]    Jon Stewart argues that critiques of Hegel similar to Kierkegaard's were present in Denmark prior to the appearance Kierkegaard's publications. Stewart also demonstrates ways in which Kierkegaard was influenced by Hegel's ideas. See Jon Stewart, *A History of Hegelianism in Golden Age Denmark*, Tome I, *The Heiberg Period: 1824–1836*, Copenhagen:

realm. In *A Philosophy of Religion*, Brightman refers readers interested in a further discussion of Kierkegaard's critique of rationality to H.R. Mackintosh's *Types of Modern Theology: Schleiermacher to Barth.*[27] The book is a study of the theologies of Schleiermacher, Hegel, Albrecht Ritschl (1822–89), Ernst Troeltsch (1865–1923), Kierkegaard and Barth. King cites Mackintosh's text in a paper on "Contemporary Continental Theology," written for his "Seminar in Systematic Theology" in the fall of 1951. Mackintosh assesses Kierkegaard as "one of those thinkers who indignantly resent all efforts to bring faith and speculative philosophy into agreement, urging with vehemence that the apologetical vindication of Christianity betrays the very genius of our faith, and that the only legitimate form of defense is frontal attack."[28] Mackintosh continues his critique by arguing that Kierkegaard has gone too far:

> The conclusion is unavoidable that, in his efforts to alter the balance of contemporary religious thought, Kierkegaard induces new distortions of belief so violent and perverse as gravely to imperil our hold on the New Testament conception of God and of the life His children are called to lead. Thus, to recur to one salient example, his individualism is of so extreme a type as largely to disqualify him from understanding actual religion. There is no sense of any kind, he asserts roundly, in which faith can pass from one life to another. Here fellowship counts for nothing; the Church, even the family, except in a purely external fashion, has no relation to the interior fact of piety. The knight of Christ rides out on a lonely quest. Whatever its momentary impressiveness, this, if taken seriously, is a caricature of Christian discipleship as the New Testament pictures it.[29]

Like Brightman, Mackintosh critiques those aspects of Kierkegaard he finds inconsistent with his own ideas about the relationship among, God, Jesus Christ, and human beings. Even his admiration of Kierkegaard as a theologian is based on spectacle and the notion of Kierkegaard as an overzealous critic of thinkers who synthesize rationality and religion.

Mackintosh is also one source for locating King's tendency to align Barth and Kierkegaard in his academic work. While Barth has indeed been influenced by Kierkegaard, King's understanding of their relationship is uncritical and borrowed from the likes of Mackintosh, Brightman, and Walter Marshall Horton, author of *Contemporary Continental Theology*. In the "Contemporary Continental Theology" paper, King includes a summary and critique of crisis theologians like Barth that are taken directly from Horton's and Mackintosh's scholarship. King writes:

> Here we can see the direct influence of existentialism on the thinking of the crisis theologians. It seems the [*sic*] Kierkegaard has arisen from the grave. For these men Biblicism takes the place of even the most exalted type of ordinary reason and experience. Philosophers and theologians are mere playboys sporting with the fad of reason. All of this is said to substantiate the view of the impotence of man. As Barth so

---

C.A. Reitzel 2007, and Jon Stewart, *A History of Hegelianism in Golden Age Denmark*, Tome II, *The Martensen Period: 1837–1842*, Copenhagen: C.A. Reitzel 2007.

[27]     H.R. Mackintosh, *Types of Modern Theology*, London: Nisbet 1937.
[28]     Ibid., p. 256.
[29]     Ibid., pp. 257–8.

often says: "God is in Heaven and man is on earth." As Kierkegaard said long before, "there is a qualitative difference between God and man."[30]

According to Mackintosh, "In Kierkegaard, it is widely recognized, we have in some degree a precursor of Karl Barth. Barth's words are often quoted: 'If we have a system, it consists in this, that always as far as the infinite qualitative difference between time and eternity, alike in its negative and positive meaning. God is in heaven, you are on earth.' "[31]

The point of this discussion is to suggest that while King often came across Kierkegaard in his studies at Crozer Theological Seminary and Boston University School of Theology, there is little evidence to suggest that these academic writings represented instances of authentic engagement between two dynamic religious thinkers. Instead, we can raise questions like, Why did not King write a paper focused solely on Kierkegaard if Kierkegaard seemed to arise in several of the discussions in his seminars and even in the debates of the Dialectical Society? Did the centrality of personalism and scholarship characterizing Kierkegaard as a fanatic prevent King from engaging in rigorous study of Kierkegaard's work? Coretta Scott King suggested that her husband did not appreciate the godlessness of existentialist thinkers, yet there are no known attempts on King's part to wrestle with the religious existentialism of Kierkegaard. It is important to remember that already at this point in his life King was known to many congregations across the eastern seaboard as a powerful preacher. Recalling his assessment of one of Barth's sermons as "boring" and full of "theological abstractions," one might ask how King reconciled the complex theological exegeses of the men he studied with his intentions in the pulpit and as a social activist. In King's papers, it is possible to locate direct moments in which he either aligns himself with or rejects certain ideas of Plato, Hegel, Nietzsche, Barth, Tillich, and others. The same cannot be said of his engagement with Kierkegaard.

### III. Tillich and Niebuhr

Two important theologians who impacted King's social philosophy are Reinhold Niebuhr and Paul Tillich, and he exchanged letters and communicated with both religious thinkers during and after his doctoral studies.[32] King read their work extensively, and each thinker relied heavily on Kierkegaard's philosophy. King wrote about Niebuhr at both Crozer and Boston, and presented a paper on him to the members of the Dialectical Society. For King

---

[30]     King, *The Papers of Martin Luther King, Jr.*, vol. 2, p. 133.

[31]     Ibid., pp. 218–19.

[32]     For King's correspondence with Niebuhr, see *The Papers of Martin Luther King, Jr.*, vol. 5, pp. 102–3. His correspondence with Tillich is printed in vol. 2, pp. 203–4; p. 300; p. 310. In his notes on Niebuhr, King wrote the following about Niebuhr's influences: "Deeply influenced in his pastoral years by the plight of the worker in the Ford plant. Theological influences; Luther, Calvin, Augustine. Philosophical influences: Hegel (dialectics); Marxism; Heidegger; Kierkegaard." See " 'Reinhold Niebuhr' an outline," *The Papers of Martin Luther King, Jr.*, vol. 2, p, 140.

Niebuhr's great contribution to theology is that he has refuted the false optimism characteristic of a great segment of Protestant liberalism. Moreover, Niebuhr has extraordinary insight into human nature, especially the behavior of nations and social groups. He is keenly aware of the complexity of human motives and of the relation between morality and power.[33]

King said Niebuhr, who rejected pacifism as "submission to evil power," helped him to develop a "realist pacifism," that took into account "the reality of sin on every level of man's existence."[34] King knew that Niebuhr's anthropology of sin derived in part from Kierkegaard, and his presentation to the Dialectical Society focused on Niebuhr's use of *The Concept of Anxiety* in several of Niebuhr's texts: *Moral Man and Immoral Society, Faith and History: A Comparison of Christian and Modern Views of History, The Nature and Destiny of Man, Beyond Tragedy: Essays on the Christian Interpretation of History, Reflections on the End of an Era,* and *Interpretation of Christian Ethics.* King writes:

> Niebuhr never wearies of pointing out that man is a sinner. He points out that such modern thinkers as Kierkegaard, Nietzsche, and Sigmund Freud, in their explorations of the dark depths of the human heart, confirm afresh the biblical doctrine of the sinfulness of man. Niebuhr sees sin as what results when man tries to find security for himself outside the tension of the dialectical relation between time and eternity.[35]

Niebuhr's *The Nature and Destiny of Man,* for example, quotes heavily from *The Concept of Anxiety, Fear and Trembling,* the *Concluding Unscientific Postscript,* and *Either/Or.* He informs his readers that "Modern psycho-analysts might learn much about the basic character of anxiety and its relation to human freedom from the greatest of Christian psychologists, Soren Kierkegaard, who devoted a profound study to this problem: *Der Begriff der Angst.*"[36] Throughout his paper on Niebuhr, King paraphrases ideas that are indeed Niebuhr's, but derive from the influence Kierkegaard had on Niebuhr, particularly concerning the concept of sin. Locating one connection between Kierkegaard and Niebuhr, King asserts that Niebuhr "resorts to the formula of 'original sin' to explain why evil in history belongs to man."[37] Sin is a major theme in the sermons and writings of King, and he often references Niebuhr when raising the issue. In the "Pilgrimage to Nonviolence" essay, King writes: "the works of Reinhold Niebuhr made me aware of the complexity of human motives and the reality of sin on every level of man's existence."[38] This represents one indirect connection between King and Kierkegaard.

---

[33]  King, *The Autobiography of Martin Luther King. Jr.*, p. 27.

[34]  Ibid.

[35]  King, "The Theology of Reinhold Niebuhr," *The Papers of Martin Luther King, Jr.*, vol. 2, p. 273.

[36]  Reinhold Niebuhr, *The Nature of the Destiny of Man: A Christian Interpretation*, vol. 1, *Human Nature*, New York: Scribner 1941, p. 46, note.

[37]  King, "The Theology of Reinhold Niebuhr," p. 273.

[38]  Martin Luther King, Jr., "Pilgrimage to Nonviolence," *Christian Century*, vol. 77, 1960, p. 420.

Though personalism was a major influence on King during his time in Boston, he chose to write his dissertation on "A Comparison of the Conception of God in the Thinking of Paul Tillich and Henry Nelson Wieman." According to King, he chose to write about God because of the reoccurring questions raised about "the God concept."[39] He focused on Tillich and Wieman due to the influence of their ideas in "theological and philosophical thought."[40] Wieman and Tillich were both aware of Kierkegaard, though the majority of King's intellectual contact with Kierkegaard in his study would come through Tillich. Wieman's article, "Interpretation of Kierkegaard," appeared in a 1939 edition of *Christian Century*, and Tillich is widely acknowledged as a leading existential religious thinker borrowing from the work of Kierkegaard.[41] For his dissertation, King read all of Tillich's published work available to him. He also read in-progress material provided in course seminars and even wrote to Tillich (and Wieman), asking for references King was not able to find.[42] In his dissertation, King cites a connection between Kierkegaard and Tillich on the concept of the finite/infinite. King found the idea in Tillich's *Systematic Theology* and David E. Roberts' essay, "Tillich's Doctrine of Man." What appears in King's dissertation is a mixture of Tillich's and Roberts' words:

> Finitude is the ontological basis of human anxiety. Therefore anxiety is as omnipresent as is finitude. As such it must be distinguished from fear which is directed toward definite objects and can be removed by action. Anxiety cannot be overcome by action, for no finite being can conquer its finitude. Anxiety is ontological; fear is psychological. Like Kierkegaard and Heidegger, Tillich regards anxiety as directed toward "nothingness." Though ineradicable, it can be accepted and used creatively as a part of what it means to be human.[43]

---

[39]   King, *The Autobiography of Martin Luther King, Jr.*, p. 32.

[40]   Ibid.

[41]   See Henry Nelson Wieman, "Interpretation of Kierkegaard," *Christian Century*, vol. 56, 1939, pp. 444–6. In *My Search for Absolutes* (New York: Simon & Schuster 1967, p. 37), Paul Tillich writes, "Important influences on our theological existence came from other sides. One of them was our discovery of Kierkegaard and the shaking impact of his dialectical psychology. It was a prelude to what happened in the 1920s when Kierkegaard became the saint of the theologians as well as of the philosophers. But it was only a prelude; for the spirit of the nineteenth century still prevailed, and we hoped that the great synthesis between Christianity and humanism could be achieved with the tools of German classical philosophy. Another prelude to things to come occurred in the period between my student years and the beginning of the First World War. It was the encounter with Schelling's second period, especially with his so-called 'Positive Philosophy.' Here lies the philosophically decisive break with Hegel and the beginning of that movement which today is called Existentialism. I was ready for it when it appeared in full strength after the First World War, and I saw it in the light of that general revolt against Hegel's system of reconciliation which occurred in the decades after Hegel's death and which, through Kierkegaard, Marx, and Nietzsche, has become decisive for the destiny of the twentieth century."

[42]   Wieman's response to King is transcribed on page 203 in vol. 2 of *The Papers of Martin Luther King, Jr.*

[43]   David E. Roberts, "Tillich's Doctrine of Man," In *The Theology of Paul Tillich*, ed. by Charles W. Kegley and Robert W. Bretall, New York: Macmillan 1964, pp. 108–30. King's

King's interpretation of Tillich leads him to use concepts and assertions found across Kierkegaard's authorship in texts like *Either/Or* and *The Concept of Anxiety*. Discussing the relationship of human beings to God, Kierkegaard writes in "The Ultimatum" that every human being is finite, and their relationship is a finite relationship that consists in a more or less."[44] In *The Concept of Anxiety*, Kierkegaard calls anxiety "the dizziness of freedom, which emerges when the spirit wants to posit the synthesis and freedom looks down into its own possibility, laying hold of finiteness to support itself."[45] These concepts King would apply to his theology of social action in his battle against segregation, poverty, and inequality. King takes a concept like anxiety, abstract and elusive in the work of Kierkegaard, and, through Tillich, applies it to the "social leprosy that segregation inflicts" upon human beings, cutting off their freedom, which is the essence of their existence.[46]

King appropriates Tillich's ideas for what would be one of his only published references to Kierkegaard, "Pilgrimage to Nonviolence," which appears in revised and reprinted editions from 1959. King attributes his first knowledge of existentialism to

> my reading of Kierkegaard and Nietzsche. Later I turned to a study of Jaspers, Heidegger and Sartre. All of these thinkers stimulated my thinking; while finding things to question in each, I nevertheless learned a great deal from study of them. When I finally turned to a serious study of the works of Paul Tillich I became convinced that existentialism, in spite of the fact that it had become all too fashionable, had grasped certain basic truths about man and his condition that could not be permanently overlooked.
>
> Its understanding of the "finite freedom" of man is one of existentialism's most lasting contributions, and its perception of the anxiety and conflict produced in man's personal and social life as a result of the perilous and ambiguous structure of existence is especially meaningful for our time. The common point in all existentialism, whether it is atheistic or theistic, is that man's existential situation is a state of estrangement from his essential nature. In their revolt against Hegel's essentialism, all existentialists contend that the world is fragmented. History is a series of unreconciled conflicts and man's existence is filled with anxiety and threatened with meaninglessness. While the ultimate Christian answer is not found in any of these existential assertions, there is much here that the theologian can use to describe the true state of man's existence.[47]

King's genealogy of his own understanding of existentialism can be traced to his training in seminary and at the university. In the midst of his academic work, he came across Kierkegaard on many occasions and accepted the secondary analyses of Kierkegaard provided to him by theologians he admired, studied with or wrote

---

paragraph on Tillich appears in Chapter III, "Tillich's Conception of God," of his dissertation. See *The Papers of Martin Luther King, Jr.*, vol. 2, p. 398. The editors show where King has plagiarized from Roberts and Tillich.

[44]     *SKS* 3, 331 / *EO2*, 352.

[45]     *SKS* 4, 365 / *CA*, 61.

[46]     Martin Luther King, Jr., *Where Do We Go From Here: Chaos or Community*, New York: Harper & Row 1967, p. 105.

[47]     King Jr., "Pilgrimage to Nonviolence," pp. 439–41. Reprinted in *The Papers of Martin Luther King, Jr.*, vol. 5, *Threshold of A New Decade, January 1959–December 1960*, pp. 419–24.

about. In my concluding section, I want to point briefly to ways in which we can find a primary relationship between Kierkegaard and King. In addition to King's academic introduction to Kierkegaard, I suggest that King read Kierkegaard and then melded his ideas into the rich array of metaphors, allusions, and references, named or unnamed, that make up the heart and soul of King's sermons, and speeches. By turning to King's sermons, speeches and memoirs, and thinking about them in relationship to Kierkegaard's authorship—namely pseudonymous texts like *Either/ Or*, *Fear and Trembling*, *The Concept of Anxiety*, and *The Sickness unto Death*, but also *Works of Love*, and *Upbuilding Discourses in Various Spirits*—I believe we can point to connections and influences otherwise unavailable in King's academic record. This approach affirms both the power of intellectual inquiry in the academy on King and the significance of cultural forms and traditions less reliant on footnotes and abstraction, namely, the African-American sermon. In 1957 King delivered a sermon at Dexter Avenue Baptist Church that would later turn into Chapter 14 of *Strength to Love*, with the title "The Mastery of Fear or Antidotes of Fear."[48] In an early draft, King writes that the

> abnormal fears and phobias that express themselves in *neurotic anxiety* can be cured by psychiatry, but the fear of death, nonbeing and nothingness which expresses itself in *existential anxiety* can only be cured by a positive religious faith. Such a faith imbues us with a sense of the trustworthiness of the universe, and a feeling of relatedness to God.[49]

The passage is among the many found in *Strength to Love* and other King homiletics that bear resemblance to ideas found in Kierkegaard. Condemning segregation in a 1960 address to Spelman college students, King said: "An individual who is not concerned about his selfhood and his freedom is at that moment committing moral and spiritual suicide."[50] In the same year, making remarks that echo themes from Kierkegaard's *Either/Or*, King told an audience at the Unitarian Church of Germantown in Philadelphia that "We have a legitimate obligation to set out in life to see what we are made for, to find that center of creativity, for there is within all of us a center of creativity seeking to break forth, and we have the responsibility of discovering this, discovering that life's work."[51] In a sermon titled "Loving Your Enemies" King emphasizes to his audience that "Love serves to build up."[52]

---

[48]    King, "Draft of Chapter XIV, 'The Mastery of Fear or Antidotes for Fear,' " in *The Papers of Martin Luther King, Jr.*, vol. 6, p. 542.
[49]    See *The Papers of Martin Luther King, Jr.*, vol. 6, p. 542. According to editors of the King papers, earlier drafts of King's sermons restore important content—critiques of war, capitalism and colonialism, for example—that was omitted or altered by publishers of King texts like *Strength to Love* (New York: Harper & Row 1963) and *Stride to Freedom* (New York: Harper & Row 1958).
[50]    King, " 'Keep Moving From This Mountain,' Address at Spelman College on 10 April 1960," in *The Papers of Martin Luther King, Jr.*, vol. 2, p. 414.
[51]    King, " 'The Three Dimensions of a Complete Life,' Sermon Delivered at the Unitarian Church of Germantown on 11 December 1960," in *The Papers of Martin Luther King, Jr.*, vol. 5, p. 572.
[52]    King, " 'Loving Your Enemies,' Sermon Delivered at the Detroit Council of Churches' Noon Lenten Services on 7 March 1961," in *The Papers of Martin Luther King, Jr.*, vol. 6, p. 427.

1 Corinthians 8:1 is also an important biblical passage for Kierkegaard in *Works of Love*. He begins the second half of *Works of Love* with a section titled "Love Builds Up."[53] Although King's academic record shows substantial encounters with Kierkegaard, his sermons on love, which do not refer to Kierkegaard directly, are the main source for discovering allusions to Kierkegaard's ideas. In other sermons, King speaks of the "purity of heart"[54] that man must have in order to know God, and he tells of seeing God in "the birds of the air."[55] A reading of *Upbuilding Discourses in Various Spirits* would reveal that King and Kierkegaard are using the same parables, drawing similar conclusions and making complementary demands upon their respective audiences, readers, and parishioners alike.

By understanding King's introduction to Kierkegaard as well as his lifelong negotiation of African-American cultural traditions and various philosophical and religious traditions from across the globe, we enrich our ability to interpret King's vision, philosophy of nonviolence, and lifelong struggle to make freedom and equality a reality for all human beings. In his 1964 Nobel lecture, for example, King makes reference to existentialist ideas with a religious solution. For King, human beings inhabit

> two realms, the internal and the external. The internal is that realm of spiritual ends expressed in art, literature, morals, and religion. The external is that complex of devices, techniques, mechanisms, and instrumentalities by means of which we live. Our problem today is that we have allowed the internal to become lost in the external. We have allowed the means by which we live to outdistance the ends for which we live.[56]

The passage is at once informed by Hegel's dialectic, Kant's categorical imperative, and Kierkegaard's ethical, aesthetic, and religious subjectivities. It was delivered orally in Oslo by a man steeped in African-American religious traditions and freedom struggles. The purpose of this article has been to show that Kierkegaard is present in King's rhetoric, both literally and figuratively. King's meditations on anxiety and despair, the importance of being human, the God concept, neighborliness, and love suggest that the echoes of Kierkegaard in his voice are quite authentic and strong.

---

53      See *SKS* 9, 212–26 / *WL*, 209–24.
54      King, "O That I Knew Where I Might Find Him," in *The Papers of Martin Luther King, Jr.*, vol. 6, p. 593.
55      Ibid., p. 594.
56      Martin Luther King, Jr., "The Quest for Peace and Justice," in *Nobel Lectures: Peace, 1951–1970*, ed. by Frederick W. Haberman, Amsterdam: Elsevier 1972, pp. 333–46.

# Bibliography

*I. References to or Uses of Kierkegaard in King's Corpus*

*A. King's Published Works*

"Pilgrimage to Nonviolence," *Christian Century*, vol. 77, 13 April 1960, pp. 439–41. (Reprinted in *The Papers of Martin Luther King, Jr.*, vol. 5, *Threshold of A New Decade, January 1959-December 1960*, ed. by Clayborne Carson, Berkeley: University of California Press 2005, pp. 419–24.

*B. King's Unpublished Writings*

*1. Martin Luther King, Jr. Papers, 1954–1968, Boston University, and the Martin Luther King, Jr., Research and Education Institute at Stanford University*
"What the Mystics Say," 22 February–6 May 1949.
"Home Quiz I, 'Philosophy of Religion,' " 27 September 1951.
"Class notes, 'Religious Teachings of the New Testament,' " 23 January–16 May 1952.
"Class notes, 'Seminar in Systematic Theology,' " 23 January–16 May 1952.
"Outline, 'Soren Kierkegaard,' " 23 January–16 May 1952.
"Class notes, 'History of Recent Philosophy,' " 26 May–5 July 1952.
"Examination answers, 'History of Recent Philosophy,' " 26 May–5 July 1952 (Printed in *The Papers of Martin Luther King, Jr.*, vol. 2, *Rediscovering Precious Values, July 1951-November 1955*, ed. by Clayborne Carson, Berkeley: University of California Press 1994, p. 152).
"Notes, 'Man, Nature and Revelation, W.R. Taylor,' " September 1951–May 1953.
"Notes on Theology and the Crisis of Culture, Modernism, and the Dialectical Theology, Chapters I–III," September 1951–May 1953.
"Final examination questions, 'History of Christian Doctrine,' " 19 May 1953 (Printed in *The Papers of Martin Luther King, Jr.*, vol. 2, *Rediscovering Precious Values, July 1951–November 1955*, ed. by Clayborne Carson, Berkeley: University of California Press 1994, p. 192).
"Draft, 'Reinhold Niebuhr,' " April 1953–June 1954.
"A Comparison of the Conceptions of God in the Thinking of Paul Tillich and Henry Nelson Wieman," 15 April 1955 (Printed in *The Papers of Martin Luther King, Jr.*, vol. 2, *Rediscovering Precious Values, July 1951–November 1955*, ed. by Clayborne Carson, Berkeley: University of California Press 1994, pp. 339–544).
"How My Mind Has Changed in the Last Decade," 7 April 1960.
"Pilgrimage to Nonviolence," 13 April 1960.

"Draft of chapter XVII, 'Pilgrimage to Nonviolence,' *Strength to Love*," July 1962–
    March 1963.

*2. King's Unpublished Writings Held at the Coretta Scott King Collection (CSKC-
INP)*
"Personal notecards on 'K' topics," [1948–1954].
"Notes from meeting of the Dialectical Society," 10 May 1954.
"Notecards on Religious Education, Dwight D (Dwight David) Eisenhower, Ethics,
    Evil, and Existentialism," [1951–1955].
"Pilgrimage to Nonviolence," 13 April 1960 Typed draft by King's hand.
"Draft, 'How My Mind Has Changed in the Last Decade,' " 13 April 1960.
"Notes, 'How My Mind Has Changed' series," 13 April 1960.

*3. King's Unpublished Writings Held at the Percy A. Carter Collection*
"Reinhold Niebuhr" [April 1953–June 1954] (Printed in *The Papers of Martin
    Luther King, Jr.*, vol. 2, *Rediscovering Precious Values, July 1951–November
    1955*, ed. by Clayborne Carson, Berkeley: University of California Press 1994,
    p. 139).

## II. Sources of King's Knowledge of Kierkegaard

Aubrey, E.E., *Present Theological Tendencies*, New York: Harper and Brothers
    1936, pp. 60–83.
Mackintosh, H.R., "The Theology of Paradox: Sören Kierkegaard," *Types of Modern
    Theology*, London: Nisbet 1937, pp. 218–62.
Niebuhr, Reinhold, *Faith and History: A Comparison of Christian and Modern
    Views of History*, New York: Scribner 1949, p. 123.
— *The Nature and Destiny of Man*, vols. 1–2, New York: Scribner 1941–43, vol. 1,
    p. 46; pp. 80–6; p. 150; pp. 175–83.
Tillich, Paul, *Love, Power, and Justice*, New York and London: Oxford University
    Press 1954, pp. 31–2; p. 118.
— *The Protestant Era*, trans. by J.L. Adams, Chicago: University of Chicago Press
    1948, p. 88; p. 193.
— *Systematic Theology I*, Chicago: University of Chicago Press 1951, p. 12; p. 57;
    p. 119; p. 154; p. 165; p. 215; p. 275.

## III. Secondary Literature on King's Relation to Kierkegaard

Ansbro, John, "Martin Luther King's Debt to Hegel," *The Owl of Minerva*, vol. 26,
    no. 1, 1994, pp. 98–100.
Sharma, Mohan Lal, "Martin Luther King: Modern America's Greatest Theologian
    of Social Action," *The Journal of Negro History*, vol. 53, no. 3, 1968, pp. 257–63.

# György Lukács:

## From a Tragic Love Story to a Tragic Life Story

András Nagy

In the studio apartment of György Lukács (1885–1971), overlooking the Danube, in the small room left the same way as it was when he got up the last time to walk to his bed before his death, right behind the writing table, packed with manuscripts, books, notes, and cigars, there is the *oeuvre* of Søren Kierkegaard,[1] just on the level that is easiest to reach by hand, right as one stands up from the armchair and turns to the bookshelves. For Hegel one has to bend, for Goethe to walk to the other room, even Marx and Engels are at a distance.

The Kierkegaard edition is the very same one the young Lukács obtained and used (printed with Gothic characters);[2] however, its meaning had radically changed throughout the (nearly seven!) decades that Lukács spent reading, understanding, absorbing, and interpreting Kierkegaard. His reaction to Kierkegaard's texts ranged from a total identification to the passionate rejection of the author and his *oeuvre*. The concrete copies of the individual books may have disappeared and appeared again, since Lukács' library had nearly as turbulent a history as its owner. He established his library first in Budapest, and then selected volumes followed him to Florence, later to Heidelberg then back to Budapest, but after a short while either the same books or newly bought copies[3] "escaped" with him to Vienna (after the fall of the Hungarian Soviet Republic in 1919), then to Berlin; he took few books with him to Moscow after the Nazi takeover, even fewer to Tashkent during the evacuation during World War II, and finally, in post-war Budapest the time came to re-establish the once existing unique collection of his books. These were important and dramatic "wandering years" for Lukács, yet he maintained a constant reference to Kierkegaard, as to the most faithful travel companion.

---

[1]     Lukács' apartment was turned into the Lukács Archive (of the Institute of Philosophy of the Hungarian Academy of Science), located at 2 Belgrád rakpart, 5th floor, Budapest.

[2]     The first volume Lukács owned by Kierkegaard was *Der Augenblick*, which appeared as vol. 12 (in 2nd printing), in Sören Kierkegaard, *Gesammelte Werke*, trans. and ed. by Hermann Gottsched and Christoph Schrempf, Jena: Diederichs 1909–22. The last work he owned by Kierkegaard was *Über den Begriff der Ironie: mit ständiger Rücksicht auf Sokrates*, which was published in 1961 as vol. 31 in Sören Kierkegaard, *Gesammelte Werke*, vols. 1–32, trans. by Emmanuel Hirsch, Düsseldorf and Cologne: Diederichs 1950–74. The catalogue of the library was available also from Lukács' time and later the Archive composed one as well.

[3]     Many books were obtained from antiquarian bookstores, as marks on the volumes suggest.

Even if the Danish philosopher's influence was probably the most visible in the social-political sphere for Lukács, the ways of understanding and thus the consequences of interpreting Kierkegaard well exceeded society and politics. This was partly due to the ideological concept of Marxism-Leninism, in which philosophy, ethics, aesthetics, and many more disciplines were integrated into a forcefully coherent and hierarchical "scientific *Weltanschauung.*" On the other hand, Lukács from the very beginning (thus before his communist "conversion") had read and "translated" for himself Kierkegaard not only as a philosopher, a writer, or a theologian but also as a master, sometimes as a model, even an example to follow, and later as a dangerous case to reject. To be able to do this, he had to disregard Kierkegaard's warnings against such interpretations. Thus Lukács ignored the use of pseudonyms and masks, and so for him everyone was Kierkegaard, from Johannes de silentio to Johannes Climacus and Anti-Climacus, from Victor Eremita to Vigilius Haufniensis, from the author of very personal journal entries to the militant public critic of Christendom. While Lukács was receptive to the concept of incognitos (particularly to moral ones in his late youth), and as a literary critic he understood the role of borrowed personalities when experimenting with ideas, concepts and, consequently, with human beings, nonetheless for him the whole *oeuvre* of Kierkegaard was somewhat "homogeneous."[4] In this manner one of the most important features of the Danish thinker remained beyond the horizon of Lukács' understanding. He tried to force coherence onto the whole body of texts that was certainly unsuited for this. Later he paid dearly for this blind spot, and so did the society he lived in, and wanted to change, and this was just the case when politics and social issues started to play the lead in this controversial interpretative process.

But at least in one sense this approach was faithful to Kierkegaard himself since the Danish thinker once angrily emphasized that Christ did not sweat blood on the cross for the habilitations of "Privatdozents."[5] Lukács also had strong reasons for taking very seriously thinking and conclusively the messianic vocation, even as a question of life and death. Yet it is also true that he did so, once his attempt at a habilitation as a "Privatdozent" at the University of Heidelberg was rejected. In the application his topic for the exam was Kierkegaard's criticism of Hegel.

*I.*

Kierkegaard's most direct influence was on the young Lukács, from his late adolescence throughout his most important formative years, up to his famous "conversion" to communism, at the age of 33. This was not only connected but sometimes even originated in the thinking of the Danish philosopher, who regularly and decisively appeared at the crossroads of his life. This happened only later when social and political issues became crucially important, since at the beginning his lonely, melancholic—Kierkegaardian—characteristics were predominant (and also

---

[4]     In the essays of his youth references and bibliographical data were not necessary, and later he referred only to the Collected Works of Kierkegaard (in German), but there is no mention of any of the pseudonyms.

[5]     *SKS* 25, 305–6, NB29:14 / *JP* 4, 4495.

the wealth of his father that allowed him to dedicate his life entirely to his studies and to his moods). In his early years Kierkegaardian philosophy was understood by the young Lukács not as a field of study or as a research project for the future, but as the kind of thinking that influences one's mentality, behavior, taste, and orientation—including inspirations, perspectives, and even when one is facing paradoxes or in love.

The very first public reference to Kierkegaard in Lukács' life and possibly in Hungarian as well, was connected to Henrik Ibsen (1828–1906), an extremely popular playwright in Hungary and an idol of the young Lukács, who was involved in the "Thalia Society" a group of talented young people whose goal was to translate, stage, and inspire contemporary drama. Ibsen was also a great filter of Kierkegaardian thoughts and paradoxes, and at the same time also a living classic. At the age of 18 Lukács visited Ibsen, with his father paying for his trip as a birthday present. In his 1906 article Kierkegaard was referred to in the context of contemporary Scandinavian drama, yet with the emphasis that he could "best express the extremes,"[6] and probably these characteristics were the most important for the young Lukács, and remained so also in the long run.

His knowledge of the texts and his—at that time probably limited—familiarity with the biography of the Danish thinker was based on a few writings available in translation, mainly in German (though Lukács read French and English as well), that the Hungarian thinker could find in university libraries, bookshops, and in philosophical magazines. But soon he began collecting the *oeuvre* of Kierkegaard, a process that very probably continued until his death. It seems, however, that the collection was never complete, nor was his knowledge of the entire *oeuvre* of Kierkegaard.[7]

Lukács was familiar with the work and activity of Georg Brandes (1842–1927), as one of the most important interpreters of Kierkegaard. However, Rudolph Kassner (1873–1959), the Austrian philosopher and writer, was more inspiring for him, when he composed his first essay on the Danish thinker. Scandinavian literature was not only known by Lukács but at that time was generally fashionable as well. He often referred to Jens Peter Jacobsen's (1847–85) writings, Henrik Pontopiddan's (1857–1943) short stories became the subject of one of his essays,[8] and he passionately read August Strindberg's (1849–1912) plays, since they expressed the deepest despair about the turn-of-the-century gender crises. However, Kierkegaard was the who one embraced the most important issues Lukács was dealing with at the time, including the role and meaning of philosophy, and its consequences for everyday

---

[6]     György Lukács, "Gondolatok Ibsen Henrikről," in *Ifjúkori művek* [Juvenilia], ed. by Árpád Tímár, Budapest: Magvető Kiadó 1977 p. 92. (English translation: "Thoughts on Henrik Ibsen," in *The Lukács Reader*, ed. by Arpad Kadarkay, Oxford and Cambridge, Massachusetts: Blackwell Publishers 1995, pp. 97–112; originally published in the Hungarian sociological periodical *Huszadik Század*, in August 1906.)

[7]     The books published by Diederichs Verlag, in German translation did not include the complete *oeuvre*. Neither Lukács' catalogue, nor the Archive's, refers to the whole set. Lukács often did go to libraries and borrow books; however, he owned the volumes he frequently referred to, and many works remained unmentioned.

[8]     György Lukács, "Pontopiddan novellái," in *Ifjúkori művek*, pp. 489–90.

life. Kierkegaard expressed the most crucial existential contradictions and boiled all these down to very personal decisions that could include writing, life, love, and the future.

The book in which the famous essay "The Foundering of Form against Life: Sören Kierkegaard and Regine Olsen" was later published, had the meaningful title *The Soul and the Forms: Experiments,*[9] referring to the most important categories for the young Lukács and to the literary form he preferred, since experiment is synonymous with essay. The essay on Kierkegaard was one of the most profound and probably the best written. Its rich "Jugendstil" style, with the hidden quotations and emphatic comments, shaped dilemmas of love, life, writing, and thinking, and staged all these in early nineteenth-century Copenhagen. This was also one of the few pieces of writing the young Lukács could publish in the most prestigious literary magazine of the time *Nyugat* (Occident) in 1910; this journal often rejected the promising young thinker's works because of his German-like argumentation, obscure style, and heavy literary manners. The text was crucial for the author himself since it was inspired by his own love affair at that time with the young painter Irma Seidler (1883–1911), whom Lukács was attracted to and also afraid of. He was probably afraid not of the woman but of the consequences of a fulfilled love, which is something he expresses in the essay: "Perhaps something inside him knew that happiness—if it was attainable—would paralyze and made him sterile forever."[10] Irma was fascinated by Lukács and made several attempts to force him to make a decision about their common future, but when it turned out to be in vain, she married one of her colleagues, who offered her more than beautiful letters, interesting essays, and one kiss in Florence, on the dark Ponte Vecchio.

The core of Lukács' dilemma was exposed right at the beginning of the essay, namely, by the "value of gesture! In other words: the value of form in life."[11] The question was whether this can be measured and can make life itself more intense. Lukács understood Kierkegaard as the one for whom "reality had nothing to do with possibilities,"[12] and who dedicated all his life to the one and only gesture. Lukács emphasized its importance:

> Perhaps the gesture—to express myself in Kierkegaard's dialectics—is the paradox: the point where reality and possibility, matter and air, the finite and infinite, form and life intersect….the gesture is the leap by which the soul passes from one into the other, and

---

[9]     György Lukács, "Sören Kierkegaard és Regine Olsen," *Nyugat*, no. 6, 1910, pp. 378–87 (in *Ifjúkori művek*, pp. 287–303; published also in Lukács, *A lélek és a formák. Kísérletek* [Soul and Form. Experiments], Budapest: Franklin 1910. pp. 129–50; English translation: "The Foundering of Form against Life. Sören Kierkegaard and Regine Olsen," in *The Lukács Reader*, pp. 11–25).

[10]     Lukács, "Sören Kierkegaard és Regine Olsen," p. 382 ("Sören Kierkegaard and Regine Olsen," p. 16.)

[11]     Lukács, "Sören Kierkegaard és Regine Olsen," p. 378. ("Sören Kierkegaard and Regine Olsen," p. 11.)

[12]     Ibid.

by which, leaving the ever relative facts of life, it reaches the eternal certainty of forms. In short, the gesture is that unique leap by which the absolutes become possible in life.[13]

To explain his thesis Lukács recalled the history of "Sören Aabye Kierkegaard" becoming engaged to the 18-year-old daughter of "State Councillor Olsen" in 1840,[14] and then suddenly breaking the engagement and leaving for Berlin, with the decision to play the role of a heartless seducer, an eccentric thinker, to be admired for his spirituality and provoking anger and hatred for his cruelty. Later in Kierkegaard's life, Lukács added, he displayed a similar mentality in attacking the State Church and provoking the same extremes publicly as he did in his personal life.[15]

"What really happened here?" asked Lukács, for whom all of Kierkegaard's writings, letters, and diaries "made the explanations easier and, at the same time, made it harder to understand."[16] Instead of explanations there is the universal meaning of the pure "gesture" Lukács claimed, following Kassner's argumentation, with the conclusion that the Danish thinker had make "a poem of his life."[17] To do so he had to reject the love of Regine Olsen, because he was "a whole eternity too old for her,"[18] but not to confess it, Kierkegaard had to put on the mask of a scoundrel that covered the real face of the penitent. Following this logic, Lukács made the distinction between "absolute" life in opposition to "relative" life, and thus anticipated the "authentic life" as presented by twentieth-century existentialist thinking, as Lucien Goldmann highlighted it, reading Lukács in the context of twentieth-century continental philosophy.[19] This separation was the basis of the "spheres of possibilities,"[20] Lukács continued, that were called stages "as Kierkegaard put it" separated from each other wholly and totally; the connection between each is "the miracle, the leap, the sudden metamorphoses of the entire being of a man."[21]

Kierkegaard's honesty, in Lukács' eyes, was that he saw absolute categories in life instead of half-hearted compromises; but is it possible to be honest against life? Lukács asked. Is it really possible "to make a poem of his life"?[22] Yet everything that happened "was done for Regine's sake,"[23] "to save her life,"[24] since he would have been

---

[13]     Lukács, "Sören Kierkegaard és Regine Olsen," p. 378. ("Sören Kierkegaard and Regine Olsen," p. 12.)

[14]     Ibid.

[15]     Ibid.

[16]     Ibid.

[17]     Lukács, "Sören Kierkegaard és Regine Olsen," p. 379. ("Sören Kierkegaard and Regine Olsen," p. 13.)

[18]     Ibid..

[19]     See Lucien Goldmann, untitled paper in *Kierkegaard vivant*, Paris: Gallimard 1966, pp. 125–64.

[20]     Lukács, "Sören Kierkegaard és Regine Olsen," p. 381. ("Sören Kierkegaard and Regine Olsen," p. 14.)

[21]     Ibid.

[22]     Lukács, "Sören Kierkegaard és Regine Olsen," p. 379. ("Sören Kierkegaard and Regine Olsen," p. 13.)

[23]     Lukács, "Sören Kierkegaard és Regine Olsen," p. 381. ("Sören Kierkegaard and Regine Olsen," p. 15.)

[24]     Ibid.

too heavy for her, and she too light for him; and the two could be fatal. Kierkegaard was worried that Regine's lightness "of spirit could have after all redeemed his great melancholy,"[25] and they could have been happy for the rest of their life. "But what would have become of him if life deprived him of his unhappiness?"[26] Lukács asked. In this sense Kierkegaard was the "sentimental Socrates," the one who only knows loving, yet he is looking for the love, in which the "object of love would not stand in love's way."[27] How can love "become absolute?"[28] Who is the one whom it is possible to love in a way that one can "never to be proved right"?[29]

Kierkegaard's answer is God. Yet Lukács does not follow this logic in the transcendent direction. Deep religious belief was unknown for him, having been born in an assimilated Jewish family, in which traditions and convictions were substituted mainly by social rituals. Yet unconditional devotion was attractive for him, and the secularization of this logic later played an important role in his thinking. Regine Olsen was a step on the way to God, as Lukács interprets Kierkegaard's conclusion, and the sense of guilt made this process more dramatic. "I thank you for never having understood me," confesses Kierkegaard in the essay,[30] since that was necessary for his secret heroism, for him to save her for life. But Kierkegaard failed on a larger scale since he could not "create a form" of his own life. "I am struggling in vain," he wrote in Lukács' words, "my life will, after all, have been a poet's life and no more,"[31] thus "the absolute" will be missing forever.

Death took Kierkegaard at the peak of his fight, as he was confronting "the Christianity of his age." By then there was nothing else in his life but this fight, and he had nothing else to offer as a final sacrifice, but his life. Still, the question remains open whether his passing away was really and deeply necessary or if it was accidental, without destiny playing any role. If so, then even the most important gesture of Kierkegaard would not be a gesture at all—as Lukács closed his essay—but only an unanswered question.[32]

Lukács' interpretation of Kierkegaard was extremely personal, focusing on dilemmas of the young Hungarian author himself concerning "life" versus "work," a common dilemma for many intellectuals and artists from Thomas Mann to Otto Weininger. Problems of the same genre and often with a similar logic inspired many other essays of *The Soul and the Forms*, on a variety of subjects. When it was finally published, the book was dedicated to Irma Seidler, and in this way Lukács in a sense

---

25    Lukács, "Sören Kierkegaard és Regine Olsen," p. 381. ("Sören Kierkegaard and Regine Olsen," p. 16.)
26    Ibid.
27    Lukács, "Sören Kierkegaard és Regine Olsen," p. 382. ("Sören Kierkegaard and Regine Olsen," p. 17.)
28    Ibid.
29    Ibid.
30    Lukács, "Sören Kierkegaard és Regine Olsen," p. 383. ("Sören Kierkegaard and Regine Olsen," p. 18.)
31    Lukács, "Sören Kierkegaard és Regine Olsen," pp. 386–7. ("Sören Kierkegaard and Regine Olsen," p. 23.)
32    Lukács, "Sören Kierkegaard és Regine Olsen," p. 387. ("Sören Kierkegaard and Regine Olsen," p. 24.)

gave the work back to the hands from which it was received. However, the muse of the early essays did not follow the path her Danish model took by marrying her suitor and living the happy life of the "blonds and blue-eyed."[33] Ms. Siedler, after a brief and unhappy marriage, tried to re-establish her relationship with Lukács, with no success, however, and so in a bout of depression she committed suicide, throwing herself into the Danube in 1911 on a warm spring night.[34]

Lukács was deeply shocked by the tragedy and felt guilty for Irma Seidler's premature death, even if he was not the only person to bear responsibility.[35] When Irma had got married Lukács himself considered suicide in an unsent letter, but this time he understood and interpreted her final departure as a death sentence for him as well. In "The Poverty of Spirit," in a dialogical essay[36] using Kierkegaardian terminology, he drew the conclusion that human sacrifice was needed. Over the horizon of *Either/Or* then appeared *Fear and Trembling*; the sacrifice of Abraham would remain determinative for Lukács for the rest of his long life.

In the preface of the book to be published soon after Irma's death, reference was made to Kierkegaard to explain Lukács' philosophical vocation, since the Danish thinker with his imaginative journals and stories provided a model for the young Hungarian author.[37] Then Lukács bitterly added that any given age can only produce a genius like Kierkegaard but is unable to understand and appreciate him.

## II.

It took quite a while for Lukács to overcome the tragedy and to be able to continue his work, while he realized that even the despair, loss, and sense of guilt might and did turn to his benefit as a thinker. This was the point when new and different Kierkegaardian categories were integrated into Lukács' thinking, such as human sacrifice, the need for an "absolute" in life, or against it, even ideas such as using living creatures and their passions and feelings for "human experiments," and conclusively all these determined his morality and mentality.[38] The way was thus paved also for a new and overwhelming impulse that Lukács received both intellectually and emotionally at this time: Russian literature and philosophy, as revealed in the novels

---

[33]     The category for the simple and happy ones in Thomas Mann's story, *Tonio Kröger.*
[34]     On the tragedy see Ágnes Heller, "Lukács György és Seidler Irma" [György Lukács and Irma Seidler], in her *Portrévázlatok az etika történetéből* [Portrait Sketches from the History of Ethics], Budapest: Gondolat 1976, pp. 385–422. See also my essay-novel on the affair, András Nagy, *Kedves Lukács* [Dear Lukács], Budapest: Magvető Kiadó 1984.
[35]     Besides her ex-husband, the writer, poet, and aesthete Béla Balázs—Lukács' close friend of the time—was also shortly involved with her, no less controversially than the beloved and hated "Gyuri" (the nickname for Lukács).
[36]     György Lukács, "A lelki szegénységről," in *Ifjúkori művek*, pp. 537–52. (English translation: "On Poverty of Spirit," in *The Lukács Reader*, pp. 42–57.)
[37]     György Lukács, "Az esszé lényegéről és formájáról. Levél a kísérletről" [On Essence and Form of the Essay. Letter about the Experiment], in Lukács, *Ifjúkori művek*, p. 306 (the essay was first published in Lukács' essay collection *A lélek és a formák. Kísérletek*, pp. 5–23.
[38]     See András Nagy, "Abraham the Communist," in *Kierkegaard—The Self in Society*, ed. by George Pattison and Steven Shakespeare, London: Macmillan 1998, pp. 196–220.

of Dostoevsky and further elaborated by the thinkers of the so-called Russian "Silver Age." Similar dilemmas were present in Kierkegaard's works, although in a totally different intellectual and spiritual context.[39]

The parallels were sometimes even striking, as Lukács highlighted when reviewing a collection of Solovyov's essays in 1915,[40] emphasizing the strong influence of Kierkegaard on one of the key figures of Russian religious thinking—who was a probable model for Dostoevsky's Alyosha Karamasov.[41] This new orientation was soon enforced and even reshaped by an overwhelming new passion, a turbulent love story with the Ukrainian-Russian revolutionary Elena Grabenko,[42] with whom Lukács had fallen in love and later married, as if "marrying Dostoevsky"[43] by her.

At the time of the "complete sinfulness,"[44] as Lukács characterized his age before and during World War I, the need for a totally new philosophical horizon, even for an earthly "redemption," became more and more important for the young Hungarian philosopher's orientation. At the very same time Lukács, however, was considering moving to Heidelberg, the cozy German university town which was attractive for him due to the inviting spiritual atmosphere created by Max Weber (1864–1920), his wife and his circle of outstanding intellectuals. Focusing on a university career, Lukács started to work out a systematic study in aesthetics, to demonstrate his abilities as a scholar in the German sense.[45] Meanwhile he also wanted to summarize his own *Weltanschauung* that could include his ethics, aesthetics, and metaphysics. The ambitious projects were interrupted, both the aesthetic system and the planned book on Dostoevsky. The introduction of the latter was finally written and then became not only famous but influential as well, as *The Theory of the Novel*.[46]

---

[39]     On Kierkegaard's influence on Russian literature, see András Nagy, "Kierkegaard in Russia," in *Kierkegaard Revisited*, ed. by Jon Stewart and Niels Jørgen Cappelørn, Berlin and New York: Walter de Gruyter 1997 (*Kierkegaard Studies Monograph Series*, vol. 1), pp. 107–38.

[40]     György Lukács, "Vlagyimir Szolovjov, Válogatott művek, 1. kötet" [Vladimir Solovyev, Selected Works, vol. 1], in *Ifjúkori művek*, pp. 622–3.

[41]     See Endre Török, *Világtudat és regényforma* [Sense of World and Form of Novel], Budapest: Akadémiai Kiadó 1979.

[42]     Elena Andreievna Grabenko, first wife of Lukács, painter and teacher; participated in the 1905 revolution, later emigrated to the West, met and married Lukács and followed him when he emigrated after 1919. In the 1920s she returned to the USSR and later disappeared, probably in the Gulag.

[43]     Béla Balázs' remark, in *Napló 1903–1914* [Journals 1903–1914], Budapest: Magvető 1982, p. 616.

[44]     The term was used by Fichte and recycled by Lukács. See, for example, György Lukács "Novalis. Jegyzetek a romantikus életfilozófiáról" [Novalis. Notes on the Romantic Philosophy of Life], *Ifjúkori művek*, p. 131.

[45]     The systematic studies of aesthetics were published as György Lukács, *Heidelbergi esztétika és művészetfilozófia* [Heidelbergian Aesthetics and Philosophy of Art], Budapest: Magvető 1975.

[46]     Georg Lukács, "Die Theorie des Romans. Ein geschichtsphilosophischer Versuch über die Formen der großen Epik," *Zeitschrift für Aesthetik und Allgemeine Kunstwissenschaft*, vol. 11, nos. 3–4, 1916, pp. 1–89. (English translation: *The Theory of the Novel: A Historico-*

A major part of the book was only drafted, left unelaborated and forgotten, and these notes and sketches resurfaced posthumously. New philological research in connection with the critical edition[47] proves, however, that the references to Kierkegaard in the unfinished work and its parallels with that of Dostoevsky were of crucial importance, not only for the philosophical development of the young Lukács, but mainly for his radically changing political and social views as well. The concept of the so-called "second ethics," for example, the first being the one based on the Kantian ethical system (called "first ethic" by Lukács), which determines the acts of the heroes ("saints," great sinners, terrorists, etc.) of the Russian writer, is also based on Kierkegaard's views,[48] creating a mystical, unconditional, and rationally inexplicable system of laws that does not exclude sin either. On Lukács' reading of *The Sickness unto Death*, this shows itself as "reality," infiltrated through despair, with the questioning of faith, and sometimes even flirting with crime, thus in need of an incognito. The Kantian—first—ethics becomes "temptation," when Lukács analyzes Abraham's choice in *Fear and Trembling*, the author concludes in the notes that the antithesis of crime is not virtue—this would only be pagan—but faith.[49]

Atheism, according to this logic, is the last step before faith and soon will be crucial for Lukács, who refers to his Danish model: Regine Olsen brings "the breakthrough in everything,"[50] he argues. Yet faith does not mean "pure Christianity" at all, only faithlessness can ever lead to religion, as Lukács interprets Kierkegaard's *Stages* in his drafts. Conclusively, it is impossible to accept any kind of traditional form of belief since for Lukács the Danish thinker is not Christian either. The Hungarian thinker goes even further when stating that Kierkegaard "hates" any kind of "institutionalization" of faith, particularly the symbiosis of state and church.[51] Lukács interprets the Danish thinker's views about "objective spirit" as it is in itself "unconscious despair,"[52] so the "victory" of institutions is only a "trick of the Satan."[53] This leads beyond the Danish thinker's horizon, as dramatically and desperately staged in Ivan Karamasov's poem, *The Grand Inquisitor*.

The parallels of Dostoevskyian dilemmas, heroes, and philosophical questions with Kierkegaardian texts create a unique philosophical, ethical, and theological texture for the young Lukács to use when presenting his *Weltanschauung*. Yet time was not in favor of such undertakings, neither the age of the Hungarian thinker,

*Philosophical Essay on the Forms of Great Epic Literature*, trans. by Anna Bostock, Cambridge, Massachusetts: MIT Press 1971.)

47    Originally reconstructed and published as Georg Lukács, *Dostojewski, Notizen und Entwürfe*, ed. by J. Kristóf Nyíri (on the basis of Lukács' *Nachlaß*), Budapest: Akadémiai Kiadó 1985. The new edition however, edited by Miklós Mesterházi, includes many years of philological works and offers a broad overview of Lukács' thinking, in György Lukács, *A regény elmélete—Dosztojevszkij-jegyzetek* [Theory of the Novel—Notes on Dostoevsky], Budapest: Gond 2009.

48    Lukács, *A regény elmélete*, p. 106.

49    Ibid., p. 375.

50    Ibid., p. 251.

51    His reading of *The Moment* proves this; see ibid., pp. 297–8.

52    Ibid., p. 243.

53    Ibid., p. 251.

nor the age he lived in. Probably the fragmentary form was the most adequate for his views, since any systematic attempt could have undermined his unusual—often literary—logic and argumentation. It is also important to add that neither Kierkegaard was represented by his whole *oeuvre* in the drafts, nor Dostoevsky. Besides the abovementioned works of the Danish thinker, only *Philosophical Fragments*, *The Concept of Anxiety*, the *Concluding Unscientific Postscript*, and *Practice in Christianity* are referred to, and a volume with his journals.[54] Regarding Kierkegaard's *oeuvre* as a whole, Lukács briefly mentions Harald Höffding's book *Sören Kierkegaard as Philosopher*[55] (and earlier Rudoph Kassner). The Hungarian thinker could have read other texts by him and about him, but for his focus only the selected original texts and interpretations were instrumental.

His interpretation, however, can be traced by his future activity, when he was inspired by the time of complete sinfulness and was looking for a way out of it. This also helped the young Lukács to get rid of his youthful—Kierkegaardian—melancholy, that seemed to be related to the emotional state called "*acedia*" in medieval cloisters; Kierkegaard's father used to call that "silent despair."[56] But there were no cloisters for him any more, "I became a fool in the eye of the world"[57] quotes Lukács from *Practice in Christianity*. Soon the Hungarian thinker will decide that his role is to become a "sinner"[58] in the eye of the world, at least this way he would be able to solve crucial problems in practice that were unsolvable for him theoretically.

## III.

Other important parts of Lukács' draft would become significant in the years to come, like his notes about German philosophers and the war,[59] which preceded the development of his view of the responsibility that German intellectuals had in historical matters, which would be elaborated in his book *The Destruction of Reason* years later. Paradoxically enough, Kierkegaard is included in this tradition, regardless of his ethnic background.[60] Lukács disregarded his own as well and for a while wanted to find his home in this tradition. This also reflected his alien situation in Hungarian philosophical circles; thus with a group of significant outsiders Lukács

---

[54]    *Sören Kierkegaard. Buch der Richters. Seine Tagebücher 1833–1855*, trans. and ed. by Hermann Gottsched, Jena and Leipzig: Diederichs 1905.

[55]    Harald Höffding, *Sören Kierkegaard als Philosoph*, Stuttgart: Fromman 1912 [1896]. (Originally published as Harald Høffding, *Søren Kierkegaard som Filosof*, Copenhagen: Philipsen 1892.)

[56]    Lukács, *A regény elmélete—Dosztojevszkij-jegyzetek*, p. 359.

[57]    Ibid., p. 359.

[58]    Lukács referred to Hebbel's *Judith* as asking "And if God has posited between me and the world the crime, who am I to withdraw myself from His will?" See Lukács' letter written to Paul Ernst on May 4, 1915 in *Lukács Görgy Levelezése*, ed. by Éva Fekete and Éva Karádl, Budapest: Magveto 1981, pp. 595–6.

[59]    Lukács, "Jegyzetek a német filozófusokról és a háborúról" [Notes About German Philosophers and the War], in his *A regény elmélete—Dosztojevszkij-jegyzetek*, p. 451.

[60]    Ibsen will be a "German" poet in this sense as well. See ibid.

established the so-called "Sunday Circle"[61] in Budapest, which discussed important philosophical, aesthetic, and literary issues. Meanwhile, the young philosopher spent more and more time in Hungary from 1915 on, where he still continued to plan his career as a "Privatdozent" at the University of Heidelberg, completing also the paperwork for his Habilitation. His close friends in the German university town, Max Weber and Emil Lask tried to discourage him from applying, arguing that any kind of systematic work would be unsuitable for a "born essayist" like Lukács and thus it would be a mistake for him to take a university job;[62] however, the dean of the Faculty had already been approached by Lukács and, probably impressed as well, was invited to Hungary. New philological research reveals Professor Eberhard Gothein (1853–1923) could not only enjoy the hospitality of the wealthy senior Lukács in Budapest, having a driver and a car at his disposal, attending artistic and cultural events, but there was a special focus on his business interests in the Austro-Hungarian Monarchy, carefully cultivated by the father of the candidate.[63]

In the themes offered by Lukács for his Habilitation exam Kierkegaard was included with his criticism on Hegel, the difference between *Gelten* and *Sollen* was also on the list of May 1918, as well as the phenomenology of transcendental philosophy. The preparations were well on their way.

At the same time the final and complete military catastrophe was approaching Lukács' homeland, while the social and political crises also radically deepened. Strikes, demonstrations and different types of manifestations became more and more frequent, in which anarchism, syndicalism, and communism gained significant popularity. In the turbulent times another critic of Hegel appeared on the horizon, Karl Marx. In an interview in 1918 about authors influential for his thinking, Lukács still laid stress on Kierkegaard who "accompanied me from the very beginning in my intellectual development."[64] However, another name was also emphasized: "I have read Marx this time also as an enduring value."[65]

In spite of the strengthening attraction, Lukács nonetheless found unsolvable the ethical contradiction of the communist movement. In his essay *Bolshevism as a Moral Problem* the Hungarian thinker rejects the hypothesis that one could "arrive at the truth by lying,"[66] referring to Dostoevsky's *Crime and Punishment*. However,

---

[61]     Participants were Karl Mannheim, Arnold Hauser, Charles de Tolnay, Frederick Antal, Karl Polányi, and several others, the young Béla Bartók performed some of his new pieces at the circle. See *A vasárnapi kör* [The Sunday Circle], ed. by Éva Karádi and Erzsébet Vezér, Budapest: Gondolat 1980.

[62]     Júlia Bendl, "Lukács György élete a századfordulótól 1918-ig" [The Life of Lukács from the Turn of the Century until 1918], in Budapest: Scientia Humana Társulás 1994, p. 2.

[63]     This information is based on archival research at the University of Heidelberg done by Júlia Bendl, see ibid., pp. 3–4.

[64]     György Lukács, "Könyvek könyve" [Book of the Books], in *Ifjúkori művek*, p. 767.

[65]     Ibid.

[66]     György Lukács, "A bolsevizmus mint erkölcsi probléma," in his *Forradalomban: Cikkek, tanulmányok, 1918–1919* [In Revolution: Essays and Studies, 1918–1919], ed. by Miklós Mesterházi, Budapest: Magvető Kiadó 1987, pp. 36–41. (English translation: "Bolshevism as an Ethical Problem," in *The Lukács Reader*, pp. 216–22; first published in *Szabadgondolat*, 1918, pp. 228–32.)

besides reading Marx and Dostoevsky, Lukács continued reading Kierkegaard as well, and nearly at the same time he completed his other article "Tactics and Ethics."[67] In the short but important text Lukács seems to find his way out of the complete sinfulness by means of the concept of the sacrifice. The object of the sacrifice could be what was dearest for him, his morality, his intellect, and his career. Morality is not a question any more since it was not an issue for Kierkegaard; however, the secularization of the paradigm makes the argumentation utterly different from its origin.

At the same time at the University of Heidelberg the Habilitation process concluded that a born German was more welcome as a "Privatdozent," than a (Jewish) born Hungarian. The involvement of Dean Gothein backfired in the debates of the Faculty, and in December 1918 the new Dean Professor Domaszewski asked Lukács to withdraw his request. The Hungarian thinker seemed to lightheartedly accept it. "I have given myself to the disposition of the Hungarian government," he answered.[68] He demanded only the return of his documents, books, and the money he deposited for the process in a letter signed as Georg von Lukács. The ex-candidate used his baron title at the very same time, when he finally joined the Hungarian Communist Party.

This was the gesture Lukács already wrote about in his essay on the Danish thinker, but in a radically changed meaning. Later the Hungarian philosopher referred to Kierkegaard as the one helping him "to lose God,"[69] and thus the secularization originated also in his understanding of the melancholic Copenhagen seducer. This final and fatal loss of the transcendental horizon was also described in some contemporary Hungarian novels, written by fellow communists, demonstrating the explosive mixture of transcendental logic, earthly redemption, and historical conditions. "To believe is different from to know; to believe means just a consciously irrational mentality that one follows when facing one's life," thus the author reconstructs the debates in the Budapest House of Soviets in the novel *The Optimists*.[70] In another book entitled *Visegrádi Street*[71] the same group of intellectuals is called or rather stigmatized as "moralists," burdened by their ethical problems that make fighting the class struggle even more difficult.

---

[67]     György Lukács, "Taktika és etika," in *Forradalomban*, p. 132. (English translation in *Tactics and Ethics. Political Essays 1919–1929*, vols. 1–2, trans. from German by Michael McColgan, New York: Harper & Row 1972–75, vol. 1., pp. 3–11; originally published in the essay collection entitled *Taktika és ethika*, Budapest: Közoktatásiügyi Népbiztosság Kiadása 1919, pp. 5–13.)

[68]     Bendl, "Lukács György élete a századfordulótól 1918-ig," p. 7. One of the contradictions is that in December 1918 the bourgeois revolutionary leadership was in government, soon to be undermined and then replaced by the communist revolution, in which Lukács played an important role.

[69]     György Lukács, *Curriculum vitae*, ed. by János Ambrus, Budapest: Magvető Kiadó 1982, p. 281.

[70]     See Ervin Sinkó, *Optimisták: történelmi regény 1918–19-ből*, Budapest: Magvető 1965 [Újvidék: Testvériség Egylet 1953–55], p. 692.

[71]     József Lengyel, *Visegrádi utca*, Budapest: Kossuth 1957. The title of the work refers to the place where the Hungarian Communist Party was established.

Lukács' conclusion was beyond tragedy, as he interpreted Abraham's sacrifice, in opposition of Agamemnon's, and it was also beyond understanding for those who do not believe. However, Lukács went further with his fatal prognosis, as "on the basis of a mystical morality one must become a cruel politician and thus violate the absolute commandment: 'Thou shall not kill!' "[72] In 1919 he became the Hungarian Red Army's political commissar,[73] and proved his hypothesis by ordering the execution of retreating soldiers. Shortly before his conversion Lukács described his situation as a choice between sins only, and the criterion is the greatness of the needed sacrifice. "But only the murder of those can be tragically moral who know, definitely and clearly know that killing is absolutely not allowed,"[74] he wrote. Thus Kierkegaard helped him not only to lose God, but also to lose his sense of morality, humanity, and solidarity. He would soon accuse the other tradition of emerging from the Danish thinker's legacy, German philosophy, of all these things.

*IV.*

After the fall of the communist republic in 1919 some of its leaders fled from Hungary. Lukács first left for Vienna (the ex-capital of the Austro-Hungarian Monarchy became "red" at that time), and then he moved to the safer Berlin. Post-war Germany was very different from how Lukács imagined his future home to be previously, although he, now a devoted communist,[75] was also very different from the "Privatdozent" he wanted to be. History played the lead role, and Lukács' concept of history was determined by Hegel now, although he arrived at Hegel from Kierkegaard.[76]

Living in Berlin during the radicalization of the political and intellectual climate, the communist Lukács was surprised by the Nazis, growing in strength, and soon became convinced that the road of modern bourgeois philosophy was altogether leading toward fascism. To theoretically justify his political views and to play an active role in the upcoming intellectual clashes, he finally wanted to create a system. The idea and then the book conceived in this process was *The Destruction of Reason*, the generalization of his Weimar experience by a Marxist analysis of contemporary Western philosophy. This also offered him a chance to give a "theoretical accounting of Kierkegaard."[77]

Lukács became a member of the German Communist Party and was instructed to remain in Berlin after the Nazi takeover in 1933, to prepare for clandestine

---

72   Lukács' letter to Paul Ernst, May 4, 1915, in *Lukács György levelezése*, p. 595.
73   After being the deputy cultural commissar of the Republic of Hungarian Soviets.
74   Lukács, "Taktika és etika," p. 132.
75   In this "capacity" he served as a model for Naphta in Thomas Mann's novel, *The Magic Mountain*. (They met in Vienna in 1922.) See Judith Marcus, *Lukács György és Thomas Mann*, Budapest: Áron Kiadó 2009, pp. 151–2.
76   György Lukács, "Utam Marxhoz" [My Road to Marx], in *Curriculum vitae*, pp. 227–38.
77   György Lukács, *Az ész trónfosztása. Az irracionalista filozófia kritikája*, Budapest: Magvető Kiadó 1978 [1954], p. 17. (English translation: *The Destruction of Reason*, trans. by Peter Palmer, London: Merlin Press 1980.)

activity. When it proved to be hopeless, Lukács was ordered to travel to Moscow.[78] Throughout this time he started to think over the origins, the nature, and the character of the entire tradition he once felt closest to, in the flow of the tragic metamorphoses of his once imagined intellectual *Heimat*. The question *How Fascist Philosophy Originated in Germany?* was posed in an important text and further elaborated in a study *How Germany Became the Center of Reactionary Philosophy?*[79] Answering these questions, Lukács wanted to prove the responsibility of the fragile bourgeois democracy (the Nazi victory was mainly possible by using democratic means) with special emphasis on the role intellectuals, writers, and philosophers played in paving the way for Nazism. According to Lukács' reading, determined by his communist *Weltanschauung* and shocked by the speed of events in Germany, the whole process of modern Western thinking was described as leading to Hitler.

To wholly understand the book it is important to notice that he started writing in Nazi-infected Berlin, continued in the Stalinist USSR (from 1933), then came the war, and the evacuation of Lukács and his wife interrupted the creative process, so he could only finish it in Hungary in the early 1950s. Since the book was intended to be more than propagandistic or purely ideological, analysis and historical background were also provided. Thus *The Destruction of Reason* survived Stalinism and for quite a while remained a communist reference book about Western thinking, translated into a dozen of languages, offering for many readers the only significant introduction to the philosophical traditions outside the official Marxist-Leninist(-Stalinist) ideology, including also Kierkegaard. The book's protagonist was Reason itself as losing power. Lukács offered a general overview of the history of irrationalism, in which the role of the Danish thinker was crucial.

Lukács' hypothesis was that the "barbarian turn was not sudden or by coincidence,"[80] since the German philosophical tradition he defined as "irrational" was the forerunner of Fascist *Weltanschauung*. Kierkegaard was the only thinker outside the ethnic tradition, analyzed in a longer chapter. The thesis was provided already in the Preface: "there is no innocent *Weltanschauung*."[81] The lost innocence was partly the consequence of the social position of the thinker who, consciously or unconsciously, defended his class interests. Lukács himself, a son of a wealthy banker was the best example to contradict the often mechanical—one could even say, "pragmatic"[82]—logic of matching ideas with the social background of its

[78] See György Lukács, *Megélt gondolkodás* [Thinking as Lived Through], Budapest: Magvető 1989, p. 220.
[79] About the changes of the titles see Dénes Zoltai, *Egy írástudó visszatér* [An Homme des Lettres Returns], Budapest: Kossuth Kiadó 1985, p. 139; see also László Sziklai, "Lukács György trónfosztása" [Dethroning of György Lukács], in *Ész, trónfosztás, demokrácia* [Reason, Dethroning, Democracy], ed. by János Boros, Pécs: Bramhauer 2005, pp. 81–92. In Hungarian in the title *Destruction* was translated as *Dethroning*.
[80] See *Lukács György élete képekben és dokumentumokban* [György Lukács' Life in Pictures and in Documents], ed. by Éva Fekete and Éva Karádi, Budapest: Corvina 1985, p. 175.
[81] Lukács, *Az ész trónfosztása*, p. 11.
[82] See János Boros, "Az ész trónfosztása után—az ész demokráciája" [After Dethroning Reason the Democracy of Reason], in *Ész, trónfosztás, demokrácia*, pp. 23–4. Boros refers to William James in this context.

representative, yet the social reading of modern thinking was not without interesting conclusions. Lukács emphasized that "Kierkegaard was honest enough to admit this openly, at least in his journals: 'My becoming a writer is basically due to my melancholy, to that and my money,'"[83] something that was probably familiar for the once melancholic and wealthy young Lukács as well. The "connection between a 'sublime' meta-social ethics and its vulgarly bourgeois financial basis"[84] was also given for the Marxist author who characterized Schopenhauer together with Kierkegaard and Nietzsche as "writers with private means, a breed which had become important to the bourgeois literature of capitalistically advanced countries long before. Kierkegaard and Nietzsche also enjoyed an independence stemming from a private income."[85]

Based on the social and historical interpretation of philosophy, modern irrationalism was born in the economic and social crises of the turn of the nineteenth century, when post-revolutionary intellectuals went in for "thermidorian moods of the post-revolutionary intelligentsia."[86] Lukács' focus was and remained on the changes in the social structure or more exactly in the class system, and how these were expressed in theory. The dissolution of the Hegelian tradition in this respect was dominant in the 1840s, and thus Kierkegaard was analyzed in parallel with Marx's and Engels' very different criticism of Hegel.[87]

The book offered an overview from the birth of irrationalism in German philosophy until Hitler, as if politics or politicians could so concretely determine theoretical thinking. According to this logic, one of Lukács' ex-idols Kierkegaard shared the responsibility for the present and even for the upcoming horrors. From Schelling to Max Weber, many of his masters (even benefactors like the latter) were included and analyzed in this context. The atmosphere of the birth of the book greatly contributed to the psychological motifs of the radical re-evaluation by the Hungarian thinker since the first version of *The Destruction of Reason* was done in "few weeks" as Lukács recalled.[88] By 1933 the early manuscript was probably completed; however, later in his life Lukács remembered that the book was "written more or less during the Second World War,"[89] and so the process took a longer time, yet still in extreme conditions. Finally, in the "Preface" of the first Hungarian edition of 1954 the author recalled that the writing started 25 years ago,[90] pushing back the beginning of the creative process into the late 1920s, and stretching its completion to after the death of Stalin.

---

[83]    Lukács, *Az ész trónfosztása*, p. 274. (*The Destruction of Reason*, p. 292.)
[84]    Lukács, *Az ész trónfosztása*, p. 275. (*The Destruction of Reason*, pp. 304–5.)
[85]    Lukács, *Az ész trónfosztása*, p. 184. (*The Destruction of Reason*, p. 198.)
[86]    Lukács, *Az ész trónfosztása*, p. 118; p. 260. (*The Destruction of Reason*, p. 129; p. 278.)
[87]    Lukács, *Az ész trónfosztása*, p. 20. (*The Destruction of Reason*, p. 15.) Lukács rejected the views of Karl Löwith who elaborated further the similarities of the distant German and Danish contemporaries.
[88]    Quoted by Sziklai, "Lukács György trónfosztása," p. 85.
[89]    Lukács, *Megélt gondolkodás*, p. 235.
[90]    See Sziklai, "Lukács György trónfosztása," p. 85.

When Lukács escaped from Nazi Germany to the safe haven of refugee communists in 1933, the future venue of earthly Paradise was probably uninviting, since the USSR looked more like hell in the 1930s. The unfavorable working conditions for Lukács included the difficulties of normal life as well, while his disappearing comrades concretely or abstractly influenced his views, arguments, and conclusions. His thinking was certainly determined by the fragility of his existence, and for a short while he was arrested by the feared Soviet secret police, and his son was deported to Siberia. In spite of all the difficulties, Lukács kept on writing the book on irrationalism, and as much as he could or was allowed to, he continued his activity as a scholar, editor, and researcher. Lukács also defended his dissertation, and this qualified him for extra food rationing.[91]

When the German troops were making their way to Moscow in 1941, Lukács and his wife were evacuated to Tashkent with other members of the Soviet intelligentsia, to save them from the Nazis. Several drafts, earlier studies, and many notes of *The Destruction of Reason* remained in the Soviet capital, yet in the distant city and in the atmosphere of the expectation of the total collapse of the USSR,[92] Lukács made new efforts to find his way back to the history of philosophy. However "Reason" was soon destroyed again, since from the 1939 Molotov–Ribbentrop pact Soviet antifascism was somewhat pushed back for tactical reasons,[93] thus the writing was suspended until the embargo was lifted.

Lukács still remained a devoted defender of the Soviet system, and his reasons were simple and recalled the Kierkegaardian argumentation that made him join the Communist Party nearly 25 years previous: "Based on the situation [Hitler advancing to Moscow] these decisions should dominate *everything*, even if it were for me personally the dearest, if it were my own *oeuvre*, I have to obey without conditions."[94]

*V.*

The Danish thinker had a special position for Lukács, probably for a variety of reasons. Kierkegaard was and remained for him an "acute, ingenious and subjectively honest thinker,"[95] and all these provided him a more favorable description in the context of *The Destruction of Reason*. Objectively though, he must have been dishonest, serving his class interest, as it is also elaborated in the book. The same honesty already appeared in Lukács' earlier writings on Kierkegaard,[96] and so the moral evaluation

---

[91] István Hermann, *Lukács György élete* [The Life of György Lukács], Budapest: Corvina 1985, pp. 161–2.
[92] Ibid., p. 159.
[93] See János Weiss, "Zárójelet nyitva" [Opening a Brackets], in *Ész, trónfosztás, demokrácia*, p. 101.
[94] See *Lukács György élete képekben és dokumentumokban*, ed. by Fekete and Karádi, p. 161.
[95] Lukács, *Az ész trónfosztása*, p. 229. (*The Destruction of Reason*, p. 245.)
[96] Regarding transparences between the young and mature Lukács' interpretation of Kierkegaard, see Zoltán Gyenge, "Lukács Kierkegaard-felfogása a Lélek és formákban és Az

remained unchanged, while the philosophical one was radically turned around. Similarly, the importance of the "gesture in life" returned in a radically different meaning but nonetheless still maintained a central role. Existential dilemmas were also the basis of the whole argumentation of the book, even if they were covered and dominated by history and ideology.

The Hungarian thinker's outlook basically changed, yet the object did not. Lukács used the same Kierkegaard edition from the early 1900s to the 1930s and also later, while the secondary literature he refers to was also mainly from the beginning of the twentieth century.[97] The young essayist Lukács did not give exact references to the quoted Kierkegaard texts, while in the footnotes of *The Destruction of Reason* the German edition was referred to since the *Gesammelte Werke* incorporated and, in a sense "unified" the whole *oeuvre*. The quotations were from Kierkegaard, but usually heavily commented, slightly distorted, or grossly mistranslated, with very sharp polemics throughout.[98]

For the mature Lukács, Kierkegaard "possessed considerable philosophical gifts"[99] yet important features "distinguished Schopenhauer, Kierkegaard and Nietzsche from the truly great philosophers"[100] in the context of German philosophical tradition; however, he acknowledged the Danish writer's capacity in philosophy. The length of the chapter and the depth of interpretation of Kierkegaard's views provided a special place for him and indirectly referred to the significance of the Danish thinker. The integration of the *oeuvre* into the German philosophical tradition was more than controversial and due to Lukács' admitted ignorance concerning Danish society and history.[101] Thus Kierkegaard was not further analyzed in this, otherwise determinative, context. In the period from 1789 to 1848 he was defined as the founder of irrationalism—quite a compliment when one considers the title and the subject of the whole work. However, the first appearance of irrationalism as a category was ascribed to Schelling. Between Schelling—Schopenhauer—Nietzsche the Danish thinker had a decisive place, mainly for his polemics with Hegel, his originality, and radicalism.

On Lukács' interpretation, the dissolution of the Hegelian tradition meant radical irrationalism in Kierkegaard's works, since this more advanced irrationalism negates the social and historical dialectics that were present in Hegel. Lukács defines it as qualitative dialectics substituting the Hegelian one, although in the analysis of the Hungarian author it lacks all determinations that make the dialectical method really dialectical. In the Danish thinker's views as interpreted by Lukács, "he thus de-historicized and de-socialized Hegelian dialectics"[102] to focus only on "the artificially

ész trónfosztásában" [Lukács' Interpretation of Kierkegaard in *The Soul and the Forms* and in *The Destruction of Reason*], in *Ész, trónfosztás, demokrácia*, p. 42.

[97]     See above, note 2. His reference includes, for example Höffding, *Sören Kierkegaard als Philosoph*.

[98]     See the chapter on Kierkegaard, in Lukács, *Az ész trónfosztása*, pp. 227–78. (*The Destruction of Reason*, pp. 243–96.)

[99]     Lukács, *Az ész trónfosztása*, p. 182. (*The Destruction of Reason*, p. 197.)

[100]    Ibid.

[101]    Lukács, *Az ész trónfosztása*, p. 238. (*The Destruction of Reason*, p. 256.)

[102]    Lukács, *Az ész trónfosztása*, p. 239. (*The Destruction of Reason*, p. 255.)

isolated individual, the only existence that is relevant here."[103] Conclusively, in Kierkegaard's views the objectivity of history becomes "pure fatalism" for human beings, since in the theater of history God is the only spectator.[104] History is thus isolated from the individual and becomes irrational and senseless, and opposes reason; despair is the only adequate reaction to all these from the side of the individual. The criticism of Hegel from the angle of the hegemony of subjectivity was mistaken, according to Lukács' evaluation of Kierkegaard's contribution to philosophy. The Danish thinker also had doubts in approaching "objective reality,"[105] and so dialectics were turned into metaphysics and into formal logic.[106]

Kierkegaard's role was once fundamental for Lukács' concept of religious atheism and that opened the road for his secularized messianism. Atheism was a new form of religion on Lukács' interpretation in his notes on Dostoevsky, since negating God could be the last step before faith. Regarding Kierkegaard's faith, the Hungarian author argues that religion withdraws more and more into the inner dimensions of the human being, and meanwhile science dominates a bigger part of the outside world.[107] Faith can be saved only by the "inner realm" (*Innerlichkeit*),[108] concludes Lukács, and communicating it becomes impossible, as is expressed so powerfully in *Fear and Trembling*. Religion can be saved only by positing the singular above the universal as Abraham did, but in this way ethics is erased from religion and not dialectically negated,[109] Lukács concludes. An incognito is created in this process as the Hungarian thinker could well remember the conclusion of his own dilemmas some decades previous.[110]

When discussing the system of Kierkegaard's thinking, Lukács highlights the close similarity of the aesthetic and religious stages, since pure and final subjectivity is revealed in both. He describes the aesthetic sphere as a mentality or behavior not necessarily as a work of art, and considers it to be the inheritance of Romanticism. The borderlines between the aesthetic and religious are washed away, and the ethical sphere may serve only as something transitory, leading from the premature phase to the only reality of solitary existence: religion.[111] According to this logic, Christianity is neither doctrine nor teaching for Kierkegaard—since then it would be Hegelian— nor does it require community. The only characteristic of faith thus becomes the pure and final subjectivity, hiding the abyss of deep despair and final nihilism.[112]

The space for human relationships is extremely limited in Kierkegaard's works as presented in *The Destruction of Reason*, for example, the way marriage is presented in *Either/Or*.[113] Social and historical determinations in general evaporate

---

[103]    Lukács, *Az ész trónfosztása*, p. 239. (*The Destruction of Reason*, p. 256.)
[104]    Lukács, *Az ész trónfosztása*, p. 242. (*The Destruction of Reason*, p. 258.)
[105]    Lukács, *Az ész trónfosztása*, p. 247. (*The Destruction of Reason*, p. 261.)
[106]    Lukács, *Az ész trónfosztása*, p. 249. (*The Destruction of Reason*, p. 263.)
[107]    Lukács, *Az ész trónfosztása*, p. 247. (*The Destruction of Reason*, p. 261.)
[108]    Lukács, *Az ész trónfosztása*, p. 257. (*The Destruction of Reason*, p. 274.)
[109]    Lukács, *Az ész trónfosztása*, pp. 256–62. (*The Destruction of Reason*, pp. 272–8.)
[110]    Lukács, *Az ész trónfosztása*, p. 257. (*The Destruction of Reason*, p. 274.)
[111]    Lukács, *Az ész trónfosztása*, pp. 258–62. (*The Destruction of Reason*, pp. 274–9.)
[112]    Lukács, *Az ész trónfosztása*, p. 265. (*The Destruction of Reason*, p. 283.)
[113]    Lukács, *Az ész trónfosztása*, p. 253. (*The Destruction of Reason*, p. 271.)

in his *Weltanschauung*. There is no connection between souls at all, and thus despair and irrationality are the dominant forces. Lukács describes Kierkegaard's aesthetic stage as "anti-ethical," while religion by definition is "beyond ethics."[114] The human being is isolated from the historical and social context, and so remains solitary and powerless.

In the cruel logic of Lukács' book all these serve as the "the reactionary bourgeoisie's tactics"[115] to maintain its influence and to suppress lower social classes. Even if Kierkegaard was honest in a subjective sense, nonetheless he was representing such social trends that he himself was not aware of. Kierkegaard's "romantic anti-capitalism" as Lukács described his opposition to the society he lived in, was in fact an indirect defense of the existing system, since the "un-socialization" of the human being concluded in the annihilation of the ethical.[116] All these were to express the "mood of feeling of an intellectual bourgeois stratum which had become deracinated and parasitical."[117] Even when Kierkegaard was fighting against the Romantic aesthete type of his age, he was basically challenging his own mentality, in vain. By the appearance of Marxism and of the workers' movement, based on materialistic dialectics and on scientific ideology, the bourgeois views proved to be empty constructions that were unable to hold any intellectual weight. Kierkegaard's answers were nothing more than the distorted questions themselves, and his views served as "the refuge for stranded decadent aesthetes."[118]

Kierkegaard's influence on Lukács' diagnosis reached its peak on the eve of Hitler's coming to power, since before that positivism undermined the Danish thinker's popularity.[119] The political and social crises of the 1930s greatly contributed to the ideological confusion of the pre-World War II years, and made intellectuals more receptive to extreme ideas. For Kierkegaard "the fight against revolution occupied the center of his world-view."[120] This was significant for Lukács, although the two shared the criticism concerning modern mass society and bourgeois democracy. Yet the Danish thinker, according to the logic of *The Destruction of Reason*, represented "reactionary tendencies"; "his irrationality [gives rise to] a pseudo-dialectic and irrationalism is clad in pseudo-dialectical forms."[121] Kierkegaard's views in general served as the "typical form for the intelligentsia's 'reactionary neutralization,' "[122] and proved to be an indirect defense of bourgeois society. Soon all these were used by the Nazis to get into power, making intellectuals defenseless or turning them into collaborators.

Kierkegaard was, for Lukács, a pioneer of "reactionary behavior" when facing nothingness and reaching out for faith.[123] The views of his followers like Heidegger

---

114    Lukács, *Az ész trónfosztása*, p. 254. (*The Destruction of Reason*, p. 272.)
115    Lukács, *Az ész trónfosztása*, p. 271. (*The Destruction of Reason*, p. 288.)
116    Lukács, *Az ész trónfosztása*, pp. 250–63. (*The Destruction of Reason*, pp. 264–80.)
117    Lukács, *Az ész trónfosztása*, p. 271. (*The Destruction of Reason*, p. 289.)
118    Lukács, *Az ész trónfosztása*, p. 261. (*The Destruction of Reason*, p. 280.)
119    Lukács, *Az ész trónfosztása*, pp. 227–36. (*The Destruction of Reason*, pp. 235–52.)
120    Lukács, *Az ész trónfosztása*, p. 235. (*The Destruction of Reason*, p. 252.)
121    Lukács, *Az ész trónfosztása*, p. 235. (*The Destruction of Reason*, p. 252.)
122    Lukács, *Az ész trónfosztása*, p. 272. (*The Destruction of Reason*, p. 290.)
123    Lukács, *Az ész trónfosztása*, p. 264. (*The Destruction of Reason*, p. 282.)

originated in confronting absolute with relative as the Danish thinker did, and thus an abyss opened between theory and praxis, as well as between history and ethics. This was rooted in Kierkegaard's doubts in progress, and led to the conclusion that ethics was incommensurable with historical praxis.[124] This was something Lukács, based on his own experience, knew intimately about.

## VI.

*The Destruction of Reason* is a "bad book" as Francois Furet put it, maybe even the worst one Lukács had ever written.[125] It also suggests that everything outside of Marxism "is reactionary and irrational,"[126] writes Leszek Kolakowski in criticism of the fat volume. It is hardly an excuse that Lukács was less aggressive and more scholarly in dealing with bourgeois thinkers like Kierkegaard than his Soviet, Rumanian, Bulgarian, Czechoslovak, etc. colleagues,[127] and even the harsh criticism could indirectly express a certain acknowledgement or even appreciation. Unfortunately the militant tone of the book remained unchanged after World War II, and even some Cold War references were included.[128] These details were later removed from the final authorized text, and thus Stalin disappeared from the newer editions; however, Marx, Engels, and Lenin remained, as did the basic ideas. However, in the last version of the book Lukács quoted Lenin 27 times, while Kierkegaard was referred to 37 times.[129]

The real significance of *The Destruction of Reason* was in the interpretation of Western thinking, even if distorted. However, intellectuals behind the Iron Curtain could well read between the lines and reconstruct a thinker's views from heavily criticized fragments. Soon after returning from Moscow in 1945 Lukács was lecturing at Budapest University on the origins of Fascism,[130] so his students had a chance to become familiar with an important tradition of modern philosophy. "I knew much more about Kierkegaard and Nietzsche than about Marx,"[131] as one of his students later recalled these lectures. Although Lukács was soon fired from the university and silenced for quite a while just at the peak of Stalinist terror in Hungary, the forced passivity finally offered him a chance to continue his work undisturbed, even though he was watched and controlled, on the final version of *The Destruction of Reason*.

---

[124]     Lukács, *Az ész trónfosztása*, p. 249. (*The Destruction of Reason*, p. 261.)
[125]     See Weiss, "Zárójelet nyitva," p. 93.
[126]     Ibid.
[127]     See, for example, David I. Zaslavsky, "Yurodstvo i yurodnie v sovremennoy burzhoaznoy filosofi" [Idiocy and Idiots in Contemporary Bourgeois Philosophy], *Voprosy Filosofii*, no. 5, 1954, pp. 138–51.
[128]     Besides Hitler, after 1948 Tito came into the picture, as a consequence of the Soviet–Yugoslav conflict (and as a possible target of the next war planned).
[129]     Lukács, *Az ész trónfosztása*, pp. 768–9. (*The Destruction of Reason*, p. 860.)
[130]     See *Lukács György élete képekben és dokumentumokban*, ed. by Fekete and Karádi, p. 180.
[131]     Ágnes Heller, "Az ész trónfosztása 50 évvel később," in *Ész, trónfosztás, demokrácia*, p. 47.

The book was published only after Stalin's death in 1954, and once the hardcore totalitarianism started to melt, the highest Hungarian award, the Kossuth prize was given to the author for his work.[132]

In the next years Lukács had a circle of students gathered again around him, many of whom later became influential for Hungarian Kierkegaard reception. During the intellectual preparations for the 1956 revolution, at the famous "Philosophical Debate" in the Petőfi Circle, Lukács played a significant role again,[133] and even if the demands included familiarity with important Western traditions, Marxism's hegemony remained unchallenged. After the defeat of the revolution Lukács was arrested and then deported to Rumania. When he was finally allowed to return to Hungary, he was silenced again. This was the ultimate opportunity to start to work on his two major systematic studies, first his *Aesthetics* then his *Ontology*. Lukács was over 60 by then, and yet the idol of his youth, Kierkegaard was much present in both.

The indirect presence of Kierkegaard was preceded by studies on literary matters and artistic issues from the late 1950s on, in which Lukács touched upon the influence existentialism had on artists and intellectuals. In spite of several attempts to create an aesthetic system, Lukács was primarily interested in the *Weltanschauung* of the artist. While analyzing it, he recycled Marxist-Leninist dogmas also to hide his basically conservative taste. Later in the 1960s when he could be a member of the Communist Party again,[134] he was sometimes commissioned to deal with certain artistic issues, but neither ordered nor forced to draw certain conclusions. He heavily criticized the Kierkegaardian influence even on masterpieces of art, since it "symbolizes art's helplessness, the terrifying vision of anxiety based on the conviction that man is completely at the mercy of the incomprehensible and impenetrable terror"[135]—as Alastair Hannay put it, emphasizing also the "elemental Platonic horror at the sight of an alien reality."[136] The Hungarian thinker's radical criticism of Kierkegaard was applied to art, as to a more subtle, but also more penetrating tool of the decadent bourgeoisie to maintain his power over the suppressed classes, for any price.

In the systematic and impressive *chef d'oeuvre*, the "great" *Aesthetics*,[137] Kierkegaard is present with significant ambiguity. He already appears in the preface, when Lukács discusses art's autonomy. Strangely enough, in this context the Danish thinker is presented as the "born enemy" of art, rejecting it like Tertullian did centuries ago, since such autonomy of aesthetic activity would contradict the deep religious convictions.[138] Later, Kierkegaard's views are characterized as having their

---

[132]     See Hermann, *Lukács György élete*, p. 177.

[133]     Lukács served in the Imre Nagy government in 1956 as minister of culture.

[134]     It was called the Hungarian Socialist Workers' Party, and Lukács applied for re-join it, after being closed out in 1957.

[135]     See Alastair Hannay, *Kierkegaard: A Biography*, Cambridge: Cambridge University Press 2003, p. 436.

[136]     Ibid.

[137]     György Lukács, *Az esztétikum sajátossága* [The Particularity of Aesthetics], vols. 1–2, Budapest: Akadémiai Kiadó 1965.

[138]     Ibid., vol. 1, p. 24.

roots in an "atheistic and thus irrational theology,"[139] and so in art he represents "pure subjectivity,"[140] while beyond art he is protesting against any rational approach toward religion. When it is expressed in the language of art, the overall anxiety[141] becomes dominant also as an important element of the basis of bourgeois ideology. It not only excludes any kind of hope but also disarms the chances of change, and conclusively negates all possible revolutions, and their most advanced ideology, Marxism-Leninism.

Once the debate was closed with the principles of the Danish thinker, Kierkegaard reappeared as the representative of the aesthetical view or, with authentic terminology, the "aesthetic stage." Lukács refers to the famous passage in *Either/Or* about the "bull of Phalaris"[142] as a universal metaphor for the painful production of aesthetic quality, and also as revealing the abyss between the subjective intention of the artist and the objective meaning of his or her work. On Lukács' reading, this remains an unsolvable contradiction for Kierkegaard, since this is how pieces of art turn into irrational enigma. The artist's incognito in this context is a necessary phenomenon of the bourgeois alienation,[143] and when later deeply analyzed, it expresses the impossibility of approaching the inner side of the individual.[144]

The born enemy of art soon will be even more needed for the aesthetic analysis of music and in particular of opera, since, in spite of Lukács' polemics with Kierkegaard, the author of *Either/Or* is a forerunner of the aesthetics of music, anticipating important conclusions of modern times.[145] When Lukács discusses the emphasis on the "demonic," the "abstract," and the "mystical" feature of music,[146] the reference of Thomas Mann to the Danish thinker is included, as if an important though "bourgeois" authority were needed. In the later chapter "Between Aesthetics and Ethics" Kierkegaard re-emerges as representing the Romantic despair, not only opposing but wholly annihilating all the hopes of the early Romantics. Then Lukács concretely refers to the Danish thinker's "In vino veritas," interpreting it as an antithesis of Plato's *Symposium*, discussing aesthetics also. Kierkegaard, however, was "too smart"[147] to believe that illusions may serve anything in the present world, and so for him only the final despair is revealed in the conversation of the otherwise joyful company. The aging Hungarian thinker even recalls his early essay on Kierkegaard, referring to his earlier criticism of aesthetic behavior and its limited validity.

In an important segment of the book Lukács discusses the nature and characteristics of tragedy, in which the Kierkegaardian reference appears again, concerning the

---

[139]    Ibid., vol. 1, p. 61.

[140]    Ibid., vol. 1, p. 114.

[141]    Ibid., vol. 1, p. 163.

[142]    Ibid., vol. 1, pp. 626–7. See *SKS* 2, 27 / *EO1*, 19.

[143]    Lukács, *Az esztétikum sajátossága* [The Particularity of Aesthetics], vol. 1, p. 737.

[144]    Ibid., vol. 2, p. 47.

[145]    Ibid., vol. 2, p. 361. See also Ágnes Heller, "A Kierkegaard-i esztétika és a zene" [The Kierkegaardian Aesthetics and Music], in *Érték és történelem* [Value and History], vols. 1–2, Budapest: Magvető 1969, vol. 2, pp. 321–69.

[146]    Lukács, *Az esztétikum sajátossága* [The Particularity of Aesthetics], vol. 2, p. 369.

[147]    Ibid., vol. 2, p. 552.

fundamental distinction between Agamemnon's sacrifice and that of Abraham. Strangely enough, Lukács provides not only an emphatic but even a sympathetic analysis of the crucial paragraphs of *Fear and Trembling*[148] to understand the deep meaning of tragedy and the particular features of the tragic hero. Lukács' periodical returning to the core of Johannes de silentio's book reveals its central position for the Hungarian thinker, throughout his life, in spite of his social, political, or philosophical convictions.

The obligatory references to bourgeois society remain highly critical, since it had "denied its gods," and so the church is no longer the rock upon which to build faith, but more like a "God-cursing"[149] institution. At least this is the way Lukács interprets Kierkegaard's views about the church—an interpretation that he elaborates at length later,[150] touching upon the role of "revelation," which contradicts institutionalized faith. Lukács does not spare any criticism regarding the contemporary church and conclusively the "lukewarm" twentieth-century Western religiosity, defended by thinkers like Karl Jaspers.[151] Once a friend in Heidelberg, Jaspers is now polemically criticized as a bourgeois follower of Kierkegaard and a representative thinker of the corrupt, decadent modern bourgeoisie. For those philosophers the Danish thinker reveals the deepest contradiction of human destiny in a world abandoned by God, where real community does not exist, and the pure and lonely existence can hardly find any excuse for survival.[152]

## VII.

In the concluding, final works of Lukács' life the struggle with Kierkegaard was still not over. He had to settle accounts with the Danish thinker, by whom he was once so paradoxically influenced, and generations of philosophers followed his ambiguous attraction. When Lukács had put aside the continuation of his *Aesthetics* and suddenly interrupted his studies on the planned *Ethics*, he started to draft his *Ontology of Social Being*,[153] in which Kierkegaard also played an important role. This most ambitious work of his life was left unfinished when he died at the age of 86, although his thoughts and ideas were clearly expressed, and the book was published posthumously. The first volume entitled the *Historical Chapters* contains an important section on existentialism, in which Lukács discusses Heidegger's famous footnote concerning Kierkegaard in *Being and Time*. Heidegger is critical of Kierkegaard's "ontological dependence" on Hegel,[154] as Lukács reads it, and

---

[148]     Ibid., vol. 2, pp. 692–5.

[149]     Ibid., vol. 2, p. 694.

[150]     Ibid., vol. 2, p. 730; p. 752.

[151]     Ibid., vol. 2, p. 755.

[152]     Ibid., vol. 2, p. 784.

[153]     See György Lukács, *A társadalmi lét ontológiájáról*, vols. 1–3, Budapest: Magvető Kiadó 1976. (English translation: *Ontology of Social Being*, vols. 1–3, trans. from the German by David Fernbach, London: Merlin Press 1978–80.) Note that this is not a complete translation, and so in what follows the translations are my own.

[154]     Lukács, *A társadalmi lét ontológiájáról*, vol. 1, p. 189.

the German philosopher argues that the edifying writings offer more for the reader ontologically than philosophically. Lukács explains that Kierkegaard's polemics with the Hegelian experiment was against including Christianity in the dialectical philosophy, thus to save it from rationalism. When Kierkegaard attacked the church, the "religious irrationalism" became evident as Lukács argues, and it was influential for Heidegger, when trying to "purge" religion of any Christian substance.[155] Thus the criticized German colleague's categories became more abstract and even more irrational on Lukács' interpretation than Kierkegaard's own categories, and only the final despair was expressed this way, as a more modern form of religion.[156]

In the *Systematic Chapters* (second volume) Kierkegaard appears again, still in the frames of the same polemical logic in the section entitled "Religion as Alienation." The familiar irrationality plays the lead role here for Lukács, far from the dogmatic narrowness of the 1950s and in a different context than in *The Destruction of Reason*. In Lukács' views, no contemporary form of religion can offer any solution or even consolation to the problems of the present time, mainly to the phenomena of alienation. Kierkegaard's *Fear and Trembling* is the best example to demonstrate that the real social and thus rational conflict may conclude in tragedy, while man's conflict with God becomes wholly irrational.[157] Referring to the difference between Agamemnon and Abraham,[158] Lukács places a new emphasis on the personal relationship with God concerning the sacrifice of Isaac, while such a relationship does not exist with Iphigenia.

Lukács concludes that if only such a relationship can connect one to God, then it is strictly personal, with no possibility of including either society or church, and has nothing to do with revelation or with Christ's appearance. In general this view is quite distant from the present forms of faith. On Lukács' interpretation, Kierkegaard's last pamphlets deal with this issue and are "brutally open"[159] about this antinomy. A sarcastic section from *The Moment* is quoted to demonstrate that religion may include even the belief that the moon was made of blue cheese. Lukács emphasizes how a grotesque antinomy may turn into pure absurdity,[160] and how religious faith contradicts the nature of modern society.

It is tempting to read everything that Lukács wrote about Kierkegaard at the end of his life as a conclusion of sacrificing his own life on the altar of an omnipotent theory, and of its institution, the Communist Party. The old Lukács finally confesses that the individual-personal relationship with God has nothing to do with earthly institutions. He understands also that atheism, as it is represented by Kierkegaard, is the world of present-day Christianity. Then Lukács refers to the Grand Inquisitor, a familiar paradigm already for more than half a century, arguing that to follow Jesus' life would destroy the church itself. All these can be interpreted as not too

---

[155]    Ibid., vol. 1, p. 91.
[156]    Ibid., vol. 1, p. 90.
[157]    Ibid., vol. 2, p. 639.
[158]    It is interesting to notice that in the first Hungarian edition instead of "teleological suspension" of ethics "theological" was written.
[159]    Lukács, *A társadalmi lét ontológiájáról*, vol. 2, p. 639.
[160]    Ibid., vol. 2, p. 640.

hidden metaphors expressing his relationship with the institution he once believed in unconditionally, the Party.

It was already too late, the ailing Lukács was soon unable to read his own manuscript, and when his students typed it in an extreme rush he was not in a position to correct it or to answer to their questions posed also in the study *Notes to Comrade Lukács about the Ontology*. The enormous torso of text remained incomplete, as a memento for a unique ambition of a life, spent with social and political issues that relegated his philosophical efforts to an *ancilla politicae*.

Yet there were two reasons for hope, even after the tragic conclusions. One was the activity of his students, the so-called Lukács School and the presence of the next generation, the "Lukács Kindergarten," a very smart group of his followers, who focused on the brighter side of his activity. Regarding Kierkegaard, the translations, comments, studies and university courses dedicated to the Danish thinker originated in this philosophical tradition, and paved the way for the future systematic scholarship. The other, maybe more paradoxical reason for hope was the sudden and nearly dramatic posthumous appearance of a suitcase from Heidelberg, deposited by Lukács in a bank's safe on November 7, 1917. It contained the letters, diaries, drafts, and different writings of the young Lukács, in which an original, sovereign, extremely sensitive, and intelligent thinker emerged, open to the most important tendencies of his time, even preceding some of those, like early existentialism. The torso that appeared from these papers was even more impressive than that of the old Lukács; however, it tragically proves what happens if the strength of the personality cannot bear the weight of his thoughts, and fatally breaks, before starting to write his real *oeuvre*.

# Bibliography

*I. References to or Uses of Kierkegaard in Lukács' Corpus*

"Gondolatok Ibsen Henrikről," in *Ifjúkori művek* [Juvenilia], ed. by Árpád Tímár, Budapest: Magvető Kiadó 1977, p. 92. (English translation: "Thoughts on Henrik Ibsen," in *The Lukács Reader*, ed. by Arpad Kadarkay, Oxford and Cambridge, Massachusetts: Blackwell Publishers 1995, pp. 97–112; originally published in the Hungarian sociological periodical *Huszadik Század*, in August 1906.)

"Vlagyimir Szolovjov, Válogatott művek, 1. kötet" [Vladimir Solovyev, Selected Works, vol. 1], in *Ifjúkori művek* [Juvenilia], ed. by Árpád Tímár, Budapest: Magvető Kiadó 1977, pp. 622–3.

"Könyvek könyve" [Book of the Books], in *Ifjúkori művek* [Juvenilia], ed. by Árpád Tímár, Budapest: Magvető Kiadó 1977, p. 767.

"Sören Kierkegaard és Regine Olsen," *Nyugat*, no. 6, 1910, pp. 378–87 (in *Ifjúkori művek* [Juvenilia], ed. by Árpád Tímár, Budapest: Magvető Kiadó 1977, pp. 287–303; published also in *A lélek és a formák. Kísérletek* [Soul and Form. Experiments], Budapest: Franklin 1910, pp. 129–50; English translation: "The Foundering of Form against Life. Sören Kierkegaard and Regine Olsen," in *The Lukács Reader*, ed. by Arpad Kadarkay, Oxford and Cambridge, Massachusetts: Blackwell Publishers 1995, pp. 11–25).

"Taktika és etika," in *Forradalomban: Cikkek, tanulmányok, 1918–1919* [In Revolution: Essays and Studies, 1918–1919], ed. by Miklós Mesterházi, Budapest: Magvető Kiadó 1987, p. 132. (English translation: "Tactics and Ethics" in *Tactics and Ethics: Political Essays 1919–1929*, vols. 1–2, trans. from the German by Michael McColgan, New York: Harper & Row 1972–75, vol. 1. pp. 3–11.)

*Dostojewski, Notizen und Entwürfe*, ed. by J. Kristóf Nyíri (on the basis of Lukács' *Nachlaß*), Budapest: Akadémiai Kiadó 1985, pp. 35–190 (new ed. by Miklós Mesterházi as *A regény elmélete—Dosztojevszkij-jegyzetek*, [Theory of the Novel—Notes on Dostoevsky], Budapest: Gond 2009, pp. 106–451).

*Az ész trónfosztása. Az irracionalista filozófia kritikája*, Budapest: Akadémiai Kiadó 1954, pp. 199–245 (new ed., Budapest: Magvető Kiadó 1978; English translation: *The Destruction of Reason*, trans. by Peter Palmer, London: Merlin Press 1980, pp. 243–305).

*A polgári filozófia válsága* [The Crisis of the Bourgeoisie Philosophy], 2nd enlarged ed., Budapest: Hungária 1949 [1947], pp. 28–36; pp. 84–7; pp. 149–205.

*Wider den mißverstandenen Realismus*, Hamburg: Claassen 1958, p. 25.

"Kierkegaard. Aus dem in Vorbereitung befundenen Werk: Zerstörung der Vernunft," *Deutsche Zeitschrift für Philosophie*, vol. 1, 1953, pp. 286-314.

*Az esztétikum sajátossága* [The Particularity of Aesthetics], vols. 1–2, Budapest: Akadémiai Kiadó 1965, vol. 1, pp. 114–52; pp. 626–737; vol. 2, pp. 360–9, pp. 750–84.

*A társadalmi lét ontológiájáról*, vols. 1–3, Budapest: Magvető Kiadó 1976, vol. 1. pp. 37–127.

*Megélt gondolkodás* [Thinking as Lived Through], Budapest: Magvető 1989, pp. 45–55; p. 240.

*Curriculum vitae*, ed. by János Ambrus, Budapest: Magvető Kiadó 1982, pp. 74–7; pp. 415–53.

*Wie ist Deutschland zum Zentrum der reaktionären Ideologie geworden?*, ed. by László Sziklai, Budapest: Akadémiai Kiadó 1982 (*Veröffentlichungen des Lukács-Archivs aus dem Nachlaß von Georg Lukács*), pp. 21–38.

*Wie ist die faschistische Philosophie in Deutschland entstanden?*, ed. by László Sziklai, Budapest: Akadémiai Kiadó 1982 (*Veröffentlichungen des Lukács-Archivs aus dem Nachlaß von Georg Lukács*), pp. 111–49.

## II. Sources of Lukács' Knowledge of Kierkegaard

Höffding, Harald, *Sören Kierkegaard als Philosoph*, Stuttgart: Fromman 1912 [1896].

Kassner, Rudoph, *Motive. Essays*, Berlin: Fischer Verlag 1906, pp. 1–76.

Kierkegaard, Sören, *Gesammelte Werke*, trans. and ed. by Hermann Gottsched and Christoph Schrempf, Jena: Diederichs 1909–22.

— *Buch der Richters. Seine Tagebücher 1833–1855*, trans. and ed. by Hermann Gottsched, Jena and Leipzig: Diederichs 1905.

— *Gesammelte Werke*, vols. 1–32, trans. by Emmanuel Hirsch, Düsseldorf and Cologne: Diederichs 1950–74.

— *Sören Kierkegaard Írásaiból* [From Søren Kierkegaard's Writings], trans. by Tivadar Dani et al., ed. by Béla Suki, Budapest: Gondolat 1969 (2nd ed., 1982; 3rd ed., 1994).

Köpeczi, Béla (ed.), *Az egzisztencializmus* [Existentialism], Budapest: Gondolat 1965, pp. 8–59.

Márkus, György and Zádor Tordai, *Irányzatok a mai polgári filozófiában* [Trends in Contemporary Bourgeois Philosophy], Budapest: Gondolat 1964, pp. 31–45.

Mátrai, László, *Haladás és fejlődés. Filozófiai tanulmányok* [Progress and Development. Philosophical Studies], Budapest: Irodalmi és művészeti Intézet 1947, pp. 46–52.

Suki, Béla, "Isten nélküli vallásosság avagy a paradox kereszténység. Gondolatok Sören Kierkegaard nézeteiről" [Religiosity without God or the Paradox of Christianity. Thoughts about Kierkegaard's Views], *Világosság*, no. 6, 1965, pp. 328–33.

134                           *András Nagy*

III. *Secondary Literature on Lukács' Relation to Kierkegaard*

Bendl, Júlia, *Lukács György élete a századfordulótól 1918-ig* [The Life of Lukács from the Turn of the Century until 1918], Budapest: MTA/Scientia Humana Társulás 1994, pp. 103–24; pp. 169–206.

Boros, János (ed.), *Ész, trónfosztás, demokrácia* [Reason, Dethroning, Democracy], Pécs: Bramhauer 2005, pp. 15–109.

Goldmann, Lucien, untitled paper in *Kierkegaard vivant*, Paris: Gallimard 1966, pp. 125–64.

Hannay, Alastair, *Kierkegaard*, London: Routledge & Kegan Paul 1982, p. 325; p. 376.

— "Two Ways of Coming Back to Reality: Kierkegaard and Lukács," *History of European Ideas*, vol. 20, no. 3, 1995, pp. 161–6.

Heller, Ágnes, "Lukács György és Seidler Irma" [György Lukács and Irma Seidler], in her *Portrévázlatok az etika történetéből* [Portrait Sketches from the History of Ethics], Budapest: Gondolat 1976, pp. 385–422.

Hermann, István, *Lukács György élete* [The Life of György Lukács], Budapest: Corvina 1985, pp. 26–43; pp 154–64.

Heywood Thomas, J., "Lukács' Critique of Kierkegaard," in *Faith, Knowledge, and Action: Essays Presented to Niels Thulstrup on His Sixtieth Birthday*, ed. by George L. Stengren, Copenhagen: C.A. Reitzel 1984, pp. 184–98.

Hunsinger, George, "A Marxist View of Kierkegaard: George Lukács on the Intellectual Origins of Fascism," *Union Seminary Quarterly Review*, vol. 30, 1974–75, pp. 29–40.

Kampits, Peter, "A fiatal Lukács és az osztrák Kierkegaard-recepció," *Magyar Filozófiai Szemle*, vol. 3, 1987, pp. 544–50.

Klentak-Zabłocka, Małgorzata, "Etyka ofiary. O recepcji Kierkegaarda we wczesnych pismach Lukacsa" [Ethics of the Victim. About Kierkegaard's Reception in the Early Writings of Lukács], *AUNC*, vol. 262, 1993, pp. 33–47.

Marcus-Tar, Judith, *Thomas Mann und Georg Lukács*, Budapest: Corvina 1982, pp. 54–157.

Nagy, András, *Kierkegaard Budapesten* [Kierkegaard in Budapest], Budapest: Fekete Sas Kiadó 1994, pp. 7–20.

— "Abraham the Communist," in *Kierkegaard—The Self in Society*, ed. by George Pattison and Steven Shakespeare, London: Macmillan 1998, pp. 196–220.

— *Főbenjárás. Kierkegaard, Mahler, Lukács. Esszék* [Parapethetics. Kierkegaard. Mahler, Lukács. Essays], Budapest: Fekete Sas 1998.

— "The Hidden Map. Kierkegaard and East Europe," *Ukrajnskaya Kerkegaardiana*, Lviv: Centr Gumanitarih Doslidzen, University Ivan Franko 1998, pp. 63–8.

— "Hungary: The Hungarian Patient," in *Kierkegaard's International Reception*, Tome II, *Southern, Central and Eastern Europe*, ed. by Jon Stewart, Aldershot: Ashgate 2008 (*Kierkegaard Research: Sources, Reception and Resources*, vol. 8), see pp. 157–71 passim; p. 176.

— "Egy élmény története" [Lukács' Readings of Kierkegaard], in *A feledés árja alól új földeket hódítok vissza. Írások Tímár Árpád tiszteletére*, Budapest: MTA Művészettörténeti Kutatóintézet—Mission Art Galéria 2009, pp. 81–95.

Price, Zachary, "On Young Lukács on Kierkegaard. Hermeneutic Utopianism and the Problem of Alienation," *Philosophy and Social Criticism*, vol. 26, no. 6, 1999, pp. 67–82.

Ryan, Bartholomew, *Kierkegaard's Indirect Politics: A Dialogue with Lukács, Schmitt, Benjamin and Adorno*, Ph.D. Thesis, University of Aarhus, Århus 2006.

Vezér, Erzsébet and Éva Karády (ed.) *A vasárnapi kör* [The Sunday Circle], Budapest: Gondolat 1980, pp. 7–42; pp. 115–32.

Зашев, Димитър [Zashev, Dimiter], "Със и без Киркегор—една дилема на младия Лукач" [With and Without Kierkegaard—a Dilemma of the Young Lukács], *Философска мисъл*, no. 11, 1981, pp. 76–87.

Zoltai, Dénes, *Egy írástudó visszatér* [An Homme des Lettres Returns], Budapest: Kossuth Kiadó 1985, pp. 13–150.

# Herbert Marcuse:

## Social Critique, Haecker, and Kierkegaardian Individualism

### J. Michael Tilley

Herbert Marcuse (1898–1979) was an influential interpreter of Hegel, Marx, and Freud, and his work has influenced an entire generation of social and critical theorists comprising the New Left in the 1960s. Although his work displays amazing insight regarding German philosophy and social theory, his exposure to Kierkegaard was rather limited and filtered through this tradition. As a result, there are only two extended discussions of Kierkegaard in Marcuse's authorship, and in his mature thought Marcuse rejects what he identifies as Kierkegaard's view.

### I. Overview of Marcuse's Life and Works

Marcuse, a German Jew, was born in Berlin and educated at Freiburg receiving his doctoral degree in literature in 1922 and another doctoral degree in philosophy under the direction of Martin Heidegger. In Freiburg he later completed his Habilitation, *Hegel's Ontology and the Theory of Historicity* in 1932.[1] In this work, Marcuse tried to synthesize the work of Hegel, Heidegger, and Marx. Upon leaving Freiburg, he briefly joined the Frankfurt School (The Institute for Social Research) before fleeing Germany in 1934. For this point forward, he lived in the United States, working initially for the government and later teaching philosophy and politics at Columbia, Harvard, Brandeis, and the University of California, San Diego.

His work on Hegel and Neo-Marxist critical theory culminated in his seminal work, *Reason and Revolution*, where Marcuse described a critical, historical social theory grounded in Hegelian philosophy.[2] This work was influential in the revival of Hegel scholarship in the early twentieth century, and Marcuse was also one of the first to study and reinterpret Marx in light of his earlier *Political and Economic Manuscripts*. His later work, *Eros and Civilization*, reinterpreted Freud and Marx

---

[1]    Herbert Marcuse, *Hegels Ontologie und die Grundlegung einer Theorie der Geschichtlichkeit*, Frankfurt am Main: Klostermann 1932. (English translation: *Hegel's Ontology and the Theory of Historicity*, trans. by Seyla Benhabib, Cambridge, Massachusetts: MIT Press 1989.)

[2]    Herbert Marcuse, *Reason and Revolution: Hegel and the Rise of Social Theory*, New York: Oxford University Press 1941.

within the basic framework of his earlier analysis while providing a portrait of a free and rational (that is, a non-repressive) society.[3] His *One Dimensional Man* explores why his social vision has not been accomplished and why society precludes revolutionary change.[4] During the time in which these latter two works were published, Marcuse was perhaps the most influential figure in the developmental of the New Left.

## II. Marcuse's References to Kierkegaard

Although there are some passages in Marcuse's works where Kierkegaard is mentioned in passing,[5] he made only two substantive references to Kierkegaard in his *corpus*.[6] The earlier passage is a portrayal of the potential for social critique in Kierkegaard's account of the individual, culminating in Kierkegaard's critique of the State Church of Denmark, and the latter passage is an important summation and barometer of the general approach that critical theorists took toward Kierkegaard as compared to Hegel (and Marx). The first article was written in 1929, and it describes how Kierkegaard's account of human existence lays a foundation for social critique that is realized and practiced in his critique—which was addressed to ordinary people—of nationalism and the State Church in Denmark. In this early essay, Marcuse does not see Kierkegaard's project as inimical to social and political critique and analysis.

Marcuse's views on Kierkegaard change sometime before the publication of *Reason and Revolution*, where Marcuse maintained that Kierkegaard "seizes upon the isolated individual" as the fulfillment of the essence of humanity and the realization of philosophy itself, whereas Hegel "penetrates to the origins of the individual in the process of social labor and shows how the latter process is the basis of man's liberation."[7] Marcuse sets the social views articulated by Marx and Hegel against Kierkegaard's isolated individualism, and he also criticizes Kierkegaard for not getting "beyond earlier philosophical and religious approaches" for developing a deep-rooted social theory.[8]

Marcuse portrays Kierkegaard as a "fierce [opponent] to Western rationalism," since he locates truth in the particular "circumstances of individual life" rather than "with reason resident in the thinking ego and in the objective mind."[9] Although the concern for a human's actual needs and longings are a needed correction of rationalist philosophy, both existentialism (whose representative is Kierkegaard) and rationalism fail to appropriately treat a human being's "material happiness" as

---

[3]		Herbert Marcuse, *Eros and Civilization*, Boston: Beacon Press 1955.

[4]		Herbert Marcuse, *One-Dimensional Man*, London: Routledge 1964.

[5]		Herbert Marcuse, "Sartre's Existentialism," in his *Studies in Critical Philosophy*, Boston: Beacon Press 1972, pp. 188–9.

[6]		Marcuse, *Reason and Revolution*, pp. 262–7. Marcia Morgan alerted me to Marcuse's references to Kierkegaard in the following article: "Herbert Marcuse, 'Ueber konkrete Philosophie,'" *Archiv für Sozialwissenschaft und Sozialpolitik*, vol. 62, 1929, pp. 123–7.

[7]		Marcuse, *Reason and Revolution*, p. 262.

[8]		Ibid., p. 263.

[9]		Ibid.

both proposed an "introversion of reason" and prematurely accepted "the world as it is" without offering an adequate social critique.[10] Remnants of Marcuse's earlier analysis remain—that is, the importance of "concrete" philosophy in Kierkegaard's thought, but the overall evaluation of Kiekegaard has shifted.

Marcuse's portrayal of Kierkegaard in both of his significant references largely derive from the beginning of the *Concluding Unscientific Postscript* and Haecker's translation of selections from *A Literary Review* (I will address this matter in Section III).[11] The sources that Marcuse uses prefigure (and I will argue in Section III expose the limitations of) the interpretation he proposes of Kierkegaard. He maintains that, for Kierkegaard:

> The individual is not the knowing but only the "ethically existing subjectivity." The sole reality that matters to him is his own "ethical existence." Truth lies not in knowledge…. Knowledge deals only with the possible and is incapable of making anything real or even of grasping reality. Truth lies only in action and can be experienced only through action. The individual's own existence is the sole reality that can actually be comprehended, and the existing individual himself the sole subject or performer of this comprehension.[12]

The implication, according to Marcuse, is two-fold: first, it involves a denial of all sociality for the Kierkegaardian self: "Every individual, in his innermost individuality, is isolated from all others, he is essentially unique. There is no union, no community, no 'universality' to contest his dominion."[13] Second, truth is exclusively a result of an individual's decision and this decision determines the eternal fate of the individual: "Truth is forever the outcome of his own decision and can be realized only in the free acts that spring from this decision. The sole decision open to the individual is that between eternal salvation and eternal damnation."[14]

Marcuse understands this aspect of Kierkegaard's thought as both a positive and negative moment. On the one hand, since there is only one proper decision, that is, "to live a Christian life," Kierkegaard does offer a social critique. "Kierkegaard's work," it turns out, "is the last great attempt to restore religion as the ultimate organon for liberating humanity from the destructive impact of an oppressive social order."[15] Kierkegaard presents a critique of society such that the remedy for the malady foisted upon humanity by oppressive social forces can only be remedied in Christian living. This move recovers the revolutionary character of religion. It "restores to Christianity its combative and revolutionary force" insofar as the arrival of the God-man is a historical event that breaks into "a society in decay" and "eternity takes on

---

[10]     Ibid.

[11]     *SKS* 7, 275–315 / *CUP1*, 301–43. It is important to note that Marcuse ignores the pseudonymous nature of the *Concluding Unscientific Postscript*, and his interpretation of *A Literary Review* is filtered through Haecker's selective editing which will be discussed in Part III. Søren Kierkegaard, *Zur Kritik der Gegenwart*, trans. and ed. by Theodor Haecker, Innsbruck: Brenner 1922.

[12]     Marcuse, *Reason and Revolution*, p. 264.

[13]     Ibid.

[14]     Ibid.

[15]     Ibid.

a temporal aspect, while the realization of happiness becomes an immediately vital matter of daily life."[16] This is the positive upshot of Kierkegaard's portrayal.

On the other hand, the negative moment in this picture is that religion can no longer play the role that Kierkegaard envisioned for it. Kierkegaard held "to a content that could no longer take a religious form."[17] The content of social revolution is conveyed more effectively in a "concrete struggle for social liberation" rather than in religion.[18] Religious critiques are "weak and impotent," and Kierkegaard's proposal may even end up turning "against the individual it set out to save," insofar as it considers primarily "the inner world of the individual, 'the truth' gets separated from the social and political vortex in which it belongs."[19] For Marcuse, Kierkegaard's isolation of the individual ends up precluding any genuine social critique. Marcuse explains, "There is no doubt, [Kierkegaard] says, that 'the idea of socialism and community cannot save this age.' "[20]

The seeds of this critique are contained in Marcuse's earlier, positive evaluation of Kierkegaard where he glosses Kierkegaard's concrete philosophy as an expression of the material existence of human being;[21] but in his mature thought, Kierkegaard's critique of society and his portrayal of the single individual (as it developed among later "existentialists") ultimately supports that which it initially criticized. Specifically, its demotion of reason—which initially was intended as a rejection of "any universally valid rational norms for state and society" and any "bond [that] joins individuals, states, and nations into a whole of mankind" made it such that "certain particularities (such as the race or the folk)" became the highest values.[22] In making this claim, Marcuse situated Kierkegaard's work as a precursor to later developments in the "existentialist" tradition, particularly, Heidegger and his association with National Socialism.

### III. Individualism and the Reception of Kierkegaard in Twentieth-Century Critical Theory

Marcuse's later reading of Kierkegaard revolves around two related claims: first, Kierkegaard is concerned primarily with the individual and inwardness. The individual alone is the locus of truth who is protected from the caprice of culture and society by the inward turn. Second, this conception of the Kierkegaardian individual is fundamentally at odds with the Hegelian image of a socially constituted self. Whereas Hegel allows for and suggests a valuable social critique, Kierkegaard only presents a weak and impotent social critique problematically grounded in a religious world- and life-view. Marcuse's earlier work saw more potential for radical social critique, but his more mature work rejects the view.

---

[16]     Ibid., p. 265.

[17]     Ibid.

[18]     Ibid., p. 266.

[19]     Ibid.

[20]     Ibid.

[21]     Marcuse, "Ueber konkrete Philosophie," p. 127.

[22]     Marcuse, *Reason and Revolution*, p. 267.

Almost three decades ago, Mark C. Taylor's *Journeys to Selfhood* made a more sophisticated defense of the mature Marcuse's basic claim that Hegel and Kierkegaard are antipodes regarding sociality and individuality. For Kierkegaard, Taylor said, "the journey to selfhood cannot culminate in spiritual community but must be a solitary sojourn that separates self from other."[23] According to Taylor, Hegel's approach to becoming a self is much more coherent and philosophically defensible because Hegel's notion of self is inherently relational and social whereas Kierkegaard's notion is fundamentally disconnected from any other(s).[24] Although it is beyond the scope of this article to fully describe why Taylor and Marcuse's claims are mistaken, it is important to note that, on the whole, Kierkegaard scholarship has clearly and definitively rejected the thesis both men presented. In particular, their theses depend on (1) their one-sided interpretations of a relatively small number of (generally pseudonymous) texts (2) ignoring the social and religious ethic described in *Works of Love* and the upbuilding discourses, and (3) severing Kierkegaard from his immediate intellectual and social context.[25]

---

[23]  Mark Taylor, *Journeys to Selfhood: Hegel and Kierkegaard*, Berkeley: University of California Press 1980, p. 179.

[24]  Ibid., p. 160.

[25]  The first sustained defense of Kierkegaard against Taylor's charge that there is no communal dimension in Kierkegaard's thought is found in Ronald Hall's essay "Language and Freedom," in *The Concept of Anxiety*, ed. by Robert Perkins, Macon, Georgia: Mercer University Press 1985 (*International Kierkegaard Commentary*, vol. 8), pp. 153–66, where he argued that Taylor fails to recognize the "role that Kierkegaard gives to language in the life of faith." Hall argues that language is inherently social and communal and that by giving it a central place in his elaboration of faith, Kierkegaard has also expressed, in part, a communal dimension to his own thought. See *Foundations of Kierkegaard's Vision of Community: Religion, Ethics, and Politics in Kierkegaard*, ed. by George Connell and C. Stephen Evans Atlantic Highlands, New Jersey: Humanities Press 1992. The Connell and Evans volume contains a significant number of the first and some of the most important challenges to the asocial reading of Kierkegaard. Perhaps the most prominent essay is Merold Westphal's account of "Religiousness C" where the inwardness of faith in "Religiousness B" must be expressed and lived out practically in the world. See also *Kierkegaard: The Self in Society*, ed. by George Pattison and Steven Shakespeare, New York: St. Martin's Press 1998. Pattison and Shakespeare's introduction to this volume of essays lays out the variety of different ways in which the atomistic, asocial reading of Kierkegaard has come under fire (cf. pp. 1–23) including a discussion of some of the articles included in the Connell and Evans volume. See also M. Jamie Ferreira, *Love's Grateful Striving*, New York: Oxford University Press 2001. Ferreira's work reveals the ethical dimension of Kierkegaard's thought in *Works of Love*, perhaps the most important of Kierkegaard's social and religious ethic. Gregory Beabout and Brad Frazier, "A Challenge to the 'Solitary Self' Interpretation of Kierkegaard," *History of Philosophy Quarterly*, vol. 17, no. 1, 2000, pp. 75–98, draws on a reading of Kierkegaard's religious ethic in order to offer a formal critique of Taylor's position. Finally, Davenport and Rudd's volume of essays on MacIntyre and Kierkegaard argues that the Dane's work is compatible with and even in many ways similar to MacIntyre's communitarianism; see *Kierkegaard After MacIntyre: Essays on Freedom, Narrative, and Virtue*, ed. by John Davenport and Anthony Rudd, Chicago: Open Court 2001.

Although recent scholarship on Kierkegaard has successfully addressed Marcuse's concern about Kierkegaard's conception of the individual, few studies have addressed the relevant intermediary sources and the social-historical context which gave rise to Marcuse's interpretation. Marcuse's work remains important regarding Kierkegaard insofar as it is a representative sample of how many critical theorists first appreciated and later reacted against Kierkegaard largely because of his historical and cultural association with figures that critical theorists were more directly critical of, such as Martin Heidegger and Emanuel Hirsch among others. Their approach to Kierkegaard scholarship has had a lasting impact on interpretations of Kierkegaard throughout most of the twentieth century, and they are only in the last three decades beginning to subside among Kierkegaard scholars.[26]

Marcuse's interpretation is likely the result of a variety of factors, but at least one was that many of the critical theorists came to understand themselves as opponents of existentialism, and they identified Kierkegaard as an important precursor to the movement, which is often characterized as lacking a social or political dimension.[27] Another important player in the development of Marcuse's views of Kierkegaard is Theodor Haecker.[28] Haecker's translation of *A Literary Review* is cited by Marcuse as the primary source for his criticism of Kierkegaard for lacking a social dimension.[29] For Marcuse, this text is the lynchpin which connects the concept of individual elaborated in the *Concluding Unscientific Postscript* with the critique of "socialism and community."[30] It provides the substance of Marcuse's objections to Kierkegaard, and therefore, a consideration of Haecker's work is helpful for understanding Marcuse's criticism of Kierkegaard as well as the general response among critical theorists.

Haecker's translation was one of the earlier translations of Kierkegaard's work into German, and in many respects, it set the tone for how Kierkegaard's thought would be received in the early and mid-twentieth century. The work was, like some English translations of the text,[31] a partial translation of select passages of Kierkegaard's *A Literary Review*. This text severed portions of the third part of

---

[26]     For an account of how Emanuel Hirsch's reception of Kierkegaard shaped the response of one critical theorist, see Marcia Morgan, "Adorno's Reception of Kierkegaard: 1929–1933," *The Søren Kierkegaard Newsletter*, no. 46, 2003, p. 9.

[27]     For an example of the common complaint that existentialists lack a social and political dimension see William McBride, "Sartre's Debts to Kierkegaard: A Partial Reckoning" in *Kierkegaard in Post/Modernity*, ed. by Martin J. Matuštík and Merold Westphal, Bloomington: Indiana University Press 1995, p. 29.

[28]     Allan Jannik's essay, "Haecker, Kierkegaard and the Early *Brenner*: A Contribution to the History of the Reception of *Two Ages* in the German-Speaking World," in *Two Ages*, ed. by Robert L. Perkins, Macon, Georgia: Mercer University Press 1984 (*International Kierkegaard Commentary*, vol. 14), pp. 189–222 is an invaluable resource describing in detail Haecker's relationship to Kierkegaard and his influence on the twentieth-century reception of Kierkegaard's thought in Europe.

[29]     Marcuse, *Reason and Revolution*, p. 266, note.

[30]     Ibid., p. 266.

[31]     Søren Kierkegaard, *The Present Age*, trans. by Alexander Dru, Oxford: Oxford University Press 1940.

the text, the theoretical account of the differences between the revolutionary age and the reflective age, from the rest of Kierkegaard's review of the novel *Two Ages* written anonymously by Thomasine Gyllembourg (1773–1856), the mother of Johan Ludvig Heiberg (1791–1860). This creative decision regarding the presentation of *A Literary Review* made the text appear more applicable to particular historical and cultural situations in Germany in the early twentieth century. Jannik writes: "Haecker published his selection from *Two Ages* in a polemical context that did much to fix the image of Kierkegaard in the sense of associating him with certain individuals and movements and dissociating him from others. The point is that *The Present Age* (and the German *Kritik der Gegenwart*) is in a sense Haecker's creation."[32]

In particular, Jannik argues that Haecker was polemical toward the degeneration of the spirit of the people: "German intellectual life, he believed, was becoming increasingly sterile as instrumental reason lost its rootedness in spiritual values.... The philosophy of inwardness was a strategy for returning *Geist* to intellectual life."[33] He saw Kierkegaard's concept of the individual as the remedy to this spiritual degeneration of his own age. "For Kierkegaard," Haecker asserts, "nothing is so unutterably real, so eternal and indestructible as the spiritual self of the individual man, the Ego that is here the highest reality and the opposite of an abstraction."[34] Jannik explains how this philosophy of inwardness functions:

> Inwardness is the recognition in practice: in concrete ethical action, that intelligence is fundamentally spiritual. As we have seen, the philosophy of inwardness proceeds from a curious critique of reason and entails a subordination of the intellectual (science and technology) to the spiritual (religious). There are three basic aspects of inwardness.... They are ethical individualism, radical adherence to Christianity, and virulent opposition to aestheticism. So intense is the inward man's commitment to his beliefs that they can neither be understood nor evaluated apart from his personality. Thus, it is not difficult to see why Kierkegaard should become the paragon of inwardness for Haecker.[35]

This image of Kierkegaard is reproduced in Marcuse's positive evaluation of the Dane in his earlier work and his critical evaluation in *Reason and Revolution*. He specifically refers to Kierkegaard as an opponent of Western rationalism where the truth is located in a particular individual.[36] In his turn to the individual, Kierkegaard is said to have accepted "the world as it is" without offering an adequate social critique.[37] The inward turn, as Haecker seemed to portray it, isolates the individual from others. Marcuse draws on this idea when he expresses Kierkegaard's view as follows: "Every individual, in his innermost individuality, is isolated from all others, he is essentially unique. There is no union, no community, no 'universality' to

---

[32]   Jannik, "Haecker, Kierkegaard and the Early *Brenner*," p. 191.

[33]   Ibid., p. 196.

[34]   Ibid., p. 202. Jannik cites Theodor Haecker, *Søren Kierkegaard und die Philosophie der Innerlichkeit*, Munich: Schreiber 1913, p. 15.

[35]   Jannik, "Haecker, Kierkegaard and the Early *Brenner*," pp. 200–1.

[36]   Marcuse, *Reason and Revolution*, p. 263.

[37]   Ibid.

contest his dominion."[38] As a result, even though Kierkegaard (and Haecker as well) was explicitly critical of nationalism and other like-minded political movements, Marcuse claims the end result of the retreat to interiority is that it will preclude any normative social critique of a culture. Marcuse claims that Kierkegaard ends up turning "against the individual it set out to save" since "the inner world of the individual, 'the truth' gets separated from the social and political vortex in which it belongs."[39] Ultimately, Marcuse sees Heidegger and the alignment of existentialist thought with immoral social practices as the end result of Kierkegaard's thought.

## *IV. Conclusion*

Marcuse's reading of Kierkegaard was shaped by the way Kierkegaard was presented and described in Haecker's translations. Marcuse's portrayal of Kierkegaard is important not only because of his popularity and influence in the larger culture, but also because he provides a picture of the general approach that critical theorists have taken toward Kierkegaard in which he was initially seen as an important figure who offered resources for social critique but who is latter portrayed as an individualist who leaves no room for community or social critique. Although this image of Kierkegaard has been addressed and criticized by Kierkegaard scholars in the last three decades, it still has an impact on the way Kierkegaard is understood and perceived in the broader philosophical and academic community.

---

[38]     Ibid., p. 264.
[39]     Ibid., p. 266.

# Bibliography

*I. References to or Uses of Kierkegaard in Marcuse's Corpus*

"Ueber konkrete Philosophie," *Archiv für Sozialwissenschaft und Sozialpolitik*, vol. 62, 1929, pp. 111–28.
*Reason and Revolution: Hegel and the Rise of Social Theory*, New York: Oxford University Press 1941, pp. 262–7.
"Sartre's Existentialism," *Studies in Critical Philosophy*, Boston: Beacon Press 1972, pp. 188–9.


*II. Sources of Marcuse's Knowledge of Kierkegaard*

Heidegger, Martin, *Sein und Zeit*, Halle: Niemeyer 1927, pp. 175–96, see also p. 190, note 1; p. 235, note 1; and p. 338, note 1.
Kierkegaard, Sören, *Zur Kritik der Gegenwart*, trans. and ed. by Theodor Haecker, Innsbruck: Brenner Verlag 1922.


*III. Secondary Literature on Marcuse's Relation to Kierkegaard*

Fahrenbach, Helmut, "Kierkegaards untergründige Wirkungsgeschichte. (Zur Kierkegaardrezeption bei Wittgenstein, Bloch und Marcuse)," in *Die Rezeption Søren Kierkegaards in der deutschen und dänischen Philosophie und Theologie. Vorträge des Kolloquiums am 22. und 23. März 1982*, ed. by Heinrich Anz, Poul Lübcke, and Friedrich Schmöe, Copenhagen and Munich: Fink 1983 (*Text & Kontext*, Sonderreihe, vol. 15), pp. 30–69.
Hannay, Alastair, *Kierkegaard*, London: Routledge 1982, pp. 302–3.
— *Kierkegaard and Philosophy: Selected Essays*, London: Routledge 2003, p. 205.
Lind, Peter, *Marcuse and Freedom: The Genesis and Development of a Theory of Human Liberation*, London: Croom Helm 1985, pp. 159–60.
Matuštík, Martin J., "Kierkegaard as Socio-Political Thinker and Activist," *Man and World*, vol. 27, no. 2, 1994, p. 218.
— "Reinterpreting the Political: Continental Philosophy and Political Theory," ed. by Lenore Langsdorf, Stephen H. Watson, Karen Anne Smith, Albany, New York: State University of New York Press 1998, pp. 7–8.
Newman, Jay, *Inauthentic Culture and Its Philosophical Critics*, Montreal: McGill-Queen's University Press 1997, pp. 27–8.

Pippin, Robert B., Andrew Feenberg, and Charles Webel, *Marcuse: Critical Theory and the Promise of Utopia*, Basingstoke: Macmillan Education 1988, pp. 125–6.

Tilley, J. Michael, *Interpersonal Relationships and Community in Kierkegaard's Thought*, Ph.D. Thesis, University of Kentucky, Lexington, Kentucky 2008, pp. 5–11.

# José Ortega y Gasset:

## Meditations on "Provincial Romanticism"

Robert Puchniak

### I. General Introduction

Spanish philosopher, essayist and social critic, José Ortega y Gasset was born in Madrid in 1883. The son of novelist and journalist, José Ortega Munilla, and educated by the Jesuits, Ortega y Gasset completed his doctorate in 1904 at the Central University of Madrid. He then spent several years (1905–07) studying in Germany, where he was exposed to philosophers who were influential in shaping his own ideas, especially a group of Neo-Kantians at Marburg led by Hermann Cohen (1842–1918). In 1910 he was named the Chair in Metaphysics at Madrid and was an active participant in the rejuvenation of Spanish education and culture. Involved in academics as well as journalism, he wrote for newspapers and periodical magazines, and founded the distinguished intellectual journal, *Revista de Occidente*, in 1923. Ortega y Gasset would spend a brief time as an elected deputy to the Congress of the Second Spanish Republic (1931–32). When the Spanish Civil War began in 1936, he fled Madrid into a self-imposed exile that would take him to France, Portugal, and Argentina, before returning to his native land in 1945. His international reputation was nurtured with further visits to the United States and Germany. He died in Madrid in 1955.

Ortega called his own philosophy one of "vital reason" (*la razón vital*) that sought to distance itself from darker, more pessimistic forms of existentialism,[1] while also eschewing "abstractions" in favor of clarity, which he named "the form of courtesy that the philosopher owes."[2] The "great philosophical task of the present generation,"[3] he believed, was to bring together the temporal and the eternal within the "modern sensibility," not through rationalism or positivism, but through the use of a method he called "perspectivism."[4] Ortega lamented what he saw as

---

[1]     See José Ortega y Gasset, *El tema de nuestro tiempo*, Madrid: Espasa-Calpe 1923, p. 95 (in *Obras Completas*, vols. 1–8, ed. by Fundacion Ortega y Gasset, Centro de Estudios Orteguianos, Madrid: Revista de Occidente 1961–70, vol. 8, p. 302.) English translation: *The Modern Theme*, trans. by James Cleugh, New York: Harper 1961.

[2]     José Ortega y Gasset, *¿Qué es filosofía?* Madrid: Revista de Occidente 1958, p. 27. (English translation: *What is Philosophy?*, trans. by Mildred Adams, New York: W.W. Norton 1960, p. 19.)

[3]     Ortega y Gasset, *¿Qué es filosofía?*, p. 34. (*What is Philosophy?*, p. 28.)

[4]     Ortega y Gasset, *¿Qué es filosofía?*, p. 35. (*What is Philosophy?*, p. 28.)

an "anti-philosophical age" in the latter half of the nineteenth century. In his best known work, *The Revolt of the Masses* (first published in 1929), he described the modern rise of the "mass man" as commonplace, undifferentiated, and vulgar, that which "crushes beneath it everything that is different, everything that is excellent, individual, qualified and select."[5] Acknowledging the prominence of "the mass" and its ways of thinking, Ortega was alarmed: "Every destiny is dramatic, tragic in its deepest meaning. Whoever has not felt the danger of our times palpitating under his hand has not really penetrated to the vitals of destiny, he has merely pricked its surface."[6] The danger, he argued, came in the "leveling" power of "appetites and unconscious assumptions" which crush "aspirations and ideals."[7] Those who would prefer the life of disciplined intellectual vigor are led to feel anguish in such times. The essential fact of human existence can therein be forgotten, namely, "that our existence is at every instant and primarily the consciousness of what is possible to us,"[8] within whatever "circumstances"[9] an individual finds himself or herself. Such consciousness has become, however, more complicated in the emerging modern world with increased exposure to "more problems, more data, more sciences, more points of view,"[10] a "fabulous potentiality."[11] "We live," he wrote, "at a time when man believes himself fabulously capable of creation, but he does not know what to create. Lord of all things, he is not lord of himself. He feels lost amid his own abundance."[12]

Faced with such a wide "horizon of possibilities," yet lacking any sense of purpose, each person is faced with the choice of how to exercise their freedom. Mass man "simply goes drifting along."[13] Ortega seemed at once resigned to the impossibility of "educating" mass man, and feared a collective regression into "barbarism," made possible by a sort of "technicism"—which has evolved with the confluence of liberal democracy, scientific experiment, and industrialism.[14] Mass man has become, he argued, beset by an illusory feeling of "spontaneous, inexhaustible power of increase," fueled by ever-increasing appetites, to produce the "psychology of the spoilt child."[15] In contrast to this, Ortega advocated the revitalization of what he called "the noble life," one in which the human person "feels himself limited," and accepts "authority external to himself."[16] The "select man" (as opposed to the "mass man") "is urged, by interior necessity, to appeal from himself to some standard

---

[5]        José Ortega y Gasset, *La rebelión de las masas*, Madrid: Revista de Occidente 1929, p. 20 (English translation: *The Revolt of the Masses*, anonymous trans., New York: W.W. Norton 1932, p. 18.)
[6]        Ortega y Gasset, *La rebelión de las masas*, p. 27. (*The Revolt of the Masses*, p. 21.)
[7]        Ortega y Gasset, *La rebelión de las masas*, p. 31. (*The Revolt of the Masses*, p. 23.)
[8]        Ortega y Gasset, *La rebelión de las masas*, p. 61. (*The Revolt of the Masses*, p. 40.)
[9]        Ortega y Gasset, *La rebelión de las masas*, p. 62. (*The Revolt of the Masses*, p. 41.)
[10]        Ortega y Gasset, *La rebelión de las masas*, p. 63. (*The Revolt of the Masses*, p. 41.)
[11]        Ortega y Gasset, *La rebelión de las masas*, p. 66. (*The Revolt of the Masses*, p. 43.)
[12]        Ortega y Gasset, *La rebelión de las masas*, p. 68. (*The Revolt of the Masses*, p. 44.)
[13]        Ortega y Gasset, *La rebelión de las masas*, p. 77. (*The Revolt of the Masses*, p. 49.)
[14]        Ortega y Gasset, *La rebelión de las masas*, p. 89. (*The Revolt of the Masses*, p. 56.)
[15]        Ortega y Gasset, *La rebelión de las masas*, p. 93. (*The Revolt of the Masses*, p. 58.)
[16]        Ortega y Gasset, *La rebelión de las masas*, p. 100. (*The Revolt of the Masses*, p. 63.)

beyond himself, superior to himself, whose service he freely accepts."[17] The "noble man" is not obsessed with his private life and its pleasures, but rather sees himself "ever set on excelling...in passing beyond what one is to what one sets up as a duty and an obligation."[18] The "noble man" is perpetually "striving," never blinded by "novelties," engaged through reason with ideas and history, not allowing his mind to be dulled by material luxuries. A life without struggle, he thought, will inevitably lead to self-satisfaction and lose all "authenticity":[19]

> Human life, by its very nature, has to be dedicated to something, an enterprise glorious or humble, a destiny illustrious or trivial. We are faced with a condition, strange but inexorable, involved in our very existence. On the one hand, to live is something which each one does of himself and for himself. On the other hand, if that life of mine, which only concerns myself, is not directed by me towards something, it will be disjointed, lacking in tension and in "form."[20]

As he stated elsewhere, "*to live* means having to be outside of myself, in the absolute 'outside' that is the circumstance or world; it is having, like it or not, constantly and incessantly to face and clash with whatever makes up the world."[21] Perhaps his most famous idea, a summation of his philosophy, is: "I am myself plus my circumstances."[22] As a non-theistic writer, Ortega resisted any revealed world-view: "Life is given to us; we do not give it to ourselves, rather we find ourselves in it, suddenly and without knowing how...we must make it for ourselves, each one his own. Life is a task."[23] He defines the human condition by saying "in the fact [the human person] has no choice but to force himself to know, to build a science, good or bad, in order to resolve the problem of his own being."[24] Each human being is always faced with the task of struggling within "a set of fixed surrounding," a "drama" which he must interpret.[25]

---

[17]   Ibid.

[18]   Ortega y Gasset, *La rebelión de las masas*, p. 104. (*The Revolt of the Masses*, p. 65.)

[19]   Ortega y Gasset, *La rebelión de las masas*, p. 163. (*The Revolt of the Masses*, p. 99.)

[20]   Ortega y Gasset, *La rebelión de las masas*, p. 238. (*The Revolt of the Masses*, p. 141.)

[21]   José Ortega y Gasset, *El hombre y la gente*, Madrid: Revista de Occidente 1957, p. 71. (English translation: *Man and People*, trans. by Willard R. Trask, New York: W.W. Norton 1957, p. 48.)

[22]   José Ortega y Gasset, *Meditaciones del Quijote*, Madrid: Publicaciones de la Residencia de Estudiantes 1914, p. 43. (English translation: *Meditations on Quixote*, trans. by Evelyn Rugg and Diego Marin, introduction and notes by Julián Marías, New York: W.W. Norton 1961, p. 45.)

[23]   José Ortega y Gasset, *Historia como sistema*, Madrid: Revista de Occidente 1941, p. 9. (English translation: *History as a System and other Essays toward a Philosophy of History*, New York: W.W. Norton 1941, p. 165.) (Note that this work was first published in English.)

[24]   José Ortega y Gasset, *En torno a Galileo*, Madrid: Revista de Occidente 1956, p. 14. (English translation: *Man and Crisis*, trans. by Mildred Adams, New York: W.W. Norton 1958, p. 21.)

[25]   José Ortega y Gasset, *En torno a Galileo*, p. 23. (*Man and Crisis*, p. 22.)

Ortega y Gasset was, by his own admission, influenced by the philosophers with whom he became acquainted while studying in Germany, the likes of Friedrich Nietzsche (1844–1900), Martin Heidegger (1889–1976), and especially Edmund Husserl (1859–1938), and Wilhelm Dilthey (1833–1911). He had great fondness for the latter two.[26] He found in German philosophy the antidote for the "way the universe has become for the Spaniard something rigid, dry, sordid and deserted."[27] There was, he thought, something lacking, namely, "clarity," in Latin thought: "Mediterranean culture cannot offer products of its own comparable with Germanic science—philosophy, physics, biology."[28] Where the Latin mind is characterized by "an ardent and perpetual justification of sensuousness, of appearances, of surfaces, of the fleeting impressions which things leave on our stimulated nerves,"[29] the German reminds him that "man has a mission of clarity upon earth."[30] Though he recognized the impossibility of happily reconciling the Latin and the Germanic, he begged: "Do not incite the Iberian within me with his harsh, wild passions, against the blonde man of Germanic heritage, meditative and sentimental....I try to make peace among my inner personalities and I urge them toward collaboration."[31] Echoing G.W.F. Hegel (1770–1831) in his insistence upon a rational understanding of the totality of history, Ortega wrote: "History is a system, the system of human experiences linked in a single, inexorable chain....Every historic term whatsoever, to have exactness, must be determined as a function of all history."[32] There is a place, *must* be a place, he was convinced, within philosophy for both the Latin/Iberian soul of Spain alongside the clear thinking, highly organized mind of the German.

## II. Kierkegaard in Ortega y Gasset's Works

Ortega did not express any fondness for the writings of Kierkegaard. In fact, he was unsparing in his comments about the difficulty he had with the Danish author. Ortega's clearest statement on Kierkegaard can be found in the "Preface for Germans" ("Prologo para Alemanes") to his work, *The Modern Theme*, published in 1934.[33] There, Ortega quite simply stated his revulsion (*repugnancia*) with Kierkegaard's style; he claims to have been unable to appreciate a single book by Kierkegaard,

---

[26]     Ortega commented that with Husserl and Dilthey philosophy had "at last" reached a temperament "which was quietly preoccupied only with 'seeing' how things properly are, or better, which things we see clearly and which we do not, without fuss, without phraseology, without tragedy or comedy *pari passu* [without partiality]." *La idea de principio en Leibniz y la evolución de la teoría deductiva*, Buenos Aires: Emecé Editores 1958, p. 366. (English translation: *The Idea of Principle in Leibnitz and the Evolution of Deductive Theory*, trans. by Mildred Adams, New York: W.W. Norton 1971, p. 311.)

[27]     Ortega y Gasset, *Meditaciones del Quijote*, p. 17. (*Meditations on Quixote*, p. 33.)

[28]     Ortega y Gasset, *Meditaciones del Quijote*, p. 98. (*Meditations on Quixote*, p. 80.)

[29]     Ortega y Gasset, *Meditaciones del Quijote*, p. 102. (*Meditations on Quixote*, p. 83.)

[30]     Ortega y Gasset, *Meditaciones del Quijote*, p. 123. (*Meditations on Quixote*, p. 98.)

[31]     Ibid.

[32]     Ortega y Gasset, *Historia como sistema*, p. 67. (*History as a System*, p. 221.)

[33]     Ortega y Gasset, "Prólogo Para Alemanes" (Preface to the 3rd German edition of *El tema de nuestro tiempo*), in *Obras completas*, vol. 8, pp. 15–58.

despite having as a reader a large capacity to absorb unpleasantries.[34] Kierkegaard's "literary gesticulations" were an obstacle to the reader, he complained. The German authors, when compared with Kierkegaard, were easier to comprehend, according to Ortega, who especially objected to Kierkegaard's presentation of Christianity as an "offense" to reason. Instead, Ortega countered that Christianity, in Kierkegaard's version, has fed like a parasite off the alleged failure of reason.[35] What made Kierkegaard highly suspicious in the eyes of Ortega was that he believed "existential thinking"—like Kierkegaard's—was born of a "desperation" of thinking, relying too much upon arbitrary judgment, articulated under the guise of "direct action." Ortega doubted that any "philosophy of existence" should be called a philosophy at all.[36]

The second prominent place where readers find (unfavorable) mention of Kierkegaard is in Ortega's 1947 work, *The Idea of Principle in Leibnitz and the Evolution of Deductive Theory*. Ortega therein lamented the need of the typical existentialist (cut from the cloth of Kierkegaard) for "darkness, death, and Nothingness."[37] Kierkegaard, according to Ortega, embodied the spirit of "provincial romanticism"[38]—he was "the typical provincial 'genius'"[39]—someone "superlative at dramatizing himself,"[40] someone characterized by "swollen ostentation" and "moral tumescence which usually afflicts the intellectual tied to the provincial clay which he knows he can never leave."[41] Kierkegaard uses a "customary strategy in a town that is out of the way," that is, he creates a scandal in Christianity and thereby

---

[34]     Ortega writes: "*En cuanto Kierkegaard, ni entonces ni después he podido leerle. Aunque poseo grandes fauces de lector e ingurgito con impavidez las materias menos gratas, soy incapaz de absorber un libro de Kierkegaard. Su estilo me pone enfermo a la quinta página.*" See Ortega y Gasset, "Prólogo Para Alemanes," in *La Idea de Principio en Leibniz y La Evolución de la Teoría Deductiva*, in *Obras completas*, vol. 8, p. 46.

[35]     He continues (ibid.): "*Sospecho, además, dos cosas que someto a la sentencia de los lectores alemanes más entendidos que yo en Kierkegaard: una es que se trata de ese eterno cristiano que fundamenta su cristianismo en algo positivo, ingenuo, generoso, y fresco, sino precisamente en el hecho de que la razón sea algo limitado y trágico. Es decir, que ese cristianismo es mera objeción que presume de ser cosa positiva y vivir por si. Mas toda objeción no es sino parásito. Ese cristianismo se alimenta exclusivamente del presunto fracaso de la razón, se nutre de un cadáver.*"

[36]     He continues (ibid.): "*La otra cosa que en Kierkegaard sospecho es esta: lo que él llama 'pensar existencial,' nacido de la desesperación del pensar, tiene todas las probabilidades de no ser, en absoluto, pensar, sino una resolución arbitraria y exasperada, también 'acción directa'. Por eso dudo mucho que pueda una filosofía llamarse adecuadamente 'filosofía de la existencia.'*"

[37]     Ortega y Gasset, *La idea de principio en Leibniz y la evolución de la teoría deductiva*, p. 367. (*The Idea of Principle in Leibnitz*, p. 311.)

[38]     Ortega y Gasset, *La idea de principio en Leibniz y la evolución de la teoría deductiva*, p. 370. (*The Idea of Principle in Leibnitz*, p. 315.)

[39]     Ibid.

[40]     Ortega y Gasset, *La idea de principio en Leibniz y la evolución de la teoría deductiva*, p. 371. (*The Idea of Principle in Leibnitz*, p. 315.)

[41]     Ortega y Gasset, *La idea de principio en Leibniz y la evolución de la teoría deductiva*, p. 371. (*The Idea of Principle in Leibnitz*, p. 316.)

creates "*his* scandal."[42] Ortega seems to principally object to Kierkegaard's flawed perspective—"*localitis*" he calls it—wherein "the factions of the small hamlet are absurdly enlarged to ecumenical size."[43] Being a "provincial," Kierkegaard has no "real public" before which he can truly be himself and therefore falls into the trap of "provincialism"—this life is "all directed inward, it reabsorbs its own secretions and consists in a continual return to the within-ness of the within....Thus Kierkegaard in Copenhagen."[44] Provincialism, Ortega concludes, "is one of the greatest infirmities from which the Occident suffers."[45]

Ortega knew that Kierkegaard had a negative influence (as a gloomy Romantic) on his intellectual descendants, an influence most acutely evident upon his older contemporary and fellow member of the "Generation of 1898," Miguel de Unamuno (1864–1936).[46] Kierkegaard's, and thus Unamuno's, "existential thought" was not philosophy but a despair of reason, an abrogation of thinking. Ortega considered Unamuno "a man very much like Kierkegaard" in his "irrationalism."[47] Ortega's philosophy of "vital reason" was a direct attempt to respond to darker, more pessimistic forms of existentialism. Admittedly, Unamuno considered Kierkegaard a "powerful" thinker from whose "anarchism" he had taken much "sustenance."[48] Unamuno, unlike Ortega, expressed a "horror of intellectualism" and admitted (in a letter addressed to Ortega), "Every day I am less interested in ideas and things: every day I am more interested in feelings and people....My long distrust of science is turning into hatred."[49] Ortega could not have been more different in perspective. He called Unamuno's thought an "Africanist deviation,"[50] reminiscent of Tertullian or Augustine: "Unamuno's spirit is too turbulent, and drags in its racing current, along

---

[42]      Ortega y Gasset, *La idea de principio en Leibniz y la evolución de la teoría deductiva*, p. 372. (*The Idea of Principle in Leibnitz*, p. 316.)

[43]      Ortega y Gasset, *La idea de principio en Leibniz y la evolución de la teoría deductiva*, p. 372. (*The Idea of Principle in Leibnitz*, p. 317.)

[44]      Ortega y Gasset, *La idea de principio en Leibniz y la evolución de la teoría deductiva*, p. 373. (*The Idea of Principle in Leibnitz*, pp. 317–18.)

[45]      Ortega y Gasset, *La idea de principio en Leibniz y la evolución de la teoría deductiva*, p. 373. (*The Idea of Principle in Leibnitz*, p. 318.)

[46]      In *The Idea of Principle in Leibnitz*, when describing Kierkegaard's bombastic language and provincial limitations and seeing therein dissatisfaction with the restricted circumstances of the "market town" of Copenhagen, Ortega remarks: "I have known another man singularly like Kierkegaard in this, and hence I know the latter well." Ortega y Gasset, *La idea de principio en Leibniz y la evolución de la teoría deductiva*, p. 371. (*The Idea of Principle in Leibnitz*, p. 316.) He must be speaking here of Unamuno. This view is shared by John T. Graham; see his *A Pragmatist Philosophy of Life in Ortega y Gasset*, Columbia and London: University of Missouri Press 1994, p. 238.

[47]      Ortega y Gasset, *Obras Completas*, vol. 8, p. 302.

[48]      Miguel de Unamuno, "Letter to Frederico Urales" (1901), in *The Private World: Selections from the* Diario intimo *and Selected Letters*, in *Selected Works of Miguel de Unamuno*, vols. 1–7, trans. by Allen Lacy and Martin Nozick, Princeton, New Jersey: Princeton University Press 1984, vol. 2, p. 165.

[49]      Unamuno, *Selected Works*, vol. 2, p. 180.

[50]      José Ortega y Gasset, "Sobre Los Estudios Clásicos," *El Imparcial*, October 28, 1907 (in *Obras Completas*, vol. 1, p. 64).

with some gold dust, many useless and unhealthy things. We must be careful about how much we swallow."[51] Ortega believed Unamuno to be prone to "fanaticism," someone who swam "in the muddy waters of the passions."[52] In *The Idea of Principle in Leibnitz*, he wrote: "From my earliest writings I have opposed the exclusiveness of a 'tragic sense of life' which Unamuno rhetorically proclaimed, preferring a 'sportive and festive sense' of existence."[53] And further, "I do not believe in the 'tragic sense of life' as the ultimate form of existence. Life is not, cannot be a tragedy. It is within life that tragedies are produced and are possible."[54]

## III. General Interpretation

José Ortega y Gasset was an engaged and avid reader who consumed a broad sampling of European thought, all of which provided the background for his own ideas. As Julian Marias, Ortega's biographer, has put it, his philosophical predecessors "*acted on him*" (though he often did not mention them by name), "especially, of course, in the apparently passive form of the *configuration* of his world, and, consequently, of his biographical trajectory."[55] Marias considers Kierkegaard among those who created "the determining conditions of his *possibilities*."[56] Though Kierkegaard was a source that Ortega resisted much more than he assimilated, there are some interpreters who credit Kierkegaard with provoking significant insights in Ortega. José Sanchez Villaseñor, for example, claims that during an "acute transitional phase" for Ortega, wherein his "perspectivism" reached maturity, Ortega admitted Kierkegaard "into the intimate circle of his readings" and was coaxed by him to turn his attention more towards "man and his circumstances" and less so to more trivial matters of history.[57] It was Kierkegaard, according to Villaseñor, who directed Ortega's thought to the individual's quest for meaning on earth within his concrete existence and circumstance. Ortega's perspective, however, was not theistic.[58] And

---

[51]     Quoted in Julian Marias, *José Ortega y Gasset: Circumstance and Vocation*, trans. by Frances M. Lopez-Morillas, Norman: University of Oklahoma Press 1970, p. 136; Cf. Ortega y Gasset, "Sobre Los Estudios Clásicos," *El Imparcial*, October 28, 1907 (in *Obras Completas*, vol. 1, pp. 117–18).

[52]     José Ortega y Gasset, "Unamuno y Europa, Fabula," *El Imparcial*, September 27, 1909 (in *Obras Completas*, vol. 1, pp. 128–32; Marias, *José Ortega y Gasset: Circumstance and Vocation*, p. 138).

[53]     Ortega y Gasset, *La idea de principio en Leibniz y la evolución de la teoría deductiva*, pp. 365–6. (*The Idea of Principle in Leibnitz*, p. 310.)

[54]     Ortega y Gasset, *La idea de principio en Leibniz y la evolución de la teoría deductiva*, p. 368. (*The Idea of Principle in Leibnitz*, p. 313.)

[55]     Marias, *José Ortega y Gasset: Circumstance and Vocation*, p. 96.

[56]     Ibid.

[57]     José Sanchez Villaseñor, *Ortega y Gasset, Existentialist: A Critical Study of His Thought and Its Sources*, trans. by Joseph Small, Chicago: Henry Regnery 1949, pp. 31–2.

[58]     John T. Graham has noted, "Always private and reserved, [Ortega] was guarded about religion." Many theistic readers, however, have seen Ortega's philosophy as compatible with their own views. Ortega exemplified a "protoecumenical spirit," which favored "rapprochement between churches and faiths and between the world and religion too, while

though he was often classified among the "existentialists," he held "reservations and objections" about being grouped with them, seeing his own thought as more positive and less preoccupied with "crisis" and "despair."[59] In a manner similar to Albert Camus (1913–60), Ortega y Gasset "concentrated on the immanent values of this life in contrast to the Christian emphasis on the beatific 'other life.' "[60]

In his work, *The Imperative of Modernity: An Intellectual Biography of José Ortega y Gasset*, Rockwell Gray further unpacks where Kierkegaard and Ortega depart. Gray sees Ortega's philosophy as one born of doubt, which maintains its authenticity "only by refusing to accept as given a particular impression of the human situation"—Ortega "rejected that type of contemporary thought...which pivoted on the need to 'engage' or commit oneself. For him, this act of commitment was the very contradiction of a genuinely philosophical attitude, which consisted in the 'negative capability' *not* to commit oneself but to remain open to further analysis."[61] Ortega saw a religious 'leap of faith' (not unlike Kierkegaard's) as "the death of true speculation" and thus of the philosophical life; instead, according to Ortega, "philosophy cannot be conceived in a desperate state, back against the wall."[62]

Where Kierkegaard and Ortega sound uncannily alike, and where Ortega may reveal Kierkegaard's influence, is on the subject of the "masses" or the "crowd." This subject is examined in Howard Tuttle's work, *The Crowd is Untruth: The Existential Critique of Mass Society in the Thought of Kierkegaard, Nietzsche, Heidegger, and Ortega y Gasset*, in which Tuttle considers the foremost "theorists of secular leveling that characterizes modern massification."[63] Tuttle argues that both Kierkegaard and Ortega understood the present condition of modern humanity to be one of "demoralization or nihilism" produced by a lack of interior reflection (what Ortega referred to as *ensimismamiento*) and an abolition of freedom, ultimately a desertion of reason in favor of blind "action."[64] Where the two differ, however, is in Kierkegaard's assessment that the source of "leveling" within modernity lies "in the individual's abandonment of the eternal, and his attempt to seek salvation in economics, politics, and materialism."[65] By contrast, Ortega's analysis was less spiritual and more political; instead, Ortega "saw the state as a danger that is connected to the rise of the mass."[66] Tuttle's commentary, it ought to be noted, is comparative in nature and less concerned with Ortega's philosophical debt to Kierkegaard. Many of the ideas articulated by Tuttle can be found earlier in an obscure, 1960 essay by Robert

---

he personally did not commit himself wholly or exclusively to either." Cf. John T. Graham, *The Social Thought of Ortega y Gasset: A Systematic Synthesis in Postmodernism and Interdisciplinarity*, Columbia and London: University of Missouri Press 2001, p. 449.

[59]     Graham, "A Pragmatist Philosophy of Life," in *Ortega y Gasset*, pp. 231–2. Graham labels Ortega "a *reluctant* existentialist."

[60]     Ibid., p. 266.

[61]     Rockwell Gray, *The Imperative of Modernity: An Intellectual Biography of José Ortega y Gasset*, Berkeley: University of California Press 1989, p. 305.

[62]     Ibid.

[63]     Howard N. Tuttle, *The Crowd is Untruth*, New York: Peter Lang 1996, pp. 152–4.

[64]     Ibid.

[65]     Ibid.

[66]     Ibid.

O. Weiss.[67] The focus of this parallel examination is upon the *choice* given to each person, "between becoming a particle of the masses or retaining his individuality,"[68] the decision to resist "the dominance of incompetence and tyrannical unreason"[69] as well as "shallowness of purpose and a monumental indolence."[70] Again, more than deciphering the dependence of Ortega upon Kierkegaard, Weiss sees "congruent analyses" in the two.

There should be no doubt that José Ortega y Gasset was intimately familiar with Kierkegaard, offering his critical appraisal, but that this acquaintance did not lead to sympathy for Kierkegaard's style or ideas. Both he found distasteful. Kierkegaard, however, did provide a philosophical resource against which Ortega pushed back and in the process forged his own identity as an "optimistic" European, rooted in Iberian soil but not confined to it. Ortega, it must be concluded, saw in Kierkegaard a route he did *not* wish to pursue. While Kierkegaard focused his attention on the human encounter with the divine paradox of the Incarnation (*the* "offense" to reason), Ortega instead focused on the human encounter with *this* world and each individual's more immediate circumstances. There is, nonetheless, a parallel (and not convergent) track between the two philosophers, insofar as they both lamented the "leveling" of individuals within modern society and a pervasive lack of "authenticity."

---

[67]     See Robert O. Weiss, "The Leveling Process as a Function of the Masses in the View of Kierkegaard and Ortega y Gasset," *Kentucky Foreign Language Quarterly*, vol. 7, 1960, pp. 27–36.

[68]     Ibid., p. 28.

[69]     Ibid., p. 30.

[70]     Ibid., p. 32.

# Bibliography

*I. References to or Uses of Kierkegaard in Ortega y Gasset's* Corpus

"Azorín: Primores de lo Vulgar,' " in *Obras Completas*, vols. 1–8, ed. by Fundación
   Ortega y Gasset, Centro de Estudios Orteguianos, Madrid: Revista de Occidente
   1961–70, vol. 2, p. 175 (first published in *El Espectador*, 1917).
"Las Dos Grandes Metáforas," in *Obras completas*, vol. 2, p. 388 (first published in
   *El Espectador*, 1924).
"Prólogo Para Alemanes" (Preface to the 3rd German edition of *El tema de nuestro
   tiempo*), in *Obras completas*, vol. 8, p. 46.
*La idea de principio en Leibniz y la evolución de la teoría deductiva*, Buenos Aires:
   Emecé Editores 1958, pp. 361–74. (English translation: *The Idea of Principle in
   Leibnitz and the Evolution of Deductive Theory*, trans. by Mildred Adams, New
   York: W.W. Norton 1971, pp. 305–19.)
"Una Interpretación de la Historia Universal," in *Obras Completas*, vol. 9, pp. 85–6
   (first published in *Revista de Occidente*, Madrid, 1960; English translation: *An
   Interpretation of Universal History*, trans. by Mildred Adams, New York: W.W.
   Norton 1973, p. 104).

*II. Sources of Ortega y Gasset's Knowledge of Kierkegaard*

Heidegger, Martin, *Sein und Zeit*, Halle: Niemeyer 1927, pp. 175–96, see also
   p. 190, note 1; p. 235, note 1; and p. 338, note 1.
Unamuno, Miguel de, *Del sentimiento trágico de la vida en los hombres y en los
   pueblos*, Madrid: Renacimiento 1913, p. 7; p. 22; pp. 111–13; pp. 117–18; p. 124;
   p. 154; pp. 176–7; p. 197; p. 253; p. 280; p. 318.
Wahl, Jean, *Études Kierkegaardiennes*, Paris: Aubier 1938.

*III. Secondary Literature on Ortega y Gasset's Relation to Kierkegaard*

Bennett, James O., "Selves and Personal Existence in the Existential Tradition,"
   *Journal of the History of Philosophy*, vol. 37, no. 1, 1999, pp. 135–56.
Cascardi, Anthony J., "Between Philosophy and Literature: Ortega's *Meditations
   on Quixote*," *José Ortega y Gasset: Proceedings of the Espectador universal
   International Interdisciplinary Conference*, ed. by Nora de Marval-McNair, New
   York: Glenwood Press 1987, pp. 15–19.

Diaz, Janet Winecoff, *The Major Themes of Existentialism in the Work of José Ortega y Gasset*, Chapel Hill: University of North Carolina Press 1970, pp. 21–33; pp. 204–9.

Dixon, Jr., John W., "Ortega and the Redefinition of Metaphysics," *Cross Currents*, Fall 1979, pp. 281–99.

Farré, Luis, "Hegel, Kierkegaard y dos españoles: Ortega y Gasset y Unamuno," *La Nación*, Buenos Aires, July 21, 1963 (reprinted in his *Unamuno, William James, Kierkegaard y otros ensayos*, Buenos Aires: La Aurora 1967, pp. 151–60).

Graham, John T., *A Pragmatist Philosophy of Life in Ortega y Gasset*, Columbia and London: University of Missouri Press 1994, pp. 229–69.

— *The Social Thought of Ortega y Gasset: A Systematic Synthesis in Postmodernism and Interdisciplinarity*, Columbia and London: University of Missouri Press 2001, pp. 446–92.

Gray, Rockwell, *The Imperative of Modernity: An Intellectual Biography of José Ortega y Gasset*, Berkeley: University of California Press 1989, pp. 130ff.; pp. 304ff.

Marias, Julian, *José Ortega y Gasset: Circumstance and Vocation*, trans. by Frances M. Lopez-Morillas, Norman: University of Oklahoma Press 1970, pp. 56–91; pp. 174–204.

McInnes, Neil, "Ortega and the Myth of the Mass," *National Interest*, vol. 44, 1996, pp. 78–88.

Statham, E. Robert, "Ortega y Gasset's 'Revolt' and the Problem of Mass Rule," *Modern Age*, vol. 46, no. 3, 2004, pp. 219–26.

Tuttle, Howard N., *The Crowd is Untruth*, New York: Peter Lang 1996, pp. xi–xv, 152–63.

Villaseñor, José Sanchez, *Ortega y Gasset, Existentialist: A Critical Study of His Thought and Its Sources*, trans. by Joseph Small, Chicago: Henry Regnery Co. 1949, pp. 11–26; pp. 190–4.

Weigert, Andrew J., "José Ortega y Gasset on Understanding Human Life as Ultimate Reality and Meaning," *Ultimate Reality and Meaning*, vol. 18, no. 1, 1995, pp. 54–65.

Weiss, Robert O., "The Leveling Process as a Function of the Masses in the View of Kierkegaard and Ortega y Gasset," *Kentucky Foreign Language Quarterly*, vol. 7, 1960, pp. 27–36.

# Jean-Paul Sartre:

## Between Kierkegaard and Marx

### Michael O'Neill Burns

While there has been much written exploring the influence of Kierkegaard's writings on the philosophical work of French philosopher Jean-Paul Sartre (1905–80), these secondary works have dealt almost exclusively with the role Kierkegaard plays in Sartre's pre-war phenomenological and psychological work, primarily as seen in his first great work, *Being and Nothingness*.[1] While the influence of Kierkegaard on the phenomenological and psychological work of Sartre has already been explored in another volume of this series,[2] in the present article I will explore the influence of Kierkegaard in Sartre's post-war period in which he developed a Marx-inspired political philosophy, which is marked by his second great work, *Critique of Dialectical Reason*, vol. 1. While Kierkegaard's name only appears once in the *Critique of Dialectical Reason*,[3] Sartre's most extensive explicit engagements with Kierkegaard take place on either side of this text. The first comes in Sartre's essay *Search for a Method*,[4] which was originally written as an article for a Hungarian journal in 1957, and then printed in Sartre's journal *Les Temps modernes* and later published as the introduction to the French edition of the *Critique of Dialectical Reason*.[5] In this work Sartre briefly charts out the shift in his philosophical approach by explicating the shifts he sees in both Kierkegaard and Marx's responses to Hegel. The second, which was published after *Critique of Dialectical Reason*, is a conference presentation entitled "Kierkegaard: The Singular Universal" which was presented

---

[1]    Jean-Paul Sartre, *L'Être et le néant: Essai d'ontologie phénoménologique*, Paris: Gallimard 1943. (English translation: *Being and Nothingness*, trans. by Hazel E. Barnes, New York: Citadel Press 1956.)

[2]    See Manuela Hackel, "Jean-Paul Sartre: Kierkegaard's Influence on His Theory of Nothingness," *Kierkegaard's Influence on Existentialism*, ed. by Jon Stewart, Aldershot: Ashgate 2011 (*Kierkegaard Research: Sources, Reception, and Resources*, vol. 9), pp. 323–54.

[3]    Jean-Paul Sartre, *Critique de la raison dialectique*, vol. 1, *Théorie des ensembles pratiques*, Paris: Gallimard 1960, p. 117, note 1. (English translation: *Critique of Dialectical Reason*, trans. by Alan Sheridan-Smith, London: New Left Books 1976, pp. 17–18, note 6.)

[4]    Jean-Paul Sartre, "Questions de methode," *Les Temps modernes*, no. 139, September 1957, pp. 338–417; no. 140, October 1957, pp. 658–98.

[5]    Jean-Paul Sartre, "Question de Methode," in *Critique de la raison dialectique*, vol. 1, *Théorie des ensembles pratiques*, pp. 13–111. (English translation: *Search for a Method*, trans. by Hazel E. Barnes, New York: Alfred A. Knopf 1963, pp. 3–34.)

at a UNESCO conference during 1964 in Paris entitled *Kierkegaard vivant.*[6] This is Sartre's lengthiest explicit engagement with Kierkegaard, and while not overtly political in nature, Sartre highlights a few particular aspects of Kierkegaard's thought that seem to parallel some of the key theoretical developments which appear in the *Critique of Dialectical Reason.*

It is worth noting that in the eyes of most commentators there is a fairly dramatic shift that takes place in Sartre's thought that can be broadly defined by his pre- and post-war periods. Before the war much of Sartre's writings were focused primarily on a phenomenological account of the absolutely free individual, and his work lacked any strong account of the social and political relationships between multiple subjects, as well as an account of history. After the war, however, the changing political climate along with his serious reading of Marx led him to move beyond an account of the free individual in an attempt to develop a political philosophy which could account for the relationship between man and the material conditions in which he found himself, as well as providing an account for the emergence of group activity. While the Sartre of *Being and Nothingness* grounded freedom in a phenomenological-ontological lack, with the writing of *Critique of Dialectical Reason* Sartre now provides a materialist account for this lack which grounds freedom in the concept of material scarcity.

In light of this, this article will begin with a description of the intellectual and political shift taken in Sartre's work between the publication of *Being and Nothingness* and the *Critique of Dialectical Reason*; it will then examine Sartre's engagement with Kierkegaard in his book *Search for a Method* and in his lecture "Kierkegaard: The Singular Universal." The article will close with a brief consideration of further lines of research which could be taken to explore the relationship between Kierkegaard and Sartre on social and political matters. Before moving forward, however, it is worth explicitly noting that as this article is in a volume concerned specifically with Kierkegaard's influence on social-political thought, I will be confining the discussion to the way in which Kierkegaard appears to have played an influence on the development of Sartre's political philosophy. Due to this specificity, the present article will not be a survey of the influence of Kierkegaard on Sartre's entire post-war authorship, but rather a specific account of the references made to Kierkegaard in his post-war political writings.

## *I. Kierkegaard's Influence on Sartre's Political Thought*

As previously noted, while there exists a vast amount of secondary material on Kierkegaard's influence on Sartre's pre-war philosophical project, there exists little in way of serious engagement with the potential influence of Kierkegaard on Sartre's post-war political philosophy. One of the few explicit engagements is contained

---

[6]     Jean-Paul Sartre, "Kierkegaard: L'universal Singulier," in *Kierkegaard vivant. Colloque organisé par l'Unesco à Paris du 21 au 23 avril 1964*, Paris: Gallimard 1966, pp. 20–63. (English translation: "Kierkegaard: The Singular Universal," in *Between Existentialism and Marxism*, trans. by John Matthews, London: New Left Books 1974, pp. 141–69.)

in the article "Sartre's Debt to Kierkegaard: A Partial Reckoning" by William L. McBride which is contained in the volume *Kierkegaard in Post/Modernity*.[7] While the piece is a summary of the influence of Kierkegaard on Sartre throughout his entire authorship, McBride includes a section on ethics and politics which engages specifically with the two essays discussed in this article. The important point argued by McBride is that we should pay closer attention to the emphasis on community found in Kierkegaard's later works, and use this reading to reconsider the similarities between the development of Kierkegaard and Sartre's philosophical projects. While not very extensive, McBride at least raises the question of the relation between the works of Kierkegaard and Sartre's political philosophy.

Along with this, there are brief references to Kierkegaard in many of the secondary texts which provide critical commentary on Sartre's political philosophy, but most do little more than recount Sartre's mention of Kierkegaard in these post-war writings. One minor exception to this trend is the book *Sartre and Marxism* by Pietro Chioch,[8] which, while in no way containing an extensive engagement with Kierkegaard, at least extends beyond the usual treatment in other writings concerned with Sartre's political work.[9]

## II. Sartre's Political Turn

In the period separating *Being and Nothingness* from the *Critique of Dialectical Reason* there is a dramatic shift in Sartre's philosophical concerns; in simple terms, this shift could be regarded as a transition from a concern with individual and interior experience, to a focus on exterior and social experience. Whereas the individual subject (or, for-itself) in Sartre's early philosophical work was founded by its relation to a fundamental ontological lack, in his later work Sartre shifts to a material account of lack, scarcity, which characterizes the fundamental inconsistency between man and matter. To characterize this transition in even more obvious terms, we could say, as Sartre himself does in *Search for a Method*, that this transition is one from existentialism to Marxism.

In an interview conducted in 1969, Sartre was asked to describe the relationship between his early and late works, and during the interview Sartre recalls himself writing that "Whatever his circumstances, and wherever the site, a man is always free

---

[7]     William L. McBride, "Sartre's Debt to Kierkegaard: A Partial Reckoning," in *Kierkegaard in Post/Modernity*, ed. by Martin Matuštík and Merold Westphal, Bloomington: Indiana University Press 1995, pp. 18–42.

[8]     Pietro Chiodi, *Sartre and Marxism*, trans. by Kate Soper, Atlantic Highlands, New Jersey: Humanities Press 1976.

[9]     Refer to the Bibliography for references to the few texts that contain some engagement with Kierkegaard's influence on Sartre's political thought. For a wonderful summary which covers the role of Kierkegaard in Sartre's post-war writings see Jon Stewart, "France: Kierkegaard as a Forerunner of Existentialism and Poststructuralism," in *Kierkegaard's International Reception*, Tome I, *Northern and Western Europe*, ed. by Jon Stewart, Aldershot: Ashgate 2009 (*Kierkegaard Research: Sources, Reception, and Resources*, vol. 8), pp. 434–41.

to be a traitor or not...."[10] After recounting this quotation, Sartre tells the interviewer, "When I read this, I said to myself: it's incredible, I actually believed that!"[11]

Whereas the freedom of *Being and Nothingness* is an ontological and nearly limitless freedom, the experience of World War II left Sartre with a realization that his earlier view was remarkably naive in light of the world's socio-political tragedies. Rather than simply acknowledging the contingent facticity of place of birth, or the class which one is born into, in the *Critique of Dialectical Reason* Sartre relies on his newfound ally, Marx, to acknowledge the concrete social, political, and productive forces which can place concrete limits on the freedom of individuals. Along with this, Sartre introduces another new concept, the practio-inert, which allows him further to analyze the limits placed on freedom. The practico-inert is the name for the limit placed on human freedom by the material remnants of previous human praxis now inscribed into matter itself. In this sense even the human work of past generations can limit the potential and success of living human praxis. Sartre's socio-political project can in many ways be seen as an exploration of the possibility of novel and collective human praxis in light of the seemingly determined limits placed on humanity by both material scarcity and the work of past human praxis inscribed in the practio-inert.

In light of what may seem like an abandonment of his earlier project, many will be unsurprised to hear that there is but one passing footnote reference to Kierkegaard in Sartre's sprawling, and ultimately unfinished, two-volume *Critique of Dialectical Reason*.[12] What may be surprising, however, is the fact that Sartre's two most extended explicit engagements with Kierkegaard take place during his later political, or Marxist, period of his work. One of these pieces, *Search for a Method*, later served as the introduction to the French edition of the *Critique of Dialectical Reason*, and the other essay, "Kierkegaard: The Singular Universal," was presented in 1964, well into Sartre's Marxist period. While both engagements include substantial reference to Kierkegaard in general, they include limited explicit textual references, which can leave one wondering if Sartre had in fact interacted in much depth with Kierkegaard's writings, or if Kierkegaard served to represent a certain philosophical position for him.

## *III. Sartre's Interaction with Kierkegaard*

A majority of the engagement with Kierkegaard in *Search for a Method* takes place in the opening chapter, "Marxism and Existentialism." This chapter opens with a discussion of Hegel, whom Sartre sees as being the starting point for both Marxism and existentialism. Never one to avoid polemic, Sartre does not keep the reader waiting to find out which school of thought he intends to side with; only a few pages

---

[10]     Jean-Paul Sartre, "The Itinerary of a Thought," *New Left Review*, no. 58, November–December 1969, pp. 43–66. (republished in *Between Existentialism and Marxism*, pp. 33–64).
[11]     Sartre, "The Itinerary of a Thought," p. 44 (in *Between Existentialism and Marxism*, pp. 33–4).
[12]     Jean-Paul Sartre, *Critique de la raison dialectique*, vol. 1, *Théorie des ensembles pratiques*, p. 117, note. (*Critique of Dialectical Reason*, pp. 17, note–18, note.)

in Sartre lets us know that Marxism is the only philosophy of our time and that "A so called 'going beyond' Marxism will be at worst only a return to pre-Marxism."[13] After this early affirmation of Marxism, Sartre then backs up a bit to discuss Kierkegaard, specifically in the context of his reaction to Hegelian totalization. As Sartre sees it, Kierkegaard's primary opposition to the Hegelian system lies in his insistence that "the existing man cannot be assimilated by a system of ideas."[14] For Sartre, this is what is worth holding onto in the work of Kierkegaard, this emphasis on "pure unique subjectivity" which cannot merely be explained as a moment in the unfolding of the historical system. This said, Sartre still acknowledges that Kierkegaard's "anti-Hegelian" project could only emerge "within a cultural field entirely dominated by Hegelianism."[15]

He goes on to emphasize the particularly human and affective aspects of the subject in Kierkegaard, noting: "Kierkegaard is right: grief, need, passion, the pain of men, are brute realities which can be neither surpassed nor changed by knowledge."[16] The point here for Sartre is that contra Hegelianism, ideas do not change men, but rather, a passionate response to a need produced by a particular situation is what has the capacity to actualize change in an individual. Sartre goes on to argue: "Knowing the cause of a passion is not enough to overcome it; one must live it, one must oppose other passions to it, one must combat it tenaciously, in short one most 'work oneself over.' "[17] Shortly after this passage Sartre then shifts the focus of his discussion back to Marx:

> It is striking that Marxism addresses the same reproach to Hegel though from quite another point of view. For Marx, indeed, Hegel has confused objectification, the simple externalization of man in the universe, with the alienation which turns his externalization back against man. Taken by itself—Marx emphasizes this again and again—objectification would be an opening out; it would allow man, who produces and reproduces his life without ceasing and who transforms himself by changing nature, to "contemplate himself in a world which he has created."[18]

Here Sartre begins to spell out the main argument of this chapter, and the one which in many ways defines his post-war authorship. Sartre is providing a reading of Marx which emphasizes the role of the subjective, and thus he claims that "Marx puts priority of action over knowledge."[19] Sartre sees Marx as placing an emphasis on action and the subjective into Hegelian objective knowledge. Later on the same page we see Sartre arguing that Marx is thus able to take the best aspects of both Hegel and Kierkegaard, and turn this into a new philosophical and political system: "Thus Marx, rather than Kierkegaard or Hegel, is right, since he asserts with Kierkegaard the specificity of human *existence* and, along with Hegel, takes the concrete man in

---

13  Sartre, *Critique de la Raison Dialectique*, p. 17. (*Search for a Method*, p. 7.)
14  Sartre, *Critique de la Raison Dialectique*, p. 19. (*Search for a Method*, p. 10.)
15  Sartre, *Critique de la Raison Dialectique*, p. 19. (*Search for a Method*, p. 11.)
16  Sartre, *Critique de la Raison Dialectique*, pp. 19–20. (*Search for a Method*, p. 12.)
17  Sartre, *Critique de la Raison Dialectique*, p. 20. (*Search for a Method*, pp. 12–13.)
18  Sartre, *Critique de la Raison Dialectique*, p. 20. (*Search for a Method*, p. 13.)
19  Sartre, *Critique de la Raison Dialectique*, p. 21. (*Search for a Method*, p. 14.)

his objective reality."[20] At this point we see that if it was Kierkegaard who defined the overall project of Sartre's pre-war philosophy, it is undoubtedly Marx who will be the philosopher informing Sartre's post-war political thought. It is also important to note here that Sartre avoids completely abandoning Hegel or Kierkegaard by making the point that the difference between their thought is not a fundamental one, but rather a matter of standpoint or perspective. Sartre thus sees Marx as the figure in which Kierkegaard's emphasis on the singular individual and Hegel's emphasis on the absolute idea's progression towards the whole is consummated in a single philosophy.

Kierkegaard does not play a major role in *Search for a Method* after this opening chapter, and in the text this book would later serve to introduce, *Critique of Dialectical Reason*, he fails to play any substantial explicit role. But it is clear that the Marx who appears throughout the rest of Sartre's political writings is one whom Sartre sees to be carrying out a very Kierkegaardian project.

Sartre's second major interaction with Kierkegaard in his post-war period is the lecture "Kierkegaard: The Singular Universal." While in many ways this lecture lacks substantial engagement with the social and political aspects of his later philosophy, the version of Kierkegaard that Sartre develops in the lecture is one that seems to be in agreement with much of Sartre's project as laid out in the *Critique of Dialectical Reason*. Because of this, I will make some brief remarks on the lecture itself, and then highlight the implications of this reading of Kierkegaard for our purpose of examining his influence on Sartre's political philosophy in particular.

Much like the argument Sartre presents in the "Existentialism and Marxism" chapter of *Search for a Method*, he here emphasizes the role passion and lived experience play in allowing Kierkegaard to avoid being merely a historical "moment" in the system, and thus, Sartre says that Kierkegaard is a "survivor of the system and one of its prophets."[21] He goes on to exemplify that rather than a Hegelian account of the development of temporality in which philosophy is placed at the end of history and has come into being through retrospective knowledge, Kierkegaard, on the contrary, conceives of history as never "finished" in this sense, and infinitely open rather than a finished totality. For Kierkegaard, according to Sartre, rather than denying the possibility of a beginning, there is always the possibility of a new beginning which is *lived*.[22] From here Sartre goes on to explain that for Kierkegaard the existing thinker is always born into a certain "set of socio-economic, cultural, moral, religious, and other relations."[23] These predetermined relations subsequently put limits on the individual's freedom, but as Sartre develops his thought in the *Critique of Dialectical Reason*, these limits create needs which are the very things

---

[20]       Ibid.

[21]       Jean-Paul Sartre, "Kierkegaard: L'universal Singulier," in *Kierkegaard vivant*, Paris: Gallimard 1966, p. 25. (English translation: "Kierkegaard: The Singular Universal," in *Between Existentialism and Marxism*, p. 144.)

[22]       Sartre, "Kierkegaard: L'universal Singulier," p. 39. ("Kierkegaard: The Singular Universal," p. 153.)

[23]       Sartre, "Kierkegaard: L'universal Singulier," p. 40. ("Kierkegaard: The Singular Universal," p. 154.)

that enable the subject to utilize her freedom in actualizing a new possibility. Describing this in Kierkegaardian terms, Sartre says: "the Paradox, for him, is the fact that we discover the absolute in the relative."[24]

Sartre then argues that because Adam temporalizes himself by sin, or in secular terms through an act of free choice, "the foundation of History is freedom in *each man*."[25] Sartre is once again utilizing Kierkegaard's work to emphasize the theory of history he sets out in the *Critique of Dialectical Reason*. It is of utter importance for Sartre's political project that historical circumstances do not constrain the freedom of individuals, but rather that we "escape history to the extent that we make it."[26] According to Sartre's political project, the need we encounter in history is the very lack that allows freedom to move beyond history by creating new situations. In this lecture, Sartre wants to read Kierkegaard as holding to a similar theory of the role of the individual in history.

Moving forward, Sartre once again provides a reading of Kierkegaard that places him at odds with what he sees as the Hegelian conception of a totalizing historical process, noting that "every enterprise, even one brought to a triumphant conclusion, remains a *failure*, that is to say an incompletion to be completed. It lives on because it is open."[27] This once again follows Sartre's insistence in the *Critique of Dialectical Reason* that a new historical sequence inaugurated by a pledged group always becomes an institution and collapses back into seriality, meaning that any subjective enterprise will inevitably fail, and the process must once again recommence. In Sartre's political philosophy, there is no such thing as Fukuyama's "end of history."[28] The question obviously remains as to whether or not Sartre is taking an inward, subjective category in Kierkegaard and then turning it into a historical and political category.

When Sartre reaches the end of this lecture he finally returns to the reading of Kierkegaard we previously encountered in the *Search for a Method*. He closes the lecture stating: "Kierkegaard and Marx: these living-dead men condition our anchorage and institute themselves, now vanished, as our future, as the tasks that await us."[29] While we see that Sartre obviously still places philosophical importance on the work of Kierkegaard, it is equally clear that his overall project of philosophically considering political and historical sequences is one he considers to be staunchly Marxist, and Kierkegaard seems to merely re-emphasize an emphasis on freedom and openness that he already believes to be present in Marx's thought itself.

---

[24]      Sartre, "Kierkegaard: L'universal Singulier," p. 41. ("Kierkegaard: The Singular Universal," p. 155.)

[25]      Sartre, "Kierkegaard: L'universal Singulier," p. 50. ("Kierkegaard: The Singular Universal," p. 161.)

[26]      Sartre, "Kierkegaard: L'universal Singulier," p. 51. ("Kierkegaard: The Singular Universal," p. 161.)

[27]      Sartre, "Kierkegaard: L'universal Singulier," p. 62. ("Kierkegaard: The Singular Universal," p. 168.)

[28]      Francis Fukuyama, *The End of History and the Last Man*, New York: Harper 1993.

[29]      Sartre, "Kierkegaard: L'universal Singulier," p. 63. ("Kierkegaard: The Singular Universal," p. 169.)

Much of what he does here is recount his position on history and the importance of the individual subject as found in the *Critique of Dialectical Reason* through a Kierkegaardian lens, and at the end, goes back to pairing Kierkegaard with Marx and arguing that through these two men we can think the future of philosophy. The social and political importance of what Sartre does here is emphasizing the openness of the future to social and political projects, and the contingency of existing historical situations. Along with this, he lets us know that no process is ever truly complete, and in a sense, every social-political project remains a failure to be completed by another subject or group.[30]

Overall, it seems as if the importance of Kierkegaard to Sartre's social-political thought is that he reminds us that we cannot dissolve the subject into the historical process, and that the place of the subjective is the paradox which resists being taken up into an historical process, and from the position of the subject one can exploit the openness and incompleteness of past historical processes to do something new. This allows Sartre to theorize the emergence of new political situations inaugurated by the scarcity experienced by individuals.

### IV. Outlines for Further Research on Sartre's Political Use of Kierkegaard

While I have shown in the preceding sections of this article that there are only brief intimations in Sartre's political philosophy of any extensive influence by Kierkegaard, I do not think that this rules out the possibility of future lines of research into the relationship between the works of Kierkegaard and Sartre's political philosophy. In particular, I think much of the recent work which has reconsidered the social and political aspects of Kierkegaard's own authorship can allow us to consider this relationship on a more conceptual level.[31] In light of this, I will conclude this piece by offering a few particular possibilities for further research into the influence of Kierkegaard on Sartre's social and political thought.

The first possibility I see for further research would revolve around the question of the development of an account of social-political relationality in the authorships of both Kierkegaard and Sartre. While in many ways both authors began their careers with psychological writings considering the absolute and isolated individual subject, they share a common concern with the ethical that leads from a psychological account of inward subjectivity to an account of the social and political relations of subjects. While Sartre marks this transition with the publication of the *Critique of Dialectical Reason*, Kierkegaard offers a strong social critique in the essay, "The Present Age," contained in *A Literary Review of Two Ages*. Along with this critical piece, one can also see an emphasis on both the inward and outward relationality of

---

[30]     Sartre, "Kierkegaard: L'universal Singulier," p. 62. ("Kierkegaard: The Singular Universal," p. 168.)

[31]     Some of the recent works which have re-opened the question of considering the social and political aspects of Kierkegaard's thought are Merold Westphal, *Kierkegaard's Critique of Reason and Society*, University Park: Penn State University Press 1992; Mark Dooley, *The Politics of Exodus*, New York: Fordham University Press 2001; Alison Assiter, *Kierkegaard, Metaphysics and Political Theory: Unfinished Selves*, London: Continuum 2009.

subjects in Kierkegaard's 1848 writings, *The Sickness unto Death* and *Practice in Christianity*, both written with the pseudonymous pen of Anti-Climacus.

Another possibility which emerges, in particular through the discussion with which Sartre begins *Search for a Method* is the relationship between Kierkegaard and Marx. It was French philosopher Emmanuel Mounier (1905–50) who said that the future of philosophy would be the reconciliation of Marx and Kierkegaard,[32] and it seems in many ways that Sartre's post-war philosophy attempts just that. This leads to the further question about whether it even possible to reconcile the work of Kierkegaard and Marx. Are they not in fact mutually exclusive? Sartre gives us the first taste of what this unlikely pairing would look like when put to the service of developing a political philosophy which accounts for both historical process and subjective singularity.

The final possibility, and in this respect I am following a comment made by Mark Dooley, is a consideration of Kierkegaard's religious writings in the context of political theology.[33] While Sartre himself had no interest in developing any sort of theology, let alone a political one, Kierkegaard's work contains the seeds for a properly theological and/or religious political critique, and one which provides an alternative account of the role of subjective freedom in the social-political sphere to the one offered by Sartre.

---

[32]    Emmanuel Mounier, *Introduction aux Existentialismes*, Paris: Les Editions Denoël 1947.

[33]    Mark Dooley, *The Politics of Exodus*, p. 19. Dooley makes the observation that Kierkegaard's God may have a surprising proximity to the God of liberation theology.

# Bibliography

*I. References to or Uses of Kierkegaard in Sartre's Corpus*

*L'être et le néant. Essai d'ontologie phénoménologique*, Paris: Gallimard 1943 (*Bibliothèque des Idées*), pp. 58–84; pp. 94–111; pp. 115–49; pp. 150–74; pp. 291–300; pp. 508–16; pp. 529–60; pp. 639–42; pp. 643–63; pp. 669–70; pp. 720–2. (English translation: *Being and Nothingness: An Essay on Phenomenological Ontology*, trans. by Hazel E. Barnes, New York: Washington Square Press 1956, pp. 21–45; pp. 55–70; pp. 73–150; pp. 107–29; pp. 235–45; pp. 433–41; pp. 452–80; pp. 553–6; pp. 557–75; pp. 580–1; pp. 625–8.

*L'existentialisme est un humanisme*, Paris: Nagel 1946, pp. 27–33. (English translation: *Existentialism and Humanism*, trans. by Philip Mairet, New York: Haskell House Publishers 1948, pp. 31–2.)

"Un nouveau mystique," in his *Situations I*, Paris: Gallimard 1947, pp. 143–88, see pp. 154–5; pp. 162–3; pp. 168ff.

"Questions de Methode," in *Critique de la raison dialectique*, vol. 1, *Théorie des ensembles pratiques*, Paris: Gallimard 1960, pp. 13–111, see pp. 15–32. (English translation: *Search for a Method*, trans. by Hazel E. Barnes, New York: Alfred A. Knopf 1963, pp. 3–181, see pp. 3–34.)

*Critique de la raison dialectique*, vol. 1, *Théorie des ensembles pratiques*, Paris: Gallimard 1960, p. 117, note 1. (English translation: *Critique of Dialectical Reason*, trans. by Alan Sheridan-Smith, London: New Left Books 1976, pp. 17–18, note 6.)

"Kierkegaard: L'universal Singulier," in *Kierkegaard vivant. Colloque organisé par l'Unesco à Paris du 21 au 23 avril 1964*, Paris: Gallimard 1966, pp. 20–63. (English translation: "Kierkegaard: The Singular Universal," in *Between Existentialism and Marxism*, trans. by John Matthews, London: New Left Books 1974, pp. 141–69.)

*Les carnets de la drôle de guerre. Novembre 1939–Mars 1940*, Paris: Gallimard 1983, pp. 333–7; pp. 342–7; pp. 348ff.; p. 352; pp. 382–3. (English translation: *The War Diaries of Jean-Paul Sartre: November 1939–March 1940*, trans. by Quintin Hoare, New York: Pantheon Books 1984, p. 120; p. 124; p. 131; p. 132; p. 139; p. 164.)

*Lettres au Castor et à quelques autres*, vols. 1–2, ed. by Simone de Beauvoir, Paris: Gallimard 1983, vol. 1 (1926–39), p. 451; p. 491; p. 494; p. 496; p. 500; p. 518; vol. 2 (1940–63), p. 11; p. 16; pp. 38–9; pp. 40–1; p. 56; p. 111; p. 129; p. 197; p. 200; p. 215; p. 219; pp. 222–4; p. 264; p. 268; p. 279; pp. 285–6; pp. 289–90. (English translation of vol. 1: *Witness of My Life: The Letters of Jean-Paul Sartre to Simone de Beauvoir 1926–1939*, ed. by Simone de Beauvoir, trans. by Lee

Fahnestock and Normann MacAfee, Harmondsworth: Penguin 1994, p. 378; p. 413; p. 416; p. 421. English translation of vol. 2: *Quiet Moments in a War: The Letters of Jean-Paul Sartre to Simone de Beauvoir, 1940–1963*, ed. by Simone de Beauvoir, trans. by Lee Fahnestock and Norman Macafee, New York: Scribner 1993, p. 5; p. 10, note; p. 161; p. 164, note; p. 214.)

## II. Sources of Sartre's Knowledge of Kierkegaard

Beauvoir, Simone de, *Pyrrhus et Cinéas*, Paris: Gallimard 1944, p. 42; p. 63.
— *Pour une morale de l'ambiguïté*, Paris: Gallimard 1947, p. 14; p. 60; pp. 165–6.
— *Le Deuxième sexe*, vols. 1–2, Paris: Gallimard 1949, vol. 1, p. 236; p. 295, p. 387; vol. 2, p. 7; pp. 213–14; p. 564.
— *La force de l'âge*, Paris: Gallimard 1960, p. 53; p. 141; pp. 482–3; p. 561; p. 564; p. 603, note.
Camus, Albert, *Le Mythe de Sisyphe*, Paris: Gallimard 1942, p. 39; pp. 42–3; p. 51; pp. 56–61; p. 65; pp. 69–72.
Heidegger, Martin, *Sein und Zeit*, Halle: Niemeyer 1927, pp. 175–96, see also p. 190, note 1; p. 235, note 1; and p. 338, note 1.
*Kierkegaard vivant. Colloque organisé par l'Unesco à Paris du 21 au 23 avril 1964*, Paris: Gallimard 1966.
Merleau-Ponty, Maurice, *Phénoménologie de la perception*, Paris: Gallimard 1945, p. 8; p. 100.
— "Complicité objective," in *Les Temps modernes*, no. 34, 1948, pp. 1–11.
— "La querelle de l'existentialisme," in his *Sens et non-sens*, Paris: Nagel 1948, pp. 141–64, see p. 151; p. 158 (originally published in *Le Temps modernes*, no. 2, 1945, pp. 344–56).
— "L'Existentialisme chez Hegel," in his *Sens et non-sens*, Paris: Nagel 1948, pp. 125–39, see pp. 127–8 (originally published in *Les Temps modernes*, no. 7, 1946, pp. 1311–19).
— "Foi et bonne foi," in his *Sens et non-sens*, Paris: Nagel 1948, pp. 351–70, see p. 359 (originally published in *Les Temps modernes*, no. 5, 1946, pp. 769–82).
— "Sartre et l'ultra-bolchevisme," in his *Les aventures de la dialectique*, Paris: Gallimard 1955, chapter 5, pp. 136–280, see p. 148.
— "Éloge de la philosophie," in his *Éloge de la philosophie et autres essais*, Paris: Gallimard 1960, pp. 11–63, see p. 14 (originally published, *Éloge de la philosophie. Leçon inaugurale faite au Collège de France, le jeudi 15 janvier 1953*, Paris: Gallimard 1953).
— "Partout et nulle part," in his *Signes*, Paris: Gallimard 1960, p. 192 (originally published in *Les Philosophes célèbres*, ed. by Maurice Merleau-Ponty, Paris: L. Mazenod 1956, p. 186).
— *Le visible et l'invisible*, Paris: Gallimard 1964, p. 234.
Wahl, Jean, *Études Kierkegaardiennes*, Paris: Aubier 1938.

*III. Secondary Literature on Sartre's Relation to Kierkegaard*

Arnou, René, "L'existentialisme à la manière de Kierkegaard et J.P. Sartre," *Gregorianum*, vol. 27, 1946, pp. 63–88.

Aron, Raymond, *Marxism and the Existentialists*, trans. by Helen Weaver and Robert Addis, New York: Harper & Row 1969, p. 176.

Barnes, Hazel A., "Translator's Introduction" to Jean-Paul Sartre, *Being and Nothingness*, New York: Philosophical Library 1956, pp. viii–xliii.

Bernstein, Richard J., *Praxis and Action: Contemporary Philosophies of Human Activity*, Philadelphia: University of Pennsylvania Press 1971, see especially pp. 84–164.

Billeskov Jansen, Frederik Julius, "The Study in France," in *Kierkegaard Research*, ed. by Niels Thulstrup and Marie Mikulová Thulstrup, Copenhagen: C.A. Reitzel 1987 (*Bibliotheca Kierkegaardiana*, vol. 15), pp. 134–59.

— "Les études kierkegaardiennes en France," in *Kierkegaard. La découverte de l'existence*, ed. by Régis Boyer and Jean-Marie Paul, Nancy: Centre de Recherches Germaniques et Skandinaves de l'Université de Nancy II 1990, pp. 215–27.

Birkenstock, Eva, *Heißt philosophieren sterben lernen? Antworten der Existenzphilosophie. Kierkegaard, Heidegger, Sartre, Rosenzweig*, Freiburg i.Br.: Alber 1997.

Bousquet, François, "Note sur les études françaises concernant les Discours Édifiants de Kierkegaard," *Kierkegaard Studies Yearbook*, 2000, pp. 246–50.

Caron, Jacques, "Remarques sur la réception française de Kierkegaard," in *Kierkegaard aujourd'hui. Actes du Colloque de la Sorbonne*, ed. by Jacques Caron, Odense: University Press 1998, pp. 69–80.

Catalano, Joseph S., *A Commentary on Jean-Paul Sartre's Critique of Dialectical Reason*, Chicago: University of Chicago Press 1986, p. 21; p. 23; pp. 37–40; pp. 70–1; p. 214.

Caws, Peter, "Der Ursprung der Negation (49–118)," in *Jean-Paul Sartre: Das Sein und das Nichts*, ed. by Bernard N. Schumacher, Berlin: Akademie Verlag 2003 (*Klassiker auslegen*, vol. 22), pp. 45–62.

Chiodi, Pietro, *Sartre and Marxism*, trans. by Kate Soper, Atlantic Highlands, New Jersey: Humanities Press 1976, pp. 4–5; p. 17; pp. 29–30; pp. 81–2; pp. 104–5; p. 117; pp. 128–9.

Cochrane, Arthur C., *The Existentialists and God: Being and the Being of God in the Thought of Sören Kierkegaard, Karl Jaspers, Martin Heidegger, Jean-Paul Sartre, Paul Tillich, Etienne Gilson, Karl Barth*, Philadelphia: Westminster Press 1956.

Cole, James Preston, "The Function of Choice in Human Existence," *Journal of Religion*, vol. 45, 1965, pp. 196–210.

Cortese, Alessandro, "Kierkegaard-Sartre: appunti di metodologia," *Filosofia e Vita*, no. 6, 1965, pp. 31–49.

Cumming, Robert, "Existence and Communication," *Ethics*, vol. 65, no. 2, 1954–55, pp. 79–101.

Curtis, Jerry L., "Heroic Commitment, or The Dialectics of the Leap in Kierkegaard, Sartre, and Camus," *Rice University Studies*, vol. 59, no. 3, 1973, pp. 17–26.

Dandyk, Alfred, *Unaufrichtigkeit. Die existentielle Psychoanalyse im Kontext der Philosophiegeschichte*, Würzburg: Könighausen & Neumann 2002, see especially pp. 48–56; pp. 77–81; pp. 86–101; pp. 105–9; pp. 123–33; pp. 174–82.

Delgaauw, Bernard, *Denkers van deze tijd. Kierkegaard, Nietzsche, Barth, Niebuhr, Sartre, Bultmann*, Franeker: Wever 1953.

Desan, Wifrid. *The Marxism of Jean-Paul Sartre*, Garden City: Doubleday & Company 1965, pp. 44–5; p. 66.

Dowell, Roland Christensen, *Eschatological Implications in the Existentialist Philosophies of Kierkegaard, Sartre, and Marcel*, Newton: Andover Newton Theological School 1957.

Dunning, Stephen N., *Kierkegaard's Dialectic of Inwardness*, Princeton: Princeton University Press 1985, p. 261, note 4.

Erfani, Farhang, "Sartre and Kierkegaard on the Aesthetics of Boredom," *Idealistic Studies*, vol. 34, 2004, pp. 303–17.

Fingarette, Herbert, *Self-Deception*, Berkeley, Los Angeles and London: University of California Press 2000, see pp. 91–109.

Flam, Leopold, *De krisis van de burgerlijke moraal. Van Kierkegaard tot Sartre*, Antwerp: Uitg. Ontwikkeling 1956.

— "Sartre tussen Kierkegaard en Marx," *Tijdschrift van de Vrije Universiteit van Brussel*, vol. 4, 1962, pp. 1–29.

Flynn, Thomas, *Existenzialismus. Eine kurze Einführung*, Vienna: Turia + Kant 2008, see especially pp. 7–34; pp. 43–60; pp. 66ff.; pp. 71–8; pp. 93–6; p. 103; pp. 114–17; pp. 119–25; pp. 147–8.

Frank, Manfred, "Nachwort," *Selbstbewußtseinstheorien von Fichte bis Sartre*, ed. by Manfred Frank, Frankfurt am Main: Suhrkamp 1991, pp. 413–599, see especially pp. 492–599.

Gabriel, Leo, *Existenzphilosophie. Kierkegaard. Jaspers. Heidegger. Sartre. Dialog der Positionen* (2nd completely revised ed. of *Existenzphilosophie von Kierkegaard zu Sartre*), Vienna and Munich: Herold 1968.

Gemmer, Anders, "Ufordøjet Kierkegaard," *Gads danske Magasin*, 1946, pp. 377–83. (Republished in his *Filosofisk Potpourri*, Copenhagen: Skjern 1949, pp. 75–85.)

Grandjean, Louis E., "Sartre og Kierkegaard," *Berlingske Aftenavis*, November 26, 1946.

— *Fra Yokohama til Tersløse*, Copenhagen: Rasmus Navers 1948, see especially pp. 65–9.

Grangier, Edouard, "Abraham, oder Kierkegaard, wie Kafka und Sartre ihn sehen," *Zeitschrift für philosophische Forschung*, vol. 4, no. 3, 1949–50, pp. 412–21.

Griffin, Christopher O., "Bad Faith and the Ethic of Existential Action: Kierkegaard, Sartre, and a Boy Named Harry. We Were So Tiny but We Were Sincere," *The Mississippi Quarterly*, vol. 54, 2001, pp. 173–96.

Grimsley, Ronald, "French Existentialism," in *The Legacy and Interpretation of Kierkegaard*, ed. by Niels Thulstrup and Marie Mikulová Thulstrup, Copenhagen: C.A. Reitzel 1981 (*Bibliotheca Kierkegaardiana*, vol. 8), pp. 121–34.

Grooten, Johan, "Le soi chez Kierkegaard et Sartre," *Revue philosophique de Louvain*, vol. 50, 3rd series, no. 25, 1952, pp. 64–89.

Hohlenberg, Johannes, "Jean-Paul Sartre og hans forhold til Kierkegaard," *Samtiden*, vol. 56, no. 5, 1947, pp. 310–22.

Howells, Christina, "Sartre and Negative Theology," *The Modern Language Review*, vol. 76, no. 3, 1981, pp. 549–55.

Hübscher, Alfred, "Der Existenzbegriff bei Heidegger, Sartre und Kierkegaard," *Kirchenblatt für die reformierte Schweiz*, vol. 105, no. 13, 1949, pp. 194–9.

Janke, Wolfgang, *Existenzphilosophie*, Berlin and New York: Walter de Gruyter 1982, p. 93; p. 95; pp. 97–8; pp. 111–12; p. 115; p. 126.

Johnson, Howard A., "Kierkegaard and Sartre," *The American Scandinavian Review*, vol. 35, 1947, no. 3, pp. 220–5.

Jolivet, Régis, *Les doctrines existentialistes de Kierkegaard à Jean-Paul Sartre*, Abbaye de Saint-Wandrille: Editions de Fontenelle 1948.

Jonker, Christine, *The Self in the Thought of Kierkegaard, Sartre and Jung*, Stellenbosch: University of Stellenbosch 2001.

Jørgensen, Poul Henning, "Från Kierkegaard till Sartre," *Kyrkornas värld*, vol. 8, 1962, pp. 250–6.

Kaneko, Takezou, 『キェルケゴールからサルトルへ-実存思想の歩み』 [From Kierkegaard to Sartre—the Development of Existential Thought], Tokyo: Shimizu-koubun-dou 1967.

Kern, Edith, *Existential Thought and Fictional Technique: Kierkegaard, Sartre, Beckett*, New Haven, Connecticut: Yale University Press 1970.

Knopp, Peter, "Sartre und Kierkegaard: eine zeitverschobene Parallelaktion?," in *Carnets Jean-Paul Sartre. Der Lauf des Bösen*, ed. by Peter Knopp and Vincent von Wroblewsky, Frankfurt am Main: Peter Lang 2006, pp. 43–61.

König, Traugott, "Zur Neuübersetzung," epilogue to Sartre, Jean-Paul, in *Das Sein und das Nichts. Versuch einer phänomenologischen Ontologie*, ed. by Traugott König, Reinbek bei Hamburg: Rowohlt 1998, pp. 1073–88.

Koskinen, Lennart, *Søren Kierkegaard och existentialismen. om tiden, varat och evigheten*, Nora: Nya Doxa 1994, p. 8; p. 146.

Kousaka, Masaaka, 『キェルケゴールからサルトルへ—実存哲学研究』 [From Kierkegaard to Sartre—A Study of Existential Philosophy], Tokyo: Koubun-dou 1949.

Ladegaard Knox, Jeanette Bresson, "Some Remarks on the French Reception of Philosophical Fragments," *Kierkegaard Studies Yearbook*, 2004, pp. 350–5.

Lafarge, Jacques, "Kierkegaard dans la tradition française: Les conditions de sa réception dans les milieux philosophiques," in *Kierkegaard Revisited: Proceedings from the Conference "Kierkegaard and the Meaning of Meaning It," Copenhagen, May 5–9, 1996*, ed. by Niels Jørgen Cappelørn and Jon Stewart, Berlin and New York: de Gruyter 1997 (*Kierkegaard Studies Monograph Series*, vol. 1), pp. 274–90.

— "Précisions sur la réception française de Kierkegaard (réponse à J. Caron)," *Kierkegaard aujourd'hui. Actes du Colloque de la Sorbonne*, ed. by Jacques Lafarge, Odense: University Press 1998, pp. 81–90.

— "L'Édition des *Œuvres complètes* de Kierkegaard en français: contexte—historique—objectifs—conception—réalisation," *Kierkegaard Studies Yearbook*, 2000, pp. 300–16.

Larson, Curtis W.R., "Kierkegaard and Sartre," *Personalist*, vol. 35, 1954, pp. 128–36.

Lévy, Bernard-Henry, *Sartre. Der Philosoph des 20. Jahrhunderts*, Munich: dtv 2005, see especially p. 113; p. 166; p. 526; p. 538; pp. 541–2; p. 599.

Liisberg, Sune, "Den levende Kierkegaard, Den nye Sartre, Den evige..," *Slagmark—tidsskrift for idéhistorie*, no. 44, 2005, pp. 141–4.

Løgstrup, Knud Ejler, "Sartres og Kierkegaards skildring af den dæmoniske indesluttethed," *Vindrosen*, vol. 13, no. 1, 1966, pp. 28–42.

Lowrie, Walter, "Existence as Understood by Kierkegaard and/or Sartre," *Sewanee Review*, vol. 63, July–September 1950, pp. 379–401.

McBride, William L., "Sartre's Debts to Kierkegaard. A Partial Reckoning," in *Kierkegaard in Post/Modernity*, ed. by Martin J. Matuštík and Merold Westphal, Bloomington, Indianapolis: Indiana University Press 1995 (*Studies in Continental Thought*), pp. 18–42.

Mejovsek, Gabriele, *Die Metamorphose vom Dasein Existenz und der Begriff der Existenzerhellung in der Philosophie Karl Jaspers. Unter Berücksichtigung verwandter Wandlungsphänomene im Denken von Pascal, Kierkegaard, Heidegger und Sartre*, Vienna: University of Vienna 1983.

Message, Jacques, "Remarques sur la réception de *Begrebet Angest* en France (1935–1971)," *Kierkegaard Studies Yearbook*, 2001, pp. 323–9.

Muñoz, Arias, "Las bases ontológicas del conflicto intersubjetivo en J.P. Sartre," *Anales del Seminario de Metafísica*, vol. 15, 1980, pp. 11–54.

Nesiote, N.A., Ὑπαρξισμὸς καὶ χριστιανικὴ πίστις. Ἡ ὑπαρκτικὴ σκέψις ἐν τῇ φιλοσοφίᾳ καὶ ἡ χριστιανικὴ πίστις ὡς τὸ ἀναπόφευκτον καὶ βασικὸν πρόβλημα αὐτῆς κατὰ τὸν *Sören Kierkegaard* καὶ τοὺς συγχρόνους ὑπαρξιστὰς φιλοσόφους *Karl Jaspers, Martin Heidegger* καὶ *Jean-Paul Sartre*, Athens: Menuma 1985.

Pedersen, Olaf, *Fra Kierkegaard til Sartre*, Copenhagen: Arne Frost-Hansens 1947.

Pieper, Annemarie, *Einführung in die Ethik*, 5th ed., Tübingen and Basel: Francke 2003, see pp. 262–6.

— "Freiheit als Selbstinitiation," in *Jean-Paul Sartre: Das Sein und das Nichts*, ed. by Bernard N. Schumacher, Berlin: Akademie Verlag 2003 (*Klassiker auslegen*, vol. 22), pp. 195–210.

Piety, Marilyn G., "Good Faith," in *Eighteen Upbuilding Discourses*, ed. by Robert L. Perkins, Macon, Georgia: Mercer University Press 2003 (*International Kierkegaard Commentary*, vol. 5), pp. 157–79.

Politis, Hélène, *Kierkegaard en France au XXᵉ siècle: archéologie d'une reception*, Paris: Kimé 2005, p. 85; p. 108, note 95; pp. 118–19; p. 121; p. 127, note 85; pp. 135–44 passim; pp. 150–9 passim; p. 162, note 156; p. 164, note 178; p. 233, p. 235; pp. 249–50.

Poole, Roger C., "Indirect Communication I: Hegel, Kierkegaard, and Sartre," *New Blackfriars*, vol. 47, 1966, pp. 532–41.

— "The Unknown Kierkegaard: Twentieth-Century Receptions," in *The Cambridge Companion to Kierkegaard*, ed. by Alastair Hannay and Gordon D. Marino, Cambridge: Cambridge University Press 1998, pp. 48–75.

Prenter Regin, "Frihedsbegrebet hos Sartre på baggrund af Kierkegaard," in his *Ordet og Ånden. Reformatorisk kristendom. Afhandlinger og artikler*, Copenhagen: Gads Forlag 1952, pp. 177–89.

Prokopski, Jacek Aleksander, "Egzystencja i nicość. Kierkegaard, Heidegger, Sartre," in *Aktualność Kierkegaarda. W 150 rocznicę śmierci myśliciela z Kopenhagi*, ed. by Antoni Szwed, Kęty: Antyk 2006, pp. 109–39.

רבינוביץ, ישעיהו, "קירקגור וסארטר", "מולד, 4, 1950, עמ' 182–187. [Rabinowitz, Yeshiahu, "Kierkegaard and Sartre," *Molad*, no. 4, 1950, pp. 182–7.]

Reed, Ross Channing, *"Love" and Addiction: The Phenomenological Ontologies of Kierkegaard and Sartre: An Existential Theory of Addiction*, Chicago: Loyola University of Chicago 1994.

Reinhardt, Kurt Frank, *The Existentialist Revolt: The Main Themes and Phases of Existentialism. Kierkegaard, Nietzsche, Heidegger, Jaspers, Sartre, Marcel*, Milwaukee: Bruce 1952.

Roberts, David E., "Faith and Freedom in Existentialism: A Study of Kierkegaard and Sartre," *Theology Today*, vol. 8, 1951–52, pp. 469–82.

Roloff, Volker, "Existentielle Psychoanalyse als theatrum mundi. Zur Theatertheorie Sartres," in *Sartre. Ein Kongreß*, ed. by Traugott König, Reinbek bei Hamburg: Rowohlt 1988, pp. 93–106.

Schnädelbach, Herbert, "Sartre und die Frankfurter Schule," in *Sartre. Ein Kongreß*, ed. by Traugott König, Reinbek bei Hamburg: Rowohlt 1998, pp. 13–35.

Schulz, Walter, "Das Problem der Angst in der neueren Philosophie," in *Aspekte der Angst. Starnberger Gespräche 1964*, ed. by Hoimar v. Ditfurth, Stuttgart: Thieme 1965, pp. 1–23.

Seibert, Thomas, *Existenzphilosophie*, Stuttgart and Weimar: Metzler 1997 (*Sammlung Metzler*, vol. 303), pp. 17–35; pp. 126–46.

Shearson, William A., *The Notion of Encounter in Existentialist Metaphysics: An Inquiry into the Nature and Structure of Existential Knowledge in Kierkegaard, Sartre, and Buber*, Toronto: University of Toronto 1970.

סיגד, רן, " קירקגור כאכזיסטנציאליסט" בספרו: אכסיסטנצִיאליזם, ירושלים: מוסד ביאליק, 1975, עמ' 82–117. [Sigad, Ran, "Kierkegaard as Existentialist," in his *Studies in Existentialism*, Jerusalem: Bialik Institute 1975, pp. 82-117.]

Sløk, Johannes, "Om begrebet Existens hos Heidegger, Sartre og Kierkegaard," *Dansk teologisk Tidsskrift*, 1947, pp. 230–40.

— "Kierkegaard og fransk Eksistentialisme," *Kristeligt Dagblad*, January 7, 1948.

Slote, Michael A., "Existentialism and the Fear of Dying," *American Philosophical Quarterly*, vol. 12, 1975, pp. 17–28. (Reprinted in *Language, Metaphysics, and Death*, ed. by John Donnelly, New York: Fordham University Press 1978, pp. 69–87.)

Søe, Niels H., "Mennesket i historien," *For Kirke og Kultur*, vol. 56, 1951, pp. 96–106.

Søltoft, Pia, "Etika Sartre-nál és Kierkegaard-nál," *Magyar Filozófiai Szemle*, nos. 1–2, 2003, pp. 185–200.

Soper, William Wayne, *The Self and Its World in Ralph Baton Perry, Edgar Sheffield Brightman, Jean-Paul Sartre and Søren Kierkegaard,* Boston: Boston University 1962.

Sørensen, Hans, "Sartre og Kierkegaard," *Jyllandsposten,* May 9, 1946.

Spanggaard, K.D., "Eksistentialismen, J.P. Sartre og Søren Kierkegaard," *Berlingske Aftenavis,* January 23, 1946.

Theunissen, Michael and Greve, Wilfried, "Einleitung: Kierkegaards Werk und Wirkung. III. Zur Wirkungsgeschichte. 3. Philosophie. b) Existenzphilosophie," in *Materialien zur Philosophie Søren Kierkegaards,* ed. by Michael Theunissen and Wilfried Greve, Frankfurt am Main: Suhrkamp 1979, pp. 62–76.

Toeplitz, Karol, "F. Kafki i J. P. Sartre'a reinterpretacja 'Konfliktu Abrahama' " [F. Kafka and J. P. Sartre's Reinterpretation of the "Abraham conflict"], *Gdańskie Zeszyty Humanistyczne,* vol. 2, no. 28, 1985, pp. 41–55.

Toettcher, R.W., *Kierkegaard and Sartre: A Comparison of the Conception of Freedom of Two Existentialist Philosophers,* London: University of London 1963–64.

Treiber, Gerhard, *Philosophie der Existenz. Das Entscheidungsproblem bei Kierkegaard, Jaspers, Heidegger, Sartre, Camus; literarische Erkundungen von Kundera, Céline, Broch, Musil,* Frankfurt am Main: Peter Lang 2000 (*Europäische Hochschulschriften,* series 20, *Philosophie,* vol. 610), see especially pp. 15–67 (chapter "Kierkegaard"); and pp. 133–61 (chapter "Sartre").

Ussher, Arland, *A Journey Through Dread: A Study of Kierkegaard, Heidegger, and Sartre,* New York: Devin-Adair 1955.

Viallaneix, Nelly, "Lectures françaises," in *The Legacy and Interpretation of Kierkegaard,* ed. by Niels Thulstrup and Marie Mikulová Thulstrup, Copenhagen: C.A. Reitzel 1981 (*Bibliotheca Kierkegaardiana,* vol. 8), pp. 102–20.

Vloemans, Antoon, "Sartres mensbeeld en het einde van het existentialisme," *Nieuw Vlaams Tijdschrift,* vol. 22, 1969, pp. 597–615.

Wahl, Jean, *Petite histoire de "l'existentialisme": suivie de Kafka et Kierkegaard commentaires,* Paris: Editions Club Maintenant 1947, p. 13; p. 44; pp. 50–60 passim; p. 63.

— "Kierkegaard: son influence en France," in his *Kierkegaard. L'un devant l'Autre,* Paris: Hachette 1998, see especially pp. 221–5.

Weiss, Gail, "Reading/Writing between the Lines," *Continental Philosophy Review,* vol. 31, 1998, pp. 387–409.

Wesche, Tilo, *Kierkegaard. Eine philosophische Einführung,* Stuttgart: Reclam 2003, see especially pp. 62–3.

Whitmire, John Floyd, *On the Subject of Autobiography: Finding a Self in the Works of Kierkegaard, Nietzsche, Sartre, and Derrida,* Villanova University, Villanova, Pennsylvania 2005.

Zeegers, Victor, "L'existentialisme de Kierkegaard à Jean-Paul Sartre," *Revue générale belge,* no. 8, 1959, pp. 1–18.

Zimmermann, Rainer, *Kritik der interkulturellen Verkunft,* Paderborn: Mentis 2002, see especially pp. 78–81.

# Carl Schmitt:

## Zones of Exception and Appropriation

Bartholomew Ryan

*An herbstlichen Mauern, es suchen Schatten dort*
*Am Hügel das tönende Gold*
*Weidende Abendwolken*
*In der Ruh verdorrter Platanen.*
*Dunklere Tränen odmet diese Zeit,*
*Verdammnis, da des Träumers Herz*
*Überfließt von purpurner Abendröte,*
*Der Schwermut der rauchenden Stadt;*
*Dem Schreitenden nachweht goldene Kühle*
*Dem Fremdling, vom Friedhof,*
*Als folgte im Schatten ein zarter Leichnam.*[1]

"He who pauses in wonder, moved with tenderness and gratitude,
before any facet of the work of these auspicious creators, let
him know that I also paused there, I, the abominable."[2]

"Such indirect influences, which elude any documentation, are
the strongest and by far the most authentic."[3]

The name Carl Schmitt evokes controversy, anger, and both silent and expressed
admiration from diverse and contrasting political and critical thinkers. A large bulk
of his writings have not been translated into English, and throughout the last eighty

---

[1]     Georg Trakl, "Limbo"/ "Vorhölle" (1915), in Georg Trakl, *Poems and Prose*, trans.
by Alexander Stillmark, London: Libris 2001, p. 89: "By autumnal walls, there shadows seek
/ Resonant gold by the hill, / Pasturing evening clouds / In the peace of desiccated planes. /
This age breathes darker tears, / Damnation, when the dreamer's heart / Overflows with purple
sunset, / With the melancholy of the smoking town; / A golden chill wafts after the stroller,
The stranger, from the graveyard, / Like a gentle corpse that follows in the shadows."
[2]     Jorge Luis Borges, "Deutsches Requiem," in his *Labyrinths*, Harmondsworth:
Penguin Books 1984, p. 174.
[3]     In a letter to Ernst Jünger 1947, see Jan-Werner Müller, *A Dangerous Mind: Carl
Schmitt in Post-War European Thought*, New Haven, Connecticut and London: Yale
University Press 2003, p. 1.

years, he has been censored, vilified, viewed as a relic of a particular period, in some circles glorified as *the* modern political thinker *par excellence*, and in other countries virtually unknown. He remains an interesting political thinker; he gives provocative and detailed political analyses; his critique of liberalism still needs to be answered where democracy negates liberalism and liberalism negates democracy; he reiterates the political idea of "totality," and most famously he both declares that the sovereign is he who decides on the exception and presents the friend/enemy distinction as the foundation of all politics. In the last twenty years interest in Carl Schmitt has increased with each year. Celebrated philosophers and critical theorists such as Jacques Derrida (1930–2004), Slavoj Žižek (b. 1949), Georgio Agamben (b. 1942), Jacob Taubes (1923–87), Chantal Mouffe (b. 1943), and Antonio Negri (b. 1933) have all referred to him at the end of the twentieth century and the beginning of the twenty-first century.[4] This could be due to two primary factors: the changing political climate around the world, not least the rise (and fall) of the neo-conservative movement in the United States of America, which can be traced back to Carl Schmitt and his rigorous thought,[5] and the disappearance of the reluctance of the political and academic environment to approach and appropriate Schmitt who was both an anti-Semite and Nazi for a time.

Little has actually been written on Carl Schmitt and Kierkegaard despite the reverence that Schmitt gives to the Danish thinker and given where Kierkegaard turns up in Schmitt's writing.

The fact remains that Schmitt uses Kierkegaard's "exception" (*Undtagelse* from *Fear and Trembling* and *Repetition*) as the central thesis to his project, and views Kierkegaard as the most articulate thinker on the exception and subsequently using this word "exception" to define the sovereign. Reading Schmitt reading Kierkegaard is a fruitful exercise in teasing out various unsolved issues in the latter's writings, and

---

[4]     See, for example, Slavoj Žižek, Eric J. Santner and Kenneth Reinhard, *The Neighbour, Three Inquiries in Political Theology*, Chicago: University of Chicago Press 2006; Georgio Agamben, *State of Exception*, Chicago: University of Chicago Press 2005; Jacob Taubes, *The Political Theology of Paul*, Stanford: Stanford University Press 2004; Michael Hardt and Antonio Negri, *Empire*, Cambridge, Massachusetts: Harvard University Press 2000; Jacques Derrida, *Politics of Friendship*, London and New York: Verso 1997; Jacques Derrida, "Force of Law: The 'Mystical Foundation of Authority,'" in his *Acts of Religion*, London: Routledge 2001, pp. 228–99; Chantal Mouffe, *The Challenge of Carl Schmitt*, London and New York: Verso 1999; and Nicolaus Sombart, *Die deutschen Männer und ihre Feinde: Carl Schmitt, ein deutsches Schicksal zwischen Männerbund und Matriarchatsmythos*, Munich: Hanser 1991.

[5]     Leo Strauss was a student of Schmitt's (Schmitt was instrumental in Strauss receiving a Rockefeller Fellowship) in Berlin. Strauss wrote on political theology and Spinoza at this time: *Religionskritik Spinozas als Grundlage seiner Bibelwissenschaft: Untersuchungen zu Spinozas Theologisch-politischen Traktat*, Berlin: Akademie-Verlag 1930. Strauss came to the University of Chicago, where he taught, along with a few other notably conservative philosophers (for example Allan Bloom). In the George W. Bush neo-conservative government, Paul Wolfowitz wrote his Ph.D. in political science in the University of Chicago and was taught by Strauss. Wolfowitz (with Karl Rove) very explicitly used the ideological tools gleaned from these influences to help the Republicans get Bush elected, and in spinning all news/decisions.

also adds another surprising member onto the list of radical European thinkers in the Weimar inter-war years who came under the spell of Kierkegaard and appropriated his thought in exciting and polarizing ways such as Georg Lukács (1885–1971), Ernst Bloch (1885–1977), Martin Heidegger (1889–1976), and Theodor W. Adorno (1903–69), to name but a few.

## I. A Brief Introduction to Carl Schmitt

Carl Schmitt was born in Plettenberg, Westphalia in Germany on July 11, 1888 to lower middle class Roman Catholic parents. His father, Johann, worked at the local railway station and many of his relatives were members of the Catholic Center Party.[6] Under the repression of Bismarck's *Kulturkampf* the Catholic Party was actually strengthened, and this is something Schmitt will go on to write about in his essay *Roman Catholicism and Political Form*. Schmitt's talent was recognized early on by the award of a scholarship to study at the Gymnasium, and afterwards he studied state theory and law at the Friedrich-Wilhelm University in Berlin. Like many of his contemporaries moving to the growing metropolis, Schmitt was equally fascinated and repulsed by avant-garde Berlin, forcing him to take a break from the city and spend two semesters in Munich and one in Strasbourg where he graduated in 1915. In his early writings on Friedrich Nietzsche (1844–1900), Thomas Mann (1875–1955), and Walter Rathenau (1867–1922), one can see that Schmitt's interests lay not only in law but also in modern literature and philosophy, placing him on the fringes of the radical avant-garde movements in Germany and part of the overall *Zeitgeist*. In 1916, he married a Serbian woman called Pawla Dorotić, whom he had met in the café culture scene in Munich, and volunteered for the reserve army. He did not seem to share the same kind of enthusiasm for the war as many of his peers, and remained quite detached from the fervent patriotism.[7] Perhaps it was his Catholic upbringing that placed him in such a position and, as Gopal Balakrishnan writes, "In any case, he was far too Latin to see the French as the representatives of a soulless 'civilisation' at war with German '*Kultur*.'"[8] In the aftermath of Germany's defeat in World War I, revolution in Germany itself, and in the midst of the Versailles Treaty, Schmitt wrote and published his first major work, *Political Romanticism*.[9] In this

---

[6]     For an excellent account of Schmitt's biography see Gopal Balakrishnan, *The Enemy: An Intellectual Portrait of Carl Schmitt*, London and New York: Verso 2002. In fact much of the information I give in this brief introduction to Schmitt comes from Balakrishnan's book.

[7]     Schmitt did socialize in circles and forged friendships with people that were against the war and also antipatriots. He kept in touch with some of these people even after the war such as the Dadaist Hugo Ball. See Balakrishnan, *The Enemy: An Intellectual Portrait of Carl Schmitt*, p. 17, see also p. 270, note 17: "In a tribute to the poetry of a friend, the minor Expressionist poet Theodor Däubler, Schmitt depicted the war as a manifestation of the unleashed power of the Antichrist, by which he meant a modern European society hell-bent on a re-creating the world through technology, and thus attempting to usurp the place of God."

[8]     Balakrishnan, *The Enemy: An Intellectual Portrait of Carl Schmitt*, p. 16.

[9]     Carl Schmitt, *Politische Romantik*, Berlin: Duncker und Humblot 1919. (English translation: *Political Romanticism*, trans. by Guy Oakes, Cambridge, Massachusetts: MIT

seminal text it is hard to tell what political side he will move towards, causing Georg Lukács to write a positive review of the book,[10] and it is also in this work where we first witness what he views as problems of his "lukewarm" generation of "eternal conversation" and not being able to make a decision. More of this though later. Things worsened in Germany; two days after martial law was declared in January 1919, socialists Karl Liebknecht (1871–1919) and Rosa Luxembourg (1871–1919) were tortured and brutally murdered along with hundreds of others in response to the Spartacist Uprising. The communist revolution was over, but soon after the democratic Weimar Republic (1919–33) was set up and with a new constitution (which came into law on August 11, 1919) to replace the imperialist government.

Shortly after receiving a temporary lectureship at the Handelshochschule in Munich in 1919, his marriage to Pawla disintegrated—she had run off and with many of his books! He tried unsuccessfully to annul the marriage, subsequently getting a divorce (in 1924) and as a result was excommunicated by the Catholic Church. He married his second wife, Duška Todorović (1903–50), who was also Serbian, in 1925 and they had a daughter called Anima. During these unsettling years of the 1920s, Schmitt penned his most famous works such as *The Dictator* (1921),[11] *Political Theology* (1922),[12] *Roman Catholicism and Political Form* (1923),[13] *The Crisis of Parliamentary Democracy* (1923),[14] and *The Concept of the Political* (1927).[15] Schmitt was Professor at Bonn (1922–28) and then at Berlin (1933–45).

---

Press 1986.) For more of this crucial point in German history and in the context of Carl Schmitt, see Balakrishnan, *The Enemy: An Intellectual Portrait of Carl Schmitt*, pp. 17–21.

[10]        Georg Lukács, "Carl Schmitt, *Politische Romantik*," *Archiv für die Geschichte des Sozialismus und der Arbeiterbewegung*, ed. by Carl Grünberg, vol. 13, 1928, pp. 307–8 (reprint edition, vols. 1–15, Graz: Akademische Druck und Verlagsanstalt 1964–66, vol. 8, pp. 307–8). See also Jan-Werner Müller, *A Dangerous Mind: Carl Schmitt in Post-War European Thought*, New Haven, Connecticut and London: Yale University Press 2003. After World War II, Schmitt would be treated as one of the intellectuals responsible for the "destruction of reason" and Lukács explains that the pre-war Schmitt was when he was "pre-fascist." See Georg Lukács, *The Destruction of Reason*, trans. by Robert Palmer, Atlantic Highlands, New Jersey: Humanities Press 1981, pp. 652–61 (original German: *Die Zerstörung der Vernunft*, Berlin: Aufbau Verlag 1954).

[11]        Carl Schmitt, *Die Diktatur. Von den Anfängen des modernen Souveränitätsgedankens bis zum proletarischen Klassenkampf*, Munich: Duncker und Humblot 1921.

[12]        Carl Schmitt, *Politische Theologie. Vier Kapitel zur Lehre von der Souveränität*, Berlin: Duncker und Humblot 1922. (English translation: *Political Theology. Four Chapters on the Concept of Sovereignty*, trans. by George Schwab, Chicago and London: University of Chicago Press 2005.)

[13]        Carl Schmitt, *Römischer Katholizismus und politische Form*, Hellerau: Hegner 1923. (English translation: *Roman Catholicism and Political Form*, trans. and ed. by G.L. Ulmen, Westport, Connecticut and London: Greenwood Press 1996.)

[14]        Carl Schmitt, *Die geistesgeschichtliche Lage des heutigen Parlamentarismus*, Munich.: Duncker und Humblot 1923. (English translation: *The Crisis of Parliamentary Democracy*, trans. by Ellen Kennedy, Cambridge, Massachusetts and London: MIT Press 1985.)

[15]        Carl Schmitt, *Der Begriff des Politischen*, Berlin: Duncker und Humblot 1932. (English translation: *The Concept of the Political*, trans. by George Schwab, Chicago: University of Chicago Press 1996.)

During his time at Bonn, he was an active supporter of the Catholic Center Party and also, as Guy Oakes writes in the introduction to the English translation of *Political Romanticism*, "the most articulate advocate of discretionary presidential power that would make it possible to defend the Republic under emergency conditions."[16] Moving to Berlin in 1928, Schmitt became a protégé of Johannes Popitz (1884–1945), a Prussian aristocrat and civil servant who was State Secretary in the German Ministry of Finance from 1925 to 1928. A right-wing conservative and monarchist, he would become good friends and neighbor to Schmitt in Berlin, and would be later hung by the Nazis in 1945 in the aftermath of the Hitler assassination plot led by Claus von Stauffenberg (1907–44). Though in favor of Jews disappearing from Germany, Schmitt was against the methods and measures taken to achieve this. During these Berlin years, Schmitt would host such German luminaries as writer Ernst Jünger (1895–1998) and expressionist Emil Nolde (1867–1956).

Schmitt did not take to the Nazi party immediately and in his essay *Legality and Legitimacy* (1932),[17] he actually criticizes the attempts to destroy the constitution and follows with a short essay called "The Abuse of Legality."[18] However, over the course of the next 12 years of the "thousand-year Third Reich" and beyond in post-war Germany, Schmitt would prove himself to be a most wily survivor. He was able to make the transition from legal theorist of the Weimar Republic to National Socialist by joining the Party in May 1933, the same year as Heidegger.[19] He also managed to keep his professorship in Berlin until the end of the war, even though he was a friend of Popitz. In 1933, he drafted legislation to legalize Nazi reorganization and state government less than a year after the publication of "The Abuse of Legality." Schmitt in this move revealed both his theory of the exception and also a rather sinister, opportunistic streak. After the "Night of the Long Knives" in 1936, Schmitt published an article defending the legality of Hitler's actions called "The Führer Protects the Law."[20] In the same year, due mostly to his Weimar past, Catholic background, and diverse factionalism within the Party, he did lose his government and party appointments after an inquiry, but kept his job and his life, protected by none other than Hermann Göring (1893–1946). In 1938, he published *The Leviathan in the State Theory of Thomas Hobbes: Meaning and Failure of a*

---

[16]    Guy Oakes, Introduction to Schmitt, *Political Romanticism*, p. ix.

[17]    Carl Schmitt, *Legalität und Legitimität*, Munich: Duncker und Humblot 1932. (English translation: *Legality and Legitimacy*, trans. by Jeffrey Seitzer, Durham: Duke University Press 2004.)

[18]    Carl Schmitt, "Der Missbrauch der Legalität," *Tägliche Rundschau*, July 19, 1932.

[19]    Schmitt actually received a letter from Heidegger encouraging him to join the Party, and on the May 1 both signed up together. As Balakrishnan notes, "Despite the massive influx of new members, which soon resulted in a moratorium, Schmitt and those who jumped on board were going beyond the call of duty: neither Popitz nor Jünger, nor most of Schmitt's other friends, nor even a majority of those who taught in the law faculties, ever became members, and he was in no danger of losing his position if he had chosen not to do so." Balakrishnan, *The Enemy: An Intellectual Portrait of Carl Schmitt*, p. 181.

[20]    Carl Schmitt, "Der Führer schützt das Rechts," *Deutsche Juristen-Zeitung*, 1934, pp. 945–50. In June 1934, Schmitt became editor in chief for the self-published newspaper *Deutsche Juristen-Zeitung*.

*Political Symbol.*[21] From the late 1930s onwards, Schmitt liked to view himself as a Benito Cereno character from the story by Herman Melville (1819–91). On his fiftieth birthday in 1938, Schmitt signed himself off as "Benito Cereno" in a letter.[22] The analogy is that of someone being caught in a situation they do not want to be in but have not choice. However, the fact remains that even though he was being watched by the Nazis during the war, Schmitt never thought about leaving Germany or criticizing the Nazis. He continued to see himself as a Benito Cereno being observed by the Allies after the war. However, he escaped the long court procedures of the Nuremburg Trials even though he had been an official defender of the legality of the Nazi regime and Hitler and refusing any de-Nazification down to his dying day. His only punishment was a year in an internment camp after the war and being banned from teaching. Instead, Schmitt returned to his hometown Plettenberg where he received intellectuals from all over the world from both the Left and the Right, and he continued to write prolifically, publishing such works as *The Nomos of the Earth in the International Law of the Jus Publicum Europaeum* (1950),[23] *Hamlet or Hecuba. The Intrusion of the Time Into the Play* (1956),[24] and *Political Theology II* (1970).[25] In 1962, Schmitt gave a few lectures in Francoist Spain from which *The Theory of Partisan* (1963) emerged.[26] Schmitt died on April 7, 1985 and is buried in his hometown.

## II. The Places in Schmitt's Writings where Kierkegaard is Mentioned or Used

However seldom, Kierkegaard does turn up in key points of Schmitt's writings. And the use that Schmitt makes of some of the thinking and writings of Kierkegaard are fundamental to understanding the roots and backbone of Schmitt's political thinking. This has been overlooked by most Schmittian scholars to the point even, strangely enough, of being ignored. Kierkegaard is especially prominent in the seminal works of the Weimar years both explicitly and implicitly in *Political Romanticism, Roman Catholicism and Political Form, Political Theology*, and *The Concept for the Political*. It was especially in these years, from 1909 up until the National

---

[21]     Carl Schmitt, *Der Leviathan in der Staatslehre des Thomas Hobbes*, Hamburg: Hanseatische Verlagsanstalt 1938. (English translation: *The Leviathan in the State Theory of Thomas Hobbes: Meaning and Failure of a Political Symbol*, trans. by George Schwab and Erna Hilfstein, Westport, Connecticut and London: Greenwood Press 1996.)

[22]     See Tracy B. Strong's Foreword to *Political Theology*, p. ix.

[23]     Carl Schmitt, *Der Nomos der Erde im Völkerrecht des Jus Publicum Europaeum*, Cologne: Greven 1950. (English translation: *The Nomos of the Earth in the International Law of the Jus Publicum Europaeum*, trans. by G.L. Ulmen, New York: Telos Press 2003.)

[24]     Carl Schmitt, *Hamlet oder Hekuba: Der Einbruch der Zeit in das Spiel*, Düsseldorf: Diederichs 1956. (English translation: *Hamlet or Hecuba. The Intrusion of the Time into the Play*, trans. by David Pan and Jennifer Rust, New York: Telos Press 2009.)

[25]     Carl Schmitt, *Politische Theologie II. Die Legende von der Erledigung jeder Politischen Theologie*, Berlin: Duncker und Humblot 1970.

[26]     Carl Schmitt, *Theorie des Partisanen. Zwischenbemerkung zum Begriff des Politischen*, Berlin: Duncker und Humblot 1963. (English translation: *Theory of the Partisan*, trans. by G.L. Ulmen, New York: Telos Press 2007.)

Socialists took power in 1933, that many German intellectuals were reading and being bewitched by Kierkegaard's profound and stylish writings.

Georg Lukács was one of the very first to write on Kierkegaard, and he quickly translated his essay in Hungarian into German in 1909 called "The Foundering of Form Against Life" in his first publication *Soul and Form*,[27] which represents a Kierkegaardian *Zeitgeist* by viewing his own broken love-affair in tandem with that of Kierkegaard and Regine.[28] This work was avidly read by Ernst Bloch, Walter Benjamin (1892–1940), and Adorno. Translations of Kierkegaard into German were coming out mostly via Carl Dallago (1900–48), Theodor Haecker (1879–1945), and Ludwig von Ficker (1885–1919) of the influential journal *Der Brenner* coming from Innsbruck, Austria, and Haecker also published *Søren Kierkegaard und die Philosophie der Innerlichkeit* in 1913.[29] From Schmitt's *Nachlass* and evidence in his own writings, both in his published works and his diaries, we know for certain that Schmitt had read or at least was familiar with German translations of *Either/Or*, *Repetition*, *Fear and Trembling*, The Essay "The Present Age,"[30] *Stages on Life's Way*, *The Concept of Anxiety*, *The Point of View of My Work as an Author*, *The Moment*, a 12-volume edition of Kierkegaard's *Collected Works*,[31] and a German edition called *Begriff des Auserwählten*[32] which he received as a gift from the German translator in 1918. In *Begriff des Auserwählten* alone, there are annotations all over

[27]     This essay was originally published in Hungarian as György Lukács, "Sören Kierkegaard és Regine Olsen," *Nyugat*, vol. 1, no. 6, 1910, pp. 378–87. (English translation: "The Foundering of Form against Life. Sören Kierkegaard and Regine Olsen," in *Soul and Form*, trans. by Anna Bostock, Cambridge, Massachusetts: MIT Press 1974, pp. 28–41; German translation: "Das Zerschellen der Form am Leben: Sören Kierkegaard und Regine Olsen," in *Die Seele und die Formen: Essays*, Berlin: Fleischel 1911, pp. 61–91.)

[28]     *Zeitgeist* in the sense that in the years from *Soul and Form* to *The Theory of the Novel*, the Germanic intelligentsia were finding a Regine Olsen in their own broken love affairs, and a certain Kierkegaard in themselves; Lukács and Irma Seidler, Ferdinand Ebner and Louise Karpischek, Franz Kafka and Felice Bauer, to name a few. See Richard Purkarthofer, "Zur deutschsprachigen Rezeptionsgeschichte von Kierkegaards *Nachlass*," *Kierkegaard Studies Yearbook*, 2003, pp. 316–45; See also Habib C. Malik, *Receiving Søren Kierkegaard*, Washington, D.C: Catholic University of America Press 1997, p. 364.

[29]     Theodor Haecker, *Sören Kierkegaard und die Philosophie der Innerlichkeit*, Munich: Schreiber 1913.

[30]     See Sören Kierkegaard, "Kritik der Gegenwart," trans. by Theodor Haecker, *Der Brenner*, May 15–16, 1915, pp. 691–712 and pp. 797–817. See also, Sören Kierkegaard, *Der Pfahl im Fleisch*, trans. and ed. by Theodor Haecker, Innsbruck: Brenner 1914, p. 75, note. 84. See also Carl Schmitt, *Die Militärzeit 1915 bis 1919*, ed. by Ernst Hüsmert and Gerd Geisler, Berlin: Akademie Verlag 2005, p. 66, note 71.

[31]     Sören Kierkegaard, *Gesammelte Werke*, vols. 1–12, trans. and ed. by Hermann Gottsched and Christoph Schrempf, Jena: Diederichs 1909–22. Cf. Carl Schmitt, *Tagebücher: Oktober 1912 bis Februar 1915*, ed. by Ernst Hüsmert, Berlin: Akademie Verlag 2003, p. 416, notes; and Schmitt, *Die Militärzeit 1915 bis 1919*, p. 577.

[32]     Sören Kierkegaard, *Der Begriff des Auserwählten*, trans. by Theodor Haecker, Hellerau: Hegner 1917. See Schmitt, *Tagebücher: Oktober 1912 bis Februar 1915*, p. 416.

the book.[33] As Kennedy remarks in *Constitutional Failure* regarding Schmitt and his copy of *Begriff des Auserwählten*: "He seems to have been especially interested in Kierkegaard's analysis of the newspaper readers of the time, which Kierkegaard regarded as a culture of the trivial, destructive of '*geist*' and seriousness. 'Our time shouts constantly' Kierkegaard wrote, and that is 'political, a religious problem.' "[34] In *Political Romanticism*, the name Kierkegaard is mentioned once and only in a footnote. But this one time in this case is enough to reveal the shadow of Kierkegaard that haunts the whole text. Schmitt writes:

> There was another resolution of the romantic situation, which only the great figure among the romantics (for I do not consider Kleist a romantic) met with: Kierkegaard. In Kierkegaard, all the elements of the romantic were in force: irony, the aesthetic conception of the world; the antitheses of the possible and the real, the infinite and the finite; the feeling for the concrete moment. His Protestant Christianity made him into the only individual who exists in the God of Christianity. In the immediacy of the relationship to God, every intrinsically worthy community was abolished. For political romanticism, this resolution does not come into consideration.[35]

This footnote is triggered by the closing sentence of a section (given the title "The romantic subject and the new realities" in the English translation) where Kierkegaard is already present: "With the definite renunciation and perception of an either-or, the romantic situation was brought to an end."[36] For Schmitt, not only is Kierkegaard the greatest of the Romantics but also, crucially, the only one who overcomes the "eternal conversation" and makes a decision, or turns possibility into concrete reality. In section three, we will delve deeper into Schmitt and Kierkegaard's decisionism. This decisionism will be developed further and more decisively by Schmitt in *The Concept of the Political* in his definition of the political and discussion of the friend/enemy distinction in politics.

Kierkegaard most famously appears at the end of the first chapter of Schmitt's *Political Theology*, though his name is not mentioned, but as the "Protestant theologian":

> A Protestant theologian who demonstrated the vital intensity possible in theological reflection in the nineteenth century stated: "The exception explains the general and itself. And if one wants to study the general correctly, one only needs to look around for a true exception. It reveals everything more clearly than does the general. Endless talk about the general becomes boring; there are exceptions. If they cannot be explained, then the general also cannot be explained. The difficulty is usually not noticed because the general is not thought about with passion but with a comfortable superficiality. The exception, on the other hand, thinks the general with intense passion."[37]

---

[33]     Cf. Ellen Kennedy, *Constitutional Failure: Carl Schmitt in Weimar*, Durham and London: Duke University Press 2004, p. 205.

[34]     Ibid.

[35]     Schmitt, *Politische Romantik*, p. 97. (*Political Romanticism*, p. 166, note 10.)

[36]     Schmitt, *Politische Romantik*, p. 97. (*Political Romanticism*, p. 65.)

[37]     Schmitt, *Politische Theologie*, p. 22. (*Political Theology*, p. 15.)

This quotation is taken from the end of Kierkegaard's *Repetition*,[38] though it is very slightly altered. Schmitt has modified and edited the quotation. His translation is not to be found in any German editions. Schmitt uses the word "actual" (*wirklich*) rather than the word that Kierkegaard uses which is "legitimate" (*berettiget*). Preceding this passage, Schmitt is already speaking in the language and ideas of Kierkegaard's pseudonym of *Repetition*, Constantin Constantius:

> The exception can be more important to it [a philosophy of concrete life] than the rule, not because of a romantic irony for the paradox, but because the seriousness of an insight goes deeper than the clear generalisations inferred from what ordinarily repeats itself. The exception is more interesting than the rule. The rule proves nothing; the exception proves everything.[39]

The exception (*die Ausnahme* in German and *undtagelsen* in Danish) is the central term in Schmitt's *Political Theology*. The opening sentence is probably Schmitt's most famous line: "Sovereign is he who decides on the exception."[40] I will take a closer look at the exception in the case of both Kierkegaard and Schmitt in Section III. Throughout the same text, there is mention of the "either/or," no doubt again due to the heavy and direct influence of Kierkegaard as "theologian" on Schmitt as "political and legal theorist" writing a book called *Political Theology*.[41]

In 1923, a year after *Political Theology*, Schmitt publishes a kind of sequel, *Roman Catholicism and Political Form*,[42] where again Kierkegaard is mentioned and this time by name. Kierkegaard is only mentioned once, but again with reverence. And whereas in *Political Theology*, Kierkegaard as "Protestant theologian" is mentioned at the end of the first chapter, in *Roman Catholicism and Political Form*, he is mentioned at the end in the Appendix to the essay. For Ulmen, this is an essay "concerned with the political consequences of Protestant inwardness and worldly asceticism, for which Schmitt finds an antidote in the 'political idea' of Catholicism."[43] Schmitt juxtaposes the Catholic visibility of the church with the Protestant invisibility of the church. The visibility of the church begins to be lost when it enters into a mystical, imaginary space. Again, Kierkegaard comes out unscathed here:

---

[38]   *SKS* 4, 93 / *R*, 227.
[39]   Schmitt, *Politische Theologie*, p. 22. (*Political Theology*, p. 15.)
[40]   Schmitt, *Politische Theologie*, p. 11 (*Political Theology*, p. 5): "*Souverän ist, wer über den Ausnahmezustand entscheidet.*"
[41]   For the insertion of "either/or" in *Political Theology*, see for example, Schmitt, *Politische Theologie*, p. 27; p. 69; p. 71. (*Political Theology*, p. 18; p. 53; p. 55.)
[42]   As G.L. Ulmen points out in the English translation's introduction to *Roman Catholicism and Political Form*: "The first edition of *Political Theology* (1922) contains a note indicating that Schmitt's four chapters on the theory of sovereignty were written together with an essay titled 'The Political Idea of Catholicism,' which appeared separately in 1923 under the title *Roman Catholicism and Political Form*," see introduction to Schmitt, *Roman Catholicism and Political Form*, p. xxxi.
[43]   See introduction to Schmitt, *Roman Catholicism and Political Form*, pp. xiii–xiv.

One cannot believe God became man without believing there will also be a visible Church as long as the world exists. Every religious sect which has transposed the concept of the Church from the visible community of believing Christians into a *corpus mere mysticum* basically has doubts about the humanity of the Son of God. It has falsified the historical reality of the incarnation of Christ into a mystical and imaginary process. In so doing, one of course arrives at a postulate of immediacy, namely, that Christ was not merely born in Bethlehem in Palestine in the year 1 but for every man and in every age. But that is no longer the physical, visible incarnation, which the most inward of all Christians, Kierkegaard, maintained with such fervour.[44]

So for Schmitt, in *Political Romanticism*, Kierkegaard is "the only great figure among the romantics"; in *Political Theology*, the one "who demonstrated the vital intensity possible in theological reflection in the nineteenth century"; and in *Roman Catholicism and Political Form*, "the most inward of all Christians"—high praise indeed.

Even though Kierkegaard is not actually mentioned in *The Concept of the Political*, one can see Schmitt's appropriation of Kierkegaard's philosophical-theological mission into the concrete existence into his own creation of the existential political condition. One might think of Kierkegaard in this text in Schmitt's prioritization of conflict and struggle ("What always matters is only the possibility of conflict"),[45] his disgust at the bourgeoisie ("The bourgeois is an individual who does not want to leave the apolitical riskless private sphere"),[46] and the lack of decision-making and *faux*-individualism ("An individualism in which anyone other then the free individual himself were to decide upon the substance and dimension of his freedom would be only an empty phrase").[47] Another vital and influential distinction is made by Schmitt in this text, the "friend/enemy" distinction, which is manifested in radical political manifestos around the world in the twentieth century such as Chairman Mao's *Little Red Book* and violent political organizations such as Red Army Faction[48] (better known as the Baader-Meinhof Group) who went to war with the West German Federal State, and the neo-conservative George W. Bush Presidency after the 9/11 Twin Tower bombings where the clear message was: it is us or them, either you are with us or against us, and the Iraq campaign's "Coalition of the Willing." Schmitt describes as clearly and as rigorously as ever:

[44]     Schmitt, "Die Sichtbarkeit der Kirche: Eine scholastische Erwägung," *Summa: Eine Vierteljahresschrift*, 1917, p. 75. (*Roman Catholicism and Political Form*, p. 52.)
[45]     Schmitt, *Der Begriff des Politischen*, p. 22. (*The Concept of the Political*, p. 39.)
[46]     Schmitt, *Der Begriff des Politischen*, p. 43. (*The Concept of the Political*, p. 62.)
[47]     Schmitt, *Der Begriff des Politischen*, p. 51. (*The Concept of the Political*, p. 71.)
[48]     In Chairman Mao Tse-Tung's book, *Quotations from Chairman Mao*, Beijing 1964), better known as *The Little Red Book*, he writes, "Who are our enemies? Who are our friends? This is a question of the first importance for the revolution....It is good if we are attacked by the enemy, since it proves that we have drawn a clear line of demarcation between the enemy and ourselves." See Chapter 2: "Classes and Class Struggle," p. 25 and p. 29. The motto on the cover of the Red Army Faction Manifesto (1971) quotes Mao: "A clear dividing line must be drawn between ourselves and the enemy!" See Anthony Murphy, *Red Army Fraction: The Urban Guerilla Concept*, Montreal and Quebec: Kersplebedeb 2005.

The friend and enemy concepts are to be understood in their concrete and existential sense, not as metaphors or symbols, not as mixed and weakened by economic, moral, and other conceptions, least of all in a private-individualistic sense as a psychological expression of private emotions and tendencies. They are neither normative nor pure spiritual antithesis.[49]

Again, one might see the influence of Kierkegaard on Schmitt's political thought of the either/or transformed into the friend/enemy distinction—from aesthetic possibility to ethical task, making a clear dividing line, as in the appropriation of Kierkegaard's exception from the poetic into the political realm. More of this in Section III.

Elsewhere, there are other allusions to Kierkegaard both directly and indirectly. In his essay on Hobbes in 1938, Schmitt writes at one point: "The distinction of inner and outer became for the mortal god a sickness unto death."[50] One familiar with the Kierkegaard–Schmitt connection is immediately made aware of Kierkegaard's great text on the profound analysis of despair, which is the "sickness unto death," the most intense form of which is when one does not make a decision, or, which Kierkegaard develops from his earlier works, when one makes a decision and can no longer change it, but holds onto his or her position with all the rage of a desperate person. Kierkegaard, in the form of his pseudonym (Anti-Climacus) for this text, takes the term "sickness unto death" from the Gospel of John 11:4.

Other places where Schmitt might very well be thinking of Kierkegaard is in his very early publication of *Schattenrisse* together with his friend Fritz Eisler (1883–1936) in 1913. This was a satire of Walter Rathenau who appears in 60 lines of blank verse. Rathenau's own story is a remarkable and ultimately depressing one. A German-Jewish nationalist and industrialist, Rathenau was a leading proponent of Jewish assimilation in Germany and even served as a minister in the Weimar Republic. He was assassinated in 1922 by ultra-nationalist army officers. Schmitt and Eisler's satire is a response to Rathenau's *Kritik der Zeit* (1912)—a work that argues that the times are mechanical and critique itself determines the age. Thus, division of labor, commerce and machines are the idea of the age, and in this age we have no soul. The title alone of Schmitt and Eisner's satire brings to mind the essay in the first part of *Either/Or* which has the same name in German (meaning "Silhouettes" or *Skyggerids* in the original Danish), and is right at the center of Kierkegaard's aesthetic, melancholic authorship dedicated to the "Fellowship of the Dead."[51] In addition, Schmitt's little aesthetic satire is under a pseudonym: Johannes Negelinus, Mox Doctor. Schmitt had a copy of *Either/Or* at this time, and he calls his pseudonym Johannes which is also the name of Kierkegaard's most famous pseudonyms such as the great aesthete of "The Seducer's Diary" in part one of *Either/Or*, who is probably also the "author" of "Silhouettes," and later Johannes de silentio of *Fear and Trembling* and Johannes Climacus of *Philosophical Fragments* and *Concluding Unscientific Postscript*.

[49]    Schmitt, *Der Begriff des Politischen*, p. 9. (*The Concept of the Political*, pp. 27–8.)
[50]    Schmitt, *Der Leviathan in der Staatslehre des Thomas Hobbes*, p. 99. (*The Leviathan in the State Theory of Thomas Hobbes: Meaning and Failure of a Political Symbol*, p. 65.)
[51]    *SKS* 2, 163–209 / *EO1*, 165–215.

Earlier in the year, Schmitt had written two stories called "The Mirror" and "Don Quijote und das Publikum," published in *Die Rheinlande*. These also in their titles and themes carry allusions to Kierkegaard or at least reveal more, albeit weaker, evidence of the influence of Kierkegaard on Schmitt at this time. Don Quixote holds a special place in Kierkegaard *corpus* of work, a figure who in a way drives the very soul of the *Concluding Unscientific Postscript*. Kierkegaard writes in his journal at the time of writing this massive and meandering work:

> It is a sad mistake for Cervantes to end Don Quixote by making him sensible and then letting him die. Cervantes, who himself had the superb idea of having him become a shepherd! It ought to have ended there. That is, Don Quixote should not come to an end; he ought to be presented as going full speed, so that he opens vistas upon an infinite series of new fixed ideas. Don Quixote is endlessly perfectible in madness, but the one thing he cannot become (for otherwise he could become everything and anything) is sensible. Cervantes seems not to have been dialectical enough to bring it to this romantic conclusion (that there is no conclusion).[52]

Quixote also epitomizes the close connection between lunacy and truth that Kierkegaard explores in both the *Concluding Unscientific Postscript* and *Fear and Trembling*. Schmitt's piece is also about reason and madness, and this piece is already giving signs of the more mature Schmitt of *Political Theology* in the articulation of the exception. For both Schmitt and Kierkegaard, Don Quixote is an exception. Similar to Kierkegaard, Schmitt writes: "A man who has motives other than those usual in bourgeois life will be a laughingstock…the public sees quite rightly what it laughs at; the question is only whether it is right."[53] Both Kierkegaard and Schmitt view Quixote as good, noble and honest, all elements of human greatness unlike the all-knowing *Publikum* or "crowd" (*Mængde*) of reason and "normal understanding."[54] Unlike Kierkegaard and Schmitt's exception, the *Publikum* only see the general with a "comfortable superficiality" rather than with "intense passion" as their Don Quixote does. Similarly, in his other piece, "The Mirror," Schmitt explores the limits of rationalism and its detachment from "real life." Ellen Kennedy points out that "Schmitt's literary work assumes a world in which there are no definitions, where everything is possible."[55] However, one can also add that it is in these literary experiments where Schmitt finds his voice and will appropriate these interests into his most vital elements of his political and legal thinking. Schmitt, in classical Kierkegaardian fashion, at one point in the piece asks: "But what does a rationalist know about real life?"[56]

---

[52]   *SKS* 20, 107, NB:170 / *JP* 1, 771.

[53]   Carl Schmitt, "Don Quijote und das Publikum," *Die Rheinlande*, vol. 22, 1912, pp. 348–50.

[54]   "The public" (*Publikum*), "the crowd" (*Mængde*) and "the numerical" (*det Numeriske*) are words that Kierkegaard uses especially from 1846 on. Look especially at his social critique and use of these words in *A Literary Review of Two Ages* (1846) and *The Point of View for My Work as an Author* (written ca. 1848, published posthumously in 1859).

[55]   See Kennedy, *Constitutional Failure*, p. 43.

[56]   See Carl Schmitt, "Der Spiegel," *Die Rheinlande*, vol. 22, 1912, p. 62.

Finally, there are direct references to Kierkegaard in Schmitt's diaries that give proof that Schmitt was reading Kierkegaard with passion and reverence. The diaries between 1912 and 1919 also show precisely what books Schmitt was reading. In the first volume of the diaries, published in 2003 (not yet translated), there is even a picture of Kierkegaard added in the appendix.[57] Also, the excerpt from *The Concept of Anxiety* that Schmitt refers to is included in the volume.[58] On October 3, 1914, Schmitt writes in his diary:

> I ate this evening, drank tea (luckily Schneider didn't come by), read Kierkegaard's *Stages on Life's Way*. It is ingenious in the highest sense; everything is brought out in gleaming formulation....The deceived is wiser than the not deceived, as Kierkegaard says it. Correct. The weak one is more direct than the stronger one; the considerate one is less considerate than the non-considerate. It all makes sense....[59]

The next day in his journals, Schmitt quotes from the section on the "demonic" and "inclosing reserve" (*det Indesluttede*) from Kierkegaard's *The Concept of Anxiety*:

> Kierkegaard, *The Concept of Anxiety*: The demonic is the inclosing reserve and the unfreely disclosed: "It is incredible what power the man of inclosing reserve can exercise over such people, how at last they beg and plead for just a word to break the silence, but it is also shameful to trample upon the weak in this manner." "It might be thought that inclosing reserve would have an extraordinary continuity; yet the very opposite is the case, although when compared with the vapid, enervating dissolution of oneself continually absorbed in the impression, it has the appearance of continuity."[60]

Directly after quoting these passages from *The Concept of Anxiety*, Schmitt writes in his diary:

> Why am I always so cautious and hesitating when I deal with human beings? Sometimes I am under the impression I only do that because I am afraid of my own ruthlessness, because I only know one thing: to dominate people until they are eliminated or submit to them in excitement, and when I cannot do the second I fear people will notice the first and thus I am timid and cautious.

The day after he again is reading Kierkegaard with joy: "Ate in the house in the evening, read with joy and pride Kierkegaard..."[61] On October 8, during the same

---

57     Schmitt, *Tagebücher: Oktober 1912 bis Februar 1915*, p. 325. This is the somewhat idealized and romantic image drawn in 1840 by Kierkegaard's cousin Niels Christian Kierkegaard (1806–82).

58     Ibid., pp. 385–91: The excerpt used is from chapter three, section two: "Anxiety defined Dialectically as Fate." See *SKS* 4, 399–405 / *CA*, 96–103.

59     Schmitt, *Tagebücher: Oktober 1912 bis Februar 1915*, p. 216 (October 3, 1914). My translation.

60     Ibid., p. 218 (October 4, 1914). The quotations correspond to *SKS* 4, 426–7 / *CA*, 125 and *SKS* 4, 430 / *CA*, 129–30.

61     Schmitt, *Tagebücher: Oktober 1912 bis Februar 1915*, p. 218 (October 5, 1914). See also ibid., p. 219 (October 10, 1914) for more evidence that Schmitt is reading Kierkegaard.

week, Schmitt writes down after reading *The Concept of Anxiety* again, "...read Kierkegaard and suddenly opened up on the place of destiny and genius."[62]

Seven months later, on May 11, 1915, Schmitt returns to Kierkegaard in his diary:

> Went down the street, when the Captain had left for an hour, accidentally saw a book by Kierkegaard in a shop and bought it: Critique of the Present. Was excited with joy (the translator is Theodor Haecker and lives in Munich), delved inside the book and didn't get any other work done. Ate with Cari and Georg in the Neue Börse for lunch, then we all had coffee on the first floor of cafe Bauknecht. Cari went to see the doctor, I went to the office. Horrible, this idleness; something for Däublers paper, but it's not working out yet. Eagerly reading Kierkegaard. In the evening happily at home. It's beautiful weather....[63]

From this journal entry, one can witness the feeling of excitement that Schmitt gets from discovering and reading Kierkegaard for the first time. Kierkegaard's essay on the "present age" is one of his only direct socio-political critiques that attacks different fabrics of our emerging modern society.[64] In this "review," Kierkegaard distinguishes between the "revolutionary age" (*Revolutions-Tiden*) and the "present age" (*Nutiden*),[65] and introduces terms such as "leveling" (*Nivelleringen*), the "Public" (*Publikum*) that "is a monstrous nothing," "chatter" (*at snakke*), "Formlessness" (*Formløshed*), and "Superficiality" (*Overfladiskhed*).[66] It is these terms that will provide exactly the type of characteristics that Schmitt will give to parliamentary democracy in his future writings: the chatter that turns into the "eternal conversation" and a present age that lacks passion and strength.

Two weeks later, Schmitt mentions the "thorn in the flesh" which editors Ernst Hüsmert and Gerd Geisler pick up on with the Kierkegaard reference. "Thorn in the Flesh" was a piece by Kierkegaard that was translated and with a foreword by Theodor Haecker in *Der Brenner* in July 1914.[67] In the Autumn of 1918, Schmitt writes: "Such a formation and great work on the *Ungeist* [Unsense or Nonspirit] of the 19th century were reserved for someone else: Kierkegaard, who articulated again for his time the ever same truth like a Father of the Church."[68] As late as his enormous work on the origin of the Eurocentric global order, *The Nomos of the Earth*, published in 1950, Schmitt cites Kierkegaard as one of the great nineteenth-century critics of Europe: "The great contemporary critics remained isolated and unfashionable individualists—Søren Kierkegaard as well as Donoso Cortés, Bruno Bauer as well as Jacob Burckhardt, Charles Baudelaire as ultimately also Friedrich

---

[62]     Ibid., p. 222 (October 8, 1914). He is referring again to chapter three, section two of *The Concept of Anxiety*.

[63]     See Schmitt, *Die Militärzeit 1915 bis 1919*, p. 66 (Tuesday, May 12, 1915). My translation.

[64]     See Kierkegaard's *A Literary Review* (1846).

[65]     *SKS* 8, 60–7 / *TA*, 61–8.

[66]     *SKS* 8, 80–100 / *TA*, 81–101.

[67]     Ibid., p. 73 (May 25, 1915): see footnote by Ernst Hüsmert and Gerd Geisler. See also Sören Kierkegaard, "Der Pfahl im Fleich," *Der Brenner*, vol. 4, no. 16, 1914, pp. 691–712 and no. 17, 1914, pp. 797–814.

[68]     Schmitt, *Die Militärzeit 1915 bis 1919*, p. 475 (Munich, Autumn 1918). My translation.

Nietzsche."[69] It is this perception of Kierkegaard as the supreme exception on the subject of faith and passion that would help transform Schmitt's political program of the exception of political sovereignty from Kierkegaard's remarks into *Political Theology*.

### III. A General Interpretation of Schmitt's Use of Kierkegaard

How many of Kierkegaard's ideas have been appropriated by Schmitt? For Schmitt, Kierkegaard, although from a Lutheran background, was a *Bruder in Geist*.[70] I will take a look at a few different aspects and areas in Schmitt's use of Kierkegaard and how they actually differ from each other: the existential element in the literary and philosophical sense from the possible to the concrete in the event of the either/or and the friend/enemy distinction, the critique of the Romantic movement and the bourgeoisie, and the use and transformation of the "exception."

### A. From Literature to Praxis: The Existential Moment

From the beginning of the twentieth century up to the outbreak of World War II, there was increasing disenchantment alongside experimentation in philosophy, the arts, and science amongst intellectuals. Carl Schmitt was one of the intellectuals who felt this intensely. In Germany alone, thinkers like Nietzsche and Kierkegaard were being hungrily read by the new generation. Kierkegaard's reception was late, given that he had died in 1855 relatively unknown outside his hometown of Copenhagen. But as mentioned previously, the translations of his works through *Der Brenner* were making quite an impact.

The literary quality of Kierkegaard's writing alongside the disenchantment of living in the modern world and suspicion of Hegelian philosophy rang powerfully in the ears of the gifted intellectuals growing up in the early twentieth century and living through World War I, and then witnessing the fragility of the Weimar Republic and the rise of extremists from both the Left and the Right culminating in Hitler's seizure of power in 1933. Adorno's monograph on Kierkegaard was published on the same day that Hitler took power.[71] In Heidegger's *Being and Time* (1927), Kierkegaard plays a central role in the development of the book. Most especially, Heidegger takes Kierkegaard's notion of repetition, the analysis of anxiety especially in the face of death, and the "moment." And, of course, Georg Lukács had already written the seminal essay on Kierkegaard entitled "The Foundering of Form against Life: Sören

---

69     Carl Schmitt, *Der Nomos der Erde im Völkerrecht des Jus Publikum Europaeum*, Berlin: Duncker und Humblot 1950, p. 267. (English translation: *The Nomos of the Earth in the International Law of the Jus Publicum Europaeum*, trans. by G.L. Ulmen, New York: Telos Publishing 2006, p. 292.)

70     I take up this expression following editor Ernst Hüsmert's use of it. See his introduction to *Tagebücher: Oktober 1912 bis Februar 1915*, p. 3.

71     See Theodor W. Adorno, *Kierkegaard. Konstruktion des Ästhetischen*, Tübingen: Mohr 1933.

Kierkegaard and Regine Olsen,"[72] revealing the personal quality of Kierkegaard's writing which acts as a mirror and ultimately judgment on the reader's own life.

Later, Kierkegaard is present throughout the even more influential *Theory of the Novel* (1920)[73] with the word *Innerlichkeit*[74] running through the text, and as a barely disguised expression for revolutionary praxis that Lukács will turn to straight after this text is published. In fact, over forty years later, Lukács does state in the 1962 preface to *Theory of the Novel* that "Kierkegaard always played an important role for the author of *The Theory of the Novel*."[75]

Not only is Schmitt looking at previous political thinkers in forming his political and legal thought, he is also delving into characters from literature such as Hamlet, Don Quixote, and Benito Cereno to name a few. We may add Constantin Constantius, Johannes de silentio, Vigilius Haufniensis, Anti-Climacus, Johannes the Seducer, Victor Eremita, and Judge William to this list of literary-philosophical creations. By travelling with these various particular characters and pseudonyms, Schmitt is answering the existential challenge: to turn theory into praxis. Fundamental is also the fact that Schmitt views these characters and pseudonyms, like the young Lukács and Heidegger did, as exceptional individuals suspicious of their socio-political environment, and their wish to transform it through concrete action. Unlike, Marx, who is the enemy for Schmitt, these figures are singular, sovereign individuals who do not rely on the collective, and rather than obeying the laws of history, wish to confront and confound it. For Schmitt, this *Bruder in Geist* is following in the great tradition of intensely psychological and religious poets of despair, decision, and faith such as Dante and Dostoevsky. When Schmitt is formulating his political sovereign in 1923, he writes: "…making a decision is more important than how a decision is made."[76]

Kierkegaard's first major work, *Either/Or*, marks the break with theory and the call for action and practice to the point where half way through Judge William's response to the aesthete, he tells the reader that if he understands him by now and finds him standing at the crossroad (*Skillevejen*), then he should throw away the book now and begin living, that is, by choosing.[77] Schmitt, as is evident from his

---

[72]     György Lukács, "Sören Kierkegaard és Regine Olsen." ("The Foundering of Form against Life. Sören Kierkegaard and Regine Olsen.")

[73]     Georg Lukács, *The Theory of the Novel: A Historico-Philosophical Essay on the Forms of Great Epic Literature*, trans. by Anna Bostock, Cambridge, Massachusetts: MIT Press 1971. (Originally published as *Die Theorie des Romans: ein geschichtsphilosophischer Versuch über die Formen der großen Epik*, Stuttgart: Enke 1916.)

[74]     "Inwardness," is translated from the Danish *Inderlighed* and is one of the key words in the whole of Kierkegaard's writings.

[75]     Lukács, *The Theory of the Novel*, p. 18.

[76]     Schmitt, *Politische Theologie*, p. 71. (*Political Theology*, p. 56.)

[77]     See *SKS* 3, 164 / *EO2*, 168: "As soon as a person can be brought to stand at the crossroads in such a way that there is no way out for him except to choose, he will choose the right thing. Therefore, if it should so happen that before you finish reading this somewhat lengthy exploration, which again is being sent to you in the form of a letter, you feel that the moment of choice has arrived, then throw away the remainder—do not bother with it; you have lost nothing!"

diaries and *Political Romanticism*, embraces the message of *Either/Or* and *A Literary Review of Two Ages* and attempts to bring this into law and politics.

## B. Political Romanticism and the Bourgeoisie

The seminal work *Political Romanticism* is inspired by Kierkegaard. What is political romanticism? Schmitt seeks out the etymology of the word *romantic*, and says: "The word is derived from *Roman*, a "novel," a "work of fiction," or a 'romance.'"[78] However, the human as the romantic, as distinguished from the word "romantic" must act, and Schmitt recognizes this: "It is only the romanticising subject and its activity that are of importance for the definition of the concept."[79] In the preface to *Political Romanticism*, Schmitt introduces a term to help us understand what he means by "romanticism": "The romantic attitude is most clearly characterised by means of a singular concept, that of the *occasio*. This concept can be rendered in terms of ideas such as occasion, opportunity, and perhaps also chance."[80] Schmitt calls romanticism "subjectified occasionalism." Explaining this definition, he writes: "in the romantic, the romantic subject treats the world as an occasion and an opportunity for his romantic productivity."[81]

Roman Catholicism is not romantic in the sense that Schmitt speaks of it just because it is not a product of rationalism.[82] Romanticism can also be a product of rationalism such as that in Descartes and Rousseau. The political romanticist that Schmitt discusses wishes to poeticize or aestheticize politics to the point where all conflict disappears. And, as Schmitt will write in a later work, "What always matters is only the possibility of conflict."[83] For Schmitt, political romanticism seems to have reached its culmination in the bourgeois revolutions of 1848 and the writings of Karl Marx and Friedrich Engels. These romantics look back to Rousseau and the French Revolution: "The spokesmen for the coming revolution of 1848 idolized Rousseau and the French Revolution and saw here a grand model to which they appealed."[84] The rise of political romanticism did not decline since then, but only grew with the rise of liberalism, because romanticism, according to Schmitt, depends on liberalism. Political romanticism had already reached fairytale proportions in Rousseau and Novalis, but thereafter, it also descended from activity to passivity in the allegiance of romanticism and liberalism. Schmitt, using his usual strategy of quoting another (this time Adam Müller) to make his point, writes that even revolution "is an idolisation of abstract concepts."[85] Hence, both conservatives and revolutionaries are subject to political romanticism, which leads to that 'endless discussion' that Schmitt is so repelled by, and which ultimately weakens the sovereign.

---

[78]   Schmitt, *Politische Romantik*, p. 43. (*Political Romanticism*, p. 30.)
[79]   Schmitt, *Politische Romantik*, p. 141. (*Political Romanticism*, p. 99.)
[80]   Schmitt, *Politische Romantik*, p. 22. (*Political Romanticism*, p. 16.)
[81]   Schmitt, *Politische Romantik*, p. 23. (*Political Romanticism*, p. 17.)
[82]   Schmitt, *Politische Romantik*, p. 76. (*Political Romanticism*, p. 50.)
[83]   Schmitt, *Der Begriff des Politischen*, p. 28. (*The Concept of the Political*, p. 39.)
[84]   Schmitt, *Politische Romantik*, p. 36. (*Political Romanticism*, p. 25.)
[85]   Schmitt, *Politische Romantik*, p. 41. (*Political Romanticism*, p. 28.)

Kierkegaard is also a critic of romanticism. Unlike the German romanticists, Kierkegaard is attempting to make space for such loaded terms as "responsibility," "duty" and "decision." Kierkegaard's aesthetic pseudonyms perceive the either/or but avoid it. One commentator articulates Kierkegaard's relation with the romantics: "Like the German romantics, Kierkegaard considers the poetic an intrinsic feature of the existential condition. Unlike the romantics, however, he does not believe one should endeavour to construct the self 'through experimentation and play with an infinity of possibilities.' "[86] One ultimately must come to the point of duty, decision, and responsibility, and yet both Kierkegaard and Schmitt are still interested in the use of the poetic. Both allude to Shakespeare's characters as providing a narrative to human existence. Are Kierkegaard and Schmitt then immersed in any way in political romanticism? In *Political Romanticism*, Schmitt warns that this might indeed happen and tells the reader: "Indeed, I hope this book remains aloof from every subromantic interest."[87] Yet it is not possible for Schmitt to be exempt from *every* subromantic interest. In Schmitt's thought, is the world instead an *occasion* for constructing a political world of friend and enemy? Is this not just another form of "occasionalism"? Is not Schmitt himself already aware of this when he asks the reader not to associate his writings with any "subromantic interest"? The conservative romantic is apparent when the sovereign/exception has the power to do anything, which is the same power that German romanticism wished to have and which Kierkegaard criticized: the power that seeks the "infinite possibilities." This time, romanticism is found in the realm of those who hold power, which makes their power all the more dangerous, as it allows for war, conquest, and subjugation. Might Schmitt be actually aestheticizing the exception and carving out a politically aesthetic world with the dynamic of the friend/enemy distinction which he bases on a presumed existential reality?

1848 is the year of decision for both Kierkegaard and Schmitt. Schmitt begins his final section of *Political Theology* by maintaining the German romantics' old trait—"everlasting conversation."[88] He defends the three Catholic political philosophers—Comte Joseph Marie de Maistre (1753–1821), Vicomte Louis Gabriel Ambroise de Bonald (1754–1840), and Donoso Cortés (1809–53) from accusations of political romanticism, by their emphasis on decision-making that separates them from the everlasting conversation of the political romantics: "for what characterized their counterrevolutionary political philosophy was the recognition that their times needed a decision."[89] The emphasis on decision-making is intensified by 1848, and Schmitt informs the reader that Cortés views that year as the end of royalism. Schmitt himself prioritizes the significance of 1848 and the necessity for decision in all three of his major interwar texts. The time of ruthless decision was upon Europe: "In 1848 this image [the warlike image of a bloody, definitive, destructive, decisive battle] rose up

[86]   See Mark Dooley, *Kierkegaard's Ethics of Responsibility*, New York: Fordham University Press 2001, p. 149.
[87]   Schmitt, *Politische Romantik*, p. 28. (*Political Romanticism*, p. 21.)
[88]   Schmitt, *Politische Theologie*, p. 69. (*Political Theology*, p. 53.)
[89]   Ibid.

on both sides in opposition to parliamentary constitutionalism."[90] For Schmitt, "The critical year of 1848 was a year of democracy and of dictatorship at the same time."[91] Writing in 1848, Kierkegaard explains the importance of the decision at the *Skillevej* or "crossroad." In *Christian Discourses*, the times need a decision in the face of the malaise of "cleverness" (*Klogskab*) in the modern era.[92] The decision, which is presented so starkly and with such rhetorical force in *A Literary Review of Two Ages*, distinguishes between God and world. By choosing God, one is not, to repeat, refuting the world, but paradoxically choosing the world too, not in the Hegelian sense of absorbing all, but in Kierkegaard's sense of acting honestly and decisively.

Schmitt's decision to overcome political romanticism is an attempt to hold a disintegrating world together. Political romanticism is an emotive response, but "Where political activity begins, political romanticism ends."[93] This is reminiscent of the end of *Works of Love*: "To say it is one thing: to do it is another."[94] Schmitt despises the potential passivity of liberal democracy and chooses dictatorship. His decisionism comes from the authoritarian government that is the sovereign. Kierkegaard's decisionism comes from the single individual and his or her guide that manifests itself as the prototype in Socrates and Christ. The dictatorship must remain in control of and wield the exception: "The decision on the exception is a decision in the true sense of the word."[95] In the Preface to the second edition, Schmitt writes:

> And whereas the normativist in his distortion makes of law a mere mode of operation of a state bureaucracy, and the decisionist, focusing on the moment, always runs the risk of missing the stable content inherent in every great political movement, an isolated institutional thinking leads to the pluralism characteristic of a feudal-corporate growth that is devoid of sovereignty.[96]

This description distorts our conceptions of the dangers of democracy and dictatorship. For Schmitt, the roles have been reversed—democracy becomes a bureaucratic, Kafkaesque hell in which nothing is ever done and it is impossible to find clarity let alone make decisions, while dictatorship provides the space for decision-making and clarity.

How can one rescue Kierkegaard from the same fate of so many modern intellectuals that reject the democratic age? And why should we? Do Kierkegaard's

---

[90]     See Schmitt, *Die geistesgeschichtliche Lage des heutigen Parlamentarismus*, p. 81. (*The Crisis of Parliamentary Democracy*, p. 69.)

[91]     Schmitt, *Die geistesgeschichtliche Lage des heutigen Parlamentarismus*, p. 64. (*The Crisis of Parliamentary Democracy*, p. 51.)

[92]     *SKS* 10, 31 / *CD*, 19. *SKS* 10, 41 / *CD*, 29.

[93]     Schmitt, *Politische Romantik*, p. 224. (*Political Romanticism*, p. 160.)

[94]     *SKS* 11, 373 / *WL*, 359.

[95]     Schmitt, *Politische Theologie*, p. 11. (*Political Theology*, p. 6.)

[96]     Schmitt, *Politische Theologie. Vier Kapitel zur Lehre von der Souveränität*, Berlin: Duncker und Humblot 1934, p. 8. (*Political Theology*, p. 3.)

scathing remarks on democracy[97] and liberalism[98] clash with his unwavering argument for the single individual in the world? Georgio Agamben, in his analysis of "state of exception" asks the question: "What then happens when exception and rule become undecidable?"[99] Schmitt bases his fear on man; Kierkegaard bases his fear on God, and fearlessness in the face of one's fellow man—something that dictatorship will not tolerate and democracy will. Kierkegaard and Schmitt wrote in the times of decision. For much of Europe there was an appeal to either fascism or socialism. Schmitt decides for Nazism for a time and authoritarian state, while Kierkegaard's authorship remains something undecidable, restoring the single individual as critical spirit over and above political romanticists and authoritarian theorists: "the condition of man, regarded as spirit…is always critical."[100]

In conclusion to this section, it is worth mentioning that Oakes devotes nearly all of his introduction to *Political Romanticism* to a summary of "The Seducer's Diary" from *Either/Or*, Part One. He concludes that Johannes the Seducer is the "romantic" that Schmitt is speaking of. This is the reason why Schmitt states that Kierkegaard is both the greatest of the romantics and also the only one to find a way out because the latter polemically presents the decision that each human being must make. *Either/Or* presents the alluring and seductive quality of the romantic lifestyle and shows also ultimately the emptiness and nihilism of that position. Some of Kierkegaard's most memorable depictions of the nihilistic world that the aesthete lives in are to be found in this text.[101] Consequently, as Oakes aptly puts it: "The world becomes nothing more than an occasion for the free play of the individual imagination."[102] For the aesthete, the world is divided amongst two kinds of people: the bored and the boring, which one of Schmitt's "high priests" of romanticism declares in none other than his magnum opus, *Don Juan*: "Society is now one polish'd horde, / Form'd of two

---

[97]     *Pap.* VIII–1 A 667 / *JP* 4, 4144: "Of all tyrannies a people's government is the most excruciating, the most mindless, unconditionally the downfall of everything greatness and elevation….A people's government is the true picture of hell [*En Folke-Regjering er det sande Billede paa Helvede*]."
[98]     *SKS* 18, 205, FF:204 / *KJN* 2, 105: "But, as in the fairytale, the liberals have a tongue and an empty head like the tongue in a church bell."
[99]     See Giorgio Agamben, *State of Exception*, trans. by Kevin Attell, Chicago and London: University of Chicago Press 2005, p. 58.
[100]    *SKS* 11, 142 / *SUD*, 25.
[101]    See, for example, *SKS* 2, 166 / *EO1*, 168: "Yes, would that the vortex, which is the world's core principle, even if people are not aware of it but eat and drink, marry and propagate themselves themselves with carefree industriousness, would that it might erupt with deep-seated resentment and shake off the mountains and the nations and the cultural works and man's clever inventions; would that it might erupt with the last terrible shriek that more surely than the trumpet of doom announces the downfall of everything; would that it might stir and spin this bare cliff on which we stand as light as thistledown before the breath in is nostrils."
[102]    See Oakes' introduction to Schmitt's *Political Romanticism*, p. xx. See also ibid., pp. xv–xxiv for Oakes' treatment of "The Seducer's Diary" in the context of *Political Romanticism*.

mighty tribes, the *Bores* / and *Bored*."[103] Kierkegaard reiterates this point through the aesthete in the essay "Rotation of Crops" from *Either/Or I*, but also goes even further to declare that actually "All human beings, then, are boring."[104] In Schmitt's critique of "political romanticism" with his *Bruder in Geist* for ammunition and inspired support, there is also a fundamental critique of the bourgeoisie. In the preface, Schmitt points out: "The bearer of the romantic movement is the new bourgeoisie."[105] And further:

> Psychologically and historically, romanticism is a product of bourgeois security. One could fail to recognise this only as long as one committed the error of considering as romanticism itself things that happen to be favourite romantic objects, such as chivalry and the Middle Ages—in other words, sundry themes and occasions for the romantic interest. A robber knight can be a romantic figure, but he is not romantic. The Middle Ages is a powerfully romanticized complex, but it is not romantic.[106]

This connects specifically with Kierkegaard's depiction of the bourgeoisie that hide behind that valor of others and shelter themselves in their protective *Klogskab*. Comments are rife throughout his authorship on this kind of image we get of the bourgeoisie. In order to survive, the bourgeoisie oscillates between right and left, between fascism and communism, between the either/ors—from hatred of monarchy and aristocracy and fear of being dispossessed of private property. Schmitt concludes in *Political Theology*: "He (the bourgeois) thus oscillated between his two enemies and wanted to fool both."[107]

One is reminded of the passage from the Revelation of John that closes the New Testament that Kierkegaard was very fond of: "I know thy works, that thou art neither cold nor hot: I would thou wert cold or hot. So because thou art lukewarm—The effect of lukewarm water is well known. I am about to spue thee out of my mouth."[108] Dostoevsky was also very fond of this passage and which turns up in vital moments of his great novels.[109] And in Dante's *Divine Comedy*, the lukewarm people are not

---

[103]     *Don Juan* (1821), Canto XIII, XCV, see *Byron: Poetical Works*, ed. by Frederick Page, Oxford: Oxford University Press 1970 p. 819. In *Political Romanticism*, Schmitt remarks, "We must see the three persons whose deformed visages penetrate the colourful romantic veil: Byron, Baudelaire, and Nietzsche, the three high priests, and at the same time the three sacrificial victims, of this private priesthood." See Schmitt, *Politische Romantik*, p. 27 (*Political Romanticism*, p. 20.)

[104]     *SKS* 2, 278 / *EO1*, 288.

[105]     Schmitt, *Politische Romantik*, p. 16. (*Political Romanticism*, p. 12.)

[106]     Schmitt, *Politische Romantik*, p. 141. (*Political Romanticism*, p. 99.)

[107]     Schmitt, *Politische Theologie*, p. 77. (*Political Theology*, p. 61.)

[108]     Rev 3:15–16, King James version.

[109]     See especially *Demons*, trans. by Richard Pevear and Larissa Volokhonsky, London and New York: Everyman's Library 2000, when the passage is read out at the end of the novel to the father of the two principle characters, p. 653. The character Stavrogin might represent the lukewarm figure at its most destructive, who shifts indifferently from one idea to the next, one country to another, from seducing one woman to another, and infecting all those around him like a cult and shadowy leader.

even allowed to enter hell, such is their wretchedness.[110] Schmitt carries this disdain of the "lukewarm" into political thought and for which the bourgeoisie, the liberal democrats, and the Jews are to blame. In his essay on Hobbes, it is Spinoza, "the liberal Jew," who "noticed the barely visible crack" in Hobbes' theory to conform it into liberalism.[111] Earlier in *The Concept of the Political* in stating his friend/enemy distinction in politics, Schmitt confronts this "lukewarm" bourgeois liberalism and declares: "If a part of the population declares that it no longer recognises enemies, then depending on the circumstance, it joins their side and aids them."[112]

However, Schmitt and Kierkegaard differ here ultimately. For Kierkegaard, it is the watering down of "spirit" and "passion" that is the great problem of the bourgeoisie towards faith in God and the mortality of one's life; for Schmitt this is transferred into the public and political realm. And even though we of course have the benefit of hindsight and history behind us and Schmitt was writing throughout the very unsettling Weimar Republic years, the danger still remains of eliminating the "everlasting conversation" and the "discussion class" altogether from the political realm. Instead, a whole generation of German jurists including Carl Schmitt, trained to uphold the independence of the courts, legalize murder and gave absolute power to the sovereign as exception to transcend the law and the "everlasting conversation." This brings us to the next point—on the appropriation of the exception.

## C. The Exception

### 1. The Exception in the Political Realm

What is the exception? Literally, the exception is a person or entity that is "excepted" or that does not follow a rule. There is an old proverb that Schmitt might be pleased with: "the exception proves the rule." The fact that some cases do not follow the rule proves that the rule applies in all other cases. This applies to both Constantin's poet and Schmitt's idea of the sovereign. Schmitt draws the sovereign from the exception, which in turn is drawn from the single individual. The problem emerges when Schmitt takes Constantin's exception and puts it to political use.

Constantin concludes: "the poet is ordinarily [*i Almindelighed*] an exception." It is Constantin's poet that fails as the exception, because he has failed in his experiment of repetition and remains outside society, asocial and nostalgic. He is lost in the melancholy of erotic love, he confides in a stranger he does not wish to confide in, he in no way wins back the girl, and he in no way overcomes his attachment to her; in short, he is left in a worse state than when he started out. Indeed, *Repetition*, perhaps the most aesthetic of Kierkegaard's writings, is a book whose characters—

---

[110]     See Dante's *Inferno*, Canto III, lines 34–9, in his *The Divine Comedy*, trans. by Allen Mandelbaum, London and New York: Everyman's Library 1995: "This miserable way is taken by the sorry souls of those who lived without disgrace and without praise. They now commingle with the coward angels, the company of those who were not rebels nor faithful to their God, but stood apart."

[111]     See Schmitt, *Der Leviathan in der Staatslehre des Thomas Hobbes*, p. 86. (*The Leviathan in the State Theory of Thomas Hobbes*, p. 57.)

[112]     Schmitt, *Der Begriff des Politischen*, p. 34. (*The Concept of the Political*, p. 51.)

the writer and the poet, fail in their project.[113] One can go further then to say that Kierkegaard too fails (intentionally perhaps) in his project of *Repetition*, as the writer behind the writer, and both the poet (as the exception) and the writer fail when the "exception" turns to praxis. Yet the political realm always implies praxis. This brings out a neglected point, because the focus of the discussion on the exception in Kierkegaard is almost invariably *Fear and Trembling*, where one is tempted to think that the exception—Abraham—is vindicated. Abraham is vindicated through God as the Absolute, and, as Johannes de silentio concludes, either the exception "stands in an absolute relation to the Absolute, or Abraham is lost."[114] *Repetition* suggests that, in praxis, most exceptions fail. Schmitt presumes upon the achievability of the exception in public practice, just what Kierkegaard would deny, or at least question. Nearing the end of chapter two of *Political Theology*, Schmitt points out: "What matters for the reality of legal life is who decides."[115] And yet, a few lines later, he concludes: "Finally it [the juristic form] is also not the form of aesthetic production, because the latter knows no decision."[116] But this simply alludes to the failure of *Repetition* in the attempt to put "the exception" into practice, and the failure of the exception in public affairs that differs from the aesthetic worlds of the poet, and the religious worlds of the knight of faith.

When Schmitt remarked on Kierkegaard being the one "who demonstrated the vital intensity possible in theological reflection," he overlooked the distinction that Johannes de silentio makes in Abraham's 'teleological suspension of the ethical' in relation to God and the individual's duties to the ethical in relation to the affairs of men. Taking note of Jesus' advice to the Pharisees: "Render therefore unto Caesar the things which are Caesar's, and to God the things that are God's,"[117] Kierkegaard, moving from *Fear and Trembling*, goes on to write extended discourses in 1848 on distinguishing what serves God and what serves Mammon.[118] In short, the same exception should not be used in the same way in both religion and politics. Yet, such an exception is something that Schmitt is at pains to construct/contest because, for Schmitt, all significant concepts of the modern theory of the state are secularized theological concepts. Schmitt writes: "The exception in jurisprudence is analogous to the miracle in theology."[119] What might be interpreted here, given the title he has been ascribed by both his supporters and detractors as "the Hobbes of the twentieth century," is a return to the pre-modern conception of man and state. But Schmitt is not pre-modern, but very much modern, when we view his modernity such that his thought is not based on theological argument or scientifically deduced argument. He will always be more modern than Hobbes, because Hobbes uses scientific argument as the ground for his thinking, while for Schmitt, there is only an existential ground, that is, an abyss.

---

[113]     *SKS* 6, 221 / *SLW*, 402: "...*Repetition*...a venture that did not, however, succeed, for he remained within the aesthetic."
[114]     *SKS* 4, 207 / *FT*, 120.
[115]     Schmitt, *Politische Theologie*, p. 46. (*Political Theology*, p. 34.)
[116]     Schmitt, *Politische Theologie*, p. 46. (*Political Theology*, p. 35.)
[117]     Matt 22:21.
[118]     Referring specifically to Kierkegaard's *Christian Discourses*.
[119]     Schmitt, *Politische Theologie*, p. 49. (*Political Theology*, p. 36.)

Schmitt still relies on the Catholic philosophers of the counterrevolution—Bonald, de Maistre, and Cortés—as his fellow theorists of the necessity of the exception; but it is not to return to a pre-modern conception, but to highlight the existential monstrosity of humans. The title of his most famous book, *Political Theology*, calls for a modern lawgiver who can omnipotently decide and bring out the exception, and suppress the monstrous, existential potential of his subjects. There remains a profound connection between the theological and the political, but only for practical purposes: "There always exists the same inexplicable identity: lawgiver, executive power, police, pardoner, welfare institution."[120] Democracy is, thus, the "expression of a political relativism," and is "liberated from miracles and dogmas and based on human understanding and critical doubt."[121] Render unto Caesar the things which are Caesar's and unto God the things that are God's. Democracy becomes for mortals an attempt towards providing increased possibility for equality, and towards a world that ought to be rather than that which is—despite its vast shortcomings; Schmitt's authoritarian state becomes an ultimate deification of the state designed to restrict the supposed stupidity and monstrosity of man. "The essence of the state," to quote Engels (the same quotation which Schmitt uses in *Political Theology*), "as that of religion, is mankind's fear of itself."[122] It seems, however, that in both the Schmitt and Engel states, the state becomes mankind's fear of itself, and religion mankind's hope for itself.

The solution for Schmitt, therefore, is Constantin's "exception." A year after *Political Theology*, Schmitt views his own form of progress arising from the exception. He writes: "Development and dictatorship seem to be mutually exclusive."[123] This development is in keeping with the idea of the exception central to the political realm. Agamben concisely explains the role of the exception within the political state in his text on the exception: "the state of exception appears as the legal form of what cannot have legal form....There is no doubt that his [Schmitt's] theory of sovereignty represents an attempt to anchor the state of exception unequivocally to the juridical order."[124] In connection to the passage on rendering unto Caesar what is Caesar's, Anti-Climacus (who could easily have been speaking to Schmitt here) points out:

> O worldly party passion, even if you are called holy and national, no, you do not extend so far that you can trap his [Jesus Christ's] indifference....In a worldly way they wanted to make it into a God-question...this is the way the worldly mentality is so fond of prinking itself up into [*sminke sig op*] godliness, and this is the way they had also mixed God and the emperor together in the question.[125]

---

[120]    Schmitt, *Politische Theologie*, p. 51. (*Political Theology*, p. 38.)

[121]    Schmitt, *Politische Theologie*, p. 55. (*Political Theology*, p. 42.)

[122]    Schmitt, *Politische Theologie*, p. 65. (*Political Theology*, p. 51.) The quotation is from Frederich Engels, *Schriften aus der Frühzeit*, ed. by Gustav Mayer, Berlin: Springer 1920, p. 281.

[123]    Schmitt, *Die geistesgeschichtliche Lage des heutigen Parlamentarismus*, p. 68. (*The Crisis of Parliamentary Democracy*, p. 56.)

[124]    Agamben, *State of Exception*, p. 1; p. 35.

[125]    *SKS* 12, 173 / *PC*, 169.

In a journal entry from 1848, Kierkegaard reflects on the same danger of ascribing divine qualities to the state: "and yet it is by no means so that it is the witness to the truth who claims to be more than human: it is an acoustic illusion; the flaw is in the establishment's imagining itself to be the divine."[126]

## 2. The "Exceptionless Exception"
Giorgio Agamben writes in *State of Exception*:

> Two theses [the right of resistance and the state of exception] are at odds here: One asserts that law must coincide with the norm, and the other holds that the sphere of law exceeds the norm. But in the last analysis, the two positions agree in ruling out the existence of a sphere of human action that is entirely removed from law.[127]

Can Kierkegaard's exception become the right of resistance to Schmitt's state of exception? In the case of Abraham in *Fear and Trembling*, the law of the state was nearly broken, and Johannes Climacus assures the reader in his concluding remarks in the *Postscript* that he is in favor of the well-ordered state that keeps out any idea of a people's rule.[128] Kierkegaard's exception is most needed when stability seems most assured. Also, unlike Schmitt's exception being the decision of the sovereign, and thus the exception becoming the ruler governing a country, Kierkegaard's exception acts as the critic in the face of the universal or norm—and *in extremis*—in the face of political totality, thus giving the exception to the individual being governed rather than to the powers that govern. Kierkegaard's exception emerges in normality, or when society assures itself that it is stable and secure, in the case of the political realm, in times of peace, in times of stability; the exception ought to provide the exception to the rule, as the Socratic gadfly (*Bremse*) that confronts the ruling powers, the one that speaks out, responsible for themselves as individuals rather than as members of a faceless public. However, it is contrary also to the modern phenomenon of the paparazzi which reveals the absence of the exception in those who are governed in their claim for no responsibility toward whatever celebrity or figure they are chasing; they claim they are only responding to a demand, and the public reader claims no responsibility either because they claim that they don't chase the figure in question, they only read about them. This example helps us understand Kierkegaard's point on journalism being the "evil principle of the world."[129]

Schmitt goes as far as to turn the exception into an "exceptionless exception,"[130] where exception becomes the norm. When the sovereign defines the exception and rules in a constant state of emergency as an "exceptionless exception," then it can no longer be considered an exception. It is in Schmitt's *Political Theology* and *The Concept of the Political* where the authoritarian "exceptionless exception" is

---

[126]     *Pap.* IX B 51:4.

[127]     Agamben, *State of Exception*, p. 11.

[128]     *SKS* 7, 563 / *CUP1*, 620–1.

[129]     *SV1* XIII, 555 / *PV*, 69.

[130]     This expression is used by Oren Gross, "The Normless and Exceptionless Exception: Carl Schmitt's Theory of Emergency Powers and the 'Norm–Exception' Dichotomy," *Cardozo Law Review*, vol. 21, 2000, p. 1825.

presented most clearly. When emergency governments become the norm, politics has failed. It is in times of normality (security, stability, and supposed tranquility) where exceptions are needed within those that are ruled, and not within dictatorships by those who rule. This is where Kierkegaard's exception might find its space in actual existence. However, Schmitt's exception emerges in a world of exceptions and crises and desires to consolidate its power; it feasts on crisis and catastrophe and waits for the opportune moment to wield its "lawful" power. Agamben poses the pertinent question: "What then happens when exception and rule become undecidable?" By way of an answer, he responds: "When exception becomes the rule, the machine can no longer function."[131] When the "exceptionless exception" finds itself embodied in one individual with that authoritarian power, then one can see that Kierkegaard's exception is far removed from Schmitt's. Again, Agamben points out this danger too: "But when they tend to coincide in a single person, when the state of exception, in which they are bound and blurred together, becomes the rule, then the juridical-political system transforms itself into a killing machine."[132]

Kierkegaard's exception emerges in a world of *Klogskab* and reflection—both for and by the stranger[133]—thus distinguishing Kierkegaard from Schmitt. So far, Kierkegaard's exception fails as an authority within the powers that be when implemented in or articulated by human affairs—witness the blunders of Constantin and his poet, or the teleological suspension by Abraham with his knife. Nor does Kierkegaard welcome chaos and impotency in the "exceptionless exception," but there must still remain space for the exception.

### 3. Hamlet: The Exception on the Stage

The fictional character Hamlet provides an interesting exception on the stage that both Kierkegaard and Schmitt share an interest in. Hamlet is surrounded by conceit and lies. Unable to tease out the truth from his mother and the new king, he sets about attempting to bring preparation into praxis, resulting in the death of the new king and himself (amongst others). For Schmitt, the myth of Hamlet implies a decision.[134] Schmitt even wrote a book on the immortal play: *Hamlet oder Hekuba. Der Einbruch der Zeit in das Spiel.* The motto for Schmitt's text is formed around Hamlet's soliloquy in Act II, Scene ii, where the prince mentions Hecuba, though the passage is annotated and changed by Schmitt into German:

---

[131]    Agamben, *State of Exception*, p. 58.

[132]    Ibid., p. 86.

[133]    "Stranger" in the sense of the outsider, as the gadfly (*Bremse*) such as Socrates, the eccentric, and "the emigrant from the sphere of the universal [*det Almenes Sphære*]" to quote from Johannes de silentio, see *SKS* 4, 202 / *FT* 115.

[134]    See Victoria Kahn, "Hamlet or Hecuba: Carl Schmitt's Decision," *Representations*, vol. 83, 2003, pp. 67–96.

Why doth flow from the player
the tears of his eyes?
For Hecuba!
What is Hecuba to him?
And what's he to her?
What would he have done if he had lost,
what I had lost?
If his father had been murdered and his crown
from him had been snatched?[135]

Why does Schmitt once more change the lines from a master writer? In these lines, Schmitt modifies Shakespeare's text perhaps inspired by his own poetic muse, to use the force of this soliloquy for his own purposes (or perhaps he was simply quoting from memory). Schmitt sees the great trinity of characters of modern European literature, which Kierkegaard lauds in his own authorship—Don Quixote, Faust, and Hamlet. For Schmitt, it is Hamlet who combines the other two and this makes him the more powerful myth. Don Quixote encompasses the "Spanish and purely Catholic" and Faust—the "German and Protestant," but it is Hamlet who encompasses the two. It is a "splitting," or, to use Schmitt's word, *Spaltung*, which "determines the destiny of Europe."[136] Jacques Derrida, commenting on Schmitt and this particular point, sees this "between-the-two…as a name for Germany," and a Hamlet that has been viewed, like Germany, as "torn and divided within itself."[137] In *Hamlet oder Hecuba*, Schmitt quotes from Ferdinand Freiligrath's poem "Hamlet" which begins "Deutschland ist Hamlet!" Fittingly, the poem was written in 1848. Kierkegaard's Hamlet remains an ambiguity because he is uncertain, he is placed between the Germanic Protestant and the Catholic subjugation (such are the complexities of this ambiguity that Climacus declares that to play the role of Hamlet is like praying—one might get it right only once in life)[138] and the beginning of subjective existence (Climacus interprets Hamlet as saying that existence and non-existence have subjective significance).[139] At the very end of the Hamlet/Hecuba text, Schmitt specifies that Hamlet is neither Lutheran nor Christian; instead, "Hamlet speaks of *special providence*."[140] For Schmitt, it is the sovereign who rescues the state from the

---

[135]     Schmitt's German text: *"Warum fließen diesem Schauspieler / die Tränen aus den Augen? / Um Hecuba! / Was ist ihm Hecuba? / Und was ist er ihr? / Was würde er tun, wenn er verloren hätte, / was ich verlor? / Wenn sein Vater ermordet und eine Krone / ihm entrissen wäre?"* Schmitt's motto is based around *Hamlet* 2.ii, 550–603.

[136]     Schmitt, *Hamlet oder Hekuba*, p. 54. (*Hamlet or Hecuba*, p. 98.) Jacques Derrida has already pointed this out in his *The Politics of Friendship*, London and New York: Verso 1997, see p. 169, note 32.

[137]     Ibid., p. 170.

[138]     *SKS* 7, 150 / *CUP1*, 163.

[139]     *SKS* 7, 177 / *CUP1*, 193.

[140]     Schmitt, *Hamlet oder Hekuba*, p. 63. The final section of the work is called "Exkurs 2: Über den barbarischen Character des Shakespeareschen Dramas; zu Walter Benjamin, *Ursprung des deutschen Trauerspiels*."

despair of the sixteenth-century civil wars.[141] The system is divided into *Politik* (the Political as the sovereign, *Polizei* (Police as the force of law), and *Politesse* (Political Body as citizens). Schmitt turns Hamlet into the figure for the synthesis of modern European culture into the era of decisionism and the authority of the sovereign. Kierkegaard's figure of Hamlet remains elusive and restless in his incertitude.

The state of exception is best described by Agamben: "The state of exception is the opening of a space in which application and norm reveal their separation and a pure force of law realises (that is, applies by ceasing to apply [*dis-applicando*]) a norm whose application has been suspended."[142] Schmitt, for his part, describes the exception as follows: "There will always be a vanguard of the *Weltgeist*, the apex of the development of consciousness, an avant-garde that has the right to act because it possesses correct knowledge and consciousness, not as the chosen people of a personal God, but as a moment in development."[143] Schmitt states the "reality" of democratic states when he makes the point about the British Empire: "That is the political and constitutional meaning of the nice formula 'the colonies are foreign in public law, but domestic in international law.' "[144] This is not a reason nor does it give license to form a dictatorship instead that lives by the reality that gives the Law the legal right to subjugate its citizens. Given political authority, the ones being ruled lose their authority, and these are the dangerous implications of Schmitt's exception, which is contra to Kierkegaard's exception. Agamben reminds the reader: "It is important not to forget that the modern state of exception is a creation of the democratic-revolutionary tradition and not the absolutist one."[145]

## IV. Conclusion

Walter Benjamin defined the "demonic" as the convergence of the concept of modernity with Catholicism.[146] This is interesting when reading Carl Schmitt and alongside Kierkegaard's own particular interest in the "demonic," especially in *The Concept of Anxiety* and *The Sickness unto Death*. We might also think of Schmitt, picturing himself as the Benito Cereno character that he was so fond of mentioning, reading the beautiful and evocative passage in *Philosophical Fragments* of the melancholy king falling in love with the lowly maiden,[147] and then thinking of his precious sovereign leading the lowly citizens to their glory and their doom.

---

[141]    Ibid., p. 65.
[142]    Agamben, *State of Exception*, p. 40.
[143]    Schmitt, *Die geistesgeschichtliche Lage des heutigen Parlamentarismus*, p. 70. (*The Crisis of Parliamentary Democracy*, p. 58.)
[144]    See Schmitt, "Vorbemerkung über den Gegensatz von Parlamentarismus und Democratie," in *Die geistesgeschichtliche Lage des heutigen Parlamentarismus*, 2nd printing, Munich and Leipzig: Duncker und Humblot 1926, p. 15. (*The Crisis of Parliamentary Democracy*, p. 10.)
[145]    Agamben, *State of Exception*, p. 5.
[146]    Walter Benjamin, *The Arcades Project*, Cambridge and London: Belknap Press of Harvard University Press 2002, p. 236.
[147]    See *SKS* 4 233–7 / *PF*, 26–30.

It is a fascinating journey to make in following Schmitt's use and appropriation of Kierkegaard and one that has been widely overlooked. Once upon a time, Schmitt wrote, "Everything lawful in this world destroys everything individual."[148] We can consider that Schmitt was a man who lived and wrote through two world wars and tried to define and analyze the realities of the political realm and who sought to bring Kierkegaard along, who he saw as a kind of kindred spirit, into his political writings and appropriate various elements of Kierkegaard through uncharted waters. What he forgot or abandoned along the way is that it is the human life that is the exception and not the state. This is where these two writers move fundamentally in different directions. Both writers found themselves very isolated in the latter part of their respective lives, and perhaps we can say that both took up the challenge of the either/or: Schmitt joining the Nazi Party and Kierkegaard going out on the street and selling his pamphlet *The Moment*, attacking both state and church and ultimately alienating himself from everyone in Copenhagen. History has been kinder to Kierkegaard for obvious reasons, but as we continue to live in unsettling times and as the future remains an unstable and uncertain phantom politically, socially and spiritually, we might take in Derrida's description of Schmitt as ominously relevant to our own time:

> ...this thought and this work repeatedly presaged the fearsome world that was announcing itself from as early as the 1920s. As though the fear of seeing that which comes to pass take place, in effect had honed the gaze of this besieged watchman. Following our hypothesis, the scene would be thus: lucidity and fear not only drove this terrified and insomniac watcher to anticipate the storms and seismic movements that would wreak havoc with the historical field, the political space, the borders of concepts and countries, the axiomatics of European law...etc. Such a "watcher" would thereby have been more attuned than so many others to the fragility and "deconstructible" precariousness of structures, borders and axioms that he wished to protect, restore and "conserve" at all costs.[149]

---

[148]     Schmitt, "Die Sichtbarkeit der Kirche: Eine scholastische Erwägung," *Summa: Eine Vierteljahresschrift*, 1917, p. 74. (*Roman Catholicism and Political Form*, p. 50.)

[149]     Derrida, *The Politics of Friendship*, p. 107.

# Bibliography

*I. References to or Uses of Kierkegaard in Schmitt's Corpus*

"Die Sichtbarkeit der Kirche: Eine scholastische Erwägung," *Summa: Eine Vierteljahresschrift*, no. 2, 1917, pp. 71–80; see p. 75. (English translation: "The Visibility of the Church: A Scholastic Consideration," in *Roman Catholicism and Political Form*, trans. and ed. by G.L. Ulmen, Westport, Connecticut: Greenwood Press 1996, pp. 45–60, see p. 52.)

*Politische Romantik*, Berlin: Duncker und Humblot 1919, p. 97. (English translation: *Political Romanticism*, trans. by Guy Oaks, Cambridge, Massachusetts: MIT Press 1991, p. 65; p. 166, note 10.)

*Politische Theologie. Vier Kapitel zur Lehre von der Souveränität*, Berlin: Duncker und Humblot 1922, p. 22; p. 27; p. 69; p. 71. (English translation: *Political Theology*, trans. by George Schwab, Chicago and London: University of Chicago Press 2005, p. 15; p. 18; p. 53; p. 55.)

*Der Leviathan in der Staatslehre des Thomas Hobbes*, Hamburg: Hanseatische Verlagsanstalt 1938, p. 99. (English translation: *The Leviathan in the State Theory of Thomas Hobbes: Meaning and Failure of a Political Symbol*, trans. by George Schwab and Erna Hilfstein, Westport, Connecticut: Greenwood Press 1996, p. 65.)

*Der Nomos der Erde im Völkerrecht des Jus Publikum Europaeum*, Berlin: Duncker und Humblot 1950, p. 267. (English translation: *The Nomos of the Earth in the International Law of the Jus Publicum Europaeum*, trans. by G.L. Ulmen, New York: Telos Publishing 2006, p. 292.)

*Tagebücher: Oktober 1912 bis Februar 1915*, ed. by Ernst Hüsmert, Berlin: Akademie Verlag 2003. pp. 216–19; p. 222; p. 385; p. 416.

*Die Militärzeit 1915 bis 1919*, ed. by Ernst Hüsmert and Gerd Geisler, Berlin: Akademie Verlag 2005, p. 66; p. 167; p. 475.


*II. Sources of Schmitt's Knowledge of Kierkegaard*

Dallago, Carl, *Ueber eine Schrift. Søren Kierkegaard und die Philosophie der Innerlichkeit (von Theodor Haecker)*, Innsbruck: Brenner 1914.

Haecker, Theodor, *Sören Kierkegaard und die Philosophie der Innerlichkeit*, Munich: Schreiber 1913.

Kierkegaard, Søren, *Entweder-Oder. Ein Lebens-Fragment*, trans. and ed. by Alexander Michelsen and Otto Gleiss, Leipzig: Lehmann 1885.

— *Stadien auf dem Lebenswege: Studien von Verschiedenen*, trans. by Albert Bärthold, Leipzig: Lehmann 1886.

— *Angriff auf die Christenheit*, ed. by August Dorner and Christoph Schempf, Stuttgart: Frommann 1896.

— *Zur Psychologie der Sünde, der Bekehrung und des Glaubens. Zwei Schriften Søren Kierkegaards* (includes *The Concept of Anxiey* and *Philosophical Fragments*), trans., ed., and introduced by Christoph Schrempf, Leipzig: F. Richter 1890.

— *Gesammelte Werke*, vols. 1–12, trans. and ed. by Hermann Gottsched and Christoph Schrempf, Jena: Diederichs 1909–22.

— *Stadien auf dem Lebensweg*, vol. 4 (1914) in his *Gesammelte Werke*, vols. 1–12, trans. and ed. by Hermann Gottsched and Christoph Schrempf, Jena: Diederichs 1909–22.

— "Der Pfahl im Fleisch," *Der Brenner*, no. 16, 1914, pp. 691–712 and no. 17, 1914, pp. 797–814 (also as *Der Pfahl im Fleisch*, trans. and ed. by Theodor Haecker, Innsbruck: Brenner 1914).

— *Der Begriff des Auserwählten*, trans. by Theodor Haecker, Hellerau: Hegner 1917.

— *Der Einzelne und die Kirche: über Luther und den Protestantismus*, trans. and ed. by Wilhelm Kütemeyer, Berlin: Wolff 1934.

*III. Secondary Literature on Schmitt's Relation to Kierkegaard*

Dotti, Jorge, "Menage a trois sobre la decision excepcional: Kierkegaard, Constant and Schmitt," *Deus Mortalis. Cuaderno de Filosofia Politica*, no. 4, 2005, pp. 303–79.

Kahn, Victoria; "Hamlet or Hecuba: Carl Schmitt's Decision," *Representations*, vol. 83, 2003, pp. 67–96.

Kennedy, Ellen, *Constitutional Failure. Carl Schmitt in Weimar*, Durham: Duke University Press 2004, pp. 47–8; p. 52; p. 79; p. 185; p. 205, note 49.

Oakes, Guy, "Introduction to the English Translation of Carl Schmitt's *Political Romanticism*, Cambridge, Massachusetts: MIT Press 1991, pp. xiv–xxxvi.

Ryan, Bartholomew, *Kierkegaard's Indirect Politics. A Dialogue with Lukács, Schmitt, Benjamin and Adorno*, Ph.D. Thesis, University of Aarhus, Århus 2006.

Zangerle, Ignaz, "Zur Situation der Kirche," *Der Brenner*, no. 14, 1933–34, pp. 52ff.

# Eric Voegelin:

# Politics, History, and the Anxiety of Existence

Peter Brickey LeQuire

## I. Introduction

Eric Voegelin was born Erich Hermann Wilhelm Vögelin in Cologne, Germany, in 1901, and died in California in 1985. He studied, and subsequently taught, in the Faculty of Law at the University of Vienna. His early writings ran him afoul of the Nazis, and he was forced to flee Austria following the *Anschluss* in 1938. He emigrated to the United States, becoming an American citizen in 1944, and teaching from 1942 to 1958 in the Department of Political Science at Louisiana State University. In 1958 he returned to Germany, where he filled the chair at the University of Munich that had been vacant since the death of Max Weber (1864–1920), its previous occupant. In 1969 he accepted a position at Stanford University's Hoover Institution, where he remained for the rest of his career.

Voegelin' voluminous writings range widely in scope, style, and subject matter.[1] However, while he revised his aims and methodology several times over the course of his life, all of his mature thought was a response to the political situation of his times. His early writings include a study of American intellectual culture, treatises on the modern understandings of race and state, and works in the field of legal theory. Ultimately his attempt to comprehend and address the intellectual and political climate of the modern West led him far from the conventions of modern academe. In 1938 Voegelin wrote a controversial tract in which he argued that modern totalitarian movements result from the illegitimate deification of the political sphere following the abandonment of transcendent religion; Nazism and Communism are "political religions," and can only be properly comprehended and opposed when understood as such.[2] This work set the tone for his subsequent writings.

---

[1]    Voegelin's major writings, including his works written in English, as well as translations of his German writings and a substantial portion of his personal correspondence, are available as *The Collected Works of Eric Voegelin*, vols. 1–34, ed. by Ellis Sandoz, Columbia, Missouri: University of Missouri Press 1989–2009. For comprehensive bibliographies of works by and about Voegelin, see Geoffrey L. Price, *Eric Voegelin: International Bibliography 1921–2000*, Munich: Fink 2000, and Peter J. Opitz, *Voegeliniana: Veröffentlichungen von und zu Eric Voegelin 2000–2005*, *Occasional Papers*, no. 46, Munich: Eric-Voegelin-Archiv 2005.

[2]    Eric Voegelin, *Die politischen Religionen*, Vienna: Bermann-Fischer 1938, reprinted with a new foreword as *Die politischen Religionen*, 2nd ed., Stockholm: Bermann-Fischer 1939, and translated in *Collected Works*, vol. 5.

In the 1940s Voegelin undertook to write a comprehensive *History of Political Ideas*,[3] which reached several thousand manuscript pages, but was not published in his lifetime. In it, he sought to chronicle the development of Western political thought from antiquity through the Middle Ages, and then its decline toward revolutionary modernity. In 1951 he delivered the Walgreen Lectures at the University of Chicago, published as *The New Science of Politics*.[4] This work marked a new development in his thinking, as it announced a turn in his methodology from legal theory and the history of ideas; since human existence in society is historical, Voegelin argued, political theory must become a theory, or *philosophy of history*.[5]

The thesis of this work, which Voegelin maintained for the rest of his life, is that modern thought and politics have been warped by an intellectual disease he called *gnosticism*: "The more we know about the gnosis of antiquity, the more it becomes certain that modern movements of thought, such as progressivism, Hegelianism, and Marxism, are variants of Gnosticism…today…[gnostic] intellectual movements dominate the public scene in America no less than in Europe."[6] Voegelin characterized gnosticism, in its modern form, as the denial of the world-transcendent God, the depiction of the world, in its present form, as evil and in need of salvation, and the attempt to accomplish that salvation through human means. Modern gnosis is expressed in the construction of ideological and philosophical systems closed to divine transcendence and, ultimately, in the attempt to realize an earthly salvation, either passively through the expectation of inevitable political and technological progress, or actively through violent service to apotheosized political institutions or movements, as in the cases of Nazi Germany and the Communist Revolutions.

From the 1950s onward, Voegelin sought to deepen his diagnosis of the modern intellectual and political "disorder" resulting from gnosticism, and to offer a therapy for it, by turning to the historical sources of "order" he found chiefly, although not exclusively, in Greek philosophy and Hebrew and Christian revelation. (Voegelin was raised as a Lutheran, and his writings are occasionally mistaken for those of a Roman Catholic, but as an adult he was critical of religious dogma; he understood himself to be continuing the tradition of political philosophy inaugurated by Plato and Aristotle.) He further elaborated the philosophy of history he began in *The New Science of Politics* in the five-volume *Order and History*.[7] In addition, as his thought

---

[3]      Now published in Voegelin, *Collected Works*, vols. 19–26. Part of the material appeared earlier as *From Enlightenment to Revolution*, ed. by John H. Hallowell, Durham: Duke University Press 1975.

[4]      Eric Voegelin, *The New Science of Politics: An Introduction*, Chicago: University of Chicago Press 1952 (reprinted in *Collected Works*, vol. 5).

[5]      Voegelin, *The New Science of Politics*, p. 1 (*Collected Works*, vol. 5, p. 88).

[6]      See Voegelin's Preface to the American edition of *Science, Politics, and Gnosticism: Two Essays*, Chicago: Henry Regnery Company 1968, pp. v–vi. See also Eric Voegelin, *Wissenschaft, Politik, und Gnosis*, Munich: Kösel-Verlag 1959, pp. 9–19.

[7]      Eric Voegelin, *Order and History*, vols. 1–5, Baton Rouge, Louisiana: Louisiana State University Press 1956–87. The individual volumes are: *Israel and Revelation* (1956), *The World of the Polis* (1957), *Plato and Aristotle* (1957), *The Ecumenic Age* (1974), and the posthumous *In Search of Order* (1987). The work is republished as *Collected Works*, vols. 14–18.

developed, he articulated a phenomenological *philosophy of consciousness*, chiefly in a work entitled *Anamnesis*,[8] and in the final volume of *Order and History*.

Like many German-speaking intellectuals of his generation, Voegelin was well acquainted with Søren Kierkegaard's writings in translation. Voegelin studied with Karl Jaspers (1883–1969) in Heidelberg in 1929;[9] although Voegelin was probably aware of Kierkegaard beforehand,[10] it was Jaspers who first prompted him to study his works extensively.[11] At several points in his life, Voegelin acknowledged a general intellectual debt to Kierkegaard. In the essay "Remembrance of Things Past," speaking of his intellectual formation in the 1920s, Voegelin wrote: "My own horizon was strongly formed, and informed, by…Jaspers' existentialism and, through Jaspers, by Kierkegaard."[12] And of an encounter in 1983, a student reported: "I sat myself across the table from [Voegelin] and asked him if there was a Kierkegaardian influence in his work. He got a big smile on his face…and said, 'Oh yes, oh yes.' "[13] From Voegelin's autobiographical comments the reader can assume a high level of familiarity,[14] and in

---

[8]     Eric Voegelin, *Anamnesis. Zur Theorie der Geschichte und Politik*, Munich: Piper 1966. (Abbreviated English translation: *Anamnesis*, trans. and ed. by Gerhart Niemeyer, Notre Dame, Indiana: University of Notre Dame Press 1978 (complete translation appears as *Collected Works*, vol. 6).)

[9]     Eugene Webb, *Philosophers of Consciousness: Polanyi, Lonergan, Voegelin, Ricoeur, Girard, Kierkegaard*, Seattle, Washington: University of Washington Press 1988, p. 97.

[10]     Kierkegaard's influence in early twentieth-century German-language thought, in which Voegelin was steeped, was extensive, as documented in Habib C. Malik, *Receiving Søren Kierkegaard: The Early Impact and Transmission of his Thought*, Washington: Catholic University of America Press 1997, pp. 339–96, and Heiko Schulz, "Germany and Austria: A Modest Head Start: The German Reception of Kierkegaard," in *Kierkegaard's International Reception*, Tome I, *Northern and Western Europe*, ed. by Jon Stewart, Aldershot: Ashgate 2009 (*Kierkegaard Research: Sources, Reception and Resources*, vol. 8), pp. 307–87. See Eugene Webb, *Eric Voegelin: Philosopher of History*, Seattle, Washington, D.C.: University of Washington Press 1981, p. 80: "Both [Voegelin and Wittgenstein] moved in circles where Schopenhauer, Nietzsche, and Kierkegaard were considered to represent philosophy at its most significant, and both read them with great interest. Both also read Karl Kraus and Robert Musil."

[11]     See Eugene Webb, *Eric Voegelin: Philosopher of History*, Seattle, Washington (in *Collected Works*, vol. 30, p. 822): University of Washington Press 1981, p. 20: "In Heidelberg I studied with Gundolf, Alfred Weber, and Jaspers. Via Jaspers: a thorough reading of Kierkegaard."

[12]     The essay was published as the first chapter in the English edition of *Anamnesis*, p. 5 (*Collected Works*, vol. 12, pp. 304–14).

[13]     Glenn Hughes, quoted in *Voegelin Recollected: Conversations on a Life*, ed. by Barry Cooper and Jodi Bruhn, Columbia, Missouri: University of Missouri Press 2008, p. 31.

[14]     Voegelin read Kierkegaard in German and later in English translation. His personal library, now housed at the University of Erlangen, includes the following primary works: *Gesammelte Werke*, vols. 1–12, trans. by Christoph Schempf, Jena: Eugen Diederichs Verlag 1909–22. Voegelin possessed vol. 1 (*Entweder/Oder: Ein Lebensfragment*); vol. 3 (*Furcht und Zittern / Die Wiederholung*); vol. 4 (*Stadien auf dem Lebensweg*); vol. 5 (*Der Begriff der Angst*); vol. 6 (*Philosophische Brocken / Abschließende unwissenschaftliche Nachschrift*, vol. 1); vol. 7 (*Abschließende unwissenschaftliche Nachschrift*, vol. 2); vol. 10 (*Der Gesichtspunkt für meine Wirksamkeit als Schriftsteller / Zwei Kleine ethisch-religiöse Abhandlungen / Über*

Voegelin's brief explicit discussions of Kierkegaard one can tell that Voegelin's reading of Kierkegaard was an important part of his lifelong intellectual development.[15]

Voegelin writes in 1945 that the important figures of late modern history are Hegel, Schelling, Kierkegaard, Bakunin, Marx, and Nietzsche, not only from the standpoint of the history of ideas, but also of history in general.[16] And Voegelin's *corpus* contains extensive commentary on all these thinkers—except Kierkegaard. However, as one scholar aptly notes, "In view of the clear affinity between them, it is perhaps curious that Voegelin has so little to say about Kierkegaard....But then Voegelin tends only to focus on those modern thinkers he most disagrees with."[17]

Not only does Voegelin accord Kierkegaard historical significance, but many elements of Voegelin's thought bear the stamp of Kierkegaard's influence; or, perhaps more accurately, Voegelin's works show that his reading and appropriation of Kierkegaard's thought essentially shaped his understanding of the character of human existence. However, Voegelin's appropriation of Kierkegaard was not that of a disciple, but rather that of an original and critical thinker. Despite his respect for Jaspers and Kierkegaard, he states: "I certainly did not...particularly care to become...an existentialist, Christian or otherwise."[18] Kierkegaard's thought is thus one of the resources Voegelin brings to bear on the intellectual and political crises of the twentieth century, in a philosophy of politics, history, and consciousness that is all his own.

Several scholars have noted the strong parallels between the two authors and are cited in the bibliography below; the present study will primarily address the places in Voegelin's *oeuvre* where Kierkegaard is explicitly cited, or can otherwise be

---

*meine Wirksamkeit als Schriftsteller*); and vol. 12 (*Der Augenblick*). He also possessed from Kierkegaard: *Über den Begriff der Ironie, mit ständiger Rücksicht auf Sokrates*, trans. by Hans Heinrich Schaeder, Munich: Oldenbourg 1929; *Fear and Trembling / The Sickness unto Death*, trans. by Walter Lowrie, Garden City, New York: Doubleday 1954; *Fear and Trembling / The Sickness unto Death*, trans. by Walter Lowrie, Princeton, New Jersey: Princeton University Press 1968. It is possible that Voegelin also read Theodor Haecker's translations of Kierkegaard published in *Der Brenner*.

[15]     Some of Voegelin's correspondence during the years he first studied Kierkegaard is being published as *Selected Correspondence 1924–1949*, ed. by Jürgen Gebhardt, Columbia, Missouri: University of Missouri Press 2009 (*Collected Works*, vol. 29); I was unable to consult this volume prior to the completion of the present article.

[16]     Letter to Alfred Schütz on September 17, 1945, see Alfred Schütz and Eric Voegelin, *Eine Freundschaft, die ein Leben ausgehalten hat: Briefwechsel 1938–1959*, ed. by Gerhard Wagner and Gilbert Weiss, Konstanz: UVK Verlaggesellschaft 2004, p. 265. Discussing his plans for his treatment of modernity in *The History of Political Ideas*, Voegelin writes: "*es scheint mir für eine Allgemeingeschichte gerade wichtig zu sein, auch organisatorisch zu zeigen, dass die Probleme die massenrelevant sind, darum keineswegs sachlich die Relevanz haben, die ein eigenes Kapitel an ausgezeichneter Stelle rechtfertigen würde. Die wichtige Geschichte ist durch Hegel und Schelling, Kierkegaard, Bakunin, Marx und Nietzsche gegeben, nicht durch Darwinismus, ökonomischen Liberalismus and ähnliche Phänomene, welche die öffentliche Szene beherrschen.*"

[17]     Andrew Shanks, *Hegel's Political Theology*, Cambridge: Cambridge University Press 1991, p. 213, note 56.

[18]     See Voegelin, *Anamnesis*, p. 5 (in *Collected Works*, vol. 12, p. 306).

documented as a source. After a brief survey of Voegelin's evaluation of Kierkegaard's historical significance, it will show how Voegelin's reading of Kierkegaard played a role, first, in his departure from the methodological constraints of German legal theory, second, in his attempt to comprehend the dynamics of history, and, third, in his meditations on the mysterious structure of human consciousness.

## II. Voegelin's View of Kierkegaard's Historical Significance

As a commentator on intellectual history, as just mentioned above, Voegelin accorded Kierkegaard high status as a figure in the development of modern thought. Sometimes Voegelin refers to Kierkegaard without further comment: in 1933, in a discussion of Bruno Bauer (1809–82), he gives an undocumented footnote to Kierkegaard's concept of *Bodenlosigkeit*;[19] in 1944, he mentions Kierkegaard in passing as a landmark figure in the history of religion: "the religious radicalization since Kierkegaard has transvalued the values of middle-class liberal Christianity."[20] In a seemingly critical tone, he writes of "the craving for the inner return in Kierkegaard" as one of the "*disjecta membra* of [Schelling's] experiences" that had been "held together by the strength of [Schelling's] soul."[21]

But elsewhere his occasional remarks reveal an appreciation for Kierkegaard's intellectual achievements. In a discussion of the intellectual climate of the nineteenth century, Voegelin writes: "Underneath the surface trend toward spiritual disorder, we must observe therefore the stimulation by Schelling's work that can be felt in Schopenhauer and Kierkegaard...."[22] In a critique of Friedrich Nietzsche (1844–1900), Voegelin writes: "For the highest form of martyrdom and its abysses one should compare Søren Kierkegaard, "Does a Human Being Have the Right to Be Put to Death for the Truth?"[23] In a letter of 1953, Voegelin writes: "This process of detachment [from the institutionalized spirit of the French Revolution] has progressed in varying degrees in the various national territories of Western civilization....Kierkegaard's existential revolt...belongs in this sphere,"[24] going on to list Blaise Pascal (1623–62) and Kierkegaard as European existentialists who made the "attempt to return from the disruption [of agnostic existence] to the faith of tradition, to restore it to greater purity,"[25] adding that "the nihilism of unbelief in which the existentialists of our time see the downfall of Christianity...is exactly the spiritual situation from which faith emanates—under the condition that simply-

---

[19]     Eric Voegelin, *Rasse und Staat*, Tübingen: J.C.B. Mohr 1933, p. 197, note 2 (in *Collected Works*, vol. 2, p. 196, note 30).
[20]     Eric Voegelin, "Nietzsche, the Crisis, and the War," *The Journal of Politics*, vol. 6, no. 2, 1944, p. 184 (in *Collected Works*, vol. 10, p. 132).
[21]     See Voegelin, *Collected Works*, vol. 25, p. 241.
[22]     Voegelin, *Collected Works*, vol. 25, pp. 99–100.
[23]     Voegelin, *Collected Works*, vol. 25, p. 274, note 58, referring to *SKS* 11, 59–93 / *WA* 51–89.
[24]     Voegelin, *Collected Works*, vol. 30, p. 143.
[25]     Ibid.

human existence, as in Pascal, is understood in its radical nothingness."[26] In a letter of 1967, Voegelin approvingly cites Kierkegaard's analysis of the phenomenon of despair as shedding light on the character of the unreflective bourgeois "good citizen."[27] Thus throughout his writings Voegelin maintains that Kierkegaard is a thinker of importance; indeed, he often treats him as one of the redeeming figures of nineteenth-century thought.


### III. Kierkegaard and Legal Theory

There is ample textual evidence, moreover, that certain themes first—or most profoundly—articulated by Kierkegaard prove to be central to Voegelin's thought from 1929 and onward. In a manuscript from the early 1930s, a *Rechtslehre*, or "Theory of Law,"[28] intended as part of a projected comprehensive *Staatslehre*, Voegelin approvingly quotes Friedrich Jacobi (1743–1819) against Immanuel Kant (1724–1804): "The unity of the necessity of nature with freedom in one and the same creature is simply an incomprehensible fact, a *miracle* and a *mystery* equal to creation."[29] The field of legal theory, Voegelin suggests, should be oriented by an understanding of "the mystery of life, whose abyss Kierkegaard first fully probed."[30] This text contains Voegelin's most extensive treatment of Kierkegaard. It is part of an attempt to transcend the legal positivism of the day, perhaps most famously espoused by Hans Kelsen (1881–1973), the framer of the Austrian constitution of 1920, and one of Voegelin's dissertation supervisors at Vienna. Voegelin argues that legal and political science can legitimately speak not only of the positive laws enacted by concrete societies, the logic according to which they operate, and the hypothetical norms they presuppose, as in Kelsen's thought, but also of natural law.[31]

---

[26]    Voegelin, *Collected Works*, vol. 30, p. 148.

[27]    Voegelin, *Collected Works*, vol. 30, p. 546, referring to *SKS* 11, 134–5 / *SUD*, 19.

[28]    First published in Voegelin, *Collected Works*, vol. 32, pp. 373–413 under the title "Theory of Law"; this fragmentary text has recently been issued in the original German as Erich Voegelin, *Rechtslehre, Occasional Papers*, no. 62, ed. by Peter J. Opitz, Munich: Eric-Voegelin-Archiv 2008. It was meant to be part of a comprehensive *Staatslehre*, the only other extant portion of which is published as "The Theory of Governance," *Collected Works*, vol. 32, pp. 224–372, Erich Voegelin, "Grundlagen der *Herrschaftslehre*. Ein Kapitel der Systems der Staatslehre," ed. by Peter J. Opitz, *Occasional Papers*, no. 55, Munich: Eric-Voegelin Archiv 2007, and Erich Voegelin, *Herrschaftslehre*, ed. by Peter J. Opitz, *Occasional Papers*, no. 56, Munich: Eric-Voegelin-Archiv 2007.

[29]    Friedrich H. Jacobi, *Ueber die Unzertrennlichkeit des Begriffes der Freyheit und Vorsehung von dem Begriffe der Vernunft*, in Jacobi, *Werke*, vols. 1–6, ed. by J.F. Köppen and C.J.F. Roth, Leipzig: Gerhard Fleischer 1812–25, vol. 2, p. 317. Quoted in Voegelin, *Rechtslehre*, p. 29 (in *Collected Works*, vol. 32, p. 395).

[30]    Voegelin, *Rechtslehre*, p. 29 (in *Collected Works*, vol. 32, p. 395).

[31]    Voegelin, *Rechtslehre*, p. 20 (in *Collected Works*, vol. 32, p. 386): "The common ground of essential content makes it possible to refer positive law to natural [law], to orient historical legislation to the essential core....Through the real relationship between natural law and positive law, based on their essential commonality, its system...provides us with a guiding principle for an ontology of law. Natural law itself is such an ontology."

Leaving aside the natural law and natural right traditions of antiquity and the Middle Ages (which he considers at length in later works), Voegelin turns to two disparate strands within modern natural law theory, represented by the English empiricist Thomas Hobbes (1588–1679), on the one hand, and the German idealists Kant and Friedrich Schelling on the other. Voegelin uses these sources to show how a theory of law can be based on a philosophical and anthropological understanding of the character of human existence. Through a reading of Hobbes and Schelling, he suggests that (from the standpoint of politics, at least) the most significant elements of human existence are *fear* and *freedom*. Then, in what follows, he argues that Kierkegaard and Martin Heidegger (1889–1976) have given the best accounts of these experiences. Voegelin does not go on to specify exactly how Kierkegaard's or Heidegger's thought might influence the study of law, or lead to a new natural law theory. But the fact that he approvingly cites Kierkegaard in this context shows that he regards Kierkegaard's anthropological insights as immediately relevant for the study of both empirical and normative questions within political theory.

Thomas Hobbes constructs his theory of natural law based on the anthropological premise that the strongest and most universal human motivation is fear, most importantly, fear of violent death. Voegelin writes: "Hobbes's stratification of the problem of law is distinguished by a relatively subtle differentiation that accompanies the state of human existence specified as *fear* and the *capacity for action*."[32] Freedom, for Hobbes, is the "absence of externall Impediments," which Voegelin glosses as "the power sphere that is left over after all manner of limitations [to the human capacity for action] [have been accounted for]."[33] In the state of nature—that is, in the absence of civil government—individuals are free to protect themselves by absolutely any means within their power. However, the natural right to self-protection by itself is not enough to ensure personal safety. When all people are free to protect themselves as they see fit, there ensues what Hobbes terms a war "of every man, against every man."[34] Since this is a perilous condition for all, reason dictates two primary natural laws: first, that humans ought to seek peace, and second, that, when possible, they should give up their unqualified right to self-protection when others are also willing to do so. Other laws of nature follow the first two: the performance of covenants people make with each other, in particular. Yet since "legally binding covenants between men are possible only if they are purged of fear," "the introduction of a public power that coercively enforces claims"[35] becomes necessary. But what makes these laws natural is the fact that humans know them to conduce to peace, which they seek out of fear, which in turn arises out of the

---

[32]     Voegelin, *Rechtslehre*, p. 25 (in *Collected Works*, vol. 32, p. 392), emphasis added.

[33]     Voegelin, *Rechtslehre*, p. 26 (in *Collected Works*, vol. 32, p. 392). The first bracketed interpolation is mine, and the second, the translator's. Voegelin refers to Thomas Hobbes, *Leviathan, or, The Matter, Forme, & Power of a Common-Wealth Ecclesiastical and Civil*, ed. by A.R. Waller, Cambridge: Cambridge University Press 1904, p. 86.

[34]     Thomas Hobbes, *Leviathan, or, The Matter, Forme, & Power of a Common-Wealth Ecclesiastical and Civil*, London: Andrew Crook 1651, p. 62.

[35]     Voegelin, *Rechtslehre*, p. 26 (in *Collected Works*, vol. 32, p. 393).

human being's capacity for action when left unchecked. Restraints on freedom are necessary if life and some measure of freedom are to be preserved.

In certain respects, Hobbes' approach to natural law is akin to that of the German idealist tradition of natural law.[36] However, Kant and Schelling, by contrast, derive natural law from the fact of human freedom rather than from the phenomenon of fear. Voegelin writes:

> The profound difference between the two types of system lies in the ultimate grounds for the theory of right action. The basis of Hobbes's thought is the idea of the equality of men due to their nature, due to their perishable corporeality; the systems of German idealism see the essence of man in a spirit in which all men participate equally.[37]

This second approach to natural law "directly bases the theory of law on the metaphysics of freedom."[38]

On Voegelin's account, the Kantian project, in which obligations are deduced from the human being's status as a free, self-determining moral agent, is limited because of its focus on spirit exclusively: "Kant had no feeling for the ominous presence of the human being's demonic aspect, for that which is intimately and genuinely essential to sensuality…. The body as a living thing appeared to him to be so unreal that the fact of death did not appreciably affect his speculation."[39] Schelling, following Kant, formulates the imperative: "*Be!*" in the most sublime sense of the term; cease *thou* to be a phenomenon; strive to become a "being-in-itself!"[40] However, Schelling also goes on to recognize that "the reciprocal relationship between fear and freedom becomes manifest in what he calls the *unity of life*."[41] In Schelling as well as Hobbes, "we find the same conflict between empirical human beings that necessitates restrictions being placed on the scope of freedom in order to save its form."[42] Humans are, as rational beings, capable of self-determination, but, as corporeal and passionate beings, not infinitely so. Voegelin's implication is that a satisfactory theory of natural law will take freedom as well as fear into account, recognizing that both phenomena are fundamental elements of human life.

Voegelin turns to these two sources of the modern natural law tradition to combat the legal positivism of his day, not in order to defend the particulars of either approach, but to show how a modern theory of law might proceed: beginning with a "philosophical anthropology." Hobbes and Schelling are examples of political

---

[36]     Voegelin, *Rechtslehre*, p. 27 (in *Collected Works*, vol. 32, p. 393): "Hobbes's theory, which has its point of departure in the life experience [*Erlebnis*] of the human being who is at the mercy of his perishable body, leads to the description of action and the problems associated with it. In this regard, his theory hardly differs from the second type of system…. For both systems the maxim of coexistence is the leading idea of the legal order…."

[37]     Voegelin, *Rechtslehre*, p. 27 (in *Collected Works*, vol. 32, p. 393).

[38]     ibid.

[39]     Voegelin, *Rechtslehre*, pp. 28–9 (in *Collected Works*, vol. 32, p. 395).

[40]     Schelling, *Neue Deduktion des Naturrechts* (1795), in *Werke*, ed. by Manfred Schroeter, Munich: Oldenburg 1927–54, vols. 1–12, vol. 1 (1927), §3.

[41]     Voegelin, *Rechtslehre*, p. 34 (in *Collected Works*, vol. 32, p. 400), emphasis added.

[42]     Voegelin, *Rechtslehre*, p. 34 (in *Collected Works*, vol. 32, p. 400).

thinkers who sought to base legal theory on a deep understanding of human nature, identifying the experiences of fear and of freedom and the relationship between then as fundamental to human life. However, "life" in this sense is a problematic term. Heidegger and Kierkegaard represent an advance over Kant and Hobbes, as well as Schelling, in formulating the concepts of existence (*Existenz*) and Dasein—in so doing, they "understand the human being in its unmediated unity."[43]

Voegelin first introduces Kierkegaard as a thinker with a more robust understanding of freedom:

> Let us now depart in another direction, into the realm of spirit, which Kierkegaard has described as the site of the synthesis of body and soul….In a methodically identical [to Schelling's] turn away from [inadequacies of] rational reflection and choice, Kierkegaard identifies the spiritual essence of freedom in the origin of potentiality itself.[44]

Freedom is not, as in the case of Hobbes, the mere absence of external impediment, nor, as in Kant, a faculty of rational self-determination in one's actions. Voegelin quotes: "Freedom's possibility [*Die Möglichkeit der Freiheit*] is not the ability to choose between good and evil. Such thoughtlessness is no more in the interest of Scriptures than in the interest of thought. This possibility is to *be able* [*Die Möglichkeit besteht darin, dass man* kann]."[45] "If," Voegelin writes, "freedom is rationally pictured as an abstract ego's capacity to stand above all possible goals of its action, so is it in this moment of deliberation 'not freedom, but meaningless reflection.'"[46] He quotes from *The Concept of Anxiety*:

> To assert that freedom begins with the *liberum arbitrium* [free will], that it can choose good or evil equally…makes every explanation of it impossible. To speak of good and evil as the objects of freedom makes both the freedom and the concepts of good and evil into something finite. As a matter of fact, freedom is infinite and arises out of nothingness.[47]

---

[43]　　Voegelin, *Rechtslehre*, p. 41 (in *Collected Works*, vol. 32, p. 408).

[44]　　Voegelin, *Rechtslehre*, p. 38 (in *Collected Works*, vol. 32, p. 404). The first bracketed interpolation is mine; the second is the translator's. Voegelin's reference is to *The Concept of Anxiety*, a text Martin Heidegger famously praises in *Being and Time*. In the pages immediately following in his fragmentary *Rechtslehre*, Voegelin calls Heidegger's work "[t]he most precise analysis of the phenomenon of fear, which builds upon Kierkegaard's thought" (Voegelin, *Rechtslehre*, p. 40 (*Collected Works*, vol. 32, p. 406)) but—perhaps tellingly, perhaps not— does not echo Heidegger's criticisms of Kierkegaard. Later in his career Voegelin was highly critical of Heidegger.

[45]　　Kierkegaard, *Der Begriff der Angst*, p. 44 (which corresponds to *SKS* 4, 354 / *CA*, 49). Quoted in Voegelin, *Rechtslehre*, p. 38 (in *Collected Works*, vol. 32, p. 404).

[46]　　Voegelin, *Rechtslehre*, p. 39 (in *Collected Works*, vol. 32, p. 406), quoting Kierkegaard, *Der Begriff der Angst*, p. 111 (which corresponds to *SKS* 4, 414 / *CA*, p. 112).

[47]　　Kierkegaard, *Der Begriff der Angst*, p. 111 (which corresponds to *SKS* 4, 414 / *CA*, p. 112). Quoted in Voegelin, *Rechtslehre*, pp. 39–40 (in *Collected Works*, vol. 32, p. 406).

By introducing nothingness as the basis of freedom, Voegelin suggests that an understanding of freedom must be based in an understanding of human finitude and all that it entails.

Accordingly, to understand freedom we must understand fear, and vice versa:[48] "Suspended between fear and reality lies potentiality, which is neither free possibility nor fixed reality. 'Anxiety is neither a category of freedom nor necessity; it is fettered freedom where freedom is not free in itself but tied up, not with necessity, but with itself.' "[49] As Voegelin writes later, in *The History of Political Ideas*:

> The man of Hobbes has no *summum bonum* serving as a point of orientation in his life, but he has a *summum malum*: death. Hobbes does not yet penetrate to the deepest layers of existential sentiments; we are still far from Kierkegaard's analysis of anxiety. The experience of death has not yet become the accompaniment of life in such intimacy that the sentiment of death and the sentiment of life would be inseparable and that self-conceit and the building of the shelter of pride would be itself an anxiety. Hobbes has no notion yet of indefinite objectless anxiety, but only of the definite fear of death....[50]

In large part, thus, it is Kierkegaard's analysis of the phenomenon of fear, or anxiety, that merits his rank, in Voegelin's eyes, as one of the foremost thinkers of modernity.

In the *Rechtslehre* he continues, again quoting liberally from *The Concept of Anxiety*:

> Fear may be compared to dizziness. He who gazes into the gaping abyss becomes dizzy, and the source of dizziness is equally the abyss and the one contemplating it. "Thus fear is the dizziness of freedom. It comes about when freedom...looks down into its own possibility and gropes for something finite to hold on to. In the grip of this dizziness freedom collapses in dizziness. Psychology cannot illuminate the matter any further, nor does it have the intention to." In this experience freedom's goal has not yet been determined. The ego that can act is suspended in potentiality, but due to its finiteness and place in the world [it] may, at any moment, have to enter into a decisive reality; anxiety

---

[48]    For the most part, in this text, Voegelin uses *Furcht* and *Angst* interchangeably, although with the implication that the understanding of fear as anxiety in Kierkegaard's and Heidegger's sense represents a deeper understanding of the phenomenon.

[49]    Voegelin, *Rechtslehre*, p. 38 (in *Collected Works*, vol. 32, p. 405). The quotation is from Kierkegaard, *Der Begriff der Angst*, p. 44 (which corresponds to *SKS* 4, 354 / *CA*, 49).

[50]    See Voegelin, *Collected Works*, vol. 25, p. 65. Cf. *SKS* 5, 156 / *CUP1*, 168: "...the idea [of death] must change a person's whole life if he, in order to think its uncertainty, must think it every moment in order to prepare for it...for the subject it is an act to think his death...if the task is to become subjective, then for the individual subject to think death...is an act, because the development of subjectivity consists precisely in this, that he, acting, works through himself in his thinking about his own existence...." In Voegelin's subsequent thought, the experience of death is existentially and morally formative: "Death is the liberating force.... Thanatos...orders the soul of the living, for it makes them desirous of stripping themselves of everything that is not noble and just." See Voegelin, *Order and History*, vol. 3, p. 12 (*Collected Works*, vol. 16, pp. 66–7).

is not fear of a specific threat, but fear of nothingness. "Fear and nothingness always correspond to one another."[51]

This understanding of fear represents a marked advance over the conception of Hobbes, for fear, in fact, is a much more primordial phenomenon, not directed at any object in particular, but arising from the human being's status as a spirit, a "synthesis of body and soul."[52]

Our freedom is, precisely, "to *be able*" in the manner of finite, self-relating beings, but this freedom is only discovered through the experience of anxiety, and, consists, precisely, in anxiousness, as the authentic way of being a finite, existent, being. Quoting Heidegger, Voegelin writes:

> Thus, the analysis of anxiety again brings us to the phenomenon of freedom. For "anxiety makes manifest in Dasein [existence, being, being-there] its *Being-toward* its ownmost potentiality-for-Being—that is, its *Being-free for* the freedom of choosing itself and taking hold of itself. Anxiety brings Dasein face to face with its *being free for* (*propensio in*)...the authenticity of its Being, and for this authenticity as a possibility which it always is. But at the same time, this is the Being to which Dasein as Being-in-the-world has been delivered over."[53]

Humans are not merely biological entities who fear concrete things in the world, nor are they essentially and merely free moral agents undetermined by the natural universe. Humans are both free and finite, and are best described as unitary beings who are both natural and spiritual, finding their freedom in the anxious and earnest comportment toward that fact.

Heidegger and Kierkegaard, obviously, are not natural law theorists, and unfortunately, Voegelin does not follow with a theory of natural law based on the philosophical anthropology of these thinkers. The manuscript of the *Rechtslehre* breaks off a few pages later and was never completed. Yet the implication of his treatment of Kierkegaard and Heidegger is that, perhaps, the basis for a renewed understanding of natural law might be found in an understanding of the human being not merely as naturally limited and hence fearful, as in Hobbes, nor in a metaphysics of freedom that abstracts from the human being's natural existence, but rather in a robust notion of human existence as a complex synthesis of body and soul.

[51]    Voegelin, *Rechtslehre*, pp. 38–9 (in *Collected Works*, vol. 32, p. 405), quoting Kierkegaard, *Der Begriff der Angst*, p. 57; p. 93 (which corresponds to *SKS* 4, 365–66 / *CA*, 61 and *SKS* 4, 399 / *CA*, 96).
[52]    Voegelin, *Rechtslehre*, p. 38 (in *Collected Works*, vol. 32, p. 404). Cf. *SKS* 11, 129 / *SUD*, 13 and *SKS* 4, 349 / *CA*, 43.
[53]    Voegelin, *Rechtslehre*, p. 42 (in *Collected Works*, vol. 32, p. 409), quoting Martin Heidegger, *Sein und Zeit*, Halle: Niemeyer 1927, p. 188. (English translation: *Being and Time*, trans. by John Macquarrie and Edward Robinson, San Francisco: Harpers 1962, pp. 232–3.)

## IV. Kierkegaard and the Order of History

Voegelin abandoned his *Rechtslehre* and its methodology. However, in his subsequent writings, he does go on to attempt a comprehensive theory of human existence in political society, meant to serve as an ordering force in political life, and one can see in it the fact that Voegelin absorbed Kierkegaard's understanding of the human self, and relied on his analysis of the problem and structure of existence as he followed his own intellectual course.

Two aspects of Kierkegaard's phenomenology of existence play a special role in Voegelin's philosophy of history. First, Voegelin never abandons the Kierkegaardian position that anxiety in the sense of concern about the fact of existence is fundamental to human nature. Second, he follows Kierkegaard in positing that different human beings exhibit greater and lesser degrees of existence—there are higher and lower forms of human consciousness—and that a well-ordered life involves attuning oneself to the fact of our existence and all that it entails; the anxiety of existence, if confronted, can be educative, not pathological. Voegelin's originality as a thinker consists, in part, of the way in which he attempts to use this understanding of the nature of existence for the purposes of a political theory. The experience of anxiety, Voegelin argues, can lead to a reordering of the human soul in openness to divine transcendence which, in turn, leads to a better understanding of the nature and purpose of political life.

Voegelin's masterwork, unfinished at the time of his death, is *Order and History*. Its first three volumes were published in 1956 and 1957, a fourth volume appeared in 1974, and a fifth was published posthumously. It began as an attempt to combat the putatively gnostic political ideologies that dominated popular and academic political thinking, Communism, most obviously, but also the liberal progressivism of the Western democracies—Voegelin saw the two as "brothers under the skin."[54] It turns to the intellectual resources of ancient Greek philosophy and Hebrew and Christian revelation as sources of intellectual and social order, in an attempt to diagnose and treat the disorder of the modern age. Voegelin's approach is to chronicle the historical emergence of the sources of order, which he locates in the human experience of the divine, whether conceptualized "noetically" as in Greek philosophy, or "pneumatically" as in revealed religion. A synopsis of the work under the present circumstances would be impossible, not only because of the length and scope of the work, but because Voegelin substantially revised his own understanding of the nature of history itself between the publication of volumes 3 and 4.

However, following the intuitions of his *Rechtslehre*, Voegelin begins his study of political order and disorder with a phenomenology of human existence, based on the notion that human beings' political self-understandings are based on their understandings of the structure of existence. Fundamental to Voegelin's philosophical anthropology is the premise that human existence is the mysterious participation in a "community of being" formed by "God and man, world and society."[55] As finite participants in being, human beings are essentially limited epistemically, lacking the

[54]    Voegelin, *Order and History*, vol. 1, p. xiii (in *Collected Works*, vol. 14, p. 23).
[55]    Voegelin, *Order and History*, vol. 1, p. 1 (in *Collected Works*, vol. 14, p. 39).

capacity for complete self-knowledge and for complete knowledge of the whole of being, of which they are a part. Their concerned finitude leads to the experience of anxiety: we do not have sure knowledge of ourselves, nor of our origin or destiny. Following his analysis of Kierkegaard in the earlier text, Voegelin takes anxiety to be a fundamental aspect of human existence:

> At the center of his existence man is unknown to himself, for the part of being that calls itself man could be known fully only if the community of being and its drama in time were known as a whole. Man's partnership in being is the essence of his existence, and this essence depends on the whole, of which existence is a part. Knowledge of the whole, however, is precluded by the identity of the knower with the partner, and ignorance of the whole precludes essential knowledge of the part. This situation of ignorance with regard to the decisive core of existence is more than disconcerting: It is profoundly disturbing, for from the depth of this ultimate ignorance wells up the anxiety of existence.[56]

Human existence is irreducibly participatory and fundamentally marked by ignorance.

Though Voegelin does not cite Kierkegaard in this passage, he elsewhere explicitly traces the concept of "the anxiety of existence" to Kierkegaard: "What Pascal tries to describe with [the terms *ennui*, blackness, *tristesse*, chagrin, despair], denoting the facets of a *fundamental mood* is what is called in the modern philosophy of existence since Kierkegaard the 'anxiety of existence.' "[57] The account of anxious existence in *Order and History* resonates with the discussion in the *Rechtslehre*, and, tellingly, departs from Heidegger whom, by 1959, at the very latest, Voegelin had come to regard as an atheistic modern gnostic.[58] For Voegelin, as mentioned above, the being in which human existence participates is a community of "God and man, world and society," and Voegelin's account of being "thrown" into this community suggests that human existence is grounded, and has its origin and goal, in transcendent, divine being.

Although all human beings are essentially ignorant participants in being, there are different modes of existence; Voegelin holds forth the possibility of "attunement," which is

> the state of existence when it hearkens to that which is lasting in being....We are thrown into and out of existence without knowing the Why or the How, but while in it we know that we are of the being to which we return. From this knowledge flows the experience

---

[56]  Voegelin, *Order and History*, vol. 1, p. 2 (in *Collected Works*, vol. 14, p. 40).

[57]  Voegelin, *From Enlightenment to Revolution*, p. 53 (in *Collected Works*, vol. 25, p. 282), emphasis added.

[58]  "As a result of [Heidegger's] refining process, the nature of gnostic speculation can now be understood as the symbolic expression of an anticipation of salvation in which the power of being replaces the power of God and the parousia of being, the Parousia of Christ." See Voegelin, *Wissenschaft, Politik, und Gnosis*, pp. 59–60. (*Science, Politics, and Gnosticism*, p. 48 (in *Collected Works*, vol. 5, p. 276).)

of obligation, for though this being, entrusted to our partial management in existence while it lasts and passes, may be gained by attunement, it may also be lost by default.[59]

The sources of order Voegelin seeks to draw on—the turn toward divine transcendence embodied in the Mosaic covenant and the philosophical speculation of Plato and Aristotle—are paradigmatic instances of human attunement to being. When the human being discovers that his participation in being is imperfect,

> He will experience a turning around, the Platonic *periagogé*, an inversion or conversion toward the true source of order. And this…conversion…results in more than an increase of knowledge concerning the order of being; it is a change in the order itself.…The more perfect attunement to being…is not an increase on the same scale but a qualitative leap.[60]

Voegelin, consistently throughout the first four volumes of *Order and History*, terms this the "leap in being"; it occurs in Greece and Israel, and, by extension, in the turn toward transcendence found in the writings of the Hindu sages and the teachings of the Buddha, Confucius, and Lao-tse.

It his initial discussion of attunement, Voegelin writes: "the anxiety of existence is more than a fear of death in the sense of biological extinction; it is the profounder horror of losing, with the passing of existence, the slender foothold in the partnership of being that we experience as ours while existence lasts."[61] When humans become conscious that their participation in being is imperfect, they experience "a horror indeed, compelling a radical reorientation of existence."[62] The "more perfect attunement to being"—that is, the experience of the anxiety of existence in its fullness—is the "leap in being."[63] Similarly, of conversion in the Christian sense, Voegelin writes that uncertainty is accompanied by anxiety, and "[u]ncertainty is the very essence of Christianity."[64] There is a strong parallel to *The Concept of Anxiety*, where anxiety is both a fundamental feature of human psychology and an experience that can lead to faith.

It is also known that Voegelin had Kierkegaard in mind while writing *Order and History*. In his *Autobiographical Reflections*, Voegelin writes: "In order to characterize the decisive transition from compact to differentiated truth [that is, the conversion resulting in the attunement to being] in the history of consciousness, I used, at the time, the term *leap in being*, taking the term *leap* from Kierkegaard's *Sprung*."[65] Kierkegaard often speaks of a "leap" or "qualitative leap," but the

---

[59]   Voegelin, *Order and History*, vol. 1, pp. 4–5 (in *Collected Works*, vol. 14, p. 43).

[60]   Voegelin, *Order and History*, vol. 1, p. 10 (in *Collected Works*, vol. 14, p. 48).

[61]   Voegelin, *Order and History*, vol. 1, p. 5 (in *Collected Works*, vol. 14, p. 43).

[62]   Voegelin, *Order and History*, vol. 1, p. 10 (in *Collected Works*, vol. 14, p. 48).

[63]   Ibid.

[64]   Voegelin, *The New Science of Politics*, p. 122 (in *Collected Works*, vol. 5, p. 187).

[65]   Kierkegaard has often been understood as an irrationalist, with the concept of a "leap of faith" taken to be synonymous with his thought, despite the fact that the phrase does not occur in his writings. Neither does it occur in the Schrempf translations Voegelin read, nor does Voegelin use it in this context (see Alastair McKennon, "Kierkegaard and the 'Leap of Faith,'" *Kierkegaardiana*, vol. 16, 1993, p. 116. Jaspers uses the phrase *Sprung ins Dasein* in *Psychologie der Weltanschauungen*, Berlin: Verlag von Julius Springer 1919, p. 297.

particular phrase "leap in being" (*Spring i Tilværelsen*) is found only in *Fear and Trembling*, and only once.[66] The 1954 Lowrie translation, which Voegelin owned, renders the phrase "leap in existence,"[67] but the 1923 Schrempf edition gives the explicitly ambiguous *Sprung ins Dasein*.[68] Although it is not clear whether this passage was in fact Voegelin's source, his language seems to suggest the pregnant ambiguity of Schrempf's translation, for Voegelin depicts the leap in being as "a change in the order [of being] itself," that is, a move upward in or *into* being, while insisting that "the leap upward in being is not a leap out of existence," that is, that this leap occurs *within* being, the fundamental structure of which remains the same.[69] However, lacking further evidence, one can only conjecture whether Voegelin's "leap in being" should be understood in light of the movement made by Kierkegaard's knight of resignation, whether it refers to the "qualitative leap" between innocence and sin that plays a crucial role in the analysis of anxiety and freedom in *The Concept of Anxiety*, or whether, on the other hand, Voegelin is borrowing more loosely from the notion of a "leap" in Kierkegaard's thought as it was generally understood at the time.[70]

In any case, Voegelin uses the Kierkegaardian term to denote an event that, when it occurs, drastically changes the human understanding not only of personal existence, but of the nature, goals, and limitations of political life. Prior to the historical "leap in being," humans are indeed anxious, but the fundamental anxiety of existence is muted by the concomitant experience of participation in the community of mundane and divine being: "The concern of man about the meaning of his existence in the field of being does not remain pent up in the tortures of anxiety but can vent

---

[66]     *SKS* 4, 137, note / *FT*, 42, note.

[67]     Kierkegaard, *Fear and Trembling / The Sickness Unto Death*, trans. by Walter Lowrie, Garden City, New York: Doubleday 1954, p. 53, note.

[68]     Kierkegaard, *Furcht und Zittern*, 3rd printing, trans. by Christoph Schrempf (vol. 3 in Kierkegaard, *Gesammelte Werke*), p. 38, note (which corresponds to *SKS* 4, 137, note / *FT*, 42, note), bracketed interpolation in the German text. The "*continual leap in existence*" (Schrempf: *der beständige Sprung ins Dasein*) mentioned in *Fear and Trembling* is the "*passion*" that "*explains the movement [of infinity]*" performed *not* by the knight of faith, but by the knight of infinite resignation. In the same footnote Kierkegaard writes: "Just to make the celebrated Socratic distinction between what one understands and what one does not understand requires passion; and even more, of course [passion is necessary in order] to make the authentic Socratic movement, the movement of ignorance. What our generation lacks is not reflection but passion." And in Voegelin's initial description of the "anxiety of existence," a few pages before he introduces the concept of a "leap in being," he writes: "The Socratic irony of ignorance has become the paradigmatic instance of awareness for this blind spot at the center of all human knowledge of man" (Voegelin, *Order and History*, vol. 1, p. 2 (in *Collected Works* 14, p. 40)).

[69]     Voegelin, *Order and History*, vol. 1, pp. 10–11 (in *Collected Works*, vol. 14), pp. 48–9.

[70]     See, for example, *SKS* 7 / *CUP1*, passim. *SKS* 1, 90 / *CI*, 28–9. If Voegelin is alluding to the knight of resignation in the *Fear and Trembling* passage, there may in fact be implications for the study of Voegelin, for interpreters are divided on the valence of Voegelin's references to faith, God, the divine, and transcendent being, some wishing to emphasize his attempt to restore classical rationalism, others insisting that he is fundamentally a mystic, with a more religious orientation.

itself in the creation of symbols purporting to render intelligible the relations and tensions between the distinguishable terms of the field."[71] The members of early societies interpreted their existence through cosmological myths, in which humans felt themselves to be "consubstantial" with being, including both its material and divine dimensions. The political world, too, was part of this cosmos, and political communities were understood to be analogous to the cosmos as a whole: "We move in a charmed community…where animals and plants can be men and gods, where men can be divine and gods are kings…."[72]

With the "leap in being," this pictures changes. When humans experience the "horror indeed" that Voegelin discusses, "Not only will the symbols [of cosmological myths] lose the magic of their transparency for the unseen order [of being] and become opaque, but a pallor will fall over the partial orders of mundane existence that hitherto furnished the analogies for the comprehensive order of being."[73] The "leap in being" leads away from mythology and toward, in the cases of Greece and Israel, philosophy and revelation, respectively, where (on Voegelin's account) society is no longer seen as analogous to the divinely-imbued cosmos, but is, instead, measured by the soul of the individual human being, because, in turn, the transcendent God is the measure of the human soul.

In what follows in *Order and History* volumes 1–4, Voegelin describes how the encounter with the divine ground of being leads a handful of exemplary individuals, "representatives" of humanity as a whole—philosophers, patriarchs, prophets, sages, and saints—to attempt to serve as ordering forces within their societies. Although his analysis of the phenomenon of anxiety is strongly similar to Kierkegaard's, the constructive elements of Voegelin's philosophy of history have a twofold purpose. Voegelin seeks to show how individuals have ordered their own existences by the anxious encounter with divine transcendence, but he also seeks to show how such individuals have functioned as social critics and lawgivers. Socrates' resolute acknowledgement of his own ignorance gave rise to the mystical contemplation of Plato, which in turn led to the writing of the *Republic* and the *Laws*; God's revelation to Moses provided the impetus for Israel's exodus from Egypt and establishment as a people existing freely under the Torah of transcendent God, and the Hebrew prophets sought to chasten a self-aggrandizing monarchy; in light of a "leap in being" analogous to those in Greece and Israel, the Chinese sages sought to temper governmental rule with *jen* (goodness) and to encourage the personal orientation of the political ruler not toward self, but toward the *tao*.[74]

The legacy of the "leap in being," however, is not unambiguous. It can engender intolerance. Further, if one neglects that it is not a leap out of existence, that the ontological and epistemological advances it brings do not change the status of the human being as a finite and essentially ignorant participant in being, the possibility arises that the conversion of the soul toward transcendence will be deformed into an irresponsible longing for the perfection of existence. The gnostics of antiquity

---

71    Voegelin, *Order and History*, vol. 1, p. 3 (in *Collected Works*, vol. 14, p. 41).
72    Ibid.
73    Voegelin, *Order and History*, vol. 1, p. 10 (in *Collected Works*, vol. 14, p. 48).
74    Voegelin, *Order and History*, vol. 4, p. 293 (in *Collected Works*, vol. 17, pp. 363–4).

claimed knowledge of a salvation by the good God beyond the evil world. The modern gnostics, on Voegelin's account, seek to find salvation in the here and now. His diagnosis of modern political "disorder," as discussed above, locates the catastrophes of the twentieth century in gnostic expectations of worldly perfection. Nazi and Communist totalitarianism was the deification of finite political aims and institutions, leading to zealous mass murder. More contentiously, on his picture, liberal democracies not guided by the recognition of divine transcendence (and an attendant sober view of human nature) are utopian enterprises, again, conflating the human with the divine by assuming the earthly perfection of human nature. Nevertheless, Voegelin sees in the *resolute* human experience of anxiety, an intellectual antidote to the intellectual and political "disorder" of the age.

## V. Kierkegaard in Voegelin's Philosophy of Consciousness

As mentioned above, Voegelin's thought undergoes a change following the publication of the first three volumes of *Order and History*; namely, he retreats from the grand historical narrative of his 1950s-era work. The intellectual approach he takes from the 1960s onward is usually described as a "philosophy of consciousness," consciousness being understood as "the experience of participation, participation of man in his ground of being," the part of human existence which orders the human being's whole existence in world and society.[75] Human consciousness has the twofold structure of "intentionality" and "luminosity"; consciousness is intentionally conscious of things in the world, on the one hand, but on the other hand conscious of its own participation in reality as a whole, that is, the community of "God and the world, man and society," through what Voegelin calls "the luminosity of consciousness."[76]

It is Voegelin's philosophy of consciousness that has attracted the most comparisons of him to Kierkegaard,[77] and there are strong parallels indeed, although Voegelin's explicit references to Kierkegaard are few. Yet one, in particular, is telling. In *In Search of Order*, the fifth volume of *Order and History* which was left unfinished at his death, Voegelin continues his critique of modern gnosticism,

---

[75]      Voegelin, *Anamnesis*, p. 315; p. 340. (*Anamnesis*, p. 175; p. 200 (in *Collected Works*, vol. 6, pp. 373–4; pp. 398–9).) With respect to this phase in Voegelin's thought, one scholar notes: "…Voegelin, while he makes recognizable use of Jaspers' notion of Existenz, names it with a word that, for Jaspers, meant something of the opposite—i.e. 'consciousness.' Perhaps in this choice of usage we can see Voegelin engaged in a struggle for the ownership of that word and its signification: whereas Jaspers was willing to grant the Kantian and Neo-Kantian schools an authority over a certain region in the theory of consciousness…Voegelin competes to replace the limited and distorted meaning of 'consciousness' with what he believes is a richer and truer one…essentially what Jaspers calls 'Existenz.' " Paul Kidder, "Existenz and Symbol in Jaspers and Voegelin," paper presented at the meeting of the Karl Jaspers Society of North America, March 2002, pp. 2–3.

[76]      Voegelin, *Order and History*, vol. 5, pp. 15–16 (in *Collected Works*, vol. 18, pp. 29–30).

[77]      See especially the respective works of Nagy and Webb, cited in the bibliography below.

arguing that, while the fundamental structure of human consciousness does not change, modern consciousness has become deformed, in large part by the "modern gnostic thinkers," by which Voegelin means the thinkers of the Enlightenment, subsequent revolutionaries, and the German idealists, foremost among them, G.W.F. Hegel.[78]

Hegel seeks to "overcome the deformation of philosophy, painfully obvious under Enlightenment criticism";[79] in his day "Hellenic and Judaeo-Christian symbols had been transformed into intentionalist concepts to be manipulated by propositional thinkers."[80] However, "Hegel wants to create a 'science of the experience of consciousness' and proceeds by eliminating from consciousness the philosopher's experience of being drawn into his quest for truth by the divine reality from the Beyond."[81] The "luminous" dimension of human consciousness is lost because when Hegel speaks of the "turning around [*Umkehrung*] of consciousness"[82] he departs from the Platonic model of the *periagoge* where the human soul is drawn by the world-transcendent Beyond: in Hegel's case, "the *periagoge* is *unsere Zutat*, our addition or addendum. The *periagoge* is not an assertive response but a self-assertive action."[83]

It is with respect to Hegel that Voegelin mentions Kierkegaard as one of a handful of thinkers who had made possible the critique of modern gnosticism: "Kierkegaard engaged in his summary attack on the Fichtean and Hegelian speculative existence in the name of a Christian existentialism, developing in his 'philosophical crumbs or a crumbly philosophy' the analytical importance of such symbols as anxiety, the instant (or moment), and existence...."[84] Hegel's thought represents a deformation of consciousness, and Kierkegaard's critique of Hegel laid the foundations for Voegelin's own reconstructive theory of consciousness.

## *VI. Conclusion*

Voegelin's reading of Kierkegaard is conventional, showing the influence of Jaspers and the intellectual climate of early and mid twentieth-century Germany and Austria. He does not explicitly consider the implications of the pseudonymous authorship of many of Kierkegaard's works; he regards Kierkegaard as engaged in a direct polemic against Hegel, a view which has been called into question; he consistently characterizes Kierkegaard as a "Christian existentialist," a compact expression with two incongruous, loaded terms. From the standpoint of the study of Kierkegaard, Voegelin is not an exegete or a commentator, but an original thinker whose

---

[78]     See also Eric Voegelin, "On Hegel: A Study in Sorcery," *Studium Generale*, vol. 24, 1971, pp. 335–68 (in *Collected Works*, vol. 12, pp. 213–55).

[79]     Voegelin, *Order and History*, vol. 5, p. 54 (in *Collected Works*, vol. 18, p. 74).

[80]     Voegelin, *Order and History*, vol. 5, p. 64 (in *Collected Works*, vol. 18, p. 79).

[81]     Voegelin, *Order and History*, vol. 5, p. 54 (in *Collected Works*, vol. 18, p. 74).

[82]     Hegel, *Phänomenologie des Geistes*, ed. by Johannes Hoffmeister, Hamburg: Felix Meiner 1952, p. 74.

[83]     Voegelin, *Order and History*, vol. 5, p. 56 (in *Collected Works*, vol. 18, p. 71).

[84]     Voegelin, *Order and History*, vol. 5, pp. 52–3 (in *Collected Works*, vol. 18, p. 68).

understanding of consciousness and existence nevertheless draws on several notions central to Kierkegaard's thought, particularly the concept of anxiety.

From the standpoint of the study of Voegelin, however, the foregoing analysis concretely shows that Kierkegaard stands as one of the modern thinkers who shaped the core of Voegelin's understanding of the human condition. In the 1930s Voegelin turned to Kierkegaard's anthropology as a corrective to the limitations of modern legal theory. And throughout his later career, Voegelin saw in Kierkegaard's writings an inspiring resistance to the intellectual "disorder" of the nineteenth century, perhaps best represented by the supposed gnosticism of Hegel (and later, Marx). His appropriation of Kierkegaard, of course, is embedded in his contribution to the field of *political* philosophy. Voegelin respected Kierkegaard's resolute focus on the *individual* spiritual order; in *The History of Political Ideas* he writes: "[Bodin's][85] activist temper apparently was not capable...of Kierkegaard's resigned wisdom: 'A single man cannot help an age or save it; he only can express that it perishes.' "[86] Yet Voegelin, writing in the twentieth century, argued that the disordered souls of modern Europe's intelligentsia were to blame for the atrocities committed in the gulags and concentration camps. In light of this view, he sought to show how individuals who are anxiously attuned to their own existence can serve as an ordering—though not salvific—presence in the political world. Voegelin wrote hopefully of his own *Order and History* that "[p]erhaps it will have its remedial effect—in the modest measure that, in the passionate course of events, is allowed to Philosophy."[87]

---

[85]      Jean Bodin (1530–96), French jurist and political philosopher.
[86]      Voegelin, *Collected Works*, vol. 32, p. 207, quoting *SKS* 21, 304, NB10:93 / *JP* 4, 157.
[87]      Voegelin, *Order and History*, vol. 1, p. xiv (in *Collected Works*, vol. 14, p. 24).

# Bibliography

*I. References to or Uses of Kierkegaard in Voegelin's Corpus*

*Rasse und Staat*, Tübingen: J.C.B. Mohr, 1933, p. 197, note 2. (English translation: *The Collected Works of Eric Voegelin*, vols. 1–34, ed. by Ellis Sandoz, Columbia, Missouri: University of Missouri Press 1989–2009, vol. 2, p. 196, note 30.)

Letter to Alfred Schütz, December 28, 1943, in Alfred Schütz and Eric Voegelin, *Eine Freundschaft, die ein Leben ausgehalten hat: Briefwechsel 1938–1959*, ed. by Gerhard Wagner and Gilbert Weiss, Konstanz: UVK Verlaggesellschaft 2004, p. 210.

"Nietzsche, the Crisis, and the War," *The Journal of Politics*, vol. 6, no. 2, 1944, p. 184 (in *The Collected Works of Eric Voegelin*, vol. 10, p. 132).

Letter to Alfred Schütz, September 17, 1945, in Alfred Schütz and Eric Voegelin, *Eine Freundschaft, die ein Leben ausgehalten hat: Briefwechsel 1938–1959*, ed. by Gerhard Wagner and Gilbert Weiss, Konstanz: UVK Verlaggesellschaft 2004, p. 265.

Letter to Jürgen Schüddekopf, February 27, 1953, in Eric Voegelin, *Selected Correspondence, 1950–1984*, ed. by Thomas A. Hollweck, Columbia: University of Missouri Press 2007 (*The Collected Works of Eric Voegelin*, vol. 30), pp. 142–9.

Letter to Manfred Henningsen, November 25, 1967, in Eric Voegelin, *Selected Correspondence, 1950–1984*, ed. by Thomas A. Hollweck, Columbia: University of Missouri Press, 2007 (*The Collected Works of Eric Voegelin*, vol. 30), pp. 543–6.

*From Enlightenment to Revolution*, ed. by John H. Hallowell, Durham: Duke University Press 1975, p. 53.

*Order and History*, vols. 1–5, Baton Rouge, Louisiana: Louisiana State University Press 1956–87, vol. 5, pp. 52–3 (in *The Collected Works of Eric Voegelin*, vol. 18, p. 68).

*Autobiographical Reflections*, ed. by Ellis Sandoz, Baton Rouge: Louisiana State University Press 1989, p. 79 (in *The Collected Works of Eric Voegelin*, vol. 34, p. 105).

"The Eclipse of Reality," in *What is History? and Other Late Unpublished Writings*, ed. by Thomas Hollweck and Paul Caringella, Columbia: University of Missouri Press 1990 (*The Collected Works of Eric Voegelin*, vol. 28), p. 117; p. 161.

*The History of Political Ideas*, vols. 1–8, Baton Rouge, Louisiana: Louisiana State University Press 1997–99 (*The Collected Works of Eric Voegelin*, vols. 19–26), vol. 5, p. 207; vol. 7, p. 65; pp. 199–200; p. 203; p. 241; p. 274, note; p. 282.

*Rechtslehre, Occasional Papers*, no. 56, ed. by Peter J. Opitz, Munich: Eric-Voegelin-Archiv 2008 (in *The Collected Works of Eric Voegelin*, vol. 32, pp. 373–413).

## II. Sources of Voegelin's Knowledge of Kierkegaard

Henningsen, Bernd, *Die Politik des Einzelnen: Studien zur Genese der skandinavischen Ziviltheologie: Ludvig Holberg, Søren Kierkegaard, N.F.S. Grundtvig*, Göttingen: Vandenhoeck und Ruprecht 1977.

Jaspers, Karl, *Philosophie*, vols. 1–3, Berlin: Verlag von Julius Springer 1932.

— *Psychologie der Weltanschauungen*, Berlin: Springer 1919, see especially pp. 225–6; pp. 370–80.

— *Vernunft und Existenz: fünf Vorlesungen*, Groningen: J.B. Wolters 1935.

Laing, Ronald David, *The Divided Self: An Existential Study in Sanity and Madness*, Harmondsworth: Penguin 1960.

Przywara, Erich, *Das Geheimnis Kierkegaards*, Munich: Oldenbourg Verlag 1929.

Strauss, Leo, Letter to Voegelin, December 17, 1949, in *Faith and Political Philosophy: The Correspondence between Leo Strauss and Eric Voegelin*, trans. and ed. by Peter Emberley and Barry Cooper, Columbia, Missouri: University of Missouri Press 2004, pp. 62–3.

— Letter to Voegelin, June 4, 1951, in *Faith and Political Philosophy: The Correspondence between Leo Strauss and Eric Voegelin*, trans. and ed. by Peter Emberley and Barry Cooper, Columbia, Missouri: University of Missouri Press 2004, pp. 88–91.

## III. Secondary Literature on Voegelin's Relation to Kierkegaard

Bellinger, Charles K., *The Trinitarian Self: The Key to the Puzzle of Violence*, Eugene, Oregon: Pickwick Publications 2008, see especially p. 31; p. 85; p. 87; p. 94; pp. 155–6.

Day, Jerry, *Voegelin, Schelling, and the Philosophy of Historical Existence*, Columbia, Missouri: University of Missouri Press, 2003, see especially p. 10; p. 15; p. 180, note.

Hughes, Glenn, *Mystery and Myth in the Philosophy of Eric Voegelin*, Columbia, Missouri: University of Missouri Press 1993, p. 13; p. 104; p. 114.

— *Transcendence and History: The Search for Ultimacy from Ancient Societies to Postmodernity*, Columbia, Missouri: University of Missouri Press 2003, p. 29; p. 51; p. 92; p. 164; pp. 181–2; p. 188; p. 195; pp. 205–12.

Ley, Michael, and Gilbert Weiss, *Voegelin in Wien: Frühe Schriften 1920–1938*, Vienna: Passagen Verlag 2007, pp. 85–6.

McPartland, Thomas J., *Lonergan and the Philosophy of Historical Existence*, Columbia, Missouri: University of Missouri Press 2001, pp. 142–3; p. 154; p. 170; pp. 208–14.

Nagy, Eugen L., "Noesis and Faith: Eric Voegelin and Søren Kierkegaard," in *Eric Voegelin and the Continental Tradition: Explorations in Modern Political*

*Thought*, ed. by Lee Trepanier and Steven McGuire, Columbia, Missouri: University of Missouri Press 2011, pp. 85-107.

Opitz, Peter J., "Rückkehr zur Realität: Grundzüge der politschen Philosophie Eric Voegelins," in *The Philosophy of Order: Essays on History, Consciousness and Politics*, ed. by Peter J. Opitz and Gregor Sebba, Stuttgart: Klett-Cotta 1981, p. 50.

Sebba, Gregor, "Prelude and Variations on the Theme of Eric Voegelin," *The Southern Review*, Autumn, 1977, p. 622.

Shanks, Andrew, *Hegel's Political Theology*, Cambridge and New York: Cambridge University Press 1991, pp. 125–40; pp. 176–7.

Webb, Eugene, *Eric Voegelin: Philosopher of History*, Seattle, Washington: University of Washington Press 1981, see especially pp. 24–5; pp. 80–2.

— *Philosophers of Consciousness: Polanyi, Lonergan, Voegelin, Ricoeur, Girard, Kierkegaard*, Seattle, Washington: Seattle University Press 1988.

# Cornel West:

## Kierkegaard and the Construction of a "Blues Philosophy"

### Marcia C. Robinson

African-American philosopher-activist Cornel Ronald West (b. 1953) is one of the most prominent intellectuals in the United States today.[1] Early on, his now classic works, *Prophesy Deliverance!: An Afro-American Revolutionary Christianity* (1982) and *Prophetic Fragments* (1988), offered a fresh interpretation of the black liberation movement, and established him as a religious and political thinker of note. *The American Evasion of Philosophy: A Genealogy of Pragmatism* (1989), his most important philosophical study to date, situated his new interpretation of the black liberation struggle—a Christian existentialism, humanism, and progressive

---

[1]     Since 1982, West has authored or edited nearly thirty books and countless articles, alone or with others (such as Henry Louis Gates, Jr., Bell Hooks, Roberto Mangabeira Unger, John Rajchman, and Sylvia Ann Hewlett). See bibliography for a selection of his work. He has taught at Union Theological Seminary (New York City), Yale Divinity School, the University of Paris VIII, Harvard University, and Princeton University. He has been the subject of several readers and monographs, including *The Cornel West Reader* (1999), an edited anthology of his writings compiled by himself; George Yancy's edited volume, *Cornel West: A Critical Reader* (2001); Mark David Wood's *Cornel West and the Politics of Prophetic Pragmatism* (2000); Clarence Sholé Johnson's *Cornel West and Philosophy* (2003); Rosemary Cowan's *Cornel West: The Politics of Redemption* (2003); and Keith Gilyard's *Composition and Cornel West: Notes Toward a Deep Democracy* (2008). West has also been the subject of numerous interviews, conducted by intellectuals, religious leaders, and professional journalists such as Eva Corredor, Anders Stephanson, Michael Lerner, Bill Moyers, Charlie Rose, Tavis Smiley, and Anand Naidoo (Al Jazeera), and along with his constant lecturing around the nation and the world, has become a regular commentator on Tavis Smiley's National Public Radio and Public Broadcasting Service programs. West has served as a columnist, reviewer, and correspondent for *Christianity and Crisis* and *Le Monde Diplomatique*. He has also served on the National Parenting Organization's Task Force on Parent Empowerment (as co-chair), the Democratic Socialists of America (as a long-term member and now honorary chair), President Clinton's National Conversation on Race, Al Sharpton's presidential exploratory committee, and Barack Obama's 2008 presidential campaign's Black Advisory Council. Finally, West has become an actor and recording artist, who has starred in two popular Hollywood films incorporating his ideas, *The Matrix Reloaded* and *The Matrix Revolutions*, and who has produced three albums on social issues with popular musicians such as Prince and Jill Scott, including the well-received "Never Forget: A Journey of Revelations" (2007).

Marxism—within the pragmatist tradition of John Dewey (1859–1952) and Richard Rorty (1931–2007), and created a new form of American philosophical culture criticism: "prophetic pragmatism." And his bestseller *Race Matters* (1993) broadened his stature by making his brand of pragmatism a regular part of public conversations on race, politics, economics, religion, and democracy.

Pragmatism is important to West because it allows him to address social problems in the United States. It, however, fails to acknowledge the reality of evil, and so fails to address the tragic and paradoxical nature of African-American life. Herein lies the fundamental significance of Søren Kierkegaard.

In an interview with George Yancy, West calls attention to pragmatism's failings by contending that black experience is significant to "any serious philosophy... grappling with life,"[2] especially American pragmatism, with its concerns for democracy and human betterment. Black experience, says West, offers pragmatism a "profound sense of the tragic and the comic rooted in heroic efforts to preserve human dignity on the night side, the underside of modernity."[3] That is, the spirituals, the blues, jazz, black literature, and black oratory—premier expressions of African-American life and faith, from the slave past to the present—present American pragmatism with astounding examples of absurdity and tragedy, wrenching cases of "radical contingency"[4] and "radical conditionedness,"[5] and harrowing instances of misery, of the "guttural cry"[6] of suffering individuals, while also demonstrating the power that oppressed people have to act—and to hope—against the odds.[7] In doing so, black art demonstrates without sentimentality or cynicism that being human

---

[2]      Cornel West, "On My Intellectual Vocation," in *The Cornel West Reader*, ed. by Cornel West, New York: Basic Civitas Books, Perseus Books 1999, p. 25. This interview first appeared as "Cornel West," in *African-American Philosophers: 17 Conversations*, ed. by George Yancy, New York: Routledge 1998, pp. 31–48.

[3]      West, *The Cornel West Reader*, pp. 23–5. See with Cornel West, *The American Evasion of Philosophy: A Genealogy of Pragmatism*, Madison, Wisconsin: University of Wisconsin Press 1989, pp. 226–30.

[4]      Cornel West, "Pragmatism and the Tragic," in his *Prophetic Thought in Postmodern Times*, Monroe, Maine: Common Courage Press 1993 (*Beyond Eurocentrism and Multiculturalism*, vol. 1), pp. 32–3.

[5]      West, *The Cornel West Reader*, pp. 23–4.

[6]      Ibid., p. 25.

[7]      See also West, "Pragmatism and the Tragic," in *Prophetic Thought in Postmodern Times*, p. 36; pp. 48–9; Cornel West, "Black Strivings in a Twilight Civilization," in *The Cornel West Reader*, pp. 87–119 (initially published in Henry Louis Gates, Jr. and Cornel West, *The Future of the Race*, New York: Alfred A. Knopf 1996, pp. 53–112); Cornel West, "Subversive Joy and Revolutionary Patience in Black Christianity," in *The Cornel West Reader*, pp. 435–9 (initially published in *Le Monde Diplomatique*, October 1984, pp. 24–5; and later in Cornel West, *Prophetic Fragments*, Grand Rapids, Michigan and Trenton, New Jersey: Eerdmans and Africa World Press, Inc. 1988, pp. 161–5); Cornel West, "The Spirituals As Lyrical Poetry," in *The Cornel West Reader*, pp. 463–70 (initially published as the Foreword in Richard Newman, *Go Down, Moses: A Celebration of the African-American Spiritual*, New York: Clarkson N. Potter, Crown Publishers 1998, pp. 9–17); and Cornel West, *Prophesy Deliverance!: An Afro-American Revolutionary Christianity*, Philadelphia: Westminster Press 1982, pp. 85–91.

means "mustering the courage to be oneself,"[8] affirming the goodness of life and being willing to "keep keeping on,"[9] even as one wrestles with the dark truths about human nature—indeed, even as one "catches hell."[10] Black experience, then, says West, tells pragmatism that in order to better black people's lives, one must take seriously the reality of evil and the contradictions of human existence precisely as one seeks to create more democratic forms of community.

In saying this, West clearly has in mind an American pragmatism informed by a "blues sensibility."[11] He, however, also has in mind the Christian existential philosophy of Kierkegaard. Kierkegaard's dialectical and poetic studies of "selves in discord and resolve"[12] and Christo-Socratic approach to philosophy affirm West's experiences and give him helpful ways to grapple with the enigma and the potential that is human being and the paradox and the possibility that is America.[13] That is, Kierkegaard's psychological portrayals of modern human being and becoming— particularly in terms of absurdity, anxiety, despair, and faith—highlight human striving, decision, and potential, and offer West ways to theorize black experience as modern experience. And Kierkegaard's role as gadfly to Danish Christendom promotes an open-ended, anti-foundationalist, radical historicist stance on faith and knowledge that challenges social conventions and cultural absolutes, and gives West a basic model—though not all of the resources[14]—for doing philosophy as a form

---

8      West, *The Cornel West Reader*, pp. 23–4.

9      Ibid., p. 23.

10     Ibid., p. 33.

11     Ibid., p. 25.

12     The phrase "selves in discord and resolve" comes from the title of Edward F. Mooney's book, *Selves in Discord and Resolve: Kierkegaard's Moral-Religious Psychology from Either/ Or to Sickness unto Death*, New York: Routledge 1996.

13     On considering Kierkegaard's thought in the context of race, it is important to note that his dialectical thinking is quite different from the "dichotomous" or "binary" thinking that race and gender theorists criticize. Although Kierkegaard does deal with dialectical pairs (e.g., finitude and infinitude), and does retain difference and tension within these pairs, his dialectics have nothing to do with rigid and impermeable binaries that re-enforce hierarchical and exclusionary practices (for example, black and white, male and female). See, for example, Patricia Hill Collins, *Black Feminist Thought: Knowledge, Consciousness, and the Politics of Empowerment*, 2nd ed., New York: Routledge 2000, p. 22; pp. 70–1. Rather, Kierkegaard's dialectics address the complexities and tensions within the life of a single individual, while also seeking harmony in the selfsame individual. Because of this, there can be no exclusion of that which is other or different, since each element is different from its counterpart, yet is equally constitutive of the self. See Part II below.

14     Kierkegaard does not share West's particular situation, or champion a particular political theory or cause. Therefore, West has to integrate Kierkegaard's ideas into black religion, literature, music, and so forth. See, for example, West, *The Cornel West Reader*, p. 20. Since West must also address social and political issues in the United States, he must also necessarily go to others, particularly those whose philosophical, cultural, political, and economic critiques (i.e., pragmatists, neo-pragmatists, and progressive Marxists) can in some way be aligned with Kierkegaard's ideas. (West has in mind a shared anti-foundationalist and radical historicist stance.) West has been criticized for integrating the ideas of European and Euro-American thinkers into discussions of black existence, while failing to use black

of religious culture criticism. This in effect makes Kierkegaard a fundamental part of West's overall development as an "organic public intellectual" or culture critic.[15]

Kierkegaard's influence on West, though, is not readily apparent. West does not provide extensive commentary on Kierkegaard, or fully explain his repeated claims that Kierkegaard is a major influence on him, even though he does regularly refer to the Dane in his writings, interviews, and public talks.[16] If one actually examines West and his work in some detail, though, beginning with his early encounter with Kierkegaard, one can see how Kierkegaard indeed inspires and informs his black, decidedly American, and decidedly Christian existentialism—in depth.[17] This article examines this rich, complicated, and heretofore unexplored topic by focusing on several fundamental features of Kierkegaard's influence on West: his views on the absurd, anxiety, despair, and faith—the launching point for any understanding of the role of the Dane in West's thought and activism.[18]

---

thinkers. See, for example, Lewis R. Gordon, "The Unacknowledged Fourth Tradition: An Essay on Nihilism, Decadence, and the Black Intellectual Tradition in the Existential Pragmatic Thought of Cornel West," in *Cornel West: A Critical Reader*, ed. by George Yancy, Malden, Massachusetts: Blackwell Publishing 2001, pp. 38–58. West, however, deems black writers and musicians as intellectuals. See Cornel West, "Afterword: Philosophy and the Funk of Life," in *Cornel West: A Critical Reader*, pp. 349–50.

[15]      West seems to have gotten his conception of the public intellectual—including the interchangeable terms "organic" or "public" or "organic public" intellectual—from Italian Marxist Antonio Gramsci's *Prison Notebooks*. Interestingly, though, in applying Gramsci's idea of the public intellectual to progressive American figures, West does not immediately think of his heroes among the pragmatists, particularly John Dewey and William James, or even any of the other figures whom he considers to be pragmatists or neo-pragmatists, such as W.E.B. Du Bois and Reinhold Niebuhr. Rather, he declares Martin Luther King, Jr. to be "the most significant and successful organic intellectual in American history." Later on, in his interview with David Lionel Smith, he qualifies these earlier references to Gramsci and King by praising nineteenth-century Russian writers, whom he contends "allow suffering to speak." See Cornel West, "Martin Luther King, Jr: Prophetic Christian as Organic Intellectual," in *Prophetic Fragments*, pp. 3–12; "On Christian Intellectuals," in *Prophetic Fragments*, pp. 271–2; and "Chekhov, Coltrane and Democracy," in *The Cornel West Reader*, p. 551.

[16]      See the bibliography for West's references to Kierkegaard. See especially West, *Prophesy Deliverance!*, p. 167, note 2, where he maintains that his "viewpoint is informed primarily by the work of Søren Kierkegaard, William James, and John Dewey," and even goes so far as to identify specific Kierkegaard texts (viz., the *Philosophical Fragments* and the *Concluding Unscientific Postscript*).

[17]      For West's discussions of his philosophical project as decidedly American and Christian, see West, *The Cornel West Reader*, pp. xv–xx, see especially p. xix; and West, *The American Evasion of Philosophy*, p. 233.

[18]      Scholars have made a few attempts to discuss Kierkegaard's relation to black existence in conference papers, and at least one scholar has made a substantial reference to this issue in print. For the latter, see Kevin Hoffman, "Kierkegaard, Compassion, and the Descent of Love," *International Philosophical Quarterly*, vol. 47, no. 2, 2007, pp. 178–9. To date, though, no scholar has published a serious study of West's use of Kierkegaard. The only noteworthy discussions of the role of Kierkegaard in West's thought in print are the brief references that philosophers George Yancy, Clarence Sholé Johnson, Lewis Gordon, and John Pittman make in the context of other issues. Of these brief discussions, Yancy captures best West's

## I. West's Early Encounter with Kierkegaard

West got his start as an activist-intellectual early in life. Born June 2, 1953 in Tulsa, Oklahoma, the son of Louisiana natives and the grandson of a Baptist minister, and raised in Sacramento, California in the close-knit, but segregated community of Glen Elder, West grew up in the black church and in civil rights and radical activist movements of the 1950s, 1960s, and 1970s. An admirer of Martin Luther King, Jr. and Malcolm X, and an active ally—though not a member—of the Black Panther Party, West learned early to blend the ideas, symbols, rituals, and ethical practices of the church with social activism. Racism in California had a different tenor than that elsewhere in the nation. Nevertheless, he and his family were forced to deal with unfair practices in housing, education, employment, wages, and working conditions, and had limited access to public facilities and resources. In regard to the latter, West speaks in particular of getting books from a bookmobile, as opposed to the stacks of the city's public library. Such injustices led him and his family to participate in civil-rights demonstrations. Early on, young Cornel showed a talent for civil-rights leadership, when he and three other black, high-school student body presidents launched a successful, city-wide strike for black studies in the Sacramento public schools.[19]

In all of these activities, West was supported by his family and his community. He, however, was not shielded from the ugliness of anti-black racism in California or elsewhere in the nation. During the 1950s and 1960s, he saw civil rights workers increasingly become the targets of random and organized violence. Some of the most celebrated cases were the assassination of NAACP[20] field secretary Medgar Evers in Jackson, Mississippi in 1963, when West was 10 years old; the murder of civil-rights workers James Chaney, Andrew Goodman, and Michael Schwerner in Mississippi

Kierkegaardian sensibility. See George Yancy, "Cornel West: The Vanguard of Existential and Democratic Hope," in *Cornel West: A Critical Reader*, pp. 6, 8–9; and "Religion and the Mirror of God: Historicism, Truth, and Religious Pluralism," in *Cornel West: A Critical Reader*, p. 133; p. 135; Clarence Sholé Johnson, *Cornel West and Philosophy: The Quest for Social Justice*, New York: Routledge 2003, pp. 3–4; Gordon, "The Unacknowledged Fourth Tradition," in *Cornel West: A Critical Reader*, pp. 41–3; p. 46; and John P. Pittman, " 'Radical Historicism,' Anti-Philosophy, and Marxism," in *Cornel West: A Critical Reader*, pp. 237–8. As indicated above, West himself makes such a study difficult, because he provides little commentary on Kierkegaard. The reader, then, must uncover both his indirect and direct references to Kierkegaard, in both substance and strategy; consider them in light of pertinent Kierkegaardian concepts, texts, and strategies; and draw conclusions. This is my method here. Note that the present article is part of a longer study to be published at a later time.

[19]     West, *The Cornel West Reader*, pp. 3–21, see especially pp. 3–4 and pp. 19–21; Cornel West, *The Ethical Dimensions of Marxist Thought*, New York: Monthly Review Press 1991, pp. xv–xxxiv; Stephen M. Avella, *Sacramento, Indomitable City*, Charleston, South Carolina: Arcadia Publishing 2003, p. 87; p. 99; p. 108; p. 111; pp. 130–3; and Robert O. Self, *American Babylon: Race and the Struggle for Postwar Oakland*, Princeton, New Jersey: Princeton University Press 2005.

[20]     NAACP stands for the National Association for the Advancement of Colored People. West's heroes John Dewey and W.E.B. Du Bois were founding members of this organization, established in 1909.

in 1964, when West was 11 years old; the murder of Detroit housewife and part-
time civil rights worker Viola Liuzzo in 1965 in Alabama, when West was 12 years
old; and the assassination of civil-rights leader Martin Luther King, Jr. in Memphis,
Tennessee in 1968, when West was 15 years old. A loving family and an affirming
community could not preclude the anxiety that he felt on learning about such things.
As he put it in his interview with George Yancy: "early on I was...seized by a...terror
that struck me as being at the heart of things human...."[21]

This does not mean that West viewed white people as demons, or only had them
in mind as he questioned what it meant to be human.[22] Rather, it means that the
anti-black racism that he witnessed and experienced compelled him to ask in more
pointed ways why things had to be the way that they were; why human beings had
to be the way that they are; who he was; why he was here; what he was supposed to
do; and what it all meant. Indeed, the very fact that these questions evoked issues of
"good and evil"—issues that disturb most children and adults, as Kierkegaard and
Ludwig Tieck (1773–1853) point out in their reflections on good storytelling[23]—
awakened in him a lifelong interest in theodicy:

> I was coming out of the church, and so there was always Job sitting there, Daniel sitting
> there, and...especially the Christ between Good Friday and Easter...which struck me as
> highly illuminating of what it meant to be human...what it meant to wrestle...with limit
> situations—death, dread, despair, disappointment, disease, and so on.[24]

These Old and New Testament mainstays in West's black Baptist heritage, however,
could not fully explain the "limit situations" that he was experiencing, or help
him to make sense of human nature. He needed sustained philosophical reflection
for this. In the aforementioned interview with George Yancy, West maintains that
Kierkegaard answered this need: "In reading Kierkegaard from the Bookmobile,...
here was someone who was seriously...wrestling with...this terror, this suffering
and this...sorrow. It resonated deeply with me."[25] West does not say what he read
of Kierkegaard at this time, just that he was "struck by" Kierkegaard's "honest and
candid" conception of "the human predicament."[26]

---

[21]     West, *The Cornel West Reader*, p. 20.
[22]     West maintains that his family and his community precluded this by giving him
"a chance to really revel in black humanity," so that when it came time for him to interact
with white people, he did not see them as devils or gods, but simply as human beings. See
*The Cornel West Reader*, p. 19. See also Rosemary Cowan, *Cornel West: The Politics of
Redemption*, Cambridge: Polity Press 2003, p. 2.
[23]     *SKS* 17, 122–33, BB:37 / *KJN* 1, 116–25; see also West, *The Cornel West Reader*,
p. 33. For a discussion of Kierkegaard's and Tieck's views on storytelling, see Marcia C.
Robinson, "Tieck: Kierkegaard's 'Guadalquivir' of Open Critique and Hidden Appreciation,"
in *Kierkegaard and His German Contemporaries*, Tome I, *Literature and Aesthetics*, ed.
by Jon Stewart, Aldershot: Ashgate 2008 (*Kierkegaard Research: Sources, Reception and
Resources*, vol. 6), pp. 284–95, see especially p. 288.
[24]     West, *The Cornel West Reader*, p. 20. Quotation slightly modified.
[25]     Ibid. Quotation slightly modified.
[26]     Ibid.

Depending on the accessioning and de-accessioning practices of the Sacramento Public Library, which probably operated the aforementioned "Bookmobile," and depending on how much access West actually had to its collections on a revolving basis on the bookmobile, West could have had available to him somewhere in the neighborhood of twenty translations of Kierkegaard's writings![27] This could easily have included: (1) Walter Lowrie's 1954 double edition of *Fear and Trembling* and the *Sickness unto Death*, 1944 translation of *Training in Christianity*, 1962 translation of *The Point of View for My Work as an Author*, and 1968 anthology *Kierkegaard's Attack Upon "Christendom," 1854–1855*; (2) Alexander Dru's 1959 anthology *The Journals of Kierkegaard*, and 1962 translation of "The Present Age"; (3) Robert Bretall's 1959 edition of *A Kierkegaard Anthology*; (4) Lee M. Hollander's 1960 *Selections from the Writings of Kierkegaard*; (5) David and Lilian Swenson's 1959 translation of *Either/Or*; and (6) Swenson's and Lowrie's 1941 translation of the *Concluding Unscientific Postscript* and (7) Swenson's and Howard Hong's 1962 translation of the *Philosophical Fragments*—two books West would later claim to be fundamental texts for his work as a "prophetic Christian freedom fighter."[28] Young Cornel West could easily have found in any one of these texts portrayals of the terror and despair that he felt and considered to be fundamentally human.[29] *Fear and Trembling* above all—with its pictures of frightening, violent, and seemingly meaningless separations of sons from fathers, infants from mothers, human beings from God—would have been sufficient in providing him with a vivid psychological portrait of the inscrutability of life and faith, and of the arbitrariness of authority—in Kierkegaard's case, divine authority; in West's case, both institutionalized white supremacy passing itself off as divine and a God who would allow it. And Dru's translations of Kierkegaard's journals would have exposed young Cornel to

---

[27]     See the online catalog of the Sacramento Public Library System for an impressive collection of Kierkegaard titles for a non-academic library. All 20 of their titles were published by 1968, when West was 15 years old, and 18 were published by 1967 or earlier. Thus, by the time West was 13 or 14, he could have seen most of these books, if Sacramento Public owned them and made them available on the bookmobile.

[28]     Walter Lowrie's translation of the *Concept of Dread* was originally published in 1944, and could also have been part of the Sacramento Public Library's collection of Kierkegaard's writings, when West was a teenager. Their current catalog, however, does not contain a record of this early edition, which means that if they did own it at the time West was a teenager, they have since de-accessioned it. For West's direct reference to the writings of Kierkegaard's Johannes Climacus, and characterization of himself as a "prophetic Christian freedom fighter," see West, *Prophesy Deliverance!*, p. 96; p. 167, note 2; and West, *The Cornel West Reader*, p. 214.

[29]     Hollander's and Bretall's anthologies were probably the primary works that West read as a youth. They would have given him the helpful introduction to Kierkegaard that he generally would have needed, not to mention opened him to a broad array of Kierkegaard's writings, including the *Fragments*, the *Postscript*, the journals, "The Present Age" (from *A Literary Review of Two Ages*), the literature from the attack on the Danish Church, and *The Point of View*, the last three of which would have given him a sense of Kierkegaard's view of the spiritual malaise of Copenhagen—an avowedly Christian, yet thoroughly market-oriented society not unlike his own.

Kierkegaard's own youthful questions about what his life meant and what he was to do.

Whatever West read of Kierkegaard at this time, his encounter with the Dane on the bookmobile was, as he put it, "decisive."[30] It set the stage for him to study philosophy in college and graduate school at Harvard and Princeton.[31] It gave him "a profoundly Kierkegaardian sensibility that required...that philosophizing be linked to existentially concrete situations."[32] And it gave him a basic philosophical framework—a dialectic of anxiety/faith and despair/faith—that allowed him to articulate his and his people's struggles as "experiences of the absurd," and to view faith as an appropriate response to the self-destructive tendencies in these experiences.[33] Indeed, Christianity emerged in this Kierkegaardian framework as a posture and practice of hope, able to counter life's death-dealing absurdities with a potentially life-giving absurdity—or "venture" in faith.[34]

## II. A Philosophical Framework for Dealing with Absurdity, Anxiety, and Despair

George Yancy begins his interview with West asking: "So what was it specifically about your experience of the absurd, at the age of thirteen or fourteen, that made the work of Søren Kierkegaard so attractive to you?"[35] West does not answer Yancy's question by defining "the absurd"—something he presents later in the interview as "the nullity and nothingness" of human life.[36] Rather, he discusses his aforementioned experiences of dread and sorrow as a teen, and then says that he found Kierkegaard's treatment of this same "terror and sorrow" compelling.[37] According to him, Kierkegaard demonstrated that such experiences could be understood in terms of what literary critic Prosser Hall Frye (1866–1934) called "the tragic qualm"—"a kind of vertigo, a dizziness, a sense of being staggered by the darkness that one sees in the human condition."[38] In other words, by focusing on the "darkness in the human condition," Kierkegaard showed West that his early experiences of anxiety and despair were in fact experiences of "the absurd." This calls forth several passages in Kierkegaard's *corpus*.

In a journal entry from 1850, Kierkegaard maintains that "the absurd" is a negative or limit concept that signifies the boundaries of reason. There, evoking the discussion of the absolute paradox in the *Philosophical Fragments*, Kierkegaard says:

---

[30]   West, *The Cornel West Reader*, p. 20.
[31]   Ibid., pp. 20–1; p. 26.
[32]   Ibid., p. 20.
[33]   Ibid.
[34]   *SKS* 7, 386–91 / *CUP1*, 424–9. *SKS* 11, 151–2 / *SUD*, 34–5.
[35]   West, *The Cornel West Reader*, p. 20. Quotation slightly modified.
[36]   Ibid., p. 33.
[37]   Ibid., p. 20. Quotation slightly modified.
[38]   Ibid., p. 20; and Prosser Hall Frye, *Romance and Tragedy*, Boston: Marshall Jones Company 1922, pp. 146–8.

the concept of the absurd is precisely to grasp the fact that it cannot and must not be grasped....The *absurd*, the *paradox*, is composed in such a way that reason has no power at all to dissolve it in nonsense and prove that it is nonsense; no, it is a symbol, a riddle, a compounded riddle about which reason must say: I cannot solve it....but it does not follow thereby that it is nonsense.[39]

Like his logician-humorist pseudonym Johannes Climacus, Kierkegaard identifies "the absurd" with "the paradox," and has in mind the contradiction that the god-man Jesus Christ represents: the idea of eternity coming into time. The problem of the god-man, though, is located in the problem of the existing individual, which itself involves the absurd or paradoxical dimensions of human nature. Climacus makes this apparent in the *Concluding Unscientific Postscript*.

According to him, existing individuals live over a void, perched out "over 70,000 fathoms."[40] Life is an inscrutable abyss that can only be meaningful, fulfilling, good, says Climacus, if, like Socrates, we need for it to be, believe that it can be, and seek for it to be.[41] This terrifying recognition of being saddled with the task and the responsibility of making meaning out of nothing seems to be precisely what West is referring to when he speaks of the "staggering darkness" that he saw "in the human condition" as a teen. Young Cornel West was looking into the "nullity and nothingness" of human existence.[42] He, however, was not simply thinking of the human condition in general. He was also thinking of the senseless evil and suffering brought on by human actions.

West makes this plain in a 1991 lecture entitled "Pragmatism and the Tragic," where he maintains that the "full seriousness of the problem of evil" is acknowledged by the person who has not simply "feared....for this or that moment in his life, but who has feared for all of his nature. So that he has trembled through and through and all that was most fixed in him has become shaken."[43] Like Socrates in Plato's *Phaedrus*, whom Kierkegaard's Climacus references in his discussion of the paradox in the *Fragments*, West was essentially saying that when one looks into the depths of human nature, where—à la Climacus—the "endless waste of tossing waves.... rolls cubits deep above the top of what were our highest mountains," one does not know whether we human beings are more akin to monsters or to gods.[44] On the one

---

[39]    *SKS* 23, 23–4, NB15:25 / *JP* 1, 7.

[40]    *SKS* 7, 131 / *CUP1*, 140.

[41]    *SKS* 7, 184–8 / *CUP1*, 201–6.

[42]    Meaninglessness is not the same as nonsense. As Kierkegaard rightly notes, to declare something to be nonsense is to say that it can be dismissed. The meaninglessness of human brutality and the enigma of human nature with which West was struggling as a teen could not be dismissed. Although they did not make sense to him, they nevertheless had an effect on his life, and so mattered. West underscores this point in his interview with Yancy, where he acknowledges Kant's essay on theodicy. As he sees it, Kant rightly recognizes that "the problem of evil could not be theoretically resolved at all. It was a question of coping." See West, *The Cornel West Reader*, p. 23.

[43]    West, "Pragmatism and the Tragic," p. 48.

[44]    See *SKS* 4, 243 / *PF*, 37. *SKS* 7, 131 / *CUP1*, 140. See also Plato, *Phaedrus*, 230a; and West, "Pragmatism and the Tragic," p. 48, which discusses Josiah Royce's conception of human being.

hand, we are free, rational, and sentient beings capable of effecting and appreciating "the good, the true, and the beautiful." On the other hand, as free beings, we are also capable of bringing about evil and destruction. Add to this "the tragedy of brute chance to which everything spiritual seems to be subject,"[45] and our "radical conditionedness"[46]—the fact that we find ourselves situated in a particular time and place, among particular people and issues—and behold, we find our capacity to act limited by contingency and necessity. Caught in a swirl of possibilities, chance, and history, we seem to bring forth misery, falsehood, and depravity. This, West contends, quoting Prosser Hall Frye, left him staggering as a youth. In a world plagued by "foolishness…ignorance…cruel accidents…fatal misunderstandings… chance mistakes,"[47] and social injustice, he was enveloped by "darkness."[48] Life was, as Kierkegaard rightly put it, "a compounded riddle"[49] that left him at a crossroads: either to give up in despair, to give himself over to destruction, or to try to preserve hope, compassion, and joy "in the face of the absurd....the nullity and nothingness that characterizes so much of our human endeavors."[50] West, however, did not throw in the towel; instead, he "kept alive some sense of possibility. Some sense of hope. Some sense of agency. Some sense of resistance in a moment of defeat."[51] This evokes Kierkegaard's discussion of anxiety and faith in *The Concept of Anxiety*, where anxiety is the awakening of freedom as "a kind of vertigo," and faith is the means to orient oneself.

In *The Concept of Anxiety*, Kierkegaard's pseudonym Vigilius Haufniensis, the watchman-psychologist of Copenhagen, maintains "anxiety is the dizziness of freedom, which....emerges when...freedom looks down into its own possibility, while laying hold of finiteness to support itself...succumbs...and...when it again rises...sees that it is guilty."[52] That is, anxiety's dizziness is like being perched on the edge of a cliff, while steadying oneself against some rocks, and then looking down into the chasm below. The abyss in this case is not some natural phenomenon, but a feature of oneself, namely, one's freedom or own vast capacity to act. But because one spends so much time worrying, rather than acting in an immediate and decisive way, one "is guilty."[53] Haufniensis provides a fuller explanation of this experience toward the end of the book.

In the last chapter of *The Concept of Anxiety*, he maintains that anxiety is an educator in the service of freedom or possibility that saves by faith. By this he means that anxiety teaches one what it means to be free by showing one all of freedom's possibilities, yet pointing beyond them:

---

[45]    West, "Pragmatism and the Tragic," p. 48.
[46]    See West, *The Cornel West Reader*, pp. 23–4 and West, "Pragmatism and the Tragic," pp. 32–3; p. 48.
[47]    West, "Pragmatism and the Tragic," p. 48.
[48]    West, *The Cornel West Reader*, p. 20.
[49]    *SKS* 23, 23–4, NB15:25 / *JP* 1, 7.
[50]    West, *The Cornel West Reader*, p. 33.
[51]    West, "Pragmatism and the Tragic," p. 48.
[52]    *SKS* 4, 366 / *CA*, 61. Translation slightly modified.
[53]    *SKS* 4, 366 / *CA*, 61. *SKS* 4, 439–40 / *CA*, 137–8.

> Whoever is educated by anxiety is educated by possibility, and only he who is educated by possibility is educated according to his infinitude. Therefore possibility is the weightiest of all categories....In possibility all things are equally possible, and whoever has truly been brought up by possibility has grasped the terrible as well as the joyful. So when such a person graduates from the school of possibility...he knows...that the terrible, perdition, and annihilation live next door to every man.[54]

In other words, anxiety teaches one that one could just as well do evil as do good. Haufniensis unpacks the terror of this thought by saying that our anxiety about our freedom makes our capacity for good or ill appear infinite: "When the discoveries of possibility are honestly administered, possibility will discover all the finitudes, but it will idealize them in the form of infinity and in anxiety overwhelm the individual until he again overcomes them in the anticipation of faith."[55] That is, anxiety presents us with an unending chain of discrete, possible actions, extending from a single action—in effect a habit—that could just as easily be an infinite chain of evil as an infinite chain of good.[56] Haufniensis' point here, though, is not just to say how anxiety overwhelms us, but it is also to say that we must recognize that anxiety is actually picturing the awakening of our freedom. Once we recognize this, we are in a position to allow freedom, coupled with faith, to teach us how to overcome this feeling so that we might actually become free beings:

> If an individual defrauds possibility, by which he is to be educated, he never arrives at faith....But if he does not defraud the possibility that wants to teach him and does not wheedle the anxiety that wants to save him, then he...must sink in possibility—his eye must become dizzy...confused...but then…he will emerge from the depth of the abyss lighter than all the troublesome and terrible things in life.[57]

To be oriented in one's freedom means that faith has helped one to pull oneself out of the vortex of possibilities, so that one can truly live. Learning to do this, though, is neither simple nor without risks. Suicide is a genuine possibility.[58] So too is spiritual death,[59] as West indicates in his remark about sitting in the church with

---

[54]     *SKS* 4, 455 / *CA*, 156. Quotation slightly modified.

[55]     *SKS* 4, 456 / *CA*, 157.

[56]     Note Augustine's discussion of nearly unbreakable habits and a "divided will" in Book VIII, Chapters 5, 9–11 of the *Confessions*, trans. by R.S. Pine-Coffin, Harmondsworth: Penguin 1961, pp. 164–5; pp. 172–7.

[57]     *SKS* 4, 456–7 / *CA*, 157–8. Translation slightly modified.

[58]     *SKS* 4, 457–8 / *CA*, 158–9.

[59]     *SKS* 4, 437–53 / *CA*, 136–54. Refusing to allow freedom to emerge as the ability to take responsibility for one's life, something Haufniensis calls "anxiety about the good," is also deadly. As he sees it, this "anxiety about the good" is a form of spiritual death that is at base "demonic," because it shuts out or "kills" the good altogether. According to Haufniensis, there are at least two kinds of "anxiety about the good" that lead to spiritual death, namely, "bestiality" and the more common "indolence." In regard to the former, one dies "psychically-somatically" as a spirit by deliberately allowing oneself to become like a beast. Here anxiety is expressed in not wanting to be helped out of this situation. For example, the bestial person who wakes up in "perdition" realizes that they are lost, that they cannot regain their capacity to be a responsible being, even recalls that there had been opportunities to do so, yet does

Job, Daniel, and "the Christ between Good Friday and Easter."[60] This is the reason that Haufniensis evokes the Passion story in the Gospels[61] and Socrates' trial and execution in Plato's *Apology* and *Phaedo*.[62] Both Jesus and Socrates refuse to get lost in the swirl of freedom, evil, and injustice. In spite of their fears (in Jesus' case) or others' tears (Socrates' case), both stay on the road to truth—"truth about their souls, societies, and world," as West puts it.[63]

Haufniensis concludes, then, that if one can make the difficult move of freedom by faith that Socrates made at his execution,[64] and that Jesus made in Gethsemane and before Judas,[65] one might come to "rest only in the Atonement"[66]—the being at one with "the power"—the freedom, the possibility, the God—"that posits us"[67] as free beings, to use the language of Kierkegaard's premier Christian pseudonym, Anti-Climacus, in *The Sickness unto Death*. With this, Haufniensis not only elaborates young Cornel West's anxiety, but he also gives him a fresh way to consider the black church's stress on faith in the face of "limit situations"[68] like anxiety. "Keep keeping on"[69] becomes a fresh call to believe in his own and others' potential for good, precisely as they find themselves in an earthly hell like Job, or before death like Socrates and Jesus. Kierkegaard's Anti-Climacus offers West something similar, yet more complicated in *The Sickness unto Death*.

In *The Sickness unto Death*, Anti-Climacus provides a discussion of despair that parallels Haufniensis' discussion of anxiety. Despair, however, illuminates the very structure and formation of human personality, and so is a much darker state than anxiety. As we have seen, anxiety is an amorphous and overwhelming worry about the broad range of consequences that can result from the use of one's freedom. At base, it is a fear of freedom, grounded in a lack of understanding of one's self. Despair, on the other hand, is an outright rejection of one's self. In its most basic

---

not want such freedom to be restored, even worries about such freedom being restored. In regard to the latter, one commits spiritual death "pneumatically" by deliberately drifting in indecision, by relying solely on the opinions of others, by cultivating an unfocused curiosity, by being "stupidly busy," etc. Here anxiety is the worry to keep responsibility at bay, is the need to keep putting freedom off, by using diversions. In either case, one kills one's spirit, kills the freedom that defines one as a human being, and so kills one's self by deliberately hindering one's responsible nature from coming forth at all. See especially *SKS* 4, 438–40 / *CA*, 137–8.

[60]    West, *The Cornel West Reader*, p. 20.
[61]    *SKS* 4, 454 / *CA*, 155. See also Mt 26:37, 38; Mk 14:33, 34; Mk 15:34; Jn 12:27; Jn 13:27.
[62]    *SKS* 4, 457–8 / *CA*, 159. See also Plato *Apology*, 40a–42a and Plato, *Phaedo*, 114d–118.
[63]    Cornel West, *Democracy Matters: Winning the Fight Against Imperialism*, New York: Penguin Press 2004, p. 208; with pp. 209–14. Quotation slightly modified.
[64]    *SKS* 4, 457–61 / *CA*, 159–62.
[65]    *SKS* 4, 454–5 / *CA*, 155.
[66]    *SKS* 4, 461 / *CA*, 162.
[67]    *SKS* 11, 130 / *SUD* 14. *SKS* 11, 157 / *SUD* 40. *SKS* 11, 242 / *SUD*, 131.
[68]    West, *The Cornel West Reader*, p. 20.
[69]    Ibid., p. 23. See with p. 20.

sense, despair means not being willing—or refusing—to be one's whole, multi-dimensional self as one was made to be.[70]

According to Kierkegaard, human being is composite. This includes the familiar mind (or soul)–body dialectic, which Anti-Climacus presents as the psychical and the physical, and idealist expansions on it, which Kierkegaard assumes from Georg Wilhelm Friedrich Hegel (1770–1831) and Johann Gottlieb Fichte (1762–1814), namely, infinitude and finitude, freedom and necessity, and eternity and time. On the one hand, then, human nature is constituted by that which is given, finite, necessary, and temporal, which includes the particular situation in which one is born; the people to whom one belongs (familial, ethnic, national); the historical circumstances in which one finds oneself; the unique traits that make one an individual; and so forth. On the other hand, human nature is also constituted by factors that transform or transcend one's given situation: the infinite, the free, and the eternal, to which one gains access primarily by the imagination.

Kierkegaard's complex conception of human being, though, does not entail a hierarchy of mind over body. Rather, it focuses on balancing or harmonizing the dualities of human personality. That is, Kierkegaard thinks that individuals should seek equilibrium among the dialectical elements of their composite natures by relating each element to the other, and to "the power"—God—that established them as "relating relations" or "selves."[71] We are freedom and necessity, eternity and time—at once—and before God. Indeed, this latter point—this being before God—is key. There is no balance, if faith's rhythmic pattern of inhaling and exhaling possibilities against a background of necessities is not operative. We must allow God—or "possibility in a pregnant sense"[72]—to pervade our given situations via a grace-imbued imagination. When we "get possibility" in this manner, says Anti-Climacus, we are able to "breathe," able to be transformed, if only for a moment, precisely as we need to be, so that our temporal existence is always aimed in creative and refreshing ways at wholeness and health—rather than becoming a prison in which we suffocate.[73] Herein Kierkegaard provides an important conceptual resource for West, especially as faith becomes a way to resist despair. Herein also is Kierkegaard's discussion of despair as dizziness—and as sin.

As Anti-Climacus sees it, when we "despair over something earthly or of something eternal"—either by treating our finite situation as though it were the only

---

[70]     Despair and anxiety are both ways of talking about sin for Kierkegaard, though not in the orthodox sense of sin or "sins." For him, sin is the stance or attitude that one takes toward the divine or God, not an innate state of moral and physical corruption. As such, sin is a "misrelation," a failure to relate properly to God—something that can lead to spiritual death and /or suicide. Given Kierkegaard's outlook, one might say that despair is a more intensified form of sin than anxiety, because it deals more directly with God, and so raises opposition to God—the demonic—in a more deliberate way. *SKS* 11, 217–42 / *SUD*, 105–31. Despair and anxiety, however, are not simply negative concepts for Kierkegaard. Both also mark the nobility of the human being in that both signify that one can stand upright and live in spite of the things that terrify one about human nature or that cause despair.

[71]     *SKS* 11, 129–30 / *SUD*, 13–14.

[72]     *SKS* 11, 153–7, see especially 155–7 / *SUD*, 37–41, see especially 40–1.

[73]     *SKS* 11, 154–5 / *SUD*, 38–40.

aspect of our lives, or by recognizing the limitations of our capacity to transform or transcend it, or by defiantly holding onto one or the other of these elements after realizing their deficiencies, or by refusing to allow a transcendent power to help us—we lose our equilibrium and become dizzy and confused.[74] This sense of being dizzy and confused, though, says Anti-Climacus, is a misunderstanding. We are not actually dizzy; rather, we are experiencing the results of a "misrelation," a fracturing or alienation of the self from itself, and from "the power" or "possibility" that "established it."[75] That is, as Kierkegaard puts it in a journal entry from 1848, "despair is related to spirit, to freedom, to responsibility," whereas dizziness resides in "an ambiguous joint boundary between the psychical and the physical"[76]—two dialectical components of human being that identify a person fundamentally as a rational, sentient, and bodied being, but not yet as a free being. Dizziness, then, is a disposition of the human psyche that affects the body, or vice versa. It, however, is not an appropriate way to talk about the misapplication of human freedom that occurs in despair. Despair's purported dizziness means that one is not aware of one's freedom as such. That is, one does not know that freedom is the capacity for uniting and balancing one's composite nature. Despair, then, is an unwillingness to take responsibility for one's whole self, whether one knows it or not. This, Anti-Climacus contends, is sin.[77]

Kierkegaard's position on despair seems rather harsh. A despairing person by definition is someone who is suffering, why, then, would one want to make this person responsible for her or his pain, or call this person sinful? Herein is a potential problem for West. As a person of African descent, whose people were exploited and demonized by Euro-American and European civilizations for over three hundred years, one might imagine that he would find talk about despair, sin, and responsibility inauthentic, even immoral. How can one think of blaming his people for being depressed, when entire civilizations are responsible for their despair?[78] Indeed, how can one even talk about personal sin, when the social and institutional evils done to black people need first to be confronted?

West recognizes that it is a mistake to read Kierkegaard in this way. To start, he knows that Kierkegaard is not demonizing black people—or anyone else for that matter. Unlike David Hume (1711–76) and Immanuel Kant (1724–1804), Kierkegaard never seems to have publicly disparaged persons of African descent, or claimed, as other Europeans regularly did, that black people have no souls, and so are immoral.[79] In fact,

---

[74]     *SKS* 11, 129–37 / *SUD*, 13–21. *SKS* 11, 145–87 / *SUD*, 29–74.
[75]     *SKS* 11, 130 / *SUD*, 14. *SKS* 11, 155 / *SUD*, 40.
[76]     *Pap.* VIII–2 B 168, p. 6 / *JP* 1, 749. Translation slightly modified.
[77]     *SKS* 11, 138–44 / *SUD*, 22–8. *SKS* 11, 161–3 / *SUD*, 47–9. *SKS* 11, 191–216 / *SUD*, 77–104.
[78]     In fact, Denmark itself not only participated in, but also benefitted from African chattel slavery! The Danish National Archives has an extensive collection of materials on the role of Denmark in the African slave trade and in establishing colonies and plantations in the West Indies, today's U.S. Virgin Islands.
[79]     David Hume, "Negroes...Naturally Inferior to the Whites...," and Immanuel Kant, "The Difference Between the Races," in *The Portable Enlightenment Reader*, ed. by Isaac Kramnick, New York: Penguin Books 1995, p. 629; pp. 637–9.

in spite of the fact that Denmark possessed slave-holding colonies in the West Indies, which in itself could have brought some Africans to Copenhagen in Kierkegaard's day, it seems likely that he knew very little about black people or slaves, beyond accounts or reports in newspapers and books, particularly Hegel's master–slave dialectic in the *Phenomenology of Spirit*, which privileges the position of the slave.[80]

Second, in promoting individual responsibility for the self one is or is to become, West also recognizes that Kierkegaard is not championing a "boot-strap" philosophy à la Horatio Alger.[81] Kierkegaard does not suggest that one take responsibility for improving one's life, without calling attention to the social conditions degrading and destroying one, and without calling attention to the fact that chance, contingency, and opportunity affect all of our decisions and actions. To assume such would mean ignoring Kierkegaard's contention in *Practice in Christianity* and *A Literary Review of Two Ages* that Copenhagen's avowedly Christian, yet thoroughly market-driven society effaces the individuality and integrity of its people by practicing a false equality—indeed, a false religion—that "levels" them all down into stock images or "reflections" of its values.[82] It would mean ignoring Kierkegaard's constant calls to his readers throughout his authorship to take existence seriously as "a gift" and "a task," which entails critical reflection about one's personal and social situation in time.[83] It would mean ignoring Kierkegaard's tragi-comic sensibility, especially under the pseudonym Johannes Climacus, who recognizes the uncertainty of life, the prevalence of death, the role that despair, terror, and chance play in our decisions, and especially the tragedy and comedy that come along with faith.[84] And it would mean ignoring Kierkegaard's avowed role as a gadfly to his age on all of these points.[85] Indeed, West's identification of himself in a similar role and alignment of his own cultural analyses and critiques of America's market society, particularly in Christian, Marxist, and pragmatist terms, with what he calls Kierkegaard's "quest for meaning"

---

[80]   G.W.F. Hegel, *Phenomenology of Spirit*, trans. by A.V. Miller, Oxford: Oxford University Press 1977, pp. 111–19. Unfortunately, Hegel loses his high estimation of the slave in other works. See Susan Buck-Morss, *Hegel, Haiti, and Universal History*, Pittsburgh: University of Pittsburgh Press 2009, pp. 59–75.

[81]   See Cornel West, "Nihilism in Black America," in *Race Matters*, Boston: Beacon Press 1993, pp. 11–14. Horatio Alger, Jr. was a nineteenth-century American writer of popular, dime-store novels that focused on poor, urban boys, who rose from rags to riches by means of their own ingenuity and moral courage in spite of adversity.

[82]   *SKS* 12, 96–7 / *PC*, 87–8. *SKS* 8, 78–92 / *TA*, 81–96. *SKS* 8, 98–104 / *TA*, 103–8. "Leveling" is the means by which a shrewd, self-serving, and indolent liberal society imposes its conception of what counts as a human being on individuals who, according to Kierkegaard, should instead be defined by God or the divine. As Kierkegaard sees it, our relationship to God opens us up to an authentic form of being human—"God with us" (Mt 1:23)—that is truly absolute, though not yet actual. See also Alastair Hannay, *Kierkegaard: A Biography*, Cambridge: Cambridge University Press 2001, pp. 331–9.

[83]   *SKS* 1, 312–15 / *CI*, 276–9.

[84]   Cf. *SKS* 7, 131 / *CUP1*, 140. *SKS* 7, 153–4 / *CUP1*, 166–7. *SKS* 7, 206 / *CUP1*, 225. *SKS* 7, 211 / *CUP1*, 232. *SKS* 7, 230–8 / *CUP1*, 253–62. *SKS* 4, 217 / *PF*, 8. *SKS* 4, 242–3 / *PF*, 36. *SKS* 12, 50–65 / *PC*, 36–53. *SKS* 12, 187–194 / *PC*, 187–96.

[85]   *SKS* 12, 97 / *PC*, 88. *Pap.* XI–3 B 53 / *JP* 6, 6943. *SKS* 20, 184, NB2:176 / *JP* 1, 641.

demonstrate that he does no such thing.[86] In fact, his "prophetic pragmatism"—a Marxist-inspired, Christian-oriented, philosophical culture criticism in the tradition of Ralph Waldo Emerson (1803–82), John Dewey, W.E.B. Du Bois (1868–1963), and Richard Rorty—suggests that he may well even see parallels between Kierkegaard's religious critique of his modern market society and his own religious, political, and economic critique of America's racialized market culture, since on his view, white supremacy, especially as practiced through American capitalism, is the idol that was and still is effacing the individuality and integrity of all Americans, especially people of color and young people.[87]

For West, then, Kierkegaard's discussion of despair cannot be a tirade about black people's irresponsibility, or a discussion of their inherent sinfulness as demonstrated by the blackness of their skins, but rather a way to think through the dynamics of black people's despair—particularly self-hatred. Nowhere is this more evident than in "Black Strivings in a Twilight Civilization," a long reflection on W.E.B. Du Bois that contrasts Richard Wright's early novel, *Native Son*, with Toni Morrison's masterpiece, *Beloved*.[88]

### III. Despair and Faith: West and Kierkegaard on Whole Human Being—in Hell

Toward the end of "Black Strivings in a Twilight Civilization," where he focuses on Wright's character Bigger Thomas, West presents one of his most compelling treatments of black despair. He opens by quoting a passage from Du Bois' classic, *The Souls of Black Folk*:

> This is the history of the human heart,—the tale of a black boy who many long years ago began to struggle with life that he might know the world and know himself. Three temptations he met on those dark dunes that lay gray and dismal before the wonder-eyes of the child: the Temptation of Hate, that stood out against the red dawn; the Temptation of Despair, that darkened noonday; and the Temptation of Doubt, that ever steals along with twilight. Above all, you must hear of the vales he crossed,—the Valley of Humiliation and the Valley of the Shadow of Death.[89]

As West sees it, Wright's 20-year-old Bigger Thomas does not make it through these "Temptations" and "Valleys," because he becomes the very embodiment of hate and despair.

---

[86]     Cornel West "The Indispensability, yet Insufficiency of Marxist Theory," in *The Cornel West Reader*, p. 215. This interview originally appears as Cornel West, "On the Influence of Lukács: Interview by Eva L. Corredor," in *Prophetic Reflections: Notes on Race and Power in America*, Monroe, Maine: Common Courage Press 1993 (*Beyond Eurocentrism and Multiculturalism*, vol. 2), pp. 47–71.
[87]     West, *The American Evasion of Philosophy*, pp. 211–39; *The Cornel West Reader*, pp. 115–16.
[88]     West, *The Cornel West Reader*, pp. 109–11. See with West, "Pragmatism and the Tragic," p. 48, where West discusses Josiah Royce's position on being tempted to do evil.
[89]     W.E.B. Du Bois, *The Souls of Black Folk*, New York: Fawcett Publications 1961, p. 157, as quoted in West, *The Cornel West Reader*, p. 109.

Consumed by the terror, degradation, and humiliation that encompass his and other black people's lives in segregated 1930s America, Bigger hates himself, his family, and his people—not to mention white people.[90] He and his people are pressed by law and the customs and practices of the dominant culture into squalid living conditions on the South Side of Chicago, with little chance for advancement outside of stealing, killing, or fighting.[91] Disillusioned, alone, and despairing, Bigger goes the way of stealing, killing, and fighting, but not without considerable reflection.[92] Like young Cornel West in the 1950s and 1960s, he is terrified and confused by the enigmatic nature of human beings in his world. He does not understand why whites have locked him and his people into oppressive situations that make them all despise each other.[93] In fact, he dreads this "compounded riddle," as Kierkegaard would put it, especially as it makes him an enigma to himself.[94] Bigger, however, cannot ignore this fact. He lives, breathes, and eats it.[95] Indeed, he is so overwhelmed by it, so dazed and dizzied by what racism and its negative effects may drive him and others to do, that he finds himself suffocating in this absurdity.[96] As a result, he lashes out in anger and pain by unintentionally and then intentionally killing two young women—black Bessie Mears, his girlfriend, and white Mary Dalton, the daughter of his wealthy employer and the girlfriend of his white, male, Communist friend Jan Erlone.[97]

From a Kierkegaardian perspective, which West seems certainly to have cultivated in this essay, Bigger's hatred of himself and his world comes forth initially as a kind of "despair over the earthly."[98] He wants to be rid of his black self and his anti-black world, because he sees no "possibility" in either.[99] Bigger, however, does not commit suicide, which, on Anti-Climacus' view, would be a display of "despair of the eternal," the idea that he could not "make or invent" a more authentic black self

---

[90]    Richard Wright, *Early Works: Lawd Today!, Uncle Tom's Children, Native Son*, New York: Library of America 1991, p. 45; pp. 463–5; pp. 467–72; pp. 479–83. The edition of *Native Son* in this collection is a restored version of the 1940 edition originally published by Harper and Brothers, and used by West in "Black Strivings in a Twilight Civilization." See West, *The Cornel West Reader*, pp. 109–14; pp. 577–8, notes 50–4, 57–8, 60, and 63.

[91]    Wright, *Early Works: Native Son*, pp. 447–84.

[92]    Ibid., p. 453; pp. 459–84, see especially p. 453; pp. 463–5; pp. 471–2; p. 476; pp. 771–86; pp. 844–9.

[93]    West, *The Cornel West Reader*, p. 20; 109; p. 112; Cowan, *Cornel West*, p. 2; Wright, *Early Works: Native Son*, pp. 459–465.

[94]    Wright, *Early Works: Native Son*, p. 465; pp. 732–3; cf. *SKS* 23, 24, NB15:25 / *JP* 1, 7.

[95]    Wright, *Early Works: Native Son*, p. 463.

[96]    Ibid., pp. 463–5. Indeed, Wright makes sure that the reader feels this vertigo throughout the story.

[97]    Ibid., pp. 520–32; pp. 606–16; pp. 655–69; pp. 771–80.

[98]    *SKS* 11, 165–75 / *SUD*, 50–60. Note that Anti-Climacus' explications of despair do not apply to Bigger Thomas' situation point for point. I am adapting his theories to Bigger's situation and outlook.

[99]    Wright, *Early Works: Native Son*, p. 453; p. 570; cf. *SKS* 11, 153–7 / *SUD*, 37–42. *SKS* 11, 165–75 / *SUD*, 50–60.

in America than his humiliated and despised self.[100] Rather, he tries to inflict as much pain on his world as it inflicts on him. In fact, the only time that Bigger feels alive is when he is inflicting pain on others, especially white people, because only then does he feel that he has power or agency.[101] From Anti-Climacus' perspective, this is a form of defiance—a stronger misuse of freedom than simply "despairing over the earthly" and "of the eternal."[102] Bigger wants to be himself "in accordance with his misery."[103] He believes that white people are out to get him in the same way that evil forces are out to get Job, and wants no help, not even from "God in heaven."[104] Thus, he rejects redemption as a belief in his own and others' humanity, as his attorney Boris Max puts it, and he rejects redemption as faith and forgiveness in the Christian terms in which his mother's pastor Reverend Hammond and the Catholic priest in the prison put it.[105] In a moment of damning clarity, before he is executed, and to Max's horror, he declares that others have not let him be a whole human being; therefore, he has become a killer without remorse, just like those in power. As Anti-Climacus sees it, then, Bigger presents himself as damning "evidence" against white society.[106] He gives up his humanity, indeed kills "possibility" or God, where he is concerned, which is why Max shudders.[107] Bigger shows Max at close range what a lost soul—a "deep-seated colonized mind," to use West's expression—looks like: a person who has become one with the forces of hell.[108]

West is disturbed by Richard Wright's character. He sees him in too many black youths today, and tries to give them alternatives by offering them a philosophy of hope in an accessible medium: hip-hop music.[109] He knows that they struggle to gain meaningful ground in America's empty, hedonistic culture, which tells them— and all people—that no one cares for them or for anything—except money and

---

[100]      *SKS* 11, 175–80 / *SUD*, 60–7; West, *The Cornel West Reader*, p. 110.

[101]      Wright, *Early Works: Native Son*, pp. 479–84; pp. 564–5; p. 605; p. 840; p. 845; p. 849.

[102]      *SKS* 11, 161–87 / *SUD*, 47–74.

[103]      *SKS* 11, 187 / *SUD*, 73–4.

[104]      West, *The Cornel West Reader*, p. 110; Wright, *Early Works: Native Son*, pp. 771–7; *SKS* 11, 186 / *SUD*, 72.

[105]      Wright, *Early Works: Native Son*, pp. 762–3, pp. 848–50; cf. *SKS* 11, 186 / *SUD*, 72. *SKS* 11, 187 / *SUD*, 73–4. *SKS* 11, 225–6 / *SUD*, 113–14. *SKS* 11, 236 / *SUD*, 125. *SKS* 11, 242 / *SUD*, 131.

[106]      Wright, *Early Works: Native Son*, p. 849; cf. *SKS* 11, 187 / *SUD*, 73–4.

[107]      Wright, *Early Works: Native Son*, pp. 762–3; pp. 848–50; cf. *SKS* 11, 155–7 / *SUD*, 40. *SKS* 11, 226 / *SUD*, 114. *SKS* 11, 236 / *SUD*, 125. *SKS* 11, 242 / *SUD*, 131.

[108]      West, *The Cornel West Reader*, p. 111.

[109]      West, *Democracy Matters*, p. 185. West's focus on developing the "prophetic," as opposed to "Constantinian," dimension of hip-hop and rap culture is part of the educational wing of his prophetic pragmatism. Speaking about his current production of hip-hop CDs, West says of his Sacramento-based hip-hop group, Four Black Men Who Mean Business (4BMWMB), that their "CDs are danceable education for artistic and political ends" (p. 185). This goes hand-in-hand with his remark about "channeling wisdom" into a "televisual culture" in his interview with David Smith. See West, *The Cornel West Reader*, p. 553.

power.[110] He also knows that they, like Bigger Thomas, lack viable resources for relief.[111] Indeed, as we have seen, West himself is no stranger to such struggles. Like Bigger, he grew up in a segregated society, and experienced the same rage. In fact, he regularly got into fights, and even slapped a pregnant white teacher.[112] Because of his family, his church, his community—and Kierkegaard, though, West was able to get "possibility"—or God—in a way that Bigger could not.[113] He had parents who gave him love and a stable home, who showed him the meaning of justice and compassion, and who never wondered aloud, as Bigger's mother did, why they brought him into the world.[114] His family, church, and community helped him to channel his rage into social activism.[115] And he found a modern thinker who helped him to make sense of his experiences, and who encouraged him to engage life intellectually, morally, and religiously with the focus, passion, and earnestness of a Socrates—a direction that resonated with his emerging and abiding admiration of Martin Luther King, Jr.[116] Thus, unlike Bigger, West was able to make the moves of faith that continually confront and counter despair.

West knows, though, that the moves of this kind of faith are neither made once, nor are easy to make, since they are always made precisely as one stands in hell—or out over 70,000 fathoms, where, as Climacus notes, doubt is one's constant companion.[117] Hence his primary question is always: "How do you really struggle against the suffering in a loving way, to leave a legacy in which people would be able to accent their own loving possibility in the midst of so much evil?"[118] That said, West knows that as fragile as this existential faith might be, it is nevertheless essential. This is the reason that he cautiously, yet deliberately presents Toni Morrison's character Baby Suggs, the spiritual leader of a group of ex-slaves, as a counter to Wright's Bigger Thomas.[119]

---

[110]     West, *The Cornel West Reader*, p. 112; p. 116; and West, *Democracy Matters*, pp. 179–86.

[111]     West, *The Cornel West Reader*, p. 116; *Race Matters*, pp. 14–18. See also Cornel West, "Winter in Afro-America," in *Prophetic Fragments*, pp. 35–7; West, *Race Matters*, pp. 9–20; Floyd W. Hayes, "Cornel West and Afro-Nihilism," in *Cornel West: A Critical Reader*, pp. 245–60; and West, "Afterword," in *Cornel West: A Critical Reader*, pp. 357–8, for one of West's earliest discussions of black nihilism, for West's most well-known piece on black nihilism, for a critique of West's discussions of black nihilism, and for West's response to such criticism.

[112]     Cowan, *Cornel West*, p. 2.

[113]     West, *The Cornel West Reader*, p. 20. See with Cornel West, "A Philosophical View of Easter," in *The Cornel West Reader*, pp. 418–19; West, *The American Evasion of Philosophy*, p. 233. Cf. *SKS* 11, 155–7 / *SUD*, 40.

[114]     West, *The Cornel West Reader*, pp. 3–4; pp. 19–21; Wright, *Early Works: Native Son*, p. 451.

[115]     West, *The Cornel West Reader*, pp. 3–7.

[116]     Ibid., pp. 3–4; p. 20.

[117]     Ibid., p. 108; pp. 112–13; p. 116; pp. 483–4; cf. *SKS* 7, 131 / *CUP1*, 140.

[118]     West, *The Cornel West Reader*, p. 20.

[119]     Ibid., pp. 107–8; pp. 112–13.

According to West, Baby Suggs embodies the kind of spirituality that is needed to make black people personally, socially, and politically whole.[120] She gathers her abused and exploited people in a wooded clearing in order to encourage them to see and to embrace the beauty and goodness of their persons. There, she tells them that "the only grace they could have was the grace they could imagine...if they could not see it, they would not have it."[121] Baby Suggs then elaborates this point by telling them to love their whole selves, because by doing so, they could be joyful and free, and resist a world that did not love them.[122] Or to put it in Anti-Climacus' terms, they could "get possibility" and live.[123]

Anti-Climacus' idea of "getting possibility" is not the only way that Kierkegaard's concept of human personality might be used to explicate the spirituality of Baby Suggs. His idea of a grace-imbued imagination—the foundation of his idea of "getting possibility"—presents Baby Suggs' charge to her people as a call to envision and to effect the good in the midst of evil. As Anti-Climacus sees it, "whatever of feeling, knowing, and willing" they have depends upon imagination and its vision of their "possibility" or potential as selves.[124] Thus, if they want to be whole, they must not only understand and challenge the forces that seek to destroy them, but they must also have a vision of what wholeness means, precisely as Baby Suggs suggests, and allow this vision to permeate the very way in which they think, feel, and act in the world.

Kierkegaard provides his own illustration of this point, and presents it as a matter of moral and spiritual beauty, in his 1849 discourses on the lilies and the birds—especially when read with the Christian ethic of *Works of Love* and the problems of modern Christendom discussed in *A Literary Review of Two Ages*. In *The Lily of the Field and the Bird of the Air*, Kierkegaard maintains that we human beings should be like the lily on the inhospitable heath, which obeys its Creator by blooming in all its glorious beauty in spite of its situation. We should transcend the hostile world by imagining a new way of living—an existence in which the possibility for the good, a divine love "blooming" in and filling up human life—is at the core of all human relations as the "middle" and defining term.[125] We, however, should not stay

---

[120]     West, *The Cornel West Reader*, pp. 107–8; West, *Race Matters*, p. 19. According to West, Baby Suggs exemplifies a love ethic that addresses nihilism head on as a "disease of the soul" (see West, *Race Matters*, pp. 18–19). Such a love ethic, on his view, must be part of a "politics of conversion" (see West, *Race Matters*, pp. 18–20). Morrison's picturing of such a love ethic, and its parallels in black jazz, blues, and religious music, is undoubtedly one reason why West thinks that these works are more masterful "intellectual" treatments of black experience than much of black thought. For him, they best grasp the "funk" of black life. See West, "Afterword," in *Cornel West: A Critical Reader*, pp. 349–50.

[121]     Toni Morrison, *Beloved: A Novel*, New York: New American Library 1987, pp. 87–9, as quoted in West, *The Cornel West Reader*, p. 107.

[122]     West, *The Cornel West Reader*, pp. 107–8.

[123]     Ibid.; cf. *SKS* 11, 155–7 / *SUD*, 40.

[124]     *SKS* 11, 147 / *SUD*, 31.

[125]     *SKS* 11, 31–3 / *WA*, 27–9. In *Works of Love*, Kierkegaard claims that human relations have God as "the middle term." See *SKS* 9, 110 / *WL*, 107. By this he means that we are to love each other by helping each other to love God. That is, as Augustine would say, we are

in heaven, beholding this divine vision. Rather, we should bring it back to the world, and seek to make it actual—a "transforming vision," as Jamie Ferreira might put it.[126] Like the lily, we should seek to "bloom" in all of our potential as creative beings, able to "improvise" community, to use West's terms, precisely as we stand in a society that effaces our humanity.[127] Indeed, like Henry David Thoreau's water lily or Giacomo Leopardi's poem "Broom, or the Flower of the Desert," which West quotes appreciatively in an essay on the spirituals, we should live a life whose "moral fragrance" transcends the acrid odors of an unjust society, and provides "a touch of consolation in the wasteland."[128] Is this not what Baby Suggs is saying, feeling, and doing, when she offers her suffering people "her great big heart"?:

> She told them that the only grace they could have was the grace they could imagine. That if they could not see it, they would not have it.
> "Here," she said, "in this here place, we flesh; flesh that weeps, laughs; flesh that dances on bare feet in grass. Love it. Love it hard. Yonder they do not love your flesh. They despise it. They don't love your eyes; they'd just as soon pick em out. No more do they love the skin on your back. Yonder they flay it. And O my people they do not love your hands. Those they only use, tie, bind, chop off and leave empty. Love your hands! Love them. Raise them up and kiss them. Touch others with them, pat them together, stroke them on your face 'cause they don't love that either. *You* got to love it, *you*! And no, they ain't in love with your mouth. Yonder, out there, they will see it broken and break it again. What you say out of it they will not heed. What you scream from it they do not hear. What you put into it to nourish your body they will snatch away and give you leavins instead. No, they don't love your mouth. *You* got to love it. This is flesh I'm talking about here. Flesh that needs to be loved. Feet that need to rest and to dance; backs that need support; shoulders that need arms, strong arms I'm telling you. And O my people, out yonder, hear me, they do not love your neck unnoosed and straight. So love your neck; put a hand on it, grace it, stroke it and hold it up. And all your inside parts

---

to love each other "in God," to mirror the Trinity by having a spirit of divine love in our midst, as lover-love-beloved. See *SKS* 9, 110 / *WL*, 107. *SKS* 9, 123–4 / *WL*, 120–1. See also St. Augustine, *On Christian Doctrine*, trans. by D.W. Robertson, Jr., New York: Macmillan Publishing Company 1958, pp. 18–33, see especially pp. 18–19 and pp. 23–30, which corresponds to Book I, chapters xxii–xl, see especially Book I, chapters xxii, xxvii–xxxv; see also *The Trinity*, trans. by Stephen McKenna, C.S.S.R., *The Fathers of the Church: A New Translation*, ed. by Hermigild Dressler, O.S.M., Washington, D.C.: Catholic University of America Press 1963, pp. 243–67, see especially pp. 266–7, which corresponds to Book VIII, especially chapter 10. Put in Anti-Climacus' terms, this means that as each person needs "God or possibility in the most pregnant sense," then human relations are fundamentally about making a community in which such divine possibility is at the core. Cf. *SKS* 11, 157 / *SUD*, 40; with *SKS* 9, 17–24 / *WL*, 5–16; *SKS* 9, 110 / *WL*, 107; *SKS* 9, 123–4 / *WL*, 120–1.

[126]     "Transforming vision" is part of the title and theme of M. Jamie Ferreira's book, *Transforming Vision: Imagination and Will in Kierkegaardian Faith*, Oxford: Clarendon Press 1991.

[127]     *SKS* 8, 78–92 / *TA*, 81–96. *SKS* 8, 98–104 / *TA*, 103–8. *SKS* 12, 96–7 / *PC*, 87–8. West, *The American Evasion of Philosophy*, pp. 212–14; pp. 228–35; West, *Race Matters*, pp. 18–20.

[128]     Henry David Thoreau, "Slavery in Massachusetts," *Liberator*, July 21, 1854, p. 4; and West, "The Spirituals as Lyrical Poetry," in *The Cornel West Reader*, p. 468.

that they'd just as soon slop for hogs, you got to love them. The dark, dark liver—love it, love it, and the beat and beating heart, love that too. More than eyes or feet. More than lungs that have yet to draw free air. More than your life-holding womb and your life-giving private parts, hear me now, love your heart. For this is the prize." Saying no more, she stood up then and danced with her twisted hip the rest of what her heart had to say while the others opened their mouths and gave her the music. Long notes held until the four-part harmony was perfect enough for their deeply loved flesh.[129]

Baby Suggs tells her people to imagine a divine, black love, to see a way of living in which black people's bodies and souls are cherished, and then to cherish each other—no matter what their pasts may hold. Indeed, on saying this, Baby Suggs opens a glorious moment of dancing and singing in accord with this love—something mirrored at the end of the novel in the love and hope of her daughter-in-law Sethe and Sethe's lover Paul D.[130] There, Paul D. speaks of Sethe's love gathering "the pieces" or fragments of his life, and giving them back to him "in all the right order."[131] This is nothing less than a vision of Kierkegaard's self in a moment of personal and social integration.

These images of black selves made whole by faith and imagination, though, not only evoke Anti-Climacus' image of the healthy, breathing self, who stands before God, but they also call forth Kierkegaard's idea of the beauty of the self, a kind of "harmony of the spheres."[132] This is the image of the centrifugal and centripetal movement of the planets, which he uses to address the unity of the self in itself, in society, and in relation to the divine. This is also the double movement of which Socrates speaks in his allegory of the cave, where one goes out of the cave into the sunshine, and then returns bringing the light of the sun—enlightenment—to the

---

[129]    Morrison, *Beloved*, pp. 87–9, as quoted in West, *The Cornel West Reader*, pp. 107–8. Cf. *SKS* 11, 1 47 / *SUD*, 31. *SKS* 11, 31–3 / *WA*, 27–8. *SKS* 11, 42–3 / *WA*, 38–9. *SKS* 11, 47–8 / *WA*, 44–5.

[130]    See Morrison, *Beloved*, pp. 87–9; pp. 272–3. Morrison bases Sethe on an actual nineteenth-century slave woman named Margaret Garner, who ran away with her children and husband from slavery in Kentucky in 1856, but who was tracked down in Ohio by her master and federal marshals. Instead of returning to Kentucky with them, Garner attempted to murder her children with a butcher knife. She only succeeded in killing her baby daughter. See Steven Weisenburger, *Modern Medea: A Family Story of Slavery and Child Murder from the Old South*, New York: Hill and Wang 1998. The theme of child murder in *Beloved* evokes Kierkegaard's *Fear and Trembling* with its focus on the Abraham and Isaac story (Gen 22:1–19). Morrison's Abraham and Isaac story, however, lacks the staying hand of God. In a world in which all black people are Isaacs—that is, all black people are sacrifices to a white patriarchal society and its gods or idols of slavery and money—to use the terms of Frances E.W. Harper and the leaders of Maine's political abolitionist movement—Sethe sees no possibility for her and her children, and so in desperation, tries to kill them. In light of this kind of despair, Baby Suggs' faith shines very bright indeed. Sethe, as well as the other ex-slaves in their community, were literally and spiritually living in hell. Note that Harper wrote a poem on the Margaret Garner affair that she titled, "The Slave Mother: A Tale of the Ohio."

[131]    Morrison, *Beloved*, pp. 272–3.

[132]    *Pap.* I B 2, pp. 174–5 / *JP* 5, 5116. *SKS* 8, 60–3 / *TA*, 63. *Pap.* X–5 B 5, p. 4 / *WA*, 199. See also Mooney, *Selves in Discord and Resolve*, pp. 89–103.

inhabitants who sit in darkness.[133] Baby Suggs' bringing of love to her community is just such a graceful and gracious movement of bringing light and beauty into the darkness of American society. As such, it is a presentation of the aesthetic as the fully-formed lives of ordinary black people, and as the product of religious and moral ideals and actions—a movement that evokes Kierkegaard's Christian conception of poetic living.[134]

As Kierkegaard notes, though, the vision of divine love and beauty that he illustrates, and that Morrison and West evoke, is not something we can effect once and for all, or even fully attain, even though it is something that we desperately need.[135] Nor is it something that can be validated or made objectively certain by rational arguments.[136] Rather, this vision of divine love is something to which we must always be open, something for which we must always strive, and something for which we must be willing to risk all, since promoting it means putting ourselves at odds with the idolatrous ways of the world, precisely as Socrates, Jesus—and West would add—Martin Luther King, Jr. did.[137] Faith in such a vision, then, especially when full and vibrant, is itself a light shining in the darkness, a flower blooming in the desert—or on a dung heap, and a jazz saxophonist wailing and praying at once.[138] This is the "melioristic" heart of West's "blues philosophy"—an outlook that unites the vision of black literature and music with the insights and sensibilities of a soulful Dane.[139]

---

[133] Plato, *Republic*, 7.514a–520e; cf. *SKS* 11, 146 / *SUD*, 29–30 and *SKS* 11, 32 / *WA*, 27–8, on the double movement of Kierkegaard's faithful self, who seeks to be balanced before God, and the lily's own message to the anxious individual in the double movement constituting its "additional" or spiritual beauty.

[134] Cf. Morrison, *Beloved*, pp. 87–9; pp. 272–3.

[135] The "human being's perfection," says Kierkegaard, "is to need God," because, as he sees it, needing God, which is the same as loving God, "is the highest good." See *SKS* 10, 68 / *CD*, 64. *SKS* 10, 210 / *CD*, 200.

[136] Faith, then, as Kierkegaard and his pseudonyms indicate, and West affirms, can be nothing other than a "leap into the arms of God." See *SKS* 8, 103 / *TA*, 108. See also *SKS* 7, 174–227 / *CUP1*, 188–249; West, *Prophesy Deliverance!*, pp. 96–8; and Cornel West, "On Paul Holmer's *The Grammar of Faith*," in *Prophetic Fragments*, pp. 229–33.

[137] *SKS* 7, 184–97 / *CUP1*, 201–16. *SKS* 8, 81–92 / *TA*, 84–96. *SKS* 9, 103–36 / *WL*, 99–134. *SKS* 12, 50–65 / *PC*, 36–53. *SKS* 12, 96–7 / *PC*, 87–8. *SKS* 12, 186–94 / *PC*, 186–96. West, *Democracy Matters*, pp. 201–18; West, *The Cornel West Reader*, p. 419; Cornel West, "Martin Luther King, Jr.," in *Prophetic Fragments*, p. 10.

[138] West, *The Cornel West Reader*, pp. 468–70; *SKS* 11, 31–3 / *WA*, 27–9. *SKS* 11, 40–8 / *WA*, 36–45.

[139] West, *The Cornel West Reader*, p. xvi.

# Bibliography

*I. References to or Uses of Kierkegaard in West's Corpus*

"A Philosophical View of Easter," *Dialog: A Journal of Theology*, vol. 19, no. 1, 1980, pp. 21–4.

Review of "Paul Holmer, *The Grammar of Faith* (New York: Harper and Row 1978)," *Union Seminary Quarterly Review*, vol. 35, nos. 3–4, 1980, pp. 279–85.

*Prophesy Deliverance!: An Afro-American Revolutionary Christianity*, Philadelphia, Pennsylvania: Westminster Press 1982, pp. 96–8; p. 106; p. 167, note 2.

"Joie Subversive et Patience Révolutionnaire: L'Evangile selon les Afro-Américains," *Le Monde Diplomatique*, October 1984, pp. 24–5. (English translation: "Subversive Joy and Revolutionary Patience in Black Christianity," in *Prophetic Fragments*, Grand Rapids, Michigan and Trenton, New Jersey: Eerdmans and Africa World Press, Inc. 1988, p. 161.)

Review of "Elisabeth Schüssler Fiorenza, *In Memory of Her: A Feminist Theological Reconstruction of Christian Origins* (New York: Crossroad 1983)," *Religious Studies Review*, vol. 11, no. 1, 1985, pp. 1–4.

"On Pascal's Significance," in *Prophetic Fragments*, Grand Rapids, Michigan and Trenton, New Jersey: Eerdmans and Africa World Press 1988, p. 235.

*The American Evasion of Philosophy: A Genealogy of Pragmatism*, Madison, Wisconsin: University of Wisconsin Press 1989, p. 36; p. 128; p. 152; p. 159; p. 215; p. 233.

*Keeping Faith: Philosophy and Race in America*, New York: Routledge 1993, pp. xi–xii.

"On the Influence of Lukács: Interview by Eva L. Corredor," in *Prophetic Reflections: Notes on Race and Power in America*, Monroe, Maine: Common Courage Press 1993 (*Beyond Eurocentrism and Multiculturalism*, vol. 2), p. 49.

"Cornel West," in *African-American Philosophers: 17 Conversations*, ed. by George Yancy, New York: Routledge 1998, pp. 33–4; p. 36; p. 39; pp. 44–5. (Revised and reprinted as "On My Intellectual Vocation," in *The Cornel West Reader*, ed. by Cornel West, New York: Basic Civitas Books, Perseus Book Group 1999, pp. 20–1; p. 23; p. 26; pp. 30–1.)

"Chekhov, Coltrane and Democracy," in *The Cornel West Reader*, ed. by Cornel West, New York: Basic Civitas Books, Perseus Book Group 1999, p. 554; p. 561.

"Introduction: To Be Human, Modern and American," *The Cornel West Reader*, ed. by Cornel West, New York: Basic Civitas Books, Perseus Book Group 1999, p. xvi.

## II. Sources of West's Knowledge of Kierkegaard

Barth, Karl, *The Epistle to the Romans*, trans. by Edwyn C. Hoskyns, London: Oxford University Press 1968, p. 29; p. 38; p. 57; p. 99; pp. 116–17; p. 136; p. 252; pp. 279–80; p. 338; p. 395; pp. 439–43; p. 468; pp. 495–6; p. 498.

Heidegger, Martin, *Being and Time*, trans. by John Macquarrie and Edward Robinson, New York: Harper and Row 1962, p. 492, Division One, Chapter Six, note iv; p. 494, Division Two, Section 45 [*sic*], note vi; and p. 497, Division Two, Chapter Four, note iii; referring to p. 235, note iv; p. 293, note vi; p. 388, note iii.

Holmer, Paul, *The Grammar of Faith*, New York: Harper and Row 1978.

Kierkegaard, Søren, *Philosophical Fragments*, trans. by David F. Swenson, Princeton, New Jersey: Princeton University Press 1936.

— *Concluding Unscientific Postscript*, trans. by David F. Swenson and Walter Lowrie, Princeton, New Jersey: Princeton University Press 1968.

Niebuhr, Reinhold, *The Nature and Destiny of Man: A Christian Interpretation*, vols. 1–2, New York: Charles Scribner's Sons 1964, vol. 1, p. 44, note 4; p. 75; p. 81; p. 163; pp. 170–1; p. 182; pp. 242–3; p. 245; pp. 251–2; p. 254; pp. 263–4.

Rorty, Richard, *Philosophy and the Mirror of Nature*, Princeton, New Jersey: Princeton University Press 1979, p. 367; p. 369; p. 376; p. 394.

Tillich, Paul, *Systematic Theology*, vols. 1–3, Chicago, Illinois: University of Chicago Press 1951–63, vol. 1, p. 12; p. 57, note 15; p. 119; p. 154; p. 165; p. 215; p. 275; vol. 2, p. 25; pp. 34–5; pp. 52–3; p. 75; p. 114; p. 133; vol. 3, pp. 160–1.

— *The Courage to Be*, New Haven, Connecticut: Yale University Press 1952, pp. 125–6; p. 135; p. 138; p. 142.

— *Theology of Culture*, ed. by Robert C. Kimball, London: Oxford University Press 1959, pp. 76–9; p. 83; p. 85; pp. 89–91; pp. 96–7; p. 99; pp. 101–2; pp. 109–10.

— *Dynamics of Faith*, New York: Harper Torch Books, Harper and Row 1957.

## III. Secondary Literature on West's Relation to Kierkegaard

Gordon, Lewis R., "The Unacknowledged Fourth Tradition: An Essay on Nihilism, Decadence, and the Black Intellectual Tradition in the Existential Pragmatic Thought of Cornel West," in *Cornel West: A Critical Reader*, ed. by George Yancy, Malden, Massachusetts: Blackwell Publishing 2001, pp. 41–3; p. 46.

Johnson, Clarence Sholé, *Cornel West and Philosophy: The Quest for Social Justice*, New York: Routledge 2003, pp. 3–4.

Pittman, John P., " 'Radical Historicism,' Anti-Philosophy, and Marxism," in *Cornel West: A Critical Reader*, ed. by George Yancy, Malden, Massachusetts: Blackwell Publishing 2001, pp. 237–8.

Yancy, George, "Cornel West: The Vanguard of Existential and Democratic Hope," in *Cornel West: A Critical Reader*, ed. by George Yancy, Malden, Massachusetts: Blackwell Publishing 2001, p. 6; pp. 8–9.

— "Religion and the Mirror of God: Historicism, Truth, and Religious Pluralism," in *Cornel West: A Critical Reader*, ed. by George Yancy, Malden, Massachusetts: Blackwell Publishing 2001, p. 133; p. 135.

# Richard Wright:

## Kierkegaard's Influence as Existentialist Outsider

Jennifer Elisa Veninga

### I. Biographical Introduction

Together the life and work of African-American author Richard Nathaniel Wright (1908–60) form a significant narrative in American literary, cultural, and social history.[1] In his large *corpus* of novels, short stories, and works of non-fiction, Wright offered critical and sometimes disturbing analysis of several of the most pressing issues of the twentieth century, including race relations and the legacy of slavery in the United States; the possibilities and failures of communism; and the effects of colonialism on Third World development. Wright is best known for his novel *Native Son* (1940)[2] and his autobiography *Black Boy* (1945),[3] both of which were set in the context of black America and sought to expose the harsh realities of racial violence and discrimination in the United States. Another novel, *The Outsider* (1953),[4] is less well known, but has been noted for its impact on, and reflection of, American existentialism. *The Outsider* raises pressing questions about the ultimate meaning of

---

[1]     For helpful general biographies on Wright, see Michel Fabre, *The Unfinished Quest of Richard Wright*, Urbana: University of Illinois Press 1993 [1973]; Hazel Rowley, *Richard Wright: The Life and Times*, New York: Henry Holt and Company 2001; Margaret Walker, *Richard Wright: Daemonic Genius, A Portrait of the Man: A Critical Look at His Work*, New York: Warner Books 1988; and Jerry W. Ward, Jr. and Robert J. Butler (eds.), *The Richard Wright Encyclopedia*, Westport, Connecticut: Greenwood Press 2008.

[2]     Richard Wright, *Native Son*, New York and London: Harper & Brothers 1940.

[3]     Richard Wright, *Black Boy: A Record of Childhood and Youth*, New York and London: Harper & Brothers 1945. Originally, Wright had submitted his full autobiography to Harper & Brothers under the name *American Hunger*. When his book was being considered for inclusion in the Book-of-the-Month Club, however, representatives from the Club asked him to drop sections of the book that they felt were too pessimistic about racism against African-Americans. Wright made the revisions and changed the name of his book to *Black Boy* for publication in 1945. In 1977, Harper and Row published the originally omitted sections as *American Hunger*, and in 1991 the Library of America published the restored text in its entirety as *Black Boy (American Hunger): A Record of Childhood and Youth*. For Wright's publishing history of the book, see *The Richard Wright Encyclopedia*, ed. by Jerry W. Ward, Jr. and Robert J. Butler, pp. 18–20 and pp. 42–3.

[4]     Richard Wright, *The Outsider*, New York: Harper & Brothers 1953.

life and how to find freedom in the face of despair and fear, themes that are present but less explicit in many of his other works.

The themes that arise in Richard Wright's *corpus*—even those of a more universal than particular nature—must be understood against the background of his historical context and personal biography. As biographer Margaret Walker (1915–98) notes: "Wright must be seen in terms of his times…Born black, poor, and male in white America in Mississippi in the early twentieth century—this was his human condition."[5] While Wright's life and work should not be *reduced* to these conditions, it is the case that they played a crucial role in forming his ideas and catalyzing his creative literary projects. Wright lived during the era of "Jim Crow" laws, which mandated racial segregation and encouraged discrimination of black Americans in virtually all aspects of public life. While the system was supposedly "separate but equal," the reality was that blacks suffered injustice, lack of opportunity, and were relegated to the periphery of society.

Wright was born in the midst of these conditions on a plantation in 1908 near Roxie, Mississippi. His childhood was marked by family moves between Mississippi, Arkansas, and Tennessee, and when Wright was seven, his father, an illiterate sharecropper, abandoned the family. In his autobiography, Wright describes this period and the years after it in terms of hunger, both emotional and physical. "I began to wake up at night to find hunger standing at my bedside, staring at me gauntly," he writes in *Black Boy*.[6] Wright's mother became ill during this time, and Wright and his brother lived with various relatives in the American South, including an uncle who was murdered by whites while Wright was living with him in Arkansas. Despite the pressure from his mother and a conservative Seventh-Adventist aunt and grandmother, Wright never found solace in organized religion. He was baptized in a Protestant church as a youth, but ultimately felt that this experience was meaningless, and he found Christian Bible study to be laborious.[7] Throughout his life, Wright would never find ultimate meaning in the context of the church.

While in Memphis, Wright began to explore literature for the first time. He began to read works by the American journalist and author Henry Louis Mencken (1880–1956), who criticized the South for its prejudices and discrimination. In reading Mencken, Wright discovered that words could be used as weapons, and Wright himself began to hunger for the experience of writing. "I no longer felt that the world about me was hostile, killing; I knew it," Wright explains, and concludes that the only way to deal with this experience was to write about it.[8] Shortly after his entrée into reading these and other works, Wright moved to Chicago in 1927 in hopes of creating a new life in a place that might be more open and less oppressive than the hostile American South.

Soon Wright found himself in Chicago during the Great Depression of the 1930s and was surprised to find conditions of inequality similar to those he had experienced in the South. As one scholar notes, he "lived out in his own life the betrayals of

---

5       Walker, *Richard Wright: Daemonic Genius*, p. 10.
6       Wright, *Black Boy*, p. 13.
7       Ibid., pp. 132–6.
8       Ibid., p. 220.

the Great Migration which promised blacks a new life in the North but delivered new forms of racial discrimination, social injustice, and poverty."[9] Yet Wright did find new opportunities for himself in Chicago. Perhaps the most significant was the discovery of the John Reed Club, an organization of young leftist artists and revolutionaries, for which he was recruited in 1933. The Club was welcoming and provided Wright with community, intellectual discussion, and opportunities for writing. In 1934, Wright joined the Communist Party and initially supported its philosophy of integration and equality, but later became disillusioned by its failure to recognize the reality of racial tensions.

Wright's first literary break came in the late 1930s, and he became internationally known through the publication of his most successful novel, *Native Son*, in 1940. Through the character of Bigger Thomas, Wright sought to reveal the violence that underlay race relations in the United States and to awaken the country to the impact of poverty, injustice, and discrimination on both whites and blacks. In the years that followed, Wright would continue to wrestle with themes of racial justice, evident through his autobiography, *Black Boy*, published in 1945. During this time, Wright also became interested in existentialism and began to read Søren Kierkegaard, Jean-Paul Sartre (1905–80), Albert Camus (1913–60), and Simone de Beauvior (1908–86).

Wright, his wife Ellen, and their two daughters were living in New York during the mid-1940s, which was less segregated than Chicago, but remained a place of discrimination against blacks. For some time, Wright had dreamed of moving to France where he believed he could be free from racial oppression. In 1946, he visited Paris for several months, and he and his family moved there permanently in 1947. Described by many as Wright's "exile," in France he forged personal relationships with Sartre, Camus, and de Beauvior. During his 13 years of exile, Wright produced three novels, including *The Outsider* (1953), *Savage Holiday* (1954),[10] and *The Long Dream* (1958).[11] While the first of the three received positive criticism, the other two were largely unsuccessful, and some readers accused Wright of having forgotten the struggles of his own black community in the United States.

Wright soon turned to non-fiction, publishing four books on colonialism and international development in just three years: *Black Power* (1954),[12] *The Color Curtain* (1956),[13] *Pagan Spain* (1957),[14] and *White Man, Listen!* (1957).[15] He continued to pursue several other literary projects until his death in 1960. Wright, now part of the American literary canon, is often cited as the first African-American writer to sustain himself professionally from his writings alone, as well as the first internationally celebrated black American author. American literary critic, Henry Louis Gates, Jr. (b. 1950), has described the publication of Wright's novel, *Native*

---

9       Ward and Butler, *The Richard Wright Encyclopedia*, p. 4.
10      Richard Wright, *Savage Holiday*, New York: Avon Publications 1954.
11      Richard Wright, *The Long Dream*, Garden City, New York: Doubleday 1958.
12      Richard Wright, *Black Power*, New York: Harper 1954.
13      Richard Wright, *The Color Curtain*, Cleveland: World 1956.
14      Richard Wright, *Pagan Spain*, New York: Harper 1957.
15      Richard Wright, *White Man, Listen!*, Garden City, New York: Doubleday 1957.

*Son*, as the "single most influential shaping force in modern Black literary history."[16] Beyond these accomplishments, Richard Wright continues to prompt reflection from his readers about what it means to exist in a painfully and undeniably broken world.

## II. Richard Wright's Encounter with Søren Kierkegaard

Among the influences on Richard Wright's authorship, Søren Kierkegaard played an important, if limited, role. The limit largely reflects the fact that it is most likely the case that Wright did not begin reading Kierkegaard until after he had written most of *Native Son* and *Black Boy*, his most successful novels. However, scholars who address the relationship between the two figures agree that Wright did in fact, read Kierkegaard after this point, and that he subsequently had a direct influence on Wright's authorship. This influence is most clearly seen in Wright's novel, *The Outsider*.

At the time of his death, Wright owned 14 of Kierkegaard's works[17] and several secondary sources on Kierkegaard.[18] As a Wright biographer notes, it is impossible to know exactly which books Wright actually read.[19] The only work that Wright most certainly read was *The Concept of Dread*, which as we will soon see, he quoted in *The Outsider*.[20] Wright did write in his diary that he purchased both *The Sickness unto Death* and *The Concept of Dread* on June 11, 1945.[21]

While it is uncertain when Wright purchased the other Kierkegaard works, it is likely that he acquired them sometime during or after 1944. Living in the United States during the early 1940s, Wright was exposed to the existentialist movement that had become popular in the country. Through the translations of Walter Lowrie

---

[16]     Henry Louis Gates, Jr., Preface to *Richard Wright: Critical Perspectives Past and Present*, ed. by Henry Louis Gates, Jr., and K. Anthony Appiah, New York: Amistad Press 1993, p. xi.

[17]     In *Richard Wright: Books and Writers*, Jackson: University Press of Mississippi 1990, pp. 86–8, biographer Michel Fabre notes that Wright owned several volumes. These are listed in the second rubric of the bibliography below.

[18]     Secondary sources included Theodor Haecker, *Kierkegaard the Cripple*, trans. by C. Van O. Bruyn, London: Harvill Press 1948; Walter Lowrie, *Kierkegaard*, London and New York: Oxford University Press 1938; Walter Lowrie, *A Short Life of Kierkegaard*, Oxford: H. Milford, Oxford University Press 1944; and Michael Wyschogrod, *Kierkegaard and Heidegger: The Ontology of Existence*, London: Routledge and Kegan Paul 1954.

[19]     See Russell Carl Brignano, *Richard Wright: An Introduction to the Man and His Works*, Pittsburgh: University of Pittsburgh Press 1970, p. 123: "It is difficult—in most cases impossible—and not entirely fair to reconstruct exactly how an author has applied to his own work the knowledge and thinking acquired from others. With Wright we know at least that into certain works he incorporated ideas of noted European intellectuals, although not in simple eclectic fashion. Variations, amalgamations, and even refutations occurred."

[20]     Here I note that Walter Lowrie translated the Danish *Begrebet Angest* (1844) as *The Concept of Dread* (1944) while Reidar Thomte's version is translated as *The Concept of Anxiety* (1980). When using quotations in this article, I note which version is used, but I employ the general terms "dread" and "anxiety" interchangeably throughout.

[21]     Fabre, *Richard Wright: Books and Writers*, pp. 86–7.

(1868–1959) and David Swenson (1876–1940), Americans had become familiar with Kierkegaard, and Richard Wright encountered him during this same late World War II period.[22] "Now Kierkegaard is one of the great writers of today," he is reported to have proclaimed.[23] In 1944, this popular interest led Wright to ask his friend, journalist and activist Dorothy Norman (1905–85), to instruct him on existentialism and the writings of Kierkegaard, Friedrich Nietzsche (1844–1900), and Martin Heidegger (1889–1976), whom she had read. Norman invited Paul Tillich (1886–1965) and Hannah Arendt (1906–75) to her New York home so that they could discuss existentialism with Wright. He purchased his own copies of several of Kierkegaard's works and often kept *The Concept of Dread* with him.[24]

Upon reading Kierkegaard and learning about existentialism, Wright often remarked that he was encountering ideas that he had known all along through his own experiences of despair and dread. To his friend, journalist Cyril Lionel Robert James (1901–89), Wright said of Kierkegaard: "Everything that he writes in those books, I knew before I had them."[25] When Wright moved to Paris in 1947 with his family, he brought his Kierkegaard volumes with him and continued to study Kierkegaard and existentialism until he published *The Outsider* in 1953.[26] These years are often described as Wright's "existentialist period."[27]

## III. Kierkegaard in The Outsider

### A. Plot Summary and Direct References to Kierkegaard

As noted, of all Wright's work, it is *The Outsider* that most reflects Kierkegaardian themes and contains direct references to Kierkegaard himself. "*The Outsider* (1953) deserves attention both because of its own merits and because of its role as one of the very few consciously existentialist works in American literature," wrote a reviewer in 1960.[28] *The Outsider* signaled a change from Wright's previous novels, as it shifted from explicitly race-related issues to more philosophical problems of

---

[22]     For a helpful summary of Kierkegaard's reception in the United States, see Lee C. Barrett, "The USA: From Neo-Orthodoxy to Plurality," in *Kierkegaard's International Reception*, Tome III, *The Near East, Asia, Australia and the Americas*, ed. by Jon Stewart, Aldershot: Ashgate 2009 (*Kierkegaard Research: Sources, Reception and Resources*, vol. 8), pp. 229–68.

[23]     George Cotkin, *Existential America*, Baltimore: Johns Hopkins University Press 2003, p. 163.

[24]     Fabre, *The Unfinished Quest*, p. 299.

[25]     Cyril Lionel Robert James, "Black Studies," *Radical America*, vol. 5, no. 5, 1971, p. 89.

[26]     In a letter to author Gertrude Stein (1874–1946) dated March 15, 1946, Wright anticipated his trip to Paris: "I'm bringing a good deal of the work of Kierkegaard, English translations, of course." See Michel Fabre, *Richard Wright: Books and Writers*, p. 88.

[27]     Fabre, *The Unfinished Quest*, p. 316.

[28]     Kingsley Widmer, "The Existential Darkness: Richard Wright's *The Outsider*," *Wisconsin Studies in Contemporary Literature*, vol. 1, no. 3, 1960, p. 13.

freedom and meaning. The novel tells the story of a black man named Cross Damon in Chicago who feels trapped and unhappy in his life; he is resentful of his wife, his sons, his job at the post office and a mistress whom he has just found out to be pregnant. A freak accident on a subway train allows him to pretend that he is dead and take on a series of new identities to escape his old life.

Cross then leaves for New York, where he becomes involved with the Communist Party and develops relationships with several of his new comrades. Among them are Eva and Gil Blount, with whom he lives for a period of time. Cross falls in love with Eva and later intervenes in a fight between Gil Blount and their racist landlord Langley Herndon, accidentally killing them both. Angry at the Communists, Cross kills another Party member and eventually confesses him crimes to Eva, who commits suicide. A hunchback district attorney finally discovers the truth, but lets Cross go without prosecuting him. The Communists find Cross, however, and shoot and kill him. In his final words, he says that he wanted to be free and find out what living really meant, but all he found was nothing. "The search can't be done alone," Cross says in his final breaths, "Man is a promise that he must never break."[29] Cross seems to have broken his promise to himself and encourages others not to make the same kinds of choices.

There are two direct references to Kierkegaard in *The Outsider*. The novel is divided into five "books," each of which is framed by an epigraph: Dread, Dream, Descent, Despair, and Decision. The first, "Dread," begins with a quotation from Kierkegaard: "Dread is an alien power which lays hold of an individual, and yet one cannot tear oneself away, nor has a will to do so; for one fears what one desires."[30] Walter Lowrie used this quotation in his introduction to *The Concept of Dread* which Wright read in the mid-1940s.[31] The other direct reference to Kierkegaard comes later in the novel when the hunchback district attorney, Ely Houston, explains how he finally figured out that Cross Damon had murdered the men. Houston contacted Cross' old landlord in Chicago to find out what books he had left in his room, and was "delighted" to find a clue to his guilt. "Your Nietzsche, your Hegel, your Jaspers, your Heidegger, your Husserl, your Kierkegaard, and your Dostoevsky were the clues...I said to myself that we are dealing with a man who has wallowed in guilty thought."[32]

### B. Kierkegaardian Themes in The Outsider

In addition to these two direct references, it can be argued that Kierkegaard's influence can be found indirectly in several important themes in *The Outsider*, including the persistence and effect of dread (or anxiety); the relationship between

---

[29]     Wright, *The Outsider*, p. 404.
[30]     Ibid., p. 1.
[31]     Lowrie, Introduction to *The Concept of Dread*, p. xii. In the translation by Reidar Thomte (1980), the same quotation appears in a footnote. See *CA*, Notes, p. 235. The original quotation is from an 1842 journal entry by Kierkegaard found in *SKS* 18, 311, JJ:511 / *KJN* 2, 286.
[32]     Wright, *The Outsider*, p. 388.

guilt and innocence; the relationship between despair and selfhood; and the nature of human freedom. Each theme shall be briefly examined, noting its presence in the novel and possible influences from Kierkegaard's *corpus*.[33]

That Wright opened his novel with a Kierkegaardian quotation on dread reveals the centrality of this theme in *The Outsider*. Indeed, as one scholar argues, "Wright self-consciously characterized Cross Damon as the human embodiment of Kierkegaardian dread."[34] Others have noted that Wright's choice of "Cross Damon" as the main character's name suggests a self whose conflicting impulses give rise to dread, while Wright's decision to make Cross a postal worker may be based on Kierkegaard's use of the postman as archetypal Christian, a symbol of mundane life in the world.[35]

Early in the novel Cross speaks of his anxieties related to his family and work: "His sense of life had been so heightened that desire boiled in him to a degree that made him afraid. Afraid of what? Nothing exactly, precisely...And this constituted his sense of dread."[36] Wright seems to be picking up on Kierkegaard's interpretation of the relationship between nothingness and anxiety as presented in *The Concept of Anxiety*. Kierkegaard describes the human "state of innocence" as a natural one where there is peace and nothing against which to strive. "But what effect does nothing have?" he asks. "It begets anxiety. This is the profound secret of innocence, that it is at the same time anxiety."[37] Cross Damon's sense of dread deepens throughout the novel, but when he changes his identity after the subway accident and then kills a man who recognizes him, he finds the source of his dread: "it was from within himself."[38]

The connections that Wright makes between anxiety, guilt, and innocence can also be traced to Kierkegaard's treatment of these topics in *The Concept of Anxiety*. Cross Damon's relationship to guilt appears to be a curious one; he murders four people, but never seems to feel guilt about his violent actions. Yet he does express guilt for other reasons. In the hours after murdering Gil and his landlord, Cross admits to feeling guilt, not because he had murdered but because he now holds

---

[33]     For simplicity in this analysis, I refer to Kierkegaard himself as the author of all his works rather than his pseudonyms.

[34]     Claudia C. Tate, "Christian Existentialism in *The Outsider*," in *Richard Wright: Critical Perspectives Past and Present*, ed. by Gates and Appiah, p. 371.

[35]     Scholars have interpreted Cross Damon's name in different ways, for example: "Crucified Devil" in Dan McCall, *The Example of Richard Wright*, New York: Harcourt, Brace and World 1969, p. 150; a "Cross (mixture) between Christianity (symbolized by his name, Cross) and demonic action (the last name: Damon)" in Raman K. Singh, "Christian Heroes and Anti-Heroes in Richard Wright's Fiction," *Negro American Literature Forum*, vol. 6, no. 4, 1972, p. 99; "In Damon is Adam the innocent" in Lewis Lawson, "Cross Damon: Kierkegaardian Man of Dread," *College Language Association Journal*, vol. 14, no. 3, 1971, p. 299. In *Fear and Trembling*, which Wright may have read, Kierkegaard explains that a knight of faith like Abraham is not recognizable; he looks just like any other person with a gait that "is as steady as a postman's." *SKS* 4, 134 / *FT*, 39.

[36]     Wright, *The Outsider*, pp. 16–17.

[37]     *SKS* 4, 347 / *CA*, 41.

[38]     Wright, *The Outsider*, p. 107.

power and knowledge over Eva, Gil's wife who trusts him.[39] One scholar argues that Cross is able to maintain his innocence because of "a kind of primordial relation to original sin."[40] After the subway accident, Cross makes the decision to fake his own death, which essentially renders him "really, legally and morally dead."[41] From a Kierkegaardian perspective, this death frees Cross from the guilt of sinfulness that Adam brought into the human race.[42] Even at the end of his life, Cross maintains his innocence. District Attorney Ely Houston asks him how he experienced his own life. Cross says that it was horrible, "Because in my heart…I'm…I felt…I'm innocent… That's what made the horror…"[43]

Cross knew that he had transgressed the laws of society through his crimes, yet he felt that he had committed them for a higher reason. "His crimes had carried a stamp of the absolute and if they wanted to nail him down, their [the police's] actions would have to carry a stamp of the absolute against him," Cross maintains.[44] During the police investigations, it is only Ely Houston who understands something of this idea. Before he knows that Cross is guilty, Houston seeks counsel from him about finding the murderer. Cross says that this man "is one for whom all ethical laws are suspended. He acts like a god."[45] While we cannot be certain that Richard Wright read Kierkegaard's *Fear and Trembling*, it seems likely that this idea of transcending social morality is influenced by Kierkegaard's interpretation of the story of Abraham's near-murder of Isaac as a "teleological suspension of the ethical." Abraham's faith reflected the paradox that the "single individual is higher than the universal," the ethical framework of society.[46]

Cross Damon is not a religious man, but Wright certainly creates him to be a man who is a solitary individual and relates only to the values that he feels are absolute. Thus Cross is able to maintain his innocence before the absolute even if he is guilty according to society. For Cross, the men he murdered were guilty, not him. And yet, Cross does experience feelings of dread about the prospect of being deemed guilty by others. Indeed, much of the book's narrative involves Cross' attempts to keep his crimes a secret and his anxiety about their discovery. Here we may be picking up on another idea from Kierkegaard's *The Concept of Anxiety* regarding the ambivalence of anxiety: "The individual, in anxiety not about becoming guilty but about being regarded as guilty, becomes guilty."[47] This may help to make sense of Cross' plea of innocence in the midst of acknowledging that he had in fact committed multiple murders.

[39] Ibid., pp. 217–18.
[40] Sandra Adell, "Richard Wright's *The Outsider* and the Kierkegaardian Concept of Dread," *Comparative Literature Studies*, vol. 28, no. 4, 1991, p. 384.
[41] Wright, *The Outsider*, p. 76.
[42] Adell, "Richard Wright's *The Outsider* and the Kierkegaardian Concept of Dread," p. 384.
[43] Wright, *The Outsider*, p. 405.
[44] Ibid., p. 346.
[45] Ibid., p. 260.
[46] *SKS* 4, 149 / *FT*, 55.
[47] *SKS* 4, 378 / *CA*, 75.

As might be clear from the comments above, the figure of Ely Houston plays a significant role in Cross' dialectical relationship to guilt. It also seems that Wright's creation of Houston was inspired by Kierkegaard. Cross first meets Houston on the train from Chicago to New York and immediately notices that he has a physical deformity—a hump on his back. The two speak about their experiences of being outsiders; Cross is an outsider because of his race and Houston because of his deformity. Houston remarks to Cross: "This hump on my back ought to give me some license…I know what it means to be an object outside of the normal lives of men." But, he continues, "I'd not want to give up what my peculiar situation has taught me about life. This damned hump has given me more psychological knowledge than all the books I read at the university."[48]

Throughout the novel, Houston functions as a paradoxical figure for Cross Damon. While Houston is the one who can ultimately prosecute him, he is also the one who understands Cross most deeply. This both terrifies and attracts Cross. "He was frightened of that hunchback, that outsider who understood too much."[49] In Kierkegaard, Wright most likely saw another outsider of sorts, one who critiqued his society and was simultaneously critiqued by it. Wright also owned a copy of *Kierkegaard the Cripple* by Theodor Haecker, which explored the effect of Kierkegaard's hunched back on his philosophy. Between Kierkegaard's writings and the secondary source, Wright must have found this image to be a powerful one.

In addition to the themes of dread, innocence, and guilt, Wright seems to be influenced by Kierkegaard's idea of the self and its relationship to despair. Central themes from *The Sickness unto Death* appear in *The Outsider*.[50] Primarily, we find that Wright's portrayal of Cross Damon depicts a self who is in despair.[51] For Kierkegaard, the self which is free of despair relates to itself, wills to be itself, and "rests transparently in the power that established it."[52] The self is a synthesis of infinite and finite, temporal and eternal, and freedom and necessity, and when a misrelation occurs within that synthesis, despair results. Despair is the sickness unto death: "The torment of despair is precisely this inability to die."[53] As *The Outsider* opens, Cross is so miserable in his life that he pulls out his gun and thinks of killing himself, but cannot go through with it. Later he remarks:

> If those who were pressing him knew how little like a human being he felt, they would recoil in horror; he felt unreal, scarcely alive. How long could he go on like this? Shame flooded him as he recalled his attempt with the gun. He could not even do *that*.[54]

---

[48]     Wright, *The Outsider*, p. 123.

[49]     Ibid., p. 120.

[50]     Like the other works, we cannot be sure that Wright read *The Sickness unto Death*. The fact that he noted its purchase in his journal, however, strongly suggests that he did.

[51]     Sarah Relyea examines Cross' despair in light of Kierkegaard's conception of selfhood. See Sarah Relyea, Chapter Four, "The Vanguard of Modernity: Richard Wright's *The Outsider*," in *Outsider Citizens: The Remaking of Postwar Identity in Wright, Beauvoir, and Baldwin*, New York: Routledge 2006, pp. 59–89.

[52]     *SKS* 11, 130 / *SUD*, 14.

[53]     *SKS* 11, 133 / *SUD*, 18.

[54]     Wright, *The Outsider*, p. 43.

Kierkegaard's formula for all despair is "to despair over oneself, in despair to will to be rid of oneself," which certainly seems to be picked up by Wright and incorporated into the narrative of Cross Damon.[55]

Not only does Cross want to be rid of himself, but he later actually wishes to be someone else. The occasion for this wish to arise is the subway accident, which actually gives Cross the opportunity to enact his own death and become someone new. In Kierkegaard's schema of the relation between selfhood and despair, willing to be someone else is one of the lowest forms of conscious despair. "One who despairs in this way is very comical," Kierkegaard writes. He continues:

> Imagine a self...and then imagine that it suddenly occurs to a self that it might become someone other—than itself. And yet one in despair this way, whose sole desire is this most lunatic of lunatic metamorphoses, is infatuated with the illusion that this change can be accomplished as easily as one changes clothes.[56]

After hearing reports of his supposed "death," Cross decides to take the opportunity to shed his old life. Pondering his new identity, he thinks he "would be a Negro who had just come up fresh from the Deep South looking for work. His name? Well... Charles...Charles what? Webb...Yes, that was good enough for the time being...He repressed a smile. *He loved this!*"[57]

While this absurd opportunity provided Cross with an escape from the despair of being his old self, the actual experience of having a new identity turned out to be less liberating than Cross had hoped. Here we encounter a final Kierkegaardian theme reflected in Richard Wright's novel—the nature of human freedom. We find the influence of both *The Concept of Anxiety* and *The Sickness unto Death* in Wright's narrative of Cross' life. While he felt "an intuitive sense of freedom" just after the subway accident, Cross also "felt dizzy as he tried to encompass the totality of the idea that had come so suddenly and unsought into his mind, for its implications ramified in so many directions that he could not grasp them all at once."[58]

At different times during the novel, Cross is afflicted with this same feeling of dizziness brought on by all the possibilities he had before him. Wright may have been influenced by Kierkegaard's classification of one form of despair that occurs when possibility outweighs necessity in the balance of the self. In this case, "possibility seems greater and greater to the self....Eventually everything seems possible, but this is exactly the point at which the abyss swallows up the self."[59] Right when one possibility arises, "a new possibility appears, and finally these phantasmagoria follow one another in such rapid succession that it seems as if everything were possible, and this is exactly the final moment, the point at which the individual himself becomes a mirage."[60] Amid such possibility, Cross only finds an empty dreamworld where

---

[55]    *SKS* 11, 135 / *SUD*, 20.
[56]    *SKS* 11, 168 / *SUD*, 53.
[57]    Wright, *The Outsider*, p. 80.
[58]    Ibid., pp. 75–6. For Kierkegaard, dizziness (in the category of the psychical) corresponds to despair (in the category of the spirit). See *SKS* 11, 132 / *SUD*, 16.
[59]    *SKS* 11, 151 / *SUD*, 36.
[60]    *SKS* 11, 152 / *SUD*, 36.

he cannot find solid ground. The relationship between anxiety and freedom posited by Kierkegaard is also reflected in Cross' narrative. Again, Kierkegaard speaks of dizziness: "Anxiety is the dizziness of freedom" and this freedom "succumbs in this dizziness....In that very moment everything is changed, and freedom, when it rises again, sees that it is guilty."[61] Rather than being able to use his freedom in the way he had wanted, Cross has difficulty making decisions and experiences a near-debilitating feeling of dread: "Out of a void, anxiety rose and captured his senses."[62]

As a man whose state of dizziness over possibilities disables him from making real choices, Wright may have intended Cross to represent a person who is stuck in Kierkegaard's category of the aesthetic. Unlike the ethical or religious stages, the aesthetic is characterized by immediacy and reflection; a person simply exists moment to moment and fails to create lasting relationships with others. We cannot know how closely Wright may have read Kierkegaard's *Either/Or*, but as one scholar argues, Cross' life resembles that of the aesthete Johannes the Seducer who chases one object of desire after another.[63] "Damon lives as an aesthete, according to the values that he creates himself and with relatively little concern for the needs and rights of others," writes George Cotkin.[64] Indeed, after he sheds his old identity and is contemplating who he will be next, Cross reflects on his life of immediacy and detachment: "What really obsessed him was his nonidentity which negated his ability to relate himself to others. He realized that what was happening to him now had been buried implicitly all along in his past life, had slumbered there in the form of a habit of acute reflection."[65] In addition to the possibility that Wright was influenced by *Either/Or*, it is probable that he drew from Kierkegaard's treatment of immediacy in regard to despair as presented in *The Sickness unto Death*. In despair, "immediacy actually has no self, it does not know itself; thus it cannot recognize itself and therefore generally ends in fantasy," Kierkegaard writes.[66]

There are at least two ways in which Cross at least momentarily exercises his own freedom, and it seems that Wright may have used Kierkegaard's categories to express these actions in terms of the "leap" and in relation to the meaning of language. Several scholars have noted Wright's use of Kierkegaard's leap in *The Outsider*.[67] In *The Concept of Anxiety*, it is through a leap that Adam's sin comes into

---

[61]      *SKS* 4, 365–6 / *CA*, 61.

[62]      Wright, *The Outsider*, p. 112.

[63]      See "The Seducer's Diary" in *SKS* 2, 291–432 / *EO1*, 301–445. Cross' behavior with his wife Gladys early in the novel is also reminiscent of Johannes's behavior with his fiancée, Cordelia. Both men seek to make the women angry with them in hopes that the women themselves will end the relationships and believe it to be their idea. Kierkegaard himself engaged in this kind of behavior with Regine, his fiancée. See *The Outsider*, pp. 50–9 and *SKS* 2, 365–432 / *EO* 1, 376–445. Wright may have read about Kierkegaard's experience with Regine in Walter Lowrie's biographies of Kierkegaard which he owned.

[64]      Cotkin, *Existential America*, p. 173.

[65]      Wright, *The Outsider*, p. 131.

[66]      *SKS* 11, 168 / *SUD*, 53.

[67]      See Tate, "Christian Existentialism in *The Outsider*"; George Cotkin, " 'Cold Rage': Richard Wright and Ralph Ellison," in *Existential America*; and Lawson, "Cross Damon: Kierkegaardian Man of Dread."

the world, but it is also the leap that allows human beings to transition from a state of inactive dread to concrete action (whether positive or negative). The qualitative leap "stands outside of all ambiguity" and Kierkegaard encourages his readers not to forget that "the new is brought about through the leap."[68] Cross engages in several "leaps" that lead him to a new state: his decision to fake his death after the subway accident, his decisions to murder, and his choice to confess to Ely Houston. While the first two sets of actions may have transgressed social norms and conventions, they did help to bring Cross out of his state of dread.

The third leap, brought about through Cross' dying confession to Houston, was a decision that gave Cross a great deal of anxiety. Throughout the narrative, Cross expresses his "urge to confide and the fear of the danger of confiding," and his feeling of being completely alone in the world.[69] Cross tries to confess to Eva, but she cannot understand what he is saying. "Was there really no direct bridge between the subjective worlds of people?" Cross asks himself. "Was the possibility of communication only a kind of pretense?"[70] Here we see the possibility that Wright picked up on themes from *Fear and Trembling* and *The Concept of Anxiety*.

In *Fear and Trembling*, Kierkegaard ponders the question of whether it was ethically defensible for Abraham to have concealed his plan to sacrifice Isaac. Ultimately, his silence cannot be deemed ethically justifiable, but it can be religiously justified. "Abraham cannot speak, because he cannot say that which would explain everything," Kierkegaard writes.[71] Abraham's actions only made sense in terms of the absolute, and thus no one would understand him. Yet ethics, or the universal, demands disclosure. In *The Concept of Anxiety*, Kierkegaard describes an anxiety over the good or the ethical, which he calls the demonic. One form of the demonic is "inclosing reserve" in which a person becomes mute and closed off from others: "What the inclosed person conceals in his inclosing reserve can be so terrible that he does not dare to utter it, not even to himself."[72] At least in terms of ethics, it is only language that can save a person from this demonic inclosure: "Here disclosure is the good, for disclosure is the first expression of salvation."[73] While Cross does not necessarily find religious salvation at the end of his life, he has at least made an ethical disclosure to Ely Houston which could certainly be interpreted as a leap toward the "good."[74]

---

[68]    *SKS* 4, 349 / *CA*, 43 and *SKS* 4, 388 / *CA*, 85.
[69]    Wright, *The Outsider*, p. 107.
[70]    Ibid., p. 303.
[71]    *SKS* 4, 202 / *FT*, 115.
[72]    *SKS* 4, 429 / *CA*, 128.
[73]    *SKS* 4, 428 / *CA*, 127.
[74]    While critics like Sandra Adell have been careful to point out that neither Wright nor the character of Cross Damon are Christian, it has been noted that Kierkegaard's influence imbues *The Outsider* with a kind of religious framework. "*The Outsider* depends so much upon the psychological and religious structure of Kierkegaard that it becomes a work of secular religion," writes Cotkin in *Existential America*, p. 171.

*IV. Kierkegaard's Influence on Other Works by Wright*

As noted in the chronology above, scholars largely agree that Richard Wright did not begin reading Kierkegaard until the 1940s and began to formally engage Kierkegaard's ideas after meeting Dorothy Norman in 1944. While it is possible that Wright may have known something of Kierkegaard before that point, it is unlikely that his ideas directly influenced Wright's work before the mid-1940s. Thus, while some scholars have noted existentialist—and even Kierkegaardian themes in his early work—this can most accurately be explained by a retrospective resonance with Kierkegaard's thought rather than an influence. This is particularly true of Wright's novella, "The Man Who Lived Underground" (completed in 1942), whose main character Fred Daniels wrestles with existential questions of anxiety, guilt, freedom and alienation.[75] Wright's first novel, *Native Son*, has been noted for its existentialist themes as well; for one scholar, "The existentialism evident here is just a preview of that in *The Outsider*."[76] After reading Kierkegaard, Wright himself is said to have been surprised at the latent existentialism in his autobiography *Black Boy* (completed in 1943 and published in 1945).[77]

We have seen the direct influence of Kierkegaard on Wright in *The Outsider*, who continued to publish both fiction and non-fiction after its completion. It is difficult, however, to detect any notable influence of Kierkegaard in these late works. The exception may be his last novel, *The Long Dream*, which Wright sets back in the American South. The main character, Fishbelly, experiences a similar kind of alienation and fear to that experienced by the characters in *Native Son* and *The Outsider*, but the novel focuses more on the tensions of family relationships and sexuality than existential dread. One scholar does characterize Fishbelly as a neurotic who has lost control of his life and exhibits a kind of Kierkegaardian despair.[78] In general, however, Kierkegaard is largely absent from the novel. Aspects of Wright's early thought resembled Kierkegaard in many ways, and in Kierkegaard Wright found ideas that he had felt but not been able to articulate. After encountering

---

[75]     For an analysis of existentialist themes in "The Man Who Lived Underground," see Patricia D. Watkins, "The Paradoxical Structure of Richard Wright's 'The Man Who Lived Underground," *Black American Literature Forum*, vol. 23, no. 4, 1989, pp. 767–83 and Carla Cappetti, "Black Orpheus: Richard Wright's 'The Man Who Lived Underground,' " *MELUS*, vol. 26, no. 4, 2001, pp. 41–68. In his article, "Reassessing (W)right: A Meditation on the Black (W)hole" (in *Modern Critical Views: Richard Wright*, ed. by Harold Bloom, New York: Chelsea House Publishers 1987), Houston A. Baker, Jr. draws a parallel between Fred Daniels' experience of the transcendent "Other" and Kierkegaard's understanding of the "Wholly Other" (pp. 150–1).

[76]     Katherine Fishburn, *Richard Wright's Hero: The Faces of a Rebel-Victim*, Metuchen, New Jersey: Scarecrow Press 1977, p. 3.

[77]     Constance Webb, *Richard Wright: A Biography*, New York: G.P. Putnam's Sons 1968, pp. 279–80. While Webb mentions that Wright had just been reading Kierkegaard, she also mentions his engagement with Heidegger, Husserl, Sartre and Camus. Thus we cannot be certain if he had Kierkegaard in mind when making his comment about *Black Boy*.

[78]     Fishburn, *Richard Wright's Hero*, pp. 30–1.

Kierkegaard, it is probable that he remained an important figure for Wright until his death. But, as has been demonstrated, it is in *The Outsider* that we find Kierkegaard's most notable influence on Wright's work.

# Bibliography

*I. References to or Uses of Kierkegaard in Wright's Corpus*

*The Outsider*, New York: Harper 1953, p. 1; p. 388.

Diary Entry, June 11, 1945. Richard Wright Papers. Yale Collection of American Literature, Beinecke Rare Book and Manuscript Library.

Letter to Gertrude Stein, March 15, 1946. Richard Wright Papers. Yale Collection of American Literature, Beinecke Rare Book and Manuscript Library.


*II. Sources of Wright's Knowledge of Kierkegaard*

Haecker, Theodor, *Kierkegaard the Cripple*, trans. by C. Van O. Bruyn, London: Harvill Press 1948.

Kierkegaard, Søren, *Purify Your Hearts: A "Discourse for a Special Occasion," The First of Three "Edifying Discourses in a Different Vein,"* trans. by A.S. Aldworth and W.S. Ferrie, London: C.W. Daniel 1937.

— *The Point of View, Etc.; Including "The Point of View for My Work as an Author," "Two Notes about 'The Individual'" and "On My Work as an Author,"* trans. by Walter Lowrie, London and New York: Oxford University Press 1939.

— *Consider the Lilies: Being the Second Part of "Edifying Discourses in a Different Vein,"* trans. by S. Aldworth and W.S. Ferrie, London: C.W. Daniel 1940.

— *The Concept of Dread*, trans. by Walter Lowrie, Princeton: Princeton University Press 1944.

— *The Sickness unto Death*, trans. by Walter Lowrie, Princeton: Princeton University Press 1944.

— *Training in Christianity and The Edifying Discourse Which "Accompanied" It*, trans. by Walter Lowrie, Princeton, New Jersey: Princeton University Press 1944.

— *Stages on Life's Way*, trans. by Walter Lowrie, London: Oxford University Press 1945.

— *Attack Upon "Christendom," 1854–1855*, trans. by Walter Lowrie, Princeton: Princeton University Press 1946.

— *Either/Or: A Fragment of Life*, trans. by David F. Swenson and Lillian Marvin Swenson, Princeton, New Jersey: Princeton University Press 1946.

— *Fear and Trembling: A Dialectical Lyric by Johannes de Silentio*, trans. by Robert Payne, Oxford: Oxford University Press 1946.

— *Philosophical Fragments, Or, A Fragment of Philosophy by Johannes Climacus*, trans. by David Swenson, Princeton, New Jersey: Princeton University Press 1946.

— *Repetition: An Essay in Experimental Psychology*, trans. by Walter Lowrie, Princeton, New Jersey: Princeton University Press 1946.

— *Works of Love*, trans. by David F. Swenson and Lillian Marvin Swenson, Princeton, New Jersey: Princeton University Press 1946.

Lowrie, Walter, *Kierkegaard*, London and New York: Oxford University Press 1938.

— *A Short Life of Kierkegaard*, Oxford: H. Milford, Oxford University Press 1944.

Wyschogrod, Michael, *Kierkegaard and Heidegger: The Ontology of Existence*, London: Routledge & Kegan Paul 1954, pp. 24–50, pp. 78–100, pp. 122–56.

*III. Secondary Literature on Wright's Relation to Kierkegaard*

Abdurrahman, Umar, "Quest for Identity in Richard Wright's *The Outsider*: An Existential Approach," *The Western Journal of Black Studies*, vol. 30, no. 1, 2006, p. 27.

Adell, Sandra, "Richard Wright's *The Outsider* and the Kierkegaardian Concept of Dread," *Comparative Literature Studies*, vol. 28, no. 4, 1991, pp. 379–94.

Atteberry, Jeffrey, "Entering the Politics of the Outside: Richard Wright's Critique of Marxism and Existentialism," *Modern Fiction Studies*, vol. 51, no. 4, 2005, pp. 883–4.

Baker, Houston A., "Reassessing (W)right: A Meditation on the Black (W)hole," in *Modern Critical Views: Richard Wright*, ed. by Harold Bloom, New York: Chelsea House Publishers 1987, pp. 150–1.

Brignano, Russell Carl, *Richard Wright: An Introduction to the Man and His Works*, Pittsburgh: University of Pittsburgh Press 1970, p. 120; p. 123.

Carson, Benjamin D., "To Make a Bridge from Man to Man: Existentialism in Richard Wright's *The Outsider*," *Indian Review of World Literature in English*, vol. 4, no. 1, 2008, p. 28, p. 31, pp. 35–7.

Cobb, Nina Kressner, "Richard Wright: Exile and Existentialism," *Phylon*, vol. 40, no. 4, 1979, p. 373.

Coles, Robert A., "Richard Wright's *The Outsider*: A Novel in Transition," *Modern Language Studies*, vol. 13, no. 3, 1983, p. 55.

Cotkin, George, *Existential America*, Baltimore: Johns Hopkins University Press 2003, pp. 161–75.

Fabre, Michael, *The Unfinished Quest of Richard Wright*, Urbana, Illinois: University of Illinois Press 1993 [1973], p. xxxi; p. 299; p. 322; p. 333; p. 374.

— "Richard Wright and the French Existentialists," *MELUS*, vol. 5, no. 2, 1978, p. 40; pp. 48–50.

— *The World of Richard Wright*, Jackson, Mississippi: University Press of Mississippi 1985, pp. 159–60; pp. 163–5; p. 173.

— *Richard Wright: Books and Writers*, Jackson, Mississippi: University Press of Mississippi 1990, p. 67; pp. 86–8; p. 100; p. 176; p. 265.

Felgar, Robert, *Richard Wright*, Boston: Twayne Publishers 1980, p. 109; p. 119.

Fishburn, Katherine, *Richard Wright's Hero: The Faces of a Rebel-Victim*, Metuchen, New Jersey: Scarecrow Press 1977, p. 30; p. 79; p. 112; p. 124; pp. 129–30.

James, Cyril Lionel Robert, "Black Studies," *Radical America*, vol. 5, no. 5, 1971, p. 89.

Lawson, Lewis, "Cross Damon: Kierkegaardian Man of Dread," *College Language Association Journal*, vol. 24, no. 3, 1971, pp. 298–316.

Lynch, Michael F., "Haunted by Innocence: The Debate with Dostoevsky in Wright's 'Other Novel,' *The Outsider*," *African American Review*, vol. 30, no. 2, 1996, pp. 262–4.

Margolies, Edward, *The Art of Richard Wright*, Carbondale: Southern Illinois University Press 1969, p. 121.

McCall, Dan, *The Example of Richard Wright*, New York: Harcourt, Brace and World 1969, p. 150.

Relyea, Sarah, *Outsider Citizens: The Remaking of Postwar Identity in Wright, Beauvoir, and Baldwin*, New York: Routledge 2006, pp. 59–89.

Rowley, Hazel, *Richard Wright: The Life and Times*, New York: Henry Holt and Company 2001, p. 357.

Singh, Amritjit, "Richard Wright's *The Outsider*: Existentialist Exemplar or Critique?" *College Language Association Journal*, vol. 27, no. 4, 1984, p. 358; pp. 362–5.

Singh, Raman K., "Heroes and Anti-Heroes in Richard Wright's Fiction," *Negro American Literature Forum*, vol. 6, no. 4, 1972, p. 103.

Tate, Claudia C., "Christian Existentialism in *The Outsider*," in *Richard Wright: Critical Perspectives Past and Present*, ed. by Henry Louis Gates, Jr. and K. Anthony Appiah, New York: Amistad Press 1993, pp. 369–87.

Walker, Margaret, *Richard Wright: Daemonic Genius, A Portrait of the Man: A Critical Look at His Work*, New York: Warner Books 1988, p. 211; pp. 230–8.

Watkins, Patricia D., "The Paradoxical Structure of Richard Wright's 'The Man Who Lived Underground,' " *Black American Literature Forum*, vol. 23, no. 4, 1989, p. 771.

Ward, Jr., Jerry W. and Robert J. Butler (eds.), *The Richard Wright Encyclopedia*, Westport, Connecticut: Greenwood Press 2008, pp. 217–18.

Webb, Constance, *Richard Wright: A Biography*, New York: G.P. Putnam's Sons 1968, pp. 279–80.

Widmer, Kingsley, "The Existential Darkness: Richard Wright's *The Outsider*," *Wisconsin Studies in Contemporary Literature*, vol. 1, no. 3, 1960, pp. 13–21.

— "Black Existentialism: Richard Wright," in *Richard Wright: A Collection of Critical Essays*, ed. by Richard Macksey and Frank E. Moorer, Englewood Cliffs, New Jersey: Prentice-Hall 1984, pp. 175–9.

# Index of Persons

# Index of Subjects

154, 187, 192, 214, 221, 233, 234,
236–8, 240, 242–9 passim, 258, 261,
263, 265–7, 269.
dialectics, xiv, 1, 7, 14, 16, 21, 44, 46, 48,
92, 93, 104, 110, 123–5, 233, 238,
243–5.
dizziness (see also "vertigo"), 102, 218,
238, 240, 243, 244, 266, 267.
doubt, 35–7, 154, 200, 246, 249.
duty, 149, 194.

earnestness, 17, 249.
emancipation of women, xii.
end of history, 164, 165.
Enlightenment, 34, 79, 226.
equality, xi, xii, 14, 15, 24, 90, 104, 200,
216, 245, 259.
ethics, the ethical, ix, xi, 12, 13, 25, 35, 47,
49, 57, 58, 63–5, 75, 78, 81, 82, 93,
108, 114, 115, 117, 118, 121, 124–6,
139, 143, 161, 166, 187, 199, 250,
267, 268.
evil, 17, 100, 201, 210, 217, 218, 225, 232,
233, 236, 239–42, 249.
exception, the, 1–4, 6, 7, 13, 14, 16, 21–3,
25, 26, 33, 178, 181, 184, 185, 187,
188, 191, 194–6, 198–205 passim.
existence, 34, 35, 45, 47–9, 59, 61, 62, 96,
102, 124, 138, 139, 153, 164, 186,
203, 212, 215, 217, 219–27 passim.
existentialism, 24, 53, 92, 96, 98, 99, 102,
127, 129, 131, 138, 142, 147, 152,
161, 162, 211, 226, 231, 234, 257,
259, 261, 269.

faith, ix, x, 31, 32, 36, 37, 42, 59, 61–3, 65,
66, 79, 81, 83, 91, 98, 103, 115, 124,
126, 129, 130, 191, 192, 198, 222,
233, 234, 237, 238, 240–3, 245, 248,
249, 264.
Fall, the, 92.
fanaticism,153.
Fascism, 7, 119, 126, 196, 197.
fear, 63, 64, 101, 103, 200, 205, 215–19,
222, 242, 258, 269.

feminism, 54.
finitude, 4, 46, 59–61, 63, 65, 96, 101, 102,
110, 184, 219, 265.
Frankfurt School, 53, 74, 137.
freedom, xiv, 4, 30, 63, 64, 78, 90, 100,
102–4, 148, 160, 162, 164, 165, 167,
186, 214–19, 223, 240–4, 248, 258,
262, 263, 265–7, 269.
French Revolution, 14, 15, 193, 213.

gadfly, 201, 233, 245.
gnosticism, 210, 225–7.
God, ix, xiv, 16, 20, 23–5, 33–5, 45, 47, 48,
63, 65, 79, 80, 91–3, 96–9, 101–4,
112, 118, 119, 124, 129, 130, 184,
186, 195, 196, 198–201, 204, 210,
220, 221, 224, 225, 237, 242, 243,
248, 249, 252.
God is dead, see "death of God."
God-man, 25, 139, 140, 239.
grace, 23, 65, 243, 250–2.
guilt, 112, 113, 240, 262–5, 269.

Hegelianism, 31, 163, 210.
Historians Dispute, the, 74, 76, 77, 80.
history, 4, 7, 32, 34, 36, 97, 102, 119, 123,
124, 126, 149, 150, 153, 160, 164–6,
192, 213, 220, 240.
hope, 232, 238, 240, 248, 252.
humanism, 48, 49, 97, 231.

idealism, 96.
    German, 53, 61, 91, 216.
immanence, see "transcendence."
immediacy, 94, 184, 186, 267.
incarnation, 155, 186.
inclosing reserve, 189, 268.
incognito, 108, 115, 124, 128.
indirect communication, see "communication."
individual, the (see also "single individual"),
ix, xi-xiv, 2, 14–16, 18, 19, 23–6,
32, 34, 42, 48, 59, 63, 76–8, 80, 82,
138–40, 142–4, 161, 165, 239.

Printed in Great Britain
by Amazon

36671106R00176